GREGORY PETROVICH MAXIMOFF

THE GUILLOTINE AT WORK

VOL 1: THE LENINIST COUNTER-REVOLUTION

CIENFUEGOS PRESS

Maximoff, Gregory Petrovich
    The Guillotine at work.
    Vol. 1: The Leninist counter revolution
    1. Lenin, Vladimir Il'ich
    I. Title II. Nowlin, William G
    947.084'1'0924   DK254.L4

    ISBN 0-904564-23-1 (Hardback)
    ISBN 0-904564-22-3 (Paperback)

First published Chicago, 1940, by Alexander Berkman Fund under the title:
The Guillotine At Work : Twenty Years of Terror in Russia (Data and
Documents).
This edition published in two volumes in 1979 by Cienfuegos Press, Over the
Water, Sanday, Orkney, KW17 2BL.
Cover illustration by Flavio Costantini
Jacket design by Simon Stern

Printed and bound in Great Britain by
Redwood Burn Limited, Trowbridge & Esher

CONTENTS

THE GUILLOTINE AT WORK offers us two very important lessons. First of all, Maximoff describes the terror under Lenin. His book stands as one of the most comprehensive documentations of the terror of the early Soviet state, which began under Lenin and was not just a Stalinist development. The principal lesson Maximoff wished to communicate, though, was that marxism/leninism was a theory which, despite its revolutionary style, was in essence counter-revolutionary.

This line of argument is a difficult one for many people to accept. While all but the most dogmatic stalinists recognise and recoil at the brutality of the Stalin era, it is believed almost equally widely that this was due to a political deformation characteristic of Stalin the man and not an endemic feature of marxism/leninism itself. Lenin is permitted to retain an aura of sacrosanctity. Whoever might broadly condemn marxism leninism rather than focus their critique on the Stalin personality cult is immediately suspect as an unregenerate reactionary. To avoid this charge, Maximoff has confined the material he presents to that which emanates from socialist, anarchist and official bolshevik sources.

The idea that the great Russian Revolution was ultimately perverted and channelled into an authoritarian and repressive regime is not a new idea. Most feel this occured after Lenin's death. Even as honest and sincere a work as Roy Medvedev's *Let History Judge*, a masterful and devastating dissection of stalinist Russia, lets Lenin off scot free. It is only to "the typical bourgeois historian," suggests Medvedev, that "Stalin's activity is seen as the logical continuation of Lenin's . . ."[1] Medvedev is, legitimately, fearful that a wholesale rejection of proletarian socialism might result from attributing to marxism and leninism itself the origins of the terror and crimes of the Stalin era; however, there do exist other forms of proletarian socialism than marxism and leninism and the dedicated revolutionary must hold each and every one up to the most penetrating criticism. Clarity of understanding is essential to the development of authentic revolutionary consciousness. If we are to learn from the mistakes of the past, we cannot exempt any tendency or any revolutionary figure from dispassionate consideration of their contributions and their shortcomings.

V

Lenin, according to Maximoff, "followed in the footsteps of the French Jacobins."[2] He believed in the necessity and even desirability of terror to implement his programme, in himself and the legitimacy of his authority. Maximoff presents scores of quotations from Lenin's published works in which Lenin urged shootings of political opponents, urged against sentimentality in the waging of political struggle and urged his fellow bolsheviks to adopt unashamedly a policy of red terror. Maximoff charges that Lenin deliberately chose to provoke civil war in the countryside, to terrorise the peasantry and force their compliance with the forced grain requisitions, to subject them to state regimentation: "That we brought civil war to the village is something that we hold up as a *merit*," wrote Lenin.[3]

The use of the death penalty was very rare in Tsarist Russia. When the bolsheviks came to power one of the first things they did (in Lenin's absence) was to abolish the death penalty. Lenin reacted furiously, "beside himself with indignation" in Trotsky's description. "How," he demanded to know, "can a revolution be made without executions?"[4] Maximoff compiles, from official bolshevik sources, statistical summaries of the number of executions in each year of Lenin's rule. Estimates based on these figures range from 200,000 to over 1,500,000 shootings during Lenin's period of leadership. Maximoff is willing to settle for the most conservative of all figures.

There is no question but that the Russian Revolution was a bloody affair. It would be unfair for anyone to attribute all of the deaths to Lenin's policies, all 10,000,000 to 12,000,000 lives. Any revolution takes lives. The white guardist counter-revolutionaries were certainly responsible for many deaths. The point is that many, if not most, of these millions of lives were shed not just because of the inevitable cost of revolutionary struggle but because Lenin insisted on implementing his own view of how that struggle should develop.

Rather than allow the people themselves to establish autonomous and federated revolutionary regimes in the various areas of the tsarist empire — in the Ukraine, in Georgia, in Siberia, and so forth — Lenin insisted that a single regime should rule over all nationalities. This despite the fact he had earlier promised full freedom to all nationalities. The tsarist empire was kept in tact with a single party asserting its political dominance — at tremendous cost. The crushing of the revolutionary peasants of the Ukraine is the best known example. By the treaty of Brest-Litovsk, Lenin ceded the Ukraine to Germany as part of his deal to gain peace. The

VI

Ukrainian people, though, organised spontaneously to resist German occupation and they were successful. They drove the Germans out of the Ukraine. They also fought off counter-revolutionary forces who tried to take over the Ukraine. Rather than allow the heroic peoples of this region to govern themselves and regulate their own lives, Lenin and Trotsky sent in the Red Army to crush the independent revolutionary movement of the Ukraine. Nestor Makhno is remembered today as one of the more courageous leaders in the fight against the Germans and counter-revolutionaries and, of tragic necessity, against bolshevik invasion as well.[5] Makhno was but one of many, and the Ukraine is simply the best known of many regions which fell under the rule of Moscow and Lenin.

Lenin insisted on the supremacy of his own revolutionary programme. Revolutionists of any other persuasion were forced out of their positions, jailed, exiled and executed. Lenin had been in Zurich when the revolution broke out, Trotsky in New York. The bolsheviks were a minority party with little real following, even among the workers.[6] The other revolutionary groups represented a threat to Lenin's domination. The left social-revolutionists had the support of by far the overwhelming mass of the peasantry. The anarchists had the most popular slogans. Lenin moved swiftly to crush both. As mentioned above, most of Maximoff's data covers the Leninist terror as directed against socialists and revolutionaries of non-bolshevik persuasions. Here the most prominent instance was the assault against the revolutionary people of Kronstadt. The sailors of Kronstadt had an unblemished record as being at the forefront of any revolutionary struggle. When they called for the bolsheviks to respect the rights of sincere revolutionists to speak and to publish, and to permit the organisation of free soviets, the response was a military assault in which thousands (up to 18,000) of the most dedicated revolutionists in all of Russia were slaughtered because they dared to challenge the uniformity of bolshevik rule. This despite the fact that the supreme military council of the bolshevik regime itself admitted, in a secret internal document which Maximoff presents, that "The Political Department of the Baltic fleet found itself isolated, not only from the masses but also from local party workers, having become a bureaucratic organ lacking any prestige and standing . . . destroyed all local initiative and brought the work down to the level of clerical routine . . . from July to November, 1920, twenty per cent of the members left the Party."[7]

Admitting they had failed here, the bolshevik leaders were afraid their supremacy would be challenged. Already strikes were spreading in Petrograd itself. So they told their troops that these were being engineered by counter-revolutionary white guardists in Kronstadt and sent them in to eliminate those who might show up the bolsheviks from a revolutionary point of view. *The Guillotine at Work* documents dozens of other instances in which the bolsheviks imprisoned and executed authentic revolutionaries who, they feared, might threaten their exclusive control. Miasnikov, a worker and leader of the bolshevik organisation of Moto-vilikha, protested against the suppression of free discussion even within the bolshevik party itself. "Those who fear to let the working class and peasantry speak out, always fear counter-revolution and see it every-where," wrote Miasnikov in a pamphlet for internal party use only.[8] A man who spent seven and a half of his eleven years of party membership in tsarist prisons, a worker who escaped from exile not to flee abroad but for party work in Russia, Miasnikov complained that it was primarily peasants and workers who were being arrested on charges of counter-revolution because they disagreed with the strict interpretation of the bolshevik line. "Don't you know that thousands of proletarians are kept in prison because they talked the way I am talking now, and that bour-geois people are not arrested on this score for the simple reason that they are never concerned with these questions?" Miasnikov was expelled from the party, imprisoned and then sent into exile.

When Lenin felt forced by events to retreat a few steps with his New Economic Policy, he could not simply admit that other revolutionists had been correct on this one point. (In fact Lenin reversed himself, against the bitter opposition of many members of his party). That admission would weaken the exclusivity of bolshevik leadership, the one thing which was never to be questioned. Accordingly Lenin developed a rationale for shooting these potential opponents. Of "the mensheviks and social-revolutionists who advocated such views," Lenin wrote that they "wonder when we tell them that we are going to shoot them for saying such things. They are amazed at it, but the question is clear: when an army is in retreat, it stands in need of discipline a hundred times more severe than when it advances because in the latter case everyone is eager to rush ahead. But if now everyone is just as eager to rush back, the result will be a catastrophe.

"And when a menshevik says: 'you are now retreating but I was always favouring a retreat, I am in full accord with you, I am one of your people, let us retreat together,' we tell them in reply: an avowal of menshevik views should be punished by our revolutionary courts with shooting, otherwise the latter are not courts, but God knows what."[10]

Lenin's desire was to see the revolution through, but only in the way he thought correct. Let us grant that he was sincere; we still have to question his self-assured single-mindedness which brooked no opposition and permitted no other approach. Looking at some of the attributes of his programme today makes one think twice about how revolutionary Lenin really was. Maximoff had no doubt on that score. He saw Lenin as a "representative of a degenerating gentry" (p.113) and even went so far as to call him "the first theoretician of fascism." (p.60). While this extreme language probably tends to alienate the unconvinced rather than to provoke thought, a good case can be made that leninist policies were essentially counter-revolutionary, that the net impact of Lenin's rule was to frustrate and stall out the authentic revolutionary momentum of the Russian people. It is an argument I have developed somewhat more fully elsewhere (see my introduction to Alexander Berkman's *The Russian Tragedy*, also published by Cienfuegos Press). Berkman's writings, Emma Goldman's works on Russia, Maximoff's *The Guillotine at Work*, and Maurice Brinton's *The Bolsheviks and Worker's Control 1917-1921 : The State and Counter-revolution* are among the books which led me to focus on this theme, one which I feel is vital to our time, which would at first glance permit us the alternative only of international cartel capitalism and marxist/leninist authoritarian bureaucratic rule.

Lenin did not stress socialism *per se*. He pushed for nationalisation, state ownership and control of the means of production. Where the workers and peasants had taken over the land and factories for themselves, and begun to institute true socialism, Lenin took a step backward by asserting state supremacy. Much of the struggle in the civil war was due to Lenin's efforts to subordinate the spontaneously created autonomous workers' councils, trade unions and peasant organisations. Maximoff quotes Lenin: "We leave to ourselves the state power, *only to ourselves* . . . it is necessary that everything should be subjected to the Soviet power and all the illusions about some kind of 'independence' on the part of detached layers of population or workers' co-operatives should be lived down as soon as possible . . . there can be no question of independence on the part of separate groups . . ." [11]. Lenin made a principle of reinstitut-ing one-man management rather than the new collective management which the workers and peasants had developed in the interests of respon-sibility to state supervision. He reinstituted higher pay and privileges for specialists and managers, as against the equality of pay in the industrial democracy which the workers themselves had promulgated. He also reintroduced piecework, the Taylor system (more precisely, elements thereof) and others of the most hated elements of capitalism.[12] Because, to his way of thinking, the party represented the real interests of the workers, it was also acceptable to outlaw strikes. Only counter-revolutionaries, he believed, would ever want to strike against a workers' state.

Capitalism was, to both Lenin and Marx, an inevitable stage of historical evolution. It was not possible to move from a fundamentally feudal system to a socialism of abundance without an intervening period of capital accumulation and centralisation. Lenin's understanding of history and economic development convinced him that a transitional stage of state capitalism ·(he did allow that the period of private capitalism could be omitted) was an historical necessity. Lenin recommended we "learn about state capitalism from the Germans, to assimilate their methods, not to spare any dictatorial methods in order to accelerate the westernisation of barbarous Russia, not to recoil from using barbarous methods of struggle against barbarism . . . govern with greater firmness than the capitalists did. Otherwise, you will not win. You must remember: your administration must be more stringent and firm than the old administration. . . This discipline included harsh, stringent measures, going as far as shootings, methods which even the old government did not visualise."[13]

It is not surprising that revolutionary workers revolted against Lenin's programme, which appeared to combine many of the worst abuses of capitalism with an "iron discipline," only justifying the regime to which the workers had to bend by proclaiming that it was issuing these orders and decrees in the name of the workers, as a government of workers. Lenin's programme of replacing factory management by the workers themselves with party committee management, and the subversion of the trade unions, robbed the workers of most of the gains they felt they had earned through struggle. The peasants felt no less betrayed. Maximoff angrily assigns to Lenin's account the millions of deaths caused by the famines which his policies of terror entailed: "by his policy of terror, by the destruction of the peasant economy, by exiling thousands of peasants from their native places, by the policy of grain requisitions, etc., Lenin prepared one of the ghastliest famines in the history of Russia, the famine of 1921, which carried away millions of lives and crippled, physically and morally, tens of millions."[17]

Maximoff following in the footsteps of Bakunin, traces the Leninist policy to "political marxism" itself. Russian socialism had always been "distinguished by its libertarian and progressive character," writes Maximoff in opening his book. "Political marxism," though, "Is an anachronism, a vestige of the dying past and is altogether reactionary in its essence. The *Communist Manifesto* of Marx and Engels is a reactionary manifesto

X

and is in striking contradiction to science, to progress in general, and humanism in particular. The demands of dictatorship, of absolute central-isation, of political and economic life in the hands of the state, of 'forming industrial armies, especially for agriculture,' of a regimented agriculture in accordance with a single plan, of raising the state to the position of an Absolute and the resulting stultification of the individual, its rights and interest — all that is nothing but the programme of reaction which is incompatible with human progress, with freedom, equality and humanism. The realisation of these demands carries with it *state slavery*."[15]

Lenin was only able to introduce "political marxism" onto the Russian scene by proclaiming other ideas. "If he had come out in 1917 with the ideas of the *Communist Manifesto*," Maximoff argues, "he would never have attained success, and like Tkachev, the Jacobin, he would have remained a rather inconspicuous figure throughout the revolution."[16] Lenin adopted the anarchist slogans in 1917, for tactical purposes pro-claiming the libertarian positions that were clearly the most popular among the Russian masses. Lenin was a brilliant politician and he pulled off this total about-face, when it was necessary to do so, even though it meant turning his back on virtually everything his party had stood for. Indeed, the other bolshevik leaders thought Lenin had lost his head.[17] The decep-tion worked, though. It was, in some cases, a number of years before it hit home with other revolutionists that Lenin had never meant the things he wrote in, for instance, *The State and Revolution*, which had convinced many that he was honestly in support of the movement of the people.

In fact, though, Lenin had not changed for any other than temporary and tactical considerations. Maximoff makes abundantly clear that Lenin never intended to change and that he employed machiavellian political tactics to consolidate himself and his party in power. Once established in power he moved firmly and unhesitatingly against the only real threat that was likely — a threat from the left. He need not have even feared such a threat had he not so doggedly and dogmatically held that only his own programmes should be applied. In time, political opposition certainly would have manifested itself but had Lenin been willing to work with other tendencies this opposition could have been comradely. Instead, as Miasnikov's insight indicates, Lenin feared the airing of views other than his own. Lenin was a most dynamic figure and the bolsheviks had won the support of many veteran anarchists who had long opposed what he had always stood for. Coming from a tradition that posed itself against Marx himself, one can read with sympathy the tragic hopes of a prominent anarchist such as Alexander Berkman who tried as long as he could to

XI

maintain revolutionary solidarity with the bolsheviks.[18] After all, it was a time of crisis: a world war, economic disruption in the extreme, counter-revolutionary invasions and plots, capitalist hostility.

It was not a simple matter of toleration. After all, the left S.-R.s assassinated Mirbach, the German Ambassador. Dora Kaplan shot and wounded Lenin. A group said to include members of the "Underground Anarchists" and the Left S-R's exploded a bomb during a meeting of the Moscow Committee of the Communist Party[18a]. These and similar acts across the country reflect determined efforts by the revolutionary opposition to challenge the direction of Bolshevik policy. Lenin seemed constitutionally unable to tolerate opposition, however, and one suspects that these incidents did not so much provoke the terroristic suppression of the revolutionary opposition as provide helpful excuses for its implementation. Well before the Revolution itself, Lenin's intolerance is easily demonstrated. He had a driving need to see his views prevail. He was absolutely and unshakably certain of their correctness and yet, at the same time, he seemed to fear an open airing of other views.

Maximoff presents us here with a great deal of material for thought. The original work, over 600 pages long, also included a second section documenting extensively the persecution of the anarchists under Lenin's regime. Although copies of the original are rather rare (it was issued in 1940 not by a commercial publishing house but by the Chicago Section of the Alexander Berkman Fund), it was decided to omit this section for this edition). Maximoff's message is contained in the first half of the book, which is here reissued in unabridged form. The second section of the book was in the nature of an appendix, a documentation which focused on the particular case of the anarchists as victims. The reader interested to explore further can now find a reasonably good selection of works offering an alternative view of the Russian Revolution, a view different from the standard one in which both the capitalists and the communists concur.[19] We hope the republication of *The Guillotine at Work* can inspire new and creative thought guided by a better understanding of the lessons of the past.

Bill Nowlin.

FOOTNOTES

1. Roy A. Medvedev, *Let History Judge,* New York, 1973.p.559.
2. See p.52 this volume. Maximoff also wrote of Lenin: "Since he was, like Marx and Engels, a Jacobin, he thought in terms and images of

XII

the latter. He could not conceive a revolution without terror and he held that the French Revolution became great only because of terror, and that the Russian revolution can be great and successful only if it pursues a terrorist policy . . ." See p.44 for more.

3. See p.71.

4. See p.28.

5. See *The Anarchism of Nestor Makhno* by Michael Palij (Seattle: 1976) for the most scholarly work on the subject. Important primary sources include Arshinov's *History of the Makhnovist Movement* (Detroit/Chicago, 1974) and Voline's *The Unknown Revolution* (Detroit/Chicago, 1974). My own summary of the literature in "The Makhnovist Movement," *Black Rose* 2 may be of interest to some.

6. As late as August 1917, even John Reed was characterising the Bolsheviks as a "small sect." See Leonard Schapiro, *Origin of the Communist Autocracy* (p.201), and Jay Sorensen, *The Life and Death of Soviet Trade Unionism.* On page 9, Sorensen writes:

"Bolshevik support quickly evaporated after 1914. By March 1917 they were little more than an isolated sect. Outside of a handful of unions . . . and a handful of worker-Bolsheviks, Lenin was hard pressed to find worker support for his party."

7. See p.169 this volume.

8. Quoted by Maximoff from p.271 of this volume. In 1924 Miasnikov wrote a letter from Tomsk Prison which is printed in *Letters From Russian Prisons.* Edited by Alexander Berkman; a reissuing of this book by Hyperion Press of Westport, Connecticut in 1978 is very welcome particularly since, for the first time, Berkman gets the credit he deserves. The Miasnikov letter appears on pages 84-5.

9. See p.270 this volume. The entire history of the Workers' Opposition in Russia is of related interest. For the best discussion of this and other early opposition to the bolshevik leadership, much from party members, see Robert V. Daniels, *The Conscience of the Revolution.*

10. See p.204 this volume.

11. See p.183

12. For any who would doubt that this was truly Lenin's policy, I would refer to Maurice Brinton's *The Bolsheviks and Workers' Control* and to my summary in my introduction to Berkman's *The Russian Tragedy.* It is not really a matter for debate. It simply

is necessary to read Lenin's writings themselves. He is the one who refers to the Taylor system *et al.* The most forthright statements of Lenin in this regard are in his pamphlet *The Immediate Tasks of the Soviet Government* which, rather than being hidden away somewhere, is available in almost any anthology of Lenin's works. Statements of this sort were not simply some temporary errant path which Lenin followed, but central to his programme.

13. See this volume pp.146-152.
14. See p.88.
15. See pp. 19, 20.
16. See p.20.
17. See, for instance, E.H. Carr, *The Bolshevik Revolution*, Vol. I, p.90.
18. Berkman's disillusionment is portrayed well in *The Russian Tragedy* but even more forcefully in his major work on revolutionary Russia, *The Bolshevik Myth.*
18a. Paul Avrich, *The Russian Anarchists*, pp. 188, 189. Other anarchists denounced the bombing, as indicated in Sam Dolgoff's introduction to this edition.
19. Consult many of the books referred to above, in particular Voline and Brinton.

GREGORY PETROVICH MAXIMOFF

Gregory Petrovich Maximoff was born 10 November 1893 in the village of Mitushenko, Smolensk Province. His parents sent him to Vladimir Theological Seminary to study for the priesthood, but a year before he was to be ordained Maximoff renounced religion in favour of science and enrolled in the St. Petersburg Agricultural Academy, graduating in 1915 as a qualified agronomist.

In his restless search for a coherent revolutionary orientation, Maximoff studied the literature of the various radical groupings. But it was the ideas of Bakunin and Kropotkin that shaped his revolutionary career. Maximoff's ideology — a synthesis of communalism and syndicalism — is based upon the teachings of Bakunin and Kropotkin. Maximoff defined this relationship:

" . . . I am a communist [because I believe in] the organisation of communal production on the basis of 'from each according to his ability' and of communal consumption on the principle of 'each according to his needs' . . . . the state would be replaced by a *confederation of free communes* . . . . I am a syndicalist [because I believe that] the means by which capitalism can be overthrown and communism installed is the seizure of production by the producers labour unions . . . *syndicalist production built around communist relations between producers* . . . . " (*Constructive Anarchism,* Chicago, 1952, pp.24, 31 — Maximoff's emphasis).

Kropotkin also confirms this relationship: ". . . I believe that the syndicalist movement will emerge as the great force . . . leading to the creation of the communist stateless society . . . ." (quoted, Paul Avrich, *The Russian Anarchists*, Princeton, 1967 p.227).

The Russian anarcho-syndicalists did not intend to become a sect of impotent grumblers. Already, remarks Maximoff:

" . . . the first two conferences of the anarcho-syndicalists in 1918 set forth clearly and in detail the political and economic characteristics of the first stages of the new social structure . . . our press was filled with articles on this subject . . . [the anarcho-syndicalists] launched a bold campaign against the chaotic, formless, disorganised and indifferent attitude [towards the constructive problems of the social-revolution] rampant among the anarchists . . . " (*Constructive Anarchism,* p.61).

XV

Maximoff's pre-eminent place in this history of Russian Anarchism rests upon his ability to adjust theory to the practical needs of the workers. He formulated workable, constructive libertarian alternatives to Bolshevism: free soviets, grass-roots housing and neighbourhood committees, workers' self-management of industry through federations of rank-and-file factory committees, industrial unions, agricultural collectives and communes, networks of non-interest, non-profit co-operatives agencies for credit and exchange, a vast network of voluntary organisations embracing the myriad operations of a complex society. (see *The Guillotine at Work;* pp.349, 353, 364-66, 374-78 — not published here: *Constructive Anarchism*, pp. 26-31, 101-47; Paul Avrich, *Anarchists in the Russian Revolution*, New York, 1973, pp.68-74, 102-6).

          *   *   *   *

Maximoff became an active anarchist propagandist, not only in student and workers' circles, but also among the peasants, where his agricultural knowledge and understanding of peasant problems proved most effective.

In 1915 Maximoff was drafted into the Czar's Army. Although his educational background qualified him for officer training school, Maximoff preferred the life of the common soldier, the better to spread anti-war, anti-militarist revolutionary propaganda among the conscripted workers and peasants.

Emma Goldman wrote that Maximoff:

" . . . an anarchist of long standing . . . participated in the revolutionary struggles beginning with the February Revolution of 1917, was one of the editors of *Golos Truda* (The Voice of Labour) and a member of the All-Russian Secretariat of Anarcho-Syndicalists . . . he is an able and popular writer and Lecturer . . . ." (*My Further Disillusionment in Russia*: New York, 1944 p.142)

In line with co-ordinating the resistance of the already spontaneously organised rank-and-file factory committees against the increasing domination of the labour movement by the state controlled unions, Maximoff played a major part in organising the first conference of the All-Russian Conference of Factory Committees (October 1917) and before that the Petrograd Factory Committees (June 1917).

Golos Truda printing collective and bookshops in Moscow and in Petrograd circulated throughout Russia translations of anarcho-syndicalist books and pamphlets; a five volume collection of Bakunin's writings and works by Kropotkin, Stepniak and other Russian anarchists. *Golos Truda*

XVI

was soon suppressed and succeded by *Volny Golos Truda* (New Voice of Labour).

*   *   *   *

No account of Maximoff's life would be adequate without recording the important part played by his wife and comrade-in-arms, Olga Freydlin. Olga was still a young girl when she became an anarchist. In 1909 she was sentenced to eight years hard labour for smuggling and spreading subversive literature. But, because of her youth she was condemned to life-banishment in Yenesink Province, Siberia.

With the release of political prisoners by the February 1917 revolution, Olga came to Moscow. She also actively participated in the revolutionary movement in Kharkov and other Ukrainian areas — particularly in the anarcho-syndicalist and co-operative m ivements. Later, Olga went to the Urals, and became active in the Ural Anarchist Federation, where she filled a responsible post in the People's Educational Committee. When it was occupied by the Czechoslovakian counter-revolutionary army, Olga returned to Moscow in 1918. She was very active in the Golos Truda Group and it was there that she first met Maximoff.

*   *   *   *

In the spring of 1919, Maximoff came to Kharkov to work with the Southern Bureau of the All-Russian Union of Metal Workers, in the department of statistics. When the trade unions mobilised trade union officials for voluntary propaganda work in the Red Army, Maximoff refused because he would be forced to spread bolshevik, not anarchist, propaganda. He agreed to serve in front-line combat against the counter-revolutionary white guards, only if he would not be obliged to participate in the suppression of workers' and peasants' strikes, demonstrations, or curtailment of civil rights. For this, and other "subversive" activities, Maximoff was arrested and saved from execution only by the threat of a general strike of the Kharkov Steelworkers Union. He was, however, thrown in the Cheka dungeons. His harrowing experience is graphically portrayed in the chapter "One Day in the Cheka's Cellas" (pp.425-31, in the original edition — to be published later as a separate title).

Although the anarchist movement condemned the bombing of the headquarters of the Moscow Committee of the Bolshevik Party, the bombings became the pretext for the wholesale arrests and persecution of anarchists all over Russia.

In 1920, Maximoff and others organised the underground Federation of Food Workers, the first step toward the establishment of a Russian

XVII

General Confederation of Labour. (Its programme is on page 369 of the original edition). In November 1920, Maximoff became the secretary of the Executive Committee of the Anarcho-Syndicalist Confederation.

With the disciplining, in 1921, of the so-called "Workers' Opposition" movement within the Russian Communist Party, and the crushing of the Kronstadt Sailors' revolt and peasant and workers' strikes and riots, the backbone of the growing anarchist movement was broken. Bookshops, printing facilities, newspapers, halls, clubs, were closed. Maximoff presents three documents protesting the attitude of the Russian Communist Party and the Red International of Trade Unions (the Profintern) towards the anarchists and anarcho-syndicalists: (1) Appeal of the All-Russian Confederation of Anarcho-Syndicalists to the Workers of All Countries; (2) The Central Committee of the Russian Communist Party; (3) the Executive Committee of the Third (Communist Party) International. (pp.440-53 of the original edition).

In July 1921, thirteen anarchist and anarcho-syndicalist prisoners in the notorious Cheka Taganka prison in Moscow, among them Maximoff, Yarchuck, Mratchny, and Volin, declared a ten day hunger strike.

Through the intervention of the syndicalist delegates to the Profintern congress, then in session, Augustin Souchy, Germany;(Armando Borghi, Italy; Orlandis and Gaston Leval, Spain; the French delegate Sirolle, among others), Lenin and Trotsky agreed to release the anarchists if they gave up their hunger strike and agreed to deportation from Russia, never to return. In this connection, we must not fail to note the part played by Emma Goldman, Alexander Berkman, Olga Maximoff and other militants in bringing the plight of the hunger strikers to the attention of the foreign syndicalist delegates. Maximoff and the other anarchists were deported in January 1922. After surmounting terrible difficulties deliberately planted by the Russian Communist Party's Cheka, they finally reached Berlin on 7 February 1922, to be welcomed and cared for by the German anarchists.

*　　　　*　　　　*　　　　*

With the arrival of the Russian anarchist exiles, Maximoff, Volin, Yarchuck, Mratchny and a few others, joined later by Alexander Schapiro, Nestor Makhno, Peter Archinoff, Emma Goldman, Alexander Berkman, Senja Fleschine, Mollie Steimer and other refugees, Berlin became the nerve centre of the International Russian Anarchist Movement, where archives and manuscripts smuggled out of Russia were deposited.

Rudolf Rocker, in his memoirs, tells how Archinoff's manuscript, *The*

XVIII

History of the Makhno Movement, and Berkman's diary of events in Russia, *The Bolshevik Myth*, sent for safekeeping until their arrival in Berlin from Russia, and deemed lost in transmission, were located, and later delivered intact. (*Revolution and Regression* — Yiddish translation, Buenos Aires 1963, Vol. I, pp.180-4).

The exiles left Russia more than ever determined to continue their struggle for the liberation of the Russian people from their new dictators. For Maximoff and his comrades, deportation signified not the end, but the beginning of new battles. This key passage from the *Guillotine at Work* illustrates the character and scope of Maximoff's activities during his three year stay in Berlin:

[While yet in Russia confined in Taganka Prison] " . . . it was decided that we go to Berlin, where there was a strong and healthy anarcho-syndicalist movement, and to launch a concerted work for Russia, acting as the Foreign Bureau of the All-Russian Anarcho-Syndicalist Confederation . . . to publish a paper for Russia . . . and also propagandistic and agitational literature . . . . we hoped that with the material and moral support of German, French, American, and other comrades, we should be able to set up a publication in one or several European languages, where the truth about the Russian Revolution would be told, where one could share one's revolutionary experience, and a series of problems brought forward by the Revolution in Russia, and where one might appeal for the organisation of an anarcho-syndicalist international based upon the principles of Bakuninism of the First International . . . ." (p.499 of the original edition).

In this they were not disappointed. Maximoff and Alexander Schapiro, who wrote its declaration of principles, contributed significantly toward organising the anarcho-syndicalist International Workingmen's Association (IWMA) as the revolutionary alternative to the Bolshevik dominated Red International of Trade Unions (Profintern). They helped establish the Joint Committee for the Defence of the Revolutionists Imprisoned in Russia.

In the Russian anarcho-syndicalist periodical *Robotny Put* (Workers' Way) which Maximoff helped establish and edited; in his pamphlet, *Instead of a Programme*; in other writings and in discussions, Maximoff emphasised that the anarchists should learn from the experience of the Russian Revolution, how to correct their mistakes and work out positive workable measures for the libertarian reconstruction of society.

*　　　　*　　　　*　　　　*

The Maximoff's left Berlin in 1924. After a few months in Paris
they arrived in the United States in 1925, settling in Chicago, under the
name Urkevich. Under the guidance of his comrade, Boris Yelensky,
Maximoff became a paperhanger, and his wife Olga found employment
in a downtown Chicago department store.

The IWMA and Maximoff regarded the Industrial Workers of the
World as part of the anarcho-syndicalist movement. The twenty thousand
member Chilean IWW did not officially affiliate, it always maintained,
and still maintains, close fraternal relations with the IWMA, and accepts
a membership card in an IWMA affiliate as the equivalent of membership
in the IWW. Shortly after settling in Chicago, Maximoff therefore became
a member of the IWW and until its suspension in 1927, edited its Russian
organ *Golos Truzhenika* (The Labourer's Voice).

When the editor of *Delo Truda* (Labour's Cause) recanted his anarchism
and with the permission of the Communist Party returned to Russia,
Delo Truda was transferred from Paris to Chicago and Maximoff became its
editor. Paul Avrich notes that under " . . . Maximoff's supervision *Delo
Truda* became the most important journal of the Russian emigres . . . ."
(*The Russian Anarchists*, Princeton, 1967, p.247). When *Delo Truda*
merged with the Detroit publication in 1940 to become *Delo Truda-
Probuzhdenie*, Maximoff stayed on as its editor until his death in 1950.

*   *   *   *

I first met Maximoff in 1926 when I congratulated him on having
learned so quickly enough English to converse, he replied that he must
perfect his English the better to participate in the building of an effective
American anarchist movement.

In discussing the basis for such a movement, Maximoff helped clarify
my ideas, introduced me to the ideas and writings of the classical
anarchists (particularly Bakunin and Kropotkin) and thus helped me
achieve a correct orientation.

Maximoff rejected the romantic glorification of conspiracy and violence
in the amoral tradition of Nechaev; total irresponsibility; excessive pre-
occupation with one's "unique life style," rejection of any form of
organisation or self-discipline and the idealisation of the most anti-social
forms of individual rebellion.

For Maximoff, anarchism was not only a standard of personal
conduct (he never underestimated its importance). Anarchism is a
social movement, a movement of the people. Like Bakunin and
Kropotkin and the classical anarchists, Maximoff defined anarchism as

XX

the truest expression of socialism. He insisted that we must work out a constructive realistic approach to the problems of the social revolution and relate anarchism to the socio-economic problems of our complex society.

We were receptive to Maximoff's ideas, not because he indoctrinated us, but because we had been led by our own experience to think along similar lines. We, too, felt the need to distinguish ourselves ideologically and organisationally from fundamentally conflicting tendencies — getting together, when necessary, for specific purposes.

In the late 1920s or early 1930s we identified ourselves as an "Anarchist-Communist" group and named our monthly organ, *Vanguard : an Anarchist-Communist Journal*. Maximoff was a regular contributor. His articles, signed or unsigned, as well as his constructive suggestions, enhanced the value of *Vanguard*, still considered one of the best radical journals of that period.

Besides his profuse writings, Maximoff strove to preserve the continuity of the Russian anarchist movement in America, periodically addressing groups in New York, New Haven, Akron, Youngstown, Gary, Philadelphia, Boston, Baltimore, Waterbury and Dobbs Ferry, and in the interim conducting a voluminous correspondence. The magnitude of Maximoff's efforts is all the more impressive when we consider that he found time to do all these things after working long hours or at weekends.

*   *   *   *

Maximoff suffered a massive heart attack and died suddenly on 10 March 1950 upon returning from his day's work. When we visited Olga Maximoff a few years before her death, she told us that she fell and broke her leg, if I am not mistaken, two or three years before. Incompetent, careless medical treatment made necessary a shortening of her foot. This, and increasing deafness, forced her to quit her job in the department store. She died on 7 May 1973. Olga left instructions not to conduct a funeral and donated her body to medical research. (Maximoff's body was cremated and interred in Waldheim cemetery near the tomb of the Chicago Haymarket martyrs.)

Irving S. Abrams, an intimate friend and comrade who had known the Maximoff's when they first came to Chicago in 1925, informed me in a recent letter that " . . . she gave all she had to the Alexander Berkman Fund for the Relief of Political Prisoners, in Russia and other countries, which the Maximoff's helped organise and under whose auspices *The Guillotine At Work* was first published in 1940.

*   *   *   *

Maximoff was a prolific writer. Besides editing and writing articles in
Delo Truda-Probuzhdenie and voluminous writings awaiting translation,
there appeared his lengthy book *The Guillotine at Work :Twenty Years
of Terror in Russia (Data and Documents)* a pioneering expose; a series
of pamphlets, among them *My Social Credo*, a concise outline of
Maximoff's ideas, *Bolshevism :Promises and Realities : The World Scene
from the Libertarian Point of View*, a collection of articles by anarchist
writers from different countries; *Bulgaria :A New Spain*, a record of the
persecution of anarchists and other dissenters etcetera.

The Political Philosophy of Bakunin, a systematic compilation of
Bakunin's constructive ideas, and *Constructive Anarchism*, an outline
of Maximoff's practical ideas, were published after his death by the
Maximoff Publication Society, organised by its secretary Irving S.
Abrams, Maximoff's wife Olga, and other comrades to honour Maximoff's
memory by publishing his works in English translation.

As I write these lines twenty-eight years after Maximoff's untimely
death, I still feel keenly the loss of the dear friend, the valiant comrade,
who inspired me (and so many others) to explore new roads to freedom.
Publication of *The Guillotine at Work* is surely an important project.
Maximoff's message is still relevant.

Sam Dolgoff.

THE GUILLOTINE AT WORK

Vol. I THE LENINIST COUNTER REVOLUTION

DEDICATED

To the Russian People.

To their Fighters for Liberty, Humanism and Justice.

To the International Proletariat.

The
GUILLOTINE
AT WORK

Twenty Years of Terror in Russia

by

G. P. MAXIMOFF

The Chicago Section of the
Alexander Berkman Fund

A Non-Profit Organization

2422 N. HALSTED ST.   CHICAGO, ILL.

1940

Translated from Russian

The March revolution subverted the power of the Romanovs and settled accounts with the Tzarist regime. In one day monarchist Russia became transformed into the freest country in the world. The Tzar's prisoners were immediately released from the prisons and penal servitude, and brought back from places of exile. The prisons became deserted. No one thought they would soon be filled again with politicals. The various societies to aid the political prisoners and exiles, the so-called Red and Black Crosses, were dissolved in Russia itself as well as abroad where political emigrants held it a duty to organize material and moral aid to their more unfortunate comrades and brothers languishing in the Tzar's numerous torture chambers.

However, those sanguine hopes were soon brought to an end. They faded before they had come to flower. The October upheaval brought Russia to a one-party dictatorship, the dictatorship of the Bolshevik party, which unwarrantedly called itself "the dictatorship of the proletariat". In the name of the dictatorship of the proletariat and under the pretense of its interests, this party unloosed a campaign of terror against any opposition. The bourgeois parties were outlawed; the socialist parties—the Social-Democrats and the Social-Revolutionists— were dubbed "entente agents" and "tuft hunters of the counter-revolution." The next logical step was to hound those parties, to suppress their papers, to arrest and expel their members from the soviets. As the civil war swept on, all non-Bolshevik elements were dubbed "petty-bourgeois and counter-revolutionary elements". Right and Left Social-Revolutionists, Social-Democrat of all shades, Maximalists, Anarchists of every tendency—all were placed in the same category of "counter-revolutionists". A campaign of slandering and baiting was launched against such "counter-revolutionists".

Soon these elements began to crowd not only the Tzar's empty prisons but the vast number of private buildings conversed by the Bolsheviks into prisons. Newly built "concentration camps," which were unknown to the Tzar's government, were quickly filled. And when this proved insufficient, the Bolsheviks restored the Tzar's exile system, having expanded it considerably.

In view of the incessant food crisis, and the unprecedented arbitrary power granted to the Bolshevik administration, political prisoners and exiles found themselves in conditions many times worse than those prevailing under the Tzar's regime. Starvation food rations, extremely unsanitary conditions in prisons and exile places, lack of proper medical care, irresponsible and high-handed prison administration, blacklisting of exiles in respect to obtaining work, all this created a desperate situation of indescribable want and starvation. Thus, out of necessity, there arose again, in Soviet Russia as well as abroad, societies to aid political prisoners and exiles.

Abroad, however, this worthy cause met with great obstacles. Suspicion and lack of confidence on the part of the liberal and radical public resulted from the campaign of slanderous Bolshevik propaganda which held that there were no political prisoners in Soviet Russia. According to this hypocritical claim, the Soviets imprisoned only common criminals, and Socialist or Anarchist renegades implicated in counter-revolutionary work.

In America for instance, even the publication of such a remarkable book as "Letters from Russian Prisons," a book replete with striking documents of unquestionable authenticity, could not overcome this mistrust and suspicion. Protests against Bolshevik persecutions of heterodox opinion, propaganda and demands for the immediate liberation of politicals, met with the rebuff of the liberal and radical circles abroad. Many liberals and radicals went so far as to defend those repressions. And in view of this indifferent or even conniving attitude of those circles, the Bolshevik government became harsher toward its victims, becoming more ruthless in its treatment of the political prisoners and exiles. In its undisguised drive to place all opposition under the knife of the dry guillotine, the Bolshevik state began to place obstacles in the work of the various aid societies in providing Soviet political prisoners and exiles with food, medicines, books, etc. This was followed by the closing of such aid societies, the arrests of their members, the banning of any correspondence with comrades abroad. The government showed special cruelty in regard to those prisoners and exiles whose names were mentioned in the protests published by the foreign press.

At the present time there is not a single organization in Russia, devoting itself to the task of providing aid for Soviet political prisoners. Until 1938, there was in existence a nonpartisan "Red Cross" society, whose origin dated back to the Tzar's time. The organization was headed by Maxim Gorky's ex-wife, Pieshkova. For many years this society had provided aid to Russian politicals to the extent of its capacity. At present, even this organization has been liquidated.

Formerly one could send material aid directly from abroad to the address of the prisoners; now, this has become absolutely impossible as a result of the fierce persecutions unloosed by the Soviet government against any one having any relations with people abroad. In the case of political prisoners, such relations entail worsened conditions of confinement, extension of term of sentence, or implication in some concocted plot, placing the Soviet political prisoner under the imminent threat of execution.

Ever since Stalin began his "bloody purge" of the Communist party, it has become more and more difficult to maintain contact with Soviet political prisoners and exiles. Connections were severed in many cases. This circumstance, coupled with some alarming news conveyed to us by temporarily released comrades who were afraid to sign the letters sent to us, leads us to think that in the hubbub of party purges, there have been executions under the guise of "Trotzkyites", "Bukharinites," and other "wreckers," of a number of Socialist and Anarchist political exiles, many of whom, like Aaron Baron, had been kept in confinement since 1920.

In the case of Aaron Baron, certain circumstances have been cropping up of late, which warrant a great deal of apprehension on our part. After more than eighteen years of confinement in various prisons, concentration camps, and other places of exile, Baron was finally established in the city of Kharkov. A year ago he was seized again and shipped to an unknown destination. Baron's wife is still denied the opportunity to visit him in prison, and up till now, his whereabouts have not been disclosed. No one knows where Aaron Baron is, or what has happened to him. And Baron's case is not the only one.

All this inspires us with fear in respect to the life of the political prisoners and exiles in Soviet Russia. At the same time we are utterly helpless in view of the indifference with which public opinion of the Western countries treat such news. During the last twenty years, such public opinion has become accustomed to the horrible persecutions in Russia and other countries and is hardened to the despairing cries for aid wafted from Bolshevik torture chambers.

What is to be done? During the last two years the attention of the protagonists of freedom and humanism has been riveted upon the pressing task of aiding the Spanish Loyalists, who waged a heroic struggle against the hordes of Italian, German and Spanish Fascism. We were forced to throw ourselves into this work of aiding the Spanish people and to set aside temporarily the crying need of the Russian politicals. And then there was another wave of terror — a wave of a savage unrestrained terror, this time against the Jews in Germany and Italy. To the many thousands of victims of political persecution have been added the victims of racial hatred, thousands and thousands of whom frantically seek asylum without being able to find it.

It is only reasonable that public opinion of the world should be thus absorbed with the fate of the new victims of Twentieth Century barbarism. Again we were forced to set aside the old crying need of prisoners of the Russian bloody dictatorship. But for how long can we keep on postponing this aid? The world is pregnant with new barbarous outbreaks, new waves of savage terror and there is no guarantee that tomorrow a new cry for help will not rise up in some new corner of the world and again detract our attention from the victims of the Bolshevik dry Guillotine.* But to forget about the Russian political prisoners, who languish during 10, 15 and 20 years in great numbers in prisons and exiles under the most horrible physical and moral conditions, is to doom them to an unavoidable death. Emaciated by hunger, and worn out by diseases, the resistance of their organism weakened to the utmost, they will inevitably succumb to the slightest attack. Already we have lost in such a manner, a number of prominent and highly esteemed figures in the Anarchist movement, people like Professor Alexey Borovoy, Nicolay Rogdayev, Ilovaysky-Kaydanov and many other less known and influential figures who had been subject to persecution by the Tzar's government. The same is true about the Socialist and non-partisan politicals.

Under these conditions, it would be nearly criminal to wait any longer. That is why **The Alexander Berkman Fund**, notwithstanding the unfavorable political situation, has decided to come out before the English-speaking world with a reminder about the pressing need of relief for Russian prisoners and exiles. In order to overcome the still latent distrust and suspicion, in order to arouse the slumbering social conscience, the **Alexander Berkman Fund** is boldly venturing forth with this work — an heroic undertaking in view of its slender financial means; it decided to present Public Opinion with documents and letters of the political prisoners and exiles, collected into a book, unfolding year after year the history and horrors of the persecutions that have been going on during the last twenty years. The authenticity of those documents and letters is beyond any question: it can be ascertained by the archives of the **Berkman Fund**, part of which is kept in Amsterdam, by the International Institute of Social History (the director of this Institute is Professor Postumus). Authenticity can also be verified through the archives of similar Aid Funds maintained

---

* As our book goes to press, war is raging in Europe and Stalin and Hitler have come to an amicable understanding. Poland has been divided, the territory of Russian terror enlarged, and the plight of the Russian political prisoners has become worse than tragic.

by the Socialist parties, especially the Social-Democrats, in whose publication "Sotzialistichesky Viestnik" ("The Socialist Courier") some of the documents we cite appeared for the first time.

When starting out to work upon this book, "The Guillotine at Work", we did not intend to confine ourselves exclusively to material dealing with the persecutions of Anarchists; what we had in mind was to give a full picture of the persecutions of non-Communists in Soviet Russia. We found, however, that neither the means at our disposal nor our organization as such were adequate for research undertaken on such a large scale. We could not undertake this work for several reasons, the principal ones among which were the following:

To collect the documents and letters of all political prisoners, irrespective of their affiliations, which would give a full picture of persecutions in Russia during the last twenty years is a task far exceeding the capacity of one person or even a single organization. Only a firmly established Scientific Institute, one solidly backed by some sort of endowment, could be able to undertake the work of getting together, editing and publishing the copious material represented by numerous documents and materials. Such a task would require not one but several books for publication. And much as we expanded our book, we found that we would still be forced to leave out numbers of important documents, letters, reminiscences, appeals, etc., all of which comprised enough material to make up another book of the same size as the present.

Another important motive impelling us to undertake this work was to stimulate an interest in the study of the Russian Terror. We hope and are still hoping that our example will be followed by other groupings: Social-Revolutionists, Social-Democrats, Maximalists, Socialist-Zionists, Tolstoyans, etc. Each of these has a great deal to tell of the persecutions and sufferings, the ghastly experience which their members went through in prisons and exile, in their struggle for elementary human and civil rights in Soviet Russia.

And the last, but not the least, reason for curtailing our original program of unfolding the history of the Soviet persecutions in the past twenty years, is the lack of financial means. The **Berkman Fund** is so limited in its financial means that were it not for the contributions of the Arbeiter Ring, the Russian and other language groups, and of a few trade unions, we would not even be able to undertake the publication of the present volume.

In placing these collected documents before the tribunal of the World's Public Opinion, we hope that our book "The Guillotine at Work" will again stimulate and revive the interest of the English-speaking public, especially that of the United States, toward the fate of Russian political prisoners and exiles. We hope that it will create a favorable atmosphere for a struggle against the horrors of a terroristic regime, as well as for the affirmation of the rights of Man and Citizen in Soviet Russia. We fervently hope that our activities will result in the release of all the political prisoners and exiled. And at the same time we trust that the success of this book (the income from which goes for the benefit of the political prisoners) will enable us to replenish the diminished treasury of the **Berkman Fund,** and thus to extend more liberal aid to the prisoners of the dreadful dictatorial regime.

The **Alexander Berkman Fund** extends its cordial thanks to the following organizations for their financial contributions toward the publication of this book:

Arbeiter Ring (Workmen's Circle) Branches: 2, 3, 19, 20, 29, 41, 45, 47, 52, 52B, 63, 65B, 79, 87, 95, 124, 126, 136, 144, 155, 161, 173, 181, 200, 207, 214, 252B, 304, 306B, 320, 362, 364, 389, 389B, 392, 475, 479, 572B, 600, 641, 650, 655, 670, 684, 695, 706, 707B, 806, 812, 816, 1908.

Branches of Russian Mutual Aid Societies (R. O. O. V.): 16, 42, 53.

Russian Groups: Los Angeles, Akron, Gary, East Akron, Philadelphia, Cleveland, Youngstown, Boston, New York, Baltimore, New Haven, San Francisco, Bethlehem, Waterbury, Dobbs Ferry.

Trade Unions: Locals 62 and 66 of the Ladies' Garment Workers, and miscellaneous Local Joint Boards of this Union in New York City.

English Speaking, and Foreign Language Groups: "Free Society", Chicago; Sunrise Colony Group; Radical Library Group, Philadelphia; The Libertarian Groups of Los Angeles; The Groups of Cleveland, Mohegan Colony, Stelton, Gary; "Freedom Group," New York; The Proletarian Group, New York; Ateneo Hispano, of New York and Wilsonville, Ill.

The Alexander Berkman Fund also extends its hearty gratitude to numerous individual contributors, whose names could not be listed in this book.

The Berkman Fund acknowledges its special gratitude to G. P. Maximoff, the author of this book for his voluntary work; to Ralph Chaplin, proletarian poet, Carl Keller, editor of "Industrial Worker," I. W. W. weekly organ, and Sophie Fagin, for their gratuitous editorial work; and to Art Hopkins, for his copy and proof-reading work.

The Chicago Section of the Alexander Berkman Fund

Author's Preface

Having something to do directly, and indirectly, with the work of aiding the political prisoners in Russia, having taken part in the organizing and reorganizing of various Aid Societies, I collected quite a number of documents of the highest authenticity and trustworthiness. Part of this material, arranged in chronological order in accordance with the explanatory notes, went into the second part of this book **"The Guillotine At Work"** which we now place before the Tribunal of Public Opinion.

The sources used in making up this book were: 1) Part of the archives of the Provisional Executive Bureau of All-Russian Anarcho-Syndicalist Confederation, which I succeeded in taking out with me when deported from Russia; 2) A small number of hitherto unpublished letters of political exiles which I have in my possession; 3) Part of the archives of the Foreign Bureau for the Setting Up of an All-Russian Anarcho-Syndicalist Confederation; 4) Documents published in the foreign press: "Der Syndicalist," Berlin; "L'Antorcha," Buenos Aires. (The documents came from Russia and its various prisons, and the author of these lines took part in the writing or the sending out of these documents); 5) Bulletins of the Aid Committee in which letters of the political prisoners and exiles appeared. The originals of most of those letters were turned over to the Amsterdam International Institute of Social History. A collection of those bulletins is in the possession of the Russian Foreign Archives in Prague.

Those bulletins are the following: a) "Bulletin of the Joint Committee for the Defense of Revolutionists imprisoned in Russia", Berlin, 1925; b) "Bulletin of the Relief Fund of the I. W. M. A. for Anarchists and Anarcho-Syndicalists, imprisoned or exiled in Russia," Berlin, 1926-32; c) "The International Workingmen's Ass'n Russian Aid Fund", 1932, and a few others. 6) "Golos Troudovogo Krestianstva" (The Voice of the Toiling Peasantry), the organ of the All-Russian Central Executive Committee of the Peasant Section of the Soviets; 7) "Znamia Trouda" (The Banner of Labor), the organ of the Central Committee of the party of the Left Social-Revolutionists-Internationalists; 8) The Publications of the Russian Anarchists: a) "Golos Anarchista" (The Voice of the Anarchists), Ekaterinoslav, 1918; b) "Nabat" (The Alarm) the organ of the Confederation of Anarchist Organizations of Ukraine, 1919; c) "Guliaypolsky Nabat," Guliay-Polie, 1919; d) "Kharkovsky Nabat," Kharkov, 1919; e) "Odessky Nabat," Odessa, 1918; f) "Universal," Moscow, 1921; g) "Pochin," a co-operative sheet, Moscow, 1923; 9) The foreign publications of the Russian Anarchists and Industrialists, in which the news of the Information Bulletin appeared: "Amerikanskiye Izvestia," New York, 1921-24; "Volna," U. S. 1921-24; "Golos Truzenika," weekly paper of Russian branch of the I.W.W., Chicago, 1919-1924; "Golos Truzenika," monthly magazine, the organ of the Russian branch of the I. W. W., Chicago, 1925-28; "Golos Truda," Buenos Aires, 1921-30; "Rabochy Put," Berlin, 1923; "Anarchichesky Viestnik," Beriln, 1923-24; "Dielo Trouda," Paris-Chicago, New York, 1925-38, and many other publications; 10) "Sotzialistichesky Viestnik," the organ of the Foreign Delegation of the Russian Social-Democratic-Workers Party, Berlin-Paris, 1921-38; 11) "Znamia Borby," the organ of the Foreign Delegation of the Party of Left Social-Revolutionists, Berlin, 1923-29. 12) A number of other press sources, which cannot be listed here.

The present work aims not only to arouse interest in the fate of the political prisoners in Soviet Russia, but to give the impetus to the study of government terror in the Russian revolution, its origin, causes, character, objectives, and consequences in the various fields of life, economic, political, cultural, as well as its effect upon the psychology of the Russian people. True, an exhaustive and adequate study of this problem is impossible, since the basic material bearing upon this problem is to be found in Russia and cannot be made accessible to the research worker. But by now there has already accumulated abroad much valuable material in the party archives, and in the archives of the various societies to aid political prisoners. The publication of this material in the collected form of a book, would lay the basis for an exhaustive study of the problem.

I shall consider my aim accomplished if other groupings and factions within the Russian Socialist movement follow our example. I shall feel highly gratified if the documents presented in this book arouse the interest of British and American students and research workers, and especially so if it will arouse a lively interest on the part of the British and American public toward the fate of all political prisoners and exiles in the U. S. S. R.

PART ONE

The Sources of the Russian Terror

(The Torquemada, Loyola, Machiavelli and Robespierre of the Russian Revolution).

CHAPTER I

LENIN'S ROAD TO POWER

The great Russian Revolution of 1917-21 was at first a 'bloodless' revolution. Nothing presaged at first that it would become most bloody in character and that by its senseless cruelty and inhumanity it would soon, as such, occupy the first place in the history of humanity. This turn of the Russian Revolution toward inhumanity, toward unrestrained and senseless bloodshed and destruction of human life is one of the historic paradoxes, for the basic trait in the character of the Russian people—that is, of the working masses— is kindness, humanness, love toward their fellow-being. This is shown even in the attitude toward criminals, who were always regarded by the Russian people as "unfortunates." Russian criminal law was doubtless one of the most humane in the world and it precluded capital punishment for common crimes. Only revolutionists were executed by the Tzar's government. Hardly any other literature was imbued as much as the Russian literature with the spirit of humanism, with the feeling of love and respect toward man. Russian Socialism, notwithstanding its tactic of revolutionary terror applied toward the Tzar's government, was never bloodthirsty, terroristic and inhumane. It never viewed society as a disciplined batallion, never lost sight of the living personality with its needs and interests. The Socialism of Chernishevsky, Bakunin, Lavrov, Kropotkin and Mikhaylovsky was based upon the ideas of individual freedom, of regional and communal federalism, and it was this kind of Socialism that always prevailed in Russia. Jacobinism, with its terror and centralization, all the great influence of the French revolution notwithstanding, was never successful in Russia, and spokesmen of Russian Jacobinism—like Tkachev, for instance—never found themselves in the main stream of Russian Socialism, never exercised a noteworthy influence upon the latter. In a word, Russian Socialism was distinguished by its libertarian and progressive character.

Reactionary notes began to sound in Russian Socialism with the appearance upon the Russian soil of political Marxism, which, to

— 19 —

my deepest conviction, is an anachronism, a vestige of the dying past, and is altogether reactionary in its essence. The "Communist Manifesto" of Marx and Engels is a reactionary manifesto and is in striking contradiction to science, to progress in general, and humanism in particular. The demands of dictatorship, of absolute centralization, of political and economic life in the hands of the State, of "forming industrial armies, especially for agriculture," of a regimented agriculture in accordance with a single plan, of raising the State to the position of an Absolute and the resulting stultification of the individual, its rights and interests—all that is nothing but the program of reaction which is incompatible with human progress, with freedom, equality and humanism. The realization of these demands inevitably carries with it *state slavery*.

This came about in Russia. Even when Lenin was still alive, Karl Kautsky, the most prominent leader of the world Social-Democracy, was led to characterize the Russian regime as state slavery; he ignored thereby the rather obvious death sentence which he, by implication, had to pass upon political Marxism and the "Communist Manifesto" of Marx and Engels. But no less harsh a verdict was passed upon the "Communist Manifesto" by another eminent Social-Democrat, E. Vandervelde, who, much before Karl Kautsky, declared that "nearly all the educated people of France would find the Socialism advocated by the 'Manifesto' rather monstrous. Fortunately, the 'Manifesto' passed almost unnoticed in the social storm which swept over Europe immediately after it was issued; the first edition having come out in a limited number of copies, the 'Manifesto' soon became a bibliographical rarity. It was only in 1872 that it began to circulate in larger numbers, spreading from one country to the other".[1] In other words, the "Manifesto" began to spread after the defeat of the Paris Commune, after the break-up of the First International, that is, at the time when the reaction was at its highest and the Social-Democracy was opportunistically adapting itself to this reaction.

Marxism came out "victorious" in the Russian Revolution, and

---

1) E. Vandervelde, "Le Jubilee du Manifeste Communiste"; appeared in "People," March 28, 1898, Brussels. The quotation is taken from V. Cherkesoff's book, "Predtechni Internazionala" (The Forerunners of the International), p. 55; 1920, Moscow.

this in itself is nothing short of a paradox: the Marxists owe their "victory" to their temporary renunciation of Marxism, effected in order to achieve their aim of seizing power.

Lenin, being a consistant Marxist and consequently a reactionary, wrote together with Plekhanov in the "Iskra" that "the Proletariat cannot and should not concern itself with federalism." If he had come out in 1917 with the ideas of the "Communist Manifesto," developing them with as much energy as he showed in developing the ideas that were contrary to the "Manifesto," he would have never attained success, and like Tkachev, the Jacobine, he would have remained a rather inconspicuous figure throughout the revolution. Lenin realized it only too well, and that is why he developed and popularized not the ideas of the "Communist Manifesto" but those of the "Civil War in France." The ideas set forth by Marx in the latter pamphlet are in full contradiction to his previous as well as subsequent writings.

The pamphlet was written under the pressure of the 1871 events in Paris and the prevailing spirit of the First International which threatened Marx with the loss of influence. By making concessions to Anarchist tendencies, Marx aimed to remove the growing dissatisfaction with his policies and to check the growing influence of the Federalists and Bakuninists in the First International. Had Marx not done it, had he based his pamphlet "The Civil War in France" upon the ideas of the "Communist Manifesto," he would have been cast aside and would have ended his days in the remote by-ways of the course of socialism and the revolutionary labor movement.

A similar fraud, perpetrated with the view of gaining the sympathies of the working masses and of seizing power in order to carry out the ideas of the "Communist Manifesto," was duplicated by Lenin in 1917. Five years later Lenin openly admitted as much. In his report on the activity of the Central Committee of the Communist Party made on March 22, 1922, he said:

"Until now we wrote programs and kept on promising. At one time that was much of a necessity. We had to present a program and to promise a world revolution. If the Whiteguards, the Mensheviks included, inveigh against us on that score, this shows only that the Mensheviks and the Socialists of the 2nd and 2½ Internationals never had any notion of how revolutions are made. We could not have started in any other way".2)

What did Lenin promise and what programs did he write in order to start the revolution? The answer is given by agitational and propagandistic writings of 1917.

In speaking about "The tasks of the Proletariat in the given revolution," Lenin wrote: "Not a parliamentary republic—this would be a step backwards as compared with the Soviet of the Workers' Deputies—but a Republic of Workers, Peasants, Farm Laborers, Soviets all over the country from top to bottom." "All power to the Soviets",3) Lenin explained to the soldiers, means that "the entire power in the State, from the lowest to the highest rungs, from the remotest village to every single ward within the city of Petrograd, must belong to the Soviets of Workers', Soldiers', Peasants' and Farm Laborer's Deputies".4) This new State will represent "a higher type of a democratic State, a State which in some respects, as Engels said, 'ceases to be a State, is no more a State in the proper sense of the word'. This is a State of the type of the Paris Commune, which replaces an army and police force set *apart* from the people with an armed people".5) In this State "the officialdom, the bureaucracy are either replaced with the direct power of the people, or, at least, are replaced under a special control, becoming not only elected deputies but ones that *can be removed* at the first popular demand, being indeed reduced to the position of pure and simple delegates. From a privileged set, receiving high emoluments on a truly bourgeois scale, they become workers discharging a certain kind of function and remunerated on a scale which *does not exceed* the regular wage of a skilled worker".6)

Lenin kept on reiterating: "not to permit the rise of totalitarian power of state officials", "not to permit the re-establishment of a standing army set apart from the people, an army which surely will be back of any attempt to rob the people of its freedom".7) That

---

2) N. Lenin (V. Uljanoff), Sobranie Sochineniy, p. 30, vol. XVIII, part 2; 1923, Moscow.

3) N. Lenin, Sobranie Sochineniy, pp. 17-18, vol. XIV, part 1.

4) N. Lenin, "A Speech Before Soldiers," p. 75, vol. XIV, part 1.

5) N. Lenin, "The Task of the Proletariat in Our Revolution," pp. 48-49, vol. XIV, part 1.

6) N. Lenin, "On Dual Power," p. 25, vol. XIV, part 1.

7) N. Lenin, "The Convention of Peasants' Deputies," p. 90, vol. XIV, part 1.

cannot be permitted to pass because "an officialdom that is appointed from above to 'direct' the local population always was, is and will be the main instigator of attempts to restore the monarchy, it being similar in this case to the standing army and the police".8)

Lenin kept on with assurances that he and the Communist Party uphold "such a Republic in which there is no police force nor a standing army, instead of which, according to my deepest conviction, there should be only universal armament of the people; nor should there be an officialdom enjoying in fact an irremovable tenure of office and privileged bourgeois remuneration for their services. We uphold the principle of election, the right to recall any official at any time and we are for proletarian standards of remunerating officials". 9)

Lenin taught that, "by state apparatus is meant first of all a standing army, police and officialdom".10) This means that Lenin, in demanding the abolition of the army, police and officialdom impressed the workers, peasants and soldiers with the idea that a Soviet Republic is an Anarchist Federation of many thousands of Communes-Soviets scattered throughout the vast expanses of Russia, and that this Republic is a full democracy, developed to its logical end—the extinction of the State. It stands to reason that he had to endow this Republic with all kinds of liberties, which, he did rather in a liberal and unstinting manner.

"The idea that it is necessary to direct the State through officials appointed from above is basically false, undemocratic, Caesaristic or is in the nature of a *Blanquist adventure.*

"The introduction of 'an appointed officialdom' should not be tolerated. Only those organs can be recognized 'which are created by the people themselves' in a given locality".11)

"In a free country the people is governed only by those who are elected by it for that purpose. . . . That is why in free countries gov-

----

8) N. Lenin, "Whither Do the Counter-Revolutionary Measures of the Provisional Government Lead Us," p. 129, vol. XIV, part 1.
    See also "A Question of Principle," p. 226.
9) N. Lenin, "Our Views," p. 92, vol. XIV, part 1.
10) "Will the Bolsheviks Retain Power?" p. 227, vol. XIV, part 2.
11) N. Lenin, Sobranie Sochineniy, p. 129, vol. XIV, part 1.

ernment of people is realized in the process of an overt struggle and free agreement among various parties".12)

"Freedom of press, means that the opinions of all citizens are given wide publicity. The state power, in the person of the Soviets, takes over *all* the printing shops, *all* the papers and distributes it *justly*. In the first place comes the State; in the second place come the big parties; in the third place, smaller parties, and then, any group of citizens enrolling a certain number of people and showing a number of signatures to that effect. This would be the real freedom for *all*, and not for rich people only".13)

"In every constitutional country citizens have an incontestable right to organize demonstrations."14)

"A government which is based in *its entirety* upon the will of the majority of the people cannot fear any demonstrations that are announced beforehand. It will certainly not revert to the policy of banning such demonstrations".15)

"Peaceful demonstrations are only a form of *agitation*, and agitation cannot be forbidden, nor can only one kind of agitation be imposed upon the people. The Constitution of Free Republics CANNOT forbid peaceful demonstrations or any display of mass power on the part of any party, any group".16)

"In order to restore democratic institutions and liberties which have been trampled upon and crushed by Kerensky, the Bolsheviks are going to build up a government which *no one* will be able to overthrow".17)

Together with Lenin the masses shouted: "Down with the social traitors!" "Long live the Bolsheviks!" "Long live the Republic of Soviets!" "For freedom, for Socialism!"

**
*

What have all those ideas in common with the ideas of the "Com-

---

12) N. Lenin, "The Lessons of the Revolution," p. 33, vol. XIV, part 1.

13) N. Lenin, Sobranie Sochineniy, "How to Assure Successful Elections to the Constituent Assembly (On Freedom of the Press)," pp. 112-113, vol. XIV, part 2.

14) N. Lenin, Sobranie Sochineniy, "The Perplexed and the Frightened," p. 254, vol. XIV, part 1.

15) N. Lenin, "Hints," p. 244, vol. XIV, part 1.

16) N. Lenin, "Contradictory Positions," p. 259, vol. XIV, part 1.

17) N. Lenin, "The Bolsheviks Have to Take the Power," p. 134, vol. XIV, part 1.

munist Manifesto"? Not a thing! Here we have federalism, and in the "Communist Manifesto", centralism; here we have democracy unfolded to its logical end, there—dictatorship; here we have all liberties, there, sheer coercion; here Communes with Soviets, there a centralized police state; here socialization, there nationalization; here persuasion, there intimidation—terror, in a word, here is freedom and there, only black reaction.

But the people had no reason to suspect Lenin and the Bolsheviks of falsehood and deceit, the more so that Lenin, as soon as he had come to power, bombarded the people with decrees, granting it the right to carry into life the promises made during the preparatory period.

At the same time each of these assurances was a deliberate lie, the greatest deliberate fraud and unprecedented deceit practiced upon the people. Lenin was following but one goal: he pressed onward to the realization of the Marx and Engels program set forth in the "Communist Manifesto"—to the so-called "Dictatorship of the Proletariat", that is, toward party dictatorship, personal dictatorship, toward centralization and state totalitarianism in every domain of life.

Having been guided in his moral actions by the principle of "the aim justifies the means," Lenin, prior to the revolution, during the factional controversies and wrangles as well as during the revolution, never showed himself overscrupulous in choosing his means of struggle against adversaries: slander, lie, deceit, breach of faith, bribery, provocation, gross abuse, willful distortion of the adversary's ideas —these were his weapons in the struggle for leadership in the party, as well as in the struggle for power in the country and for consolidation of this power. There is nothing surprising, then, that he chose such a ghastly road to power and setting up of dictatorship as perpetrating a fraud upon the people.

Lenin understood wherein lay the error of the largest and most influential party—that of the Social-Revolutionists—which tried to confine the elemental forces within the channels of "law", "order" and "discipline". He understood that those elemental forces cannot be fought against, cannot be damned up, that they will erase and destroy all impediments put in their path. Lenin saw clearly that the best policy would be not to oppose those forces but to stir them up, to float along the wave set up by them, and to be carried on the crest of that wave. He saw the advantage of letting this wave spend itself riotously so that, when becalmed and subsided, it might sink into placid and meek submission to the new master. He sought to harness it for his own purposes, to make use of some of its unspent energies for the purpose of crushing any opposition. He sought to destroy the overt and latent inciters of the elemental forces of people, the new upsurge of which might wash away the foundations of the newly established power. It was those considerations that determined Lenin's tactics during the revolution.

Lenin set himself a definite aim, having mapped out the following course for its realization: A Workers' State, to be realized via an All-Russian Commune: an absolute dictatorship, via absolute freedom; centralization via federalism; nationalization—that is, state monopoly —via socialization; terror via agitation and propaganda. In other words, the ideas set forth by Marx and Engels in the "Communist Manifesto" were to be realized via Marx's ideas of "The Civil War in France".

Lenin could not come out openly with this provocation before the masses of people nor before the leaders and the rank and file of the party. That is why many of the eminent figures and active workers of the party could not understand the drift of his policies. And that is why they rebelled against him.

At the very beginning, when Lenin made the party cast off "the dirty shirt of Social-Democracy" and put on instead the clean ones of Communism, he met opposition on the part of the editors of "Pravda," Kamenev and Stalin. And then, after he had overcome this opposition by the use of every means at his disposal, after he had infused the party with a new faith in this program based upon Marx' pamphlet "The Civil War in France," he again faced opposition when, acting in accordance with his preconceived plan, he began urging that the program be shunted once more to that of the "Communist Manifesto." Almost on the morrow of the October upheaval, contrary to what he had upheld in the pre-October tactics and propaganda, Lenin categorically rejected a coalition with the Social-Revolutionists and Social-Democrats. When he thus openly revealed that he was heading toward a party and personal dictatorship the newly formed government was split wide open by the resignation of Noghin, Rykov, Miliutin, Theodorovich, Riazanov, Derbishew and Shliapnikov, and the Central Committee of the Party was also split by the resignation of Miliutin, Zinoviev, Kamenev, Noghin and Rykov.

— 26 —

The present dictator of Russia, Lenin's heir and disciple, Stalin (Dzhugashvili) caught on to Lenin's tactics only many months after the October upheaval. He let the cat out of the bag, by declaring in one of the articles written in 1918 in which he said that they, the Bolsheviks, "are heading toward centralism via federalism." As we already pointed out, five years later Lenin admitted as much as that. Moreover, he admitted that all the decrees issued in the first period (1917-1918) after the October upheaval had the same meaning as the pre-October propaganda, that is, their object was to gain the confidence of the masses and to allay any suspicions. That was the only angle from which Lenin evaluated the decrees, hardly attributing any other significance to them and not considering himself bound by them to any extent.

"At that time," Lenin told the delegates at the party convention, "we went through a period when decrees were to us a form of propaganda. We were laughed at, we were told that the decrees were not being executed, that the White-Guardist press was full of sneers at our expense. But this was quite to be expected. It was quite logical on our part, at the time when we had just taken the power in our hands, to say to the rank and file workers and the peasants: This is the way we should like to see the state governed, here is a decree—try it out. To the ordinary worker and peasant we presented our ideas of politics in the form of decrees. The result was the gaining of the enormous confidence which we now enjoy with the masses of people. This was a necessary period at the beginning of the revolution; without this approach we should have never gained the leadership of the revolutionary war, being forced instead to lag behind it. But this period is a matter of past history—something we refused to see".18)

In addition to these admissions made by Lenin, we have his policy followed after the October upheaval, substantiating our contention that the ideas advocated by Lenin in 1917—that is, the ideas of 1917 —were viewed by him only as mere propaganda, that he did not believe in them, inveterate believer in the State that he was, he felt an organic hostility toward those ideas, using them as expe-

18) N. Lenin, Sobranie Sochineniy, "The Report on the Work of the Central Committee of the Russian Communist Party, March 27, 1922," pp. 54-55, vol. XVIII, part 2.

dients to clear the road to power, to dictatorship, the road toward the "workers" totalitarian state of Marx and Engels. And, if this is not sufficient, I shall cite here two characteristic and convincing instances.

One of Lenin's fighting slogans hurled against the Provisional Government was the demand to abolish the death penalty at the front and in the rear-guard. But no sooner did the October revolution take place, no sooner did Lenin make his appearance within the walls of the Smolny palace, than he began working himself into furious indignation when he learned of the abolition of the death penalty. Cynically and bitingly he scoffed at this mollycoddling and silliness. . . . And he quietened down only when it was decided to begin executions without revoking the decree abolishing the death penalty.

This is what L. Trotzky, next to Lenin the most prominent theoretician, ideological defender and instigator of the Russian terror tells of Lenin's endeavors in that direction. He tells it without evincing the slightest trace of indignation over such cynicism and seemingly making common cause with it.

"Upon the initiative of Kamenev, the Kerensky decree introducing capital punishment for soldiers was abrogated. I cannot remember particularly in which section of the Soviet Kamenev's motion was introduced; possibly, it was the Revolutionary War Committee, and it was discussed on the morning of October 25. As far as I can remember, there were no objections raised on my part. Lenin was not present then. This took place just before his arrival to the Smolny. (ed. note: the headquarters of the Petrograd Soviet.) When he learned about this first legislative act, he was beside himself with indignation: 'It is absurd,' he kept on repeating, 'How can a revolution be made without executions? Do you really think it is possible to get the best of our enemies by disarming ourselves? What other repressive measures do we have? Imprisonment? Who thinks it is important enough during a civil war when each side is hopeful of ultimate victory?'

"Kamenev tried to prove that what was meant by that act was to abrogate Kerensky's decree directed against soldiers who deserted from the army. But Lenin was irreconcilable on that point. It was clear to him that this act implied an inadequate realization of the unusual difficulties toward which we were heading.

"It is a mistake,' he kept on repeating, 'an inadmissible weakness, pacifist illusions, etc.' He suggested the immediate abrogation of this decree. This was argued against, the opinion being that this was liable to produce a very adverse effect. Someone said: 'It is better to fall back upon shooting when it becomes clear that there is no other way out.' And that was the final decision.

"The German aggression placed us before the difficult tasks, but as to ways of solving those tasks we had none. Nor was there the most elementary knowledge of how to discover such ways and means. We began with a manifesto. The draft of the manifesto which I wrote: 'The Socialist Fatherland is in danger,' was discussed together with the Left Social-Revolutionists. The latter, being yet green in their internationalism, were taken aback by the title. But Lenin approved it greatly: 'It shows immediately the 180 degree turn of our attitude toward the defense of the fatherland. That is the right way.' In one of the concluding passages of the draft, the manifesto demands to do away, on the spot, with everyone who is extending help to the enemy. The Left Social-Revolutionist, Steinberg, who drifted into the revolution, and the Sovnarkom (Council of People's Commissars) protested against this grim threat contained in the manifesto as militating against the 'pathos of the manifesto.' 'Just the opposite', Lenin exclaimed, 'this is the genuine revolutionary pathos! Do you really believe we shall be able to come out triumphant without the most drastic revolutionary terror?'

"At that time Lenin kept on hammering upon the idea of terror being unavoidable. Every manifestation of 'fine sentiments,' Pollyana attitudes—and there was plenty of all that—evoked his indignation not so much in themselves but as a sign that even the upper layers of the working class do not realize the monstrous difficulties facing a task that can be met only by measures of extraordinary energy. 'They, our enemies,' he used to say, 'are threatened with loss of everything they have. And at the same time they have hundreds of thousands of people who went through the school of war, well-fed, daring people who are ready for everything—officers, cadets, sons of landlords and well-to-do capitalists, police agents, village kulaks. But these so-called revolutionists—may I be excused for calling them such—imagine that we can make a revolution with good will and fine intentions. Where did those people ever study their revolutionary theories? What do they mean by dictatorship? What sort of dictatorship will they have if they are themselves of the shilly-shallying kind?' Such tirades could be heard dozens of times during the same day and they were also aimed at some one present, someone suspected of tendency toward 'pacifism.'

"Lenin never omitted the chance to repeat those ideas whenever the question of revolution and dictatorship was discussed, especially when those discussions took place at the session of the Sovnarkom (Council of People's Commissars), in the presence of Left Social-Revolutionists or some wavering Communists. 'Where do we have dictatorship?' he would say. 'Show it to me; we have a mess but not a dictatorship. Where is our Great Revolution, if we cannot shoot a few dozen White Guardists and saboteurs? Just see what the bourgeois scum write in their papers. Where is the dictatorship? Just mere prattling and a general mess.'

"Those speeches expressed his actual sentiments. In accordance with his method Lenin was hammering into the heads of the people the realization that exceptional drastic measures were needed in order to save the revolution".[19]

We have quoted L. Trotzky's article in full because of its great interest and importance. This article not only confirms what we said above about Lenin, but also reveals to us the true Lenin; not the Democrat and Socialist, but the Terrorist, the initiator and ideologist of terror in the Russian revolution modeled upon the terror of the French revolution. Of this, however, we shall write later in its proper context.

The second instance is the attempts made to set up a coalitionary Socialist government taking place immediately after the October upheaval. This is what we find about it in the 18th annotation to the 15th volume of Lenin's "Collected Works" published in accordance with the decision of the Party convention in 1922-23, under the editorship of Leo Kamenev (since shot by Stalin):

"The question of setting up a coalitionary government was brought forward by the VIKZHEL (The All-Russian Executive Committee of Railway Workers) immediately after the proletarian revolution triumphed in Petrograd. That was before the outcome of the street fighting in Moscow had become known. Nor had the situation in

19) L. Trotzky, "Lenin and the Work in the Government," "Pravda," Jan. 23, 1924, Moscow.

the active army yet become clarified by that time. (And nothing was known about the situation all over the country.—G.M.) The Left Social-Revolutionists were inclined toward such a coalition. At their insistence a series of conferences took place in the VIKZHEL, with the participation of Bolsheviks and the moderate Socialist groups. At those conferences was brought forward the project of setting up a "Socialist government" by expanding the Soviet Central Executive Committee to 150 people, this body to be supplemented by 75 delegates from the provincial Peasant Soviets, 80 from the Army and Navy, 40—from the Trade Unions, 25—from the All-Russian Professional Associations, 10—from the Central Executive Committee of the Railway Union, 5—from the Postal and Telegraph Workers and 70 deputies from the Socialist section of the Municipal Council of Petrograd. This expanded Central Executive Committee was to guarantee, according to this projected plan, 60 percent voting strength to the Bolsheviks. In the projected government, which was to be responsible before the Central Executive Committee, the Bolsheviks were to control no less than 50 percent of ministerial positions, which would include the Ministry of Labor, Ministries of Internal and Foreign Affairs. This project was taken up for discussion by the Central Executive Committee of the Communist Party on November 2. The project was rejected, it having been found that the Party could enter into coalition only with the Left Social-Revolutionists".[20]

The coalition plan was rejected notwithstanding the protests of a minority within the Central Committee of the Party and the protests of a minority within the Council of People's Commissars. The question was not brought up for discussion at the plenary sessions of the Central Executive Committee of the Soviets, nor was it laid before the party as a whole.

What does it mean? It means, first of all, that Lenin,s, pre-October propaganda, which reduced itself to the development of the ideas and principles of the Paris Commune, was nothing but a hoax and mere chicanery; it means that Lenin had in mind something altogether different when he said that, "In a free country, government of people is carried on in the process of an open struggle and free agreement among various parties"; secondly, that Lenin,

---

20) N. Lenin, Sobranie Sochineniy, "Annotations," pp. 640-641, annot. 18, vol. XV.

from the moment he arrived at power, decided upon a course of a party and personal dictatorship; thirdly, it means that Lenin declared war on the so-called Social-Democracy as well as upon the bourgeoisie and capitalists. It means that the responsibility for the continuation of the Civil War, for the destruction of the national economy, for oceans of blood, for millions of people who perished from hunger or fell on the battlefields—that the responsibility for all that falls upon Lenin and his party. This is obviously the case since an understanding among the Russian Socialists would either obviate the necessity of waging a civil war by placing the feeble Russian bourgeoisie and the military clique in a position where resistance would become nearly impossible, or it would have reduced the resistance of the counter-revolutionary elements to isolated outbreaks, which the Soviet government would find little difficulty in suppressing. This is borne out by the fact that while the "Socialist Democracy" and the masses of workers and peasants following it were still enjoying a certain measure of equality and civil liberty, they took an active part in the defense of the revolution against the onslaughts of reactionary elements. Although keeping up their ideological struggle against the Bolsheviks, they knew how to draw the line between the party struggles for power and the cause of the revolution. It was due to this attitude on the part of the revolutionary democracy that Lenin could declare on April 29, 1918, that "the main task of facing the resistance of exploiters has been solved already in the period from October 25, 1917, until February 1918 or until the surrender of General Bogayevsky".21)

The so-called October revolution was in fact but a simple upheaval. It was the seizure of power by way of organizing and engineering a plot and rebellion within the capital, in the hope that the country would follow the example of Petrograd in case the rebellion succeeded. It was a dangerous Blanquist adventure which had all the chances of success in Petrograd but not in the country as a whole. "Socialist Democracy"—Social-Revolutionists, Social-Democrats (Mensheviks)—were the dominant element. Then there was the army which, notwithstanding its war weariness, its eager longing for peace, its disorganization and the vanished influence of the officer corps, was still in the great unknown at that particular moment, the

---

21) N. Lenin, "The Next Problems of the Soviet Power," p. 195, vol. XV.

probability of an internecine strife among the various army units not being precluded. Likewise the Communist Party, being small in numbers, could not hope to take over without any resistance the government apparatus in the provinces, nor could it hope to implement it with forces of its own. The street battles in Moscow were quite symptomatic in this respect. And still, all that notwithstanding, Lenin rejected the proposal to form a coalitionary Socialist government, that is, he knowingly took a course upon civil war to be waged not only against the exploiters, but also against the "Socialist Democracy", against the great mass of workers and peasants rallied behind the banners of this democracy; he was knowingly heading toward the establishment of dictatorship and government through terror.

Lenin won, just as Hitler and Mussolini were winners before the war, because the Socialists shrank from the challenge of civil war. Russian Socialists shunned civil war because of their feeling of responsibility to the country and revolution, because of their fear of German invasion and restoration of monarchy, because of the fear of economic collapse. It was this prevailing spirit among the Socialists and the peaceful tactics they used in the struggle against the Bolsheviks that were skillfully exploited by Lenin with the view of the total annihilation of both Socialists and Anarchists.

Does not all this prove that the ideas of Federalistic Communism and genuine Libertarian Socialism advocated by Lenin prior to the seizure of power were only the means to an end, his true aim being dictatorship and the centralized totalitarian state of the "Communist Manifesto"? Indeed, it does. Lenin himself let it out in his polemic against Maxim Gorky's paper "Novaya Zhizn". "When the State has become proletarian, when it has become the apparatus of violence exercised by the workers over the bourgeoisie, then we shall affirm our allegiance to centralism and strong government".[22]

I shall cite another instance showing that Lenin never entertained the idea of realizing the "Soviet Democracy" and that, from the very moment he came into power, he placed himself and his party in the position of a dictator.

Only ten days after the seizure of power, on November 17, 1917,

22) N. Lenin, Sobranie Sochineniy, "Will the Bolsheviks Succeed in Holding the State Power," p. 241, vol. XIV, part 2.

Lenin, in his capacity of Chairman of the Council of People's Commissars, was presented with an interpellation on the part of the left Social-Revolutionists who submitted it at the session of the All-Russian Central Executive Committee of the Soviets.

". . . Of late a number of decrees were published in the name of the government. These decrees were not discussed in the Central Executive Committee nor were they sanctioned by it. The same procedure was characteristic of certain governmental acts, which, in fact, have abrogated the principles of civil freedom.

"We present therefore the following questions to the Chairman of the People's Commissars:

"1) On what ground were the drafts of the decrees and other governmental acts kept from being submitted to the Central Executive Committee for regular discussions?

"2) Does the government intend to give up the arbitrary and inadmissible procedure of decreeing laws?" [23]

The last question was not even dignified with a reply, and as to the first question, Lenin countered it with reproaching the Left Social-Revolutionists for not having entered the government, adding thereto the following characteristic declaration:

"The new power had to brush aside various formalities which might have raised serious obstacles. The moment was too serious and, under the circumstances, no delay could be permitted. No time could be wasted upon smoothing out certain rough points, all of which is really a matter of exterior finish, changing but little in the essential nature of the new measures of the government".[24]

Thus from the very first days Lenin began to ignore the Central Executive Committee, the parties represented in it and also his own party, and to "govern" and legislate in a dictatorial manner.

It is clear then that Lenin's advocacy of the ideas of the Paris Commune prior to the October upheaval were meant only for mass consumption, were meant as a bait, as a means to gain the sympathies of workers and peasants, as a weapon clearing the road to power. His aim was "Dictatorship of the Proletariat"—a dictatorship of the Party and that of his own person, a centralized "Workers' State" as a monopolist, that is, an absolute totalitarian state which governs by means of violence and terror.

---

23) N. Lenin, "The Answer to the Interpellation of the Left Social-Revolutionists," annotations, p. 27, vol. XV.

24) Ibid.

CHAPTER II

THE ABSOLUTIST AND TERRORISTIC NATURE
OF THE MARXIST STATE

While advocating the democracy of the Paris Commune, Lenin aimed at its opposite. And since Lenin was well versed, in his own dry-as-dust-scholarship manner, in the works of Marx and Engels, he certainly knew the following passage in Karl Marx's address made to the Union of Communists in March 1850:

"The democrats will either strive for a federated republic or, they cannot get along without an indivisible republic, they will at least try to weaken the central government by granting the widest measure of autonomy and initiative to the communes and provinces. As against that, the workers should strive not only for a single and undivided German republic, but the most vigorous centralization of power in the hands of the state. They should not let themselves be hooked upon the bait of this democratic chatter about the freedom of communes, self-government, etc., like France during the year 1793. The carrying out of the most vigorous centralization of present day Germany should become the task of a truly revolutionary party".[25]

In his pamphlet "State and Revolution", Lenin quotes the following lengthy excerpt from Engels' letter to Bebel, which ends in the following fashion:

"Since our [26] state is only a transitional institution which is to be used during the struggle, in the revolution, in order to suppress violently our adversaries, it would be sheer nonsense to speak of a free state of the people; as matters stand, the proletariat still

---

25) Quoted by K. Kautsky in his book: "From Democracy to State Slavery," p. 48, Russian edition, 1922, Berlin.

26) The word "our" is omitted by Lenin, who thereby distorted the meaning of the statement in which Engels is made to refer to the State in general and not to "our" State.

needs the State; he needs it not in the interests of freedom but in order to be able to suppress his enemies; freedom will be on the order of the day only when the state as such will have ceased to exist".

It was upon this canvas that Lenin drew his patterns of "Socialist" construction in Russia and built the "Dictatorship of the Proletariat". Those were the starting points of his methods of struggle not only against the *enemies* of the proletariat, not only his own enemies, but his *adversaries, as it was taught by Engels.*

Lenin thus defines the "Dictatorship of the Proletariat": "The revolutionary Dictatorship of the Proletariat is the power conquered by the proletariat and maintained through violence over the bourgeoisie, it is a power unbound by laws".[27]

When Lenin seized power he immediately began to carry out this "Dictatorship of the Proletariat" without binding himself by any laws. His reply to the interpellation of the Left Social-Revolutionists, his indignation at the abrogation of the death penalty and his turning down of the proposal to form a Socialist coalition government, could all be traced to one and the same source: the drive for autocratic power, the burning desire, born out of vanity and ambition, to make the attempt to build up the first Marxist "Workers' State" in the world, his own Bolshevik State, "Our State," as Engels wrote—that is such a State about which one might say:

". . . the State it is we, it is the proletariat, it is the vanguard of the working class". ". . . The State—that means the workers, the advanced section of the workers, it is the vanguard, it is we."[28]

"The State it is we". . . . We are the Party, and the Party—that is, the party and the party apparatus,—that is I. Consequently, the State—that is I and only I. A Marxist Louis XIV—such is the inescapable conclusion of the logical unfoldment of political Marxism in practice, in life. . . . The Workers' Socialist State, the "Dictatorship of the Proletariat" is crowned by a Louis XIV, that is, by a benevolent despotism, by absolutism. It is an inescapable logical ne-

---

27) N. Lenin, Sobranie Sochineniy, "Proletarian Revolution and the Renegade Kautsky," p. 451, vol. XV.

28) N. Lenin, Sobranie Sochineniy, "A Report on the Activity of the Central Committee of the Russian Communist Party; the Session of March 27, 1922," p. 35, vol. XVIII, part 2.

cessity. . . . "Our State" is an absolutist State built not only in order to destroy our *enemies,* but mainly in order to suppress our *"adversaries".* And there are always more adversaries than enemies. The enemies are the capitalists, landlords, generals and priests. And as to adversaries, they comprise, in the first place, those that stand outside the pale of the collective "we," that is, outside the Party. Those millions of people who are "not our people" fall into two categories of adversaries: those who do their own thinking, who have their own Socialist views and their own ideas as to the ways and means of building up Socialism. Various Socialists and Anarchist groups, parties, workers' unions, cooperatives, various societies—all those belong to the class of direct and permanent adversaries. The other group consists of the vast mass of passive elements who only at times, sporadically and on specific occasions bring forth adversaries from their midst, that is, the group of potential adversaries. It follows hence that all "adversaries" must be disfranchised and deprived of their liberties. But before that could be done they had to be crushed or physically undermined.

The Russian bourgeoisie had already been undermined in the February revolution and was finally broken by the October upheaval. The masses of the people could only sympathize with any attempt to outlaw the vanguard of the Russian bourgeoisie—the Cadet party—and so on December the first, this party was declared the "enemy of the people".

Four months later it already became clear to Lenin that, "by now the Marxist tenet has been amply demonstrated, stating that Anarchism and Anarcho-Syndicalism are *bourgeois* movements which are in irreconcilable contradiction to Socialism, Proletarian Dictatorship and Communism".[29] "The threat to restore bourgeois exploitation was held out to us only recently in the person of Kornilovs, the Gotzes, the Dutovs, Gheghechkoris, and the Bogayevskys.[30] We vanquished them. But now we are threatened with another restoration, which asserts itself in a wave of petty-bourgeois license and

29) N. Lenin, Sobranie Sochineniy, "The Tasks of the Soviet Power," p. 205, vol. XV.

30) Gotz, one of the oldest leaders of the Social-Revolutionary Party; Kornilov, former supreme commander; Dutov and Bogayevsky, Cossack generals; Gheghechkori, one of the leaders of the Social-Democratic Party of Russia and Georgia.

Anarchism, in the trivial, petty but numerous invasions and attacks of the petty-bourgeois elemental forces against proletarian discipline. This flood tide of petty-bourgeois Anarchy has to be vanquished, and we shall vanquish it".31) "The nearer we come to the full military suppression of the bourgeoisie, the more dangerous becomes to us the high flood of petty-bourgeois Anarchism. And the struggle against these elementals cannot be waged with propaganda and agitation alone, by organizing emulation, by selecting organizers; the struggle must also be waged by applying force and compulsion".32) The Anarchist movement was therefore declared to be clogged up with "bandits" of which it had no power to rid itself. And so the authorities took upon themselves this business of "purging" the Anarchist movement via a military pogrom. On the night of April 12, 1918, the backbone of the Anarchist movement was broken, its organizations were smashed, its newspapers closed up, members of the movement were arrested and some, like Khodounov, were assassinated.

The next turn came for the right sector of the Russian Socialism, whose representatives (Social-Revolutionists and Social-Democrats) according to Lenin, "could pass for Socialists only among fools or renegades like Kautsky".33) for "neither the Mensheviks nor the Social-Revolutionists (who preached Socialism) can be classed as Socialists".34) "It would be a mistake to view them as Socialists. . . . In reality they are the representatives of the Russian petty-bourgeoisie".35) Inasmuch as according to Lenin this "petty-bourgeoisie" represented millions and millions of the small toiling peasants, they were dangerous to the "Dictatorship of the Proletariat" and therefore had to be destroyed or rendered harmless. And so on June 14 the Social-Revolutionists and Social-Democrats were expelled from the All-Russian Central Executive Committee of the Soviets, that is, they were outlawed and declared "enemies of the people".

Thus there remained only the Left Social-Revolutionists who shared power with the Bolsheviks. On January 11, 1918, Lenin said the following about this party: "The party of the Left Social-Revolutionists is the only party which expresses the aspirations and inter-

31) N. Lenin, p. 221, vol. XV.
32) Ibid, p. 215.
33) N. Lenin, "Kautsky the Renegade," p. 509, vol. XV.
34) N. Lenin, "On the Petty-Bourgeoise Parties," p. 569.
35) Ibid, p. 570.

ests of the peasants".[36] And it remained such in Lenin's eyes as long as it kept on "yessing" his policies, that is, until the Brest-Litovsk peace, which it rejected and which it attempted to undermine by assassinating the German Ambassador Mirbach. It was then that the Bolshevik authorities swooped down upon it, suppressing it with most ferocious measures. It was then that they became to Lenin, "the accomplices of the Whiteguardists, landlords and capitalists".[37] Lenin promised "ruthlessly to expatriate the betrayers, the 'Socialists' in quotes who are not worth a penny."[38] "A Left Social-Revolutionist who keeps on emphasizing the fact that he is Left, who camouflages himself behind a revolutionary phrase but who ,in reality rises in revolt against the Soviet power, is a hireling of the Yaroslav Whiteguardists".[39]

Having disposed of the political parties and groups, Lenin betook himself to peasants and workers. The provocatory policy of persecution pursued by the Bolshevik authorities placed those parties and groups in a position which left but two ways out: either to take up arms or, fearing the repercussions upon the revolution which such a policy of armed defiance might produce, to sacrifice themselves by condemning themselves to legal activities of an open opposition and let themselves be crucified daily by the Bolsheviks until political and physical death should overtake them. Following these parties and groups, there came the turn of the great mass of peasants and workers. Almost the entire peasantry of Russia with very few exceptions found itself in the category of enemies. The food policy which reduced itself to grain requisitions carried out by armed detachments who were indiscriminately taking away the grain of the peasants—rich and poor alike—resulted in a number of peasant rebellions throughout the country. Fixed grain prices under conditions of great scarcity of commodities and total depreciation of currency, were in fact but a form of ordinary plunder perpetrated not only in regards of the kulaks but the entire peasantry. Rich peasants, middle peasants as well as poor peasants refused to sell grain. It was then that Lenin declared them "enemies of the people"

---

36) N. Lenin, "A Report on the Work of the Council of People's Commissars," p. 75, vol. XV.

37) N. Lenin, p. 387, vol. XV.

38) N. Lenin, "On the Situation in Soviet Russia," p. 398, vol. XV.

39) Ibid, p. 402.

and friends of the capitalists, opening up a mad campaign against peasants with the help of "the committees of poor peasants".

"Those who know what indescribable torments of hunger the people are suffering now and still refuse to sell grain at prices acceptable to the middle peasants—those are the people's enemies. They ruin the revolution and promote violence, those are the friends of the capitalists. Upon them we declare war—a ruthless war".40) And so war was unloosed upon the peasants. The "kombieds" (committees of poor peasants) wrought so much damage and did so much to provoke a sweeping wave of peasant rebellions throughout the country that by November of 1918 the government was compelled to dissolve them, but it could not undo the destructive effects of their work.

The next category of enemies and adversaries was that of workers who dared to demand that the situation in regard to food provisioning be improved. Such workers were to Lenin also scoundrels sold to the bourgeoisie.

". . . There is a question presented here in a written form; the question runs as follows: 'How is it that counter-revolutionary newspapers are still permitted to come out?' One of the reasons is that among the printing workers are certain elements that are bribed by the bourgeoisie. (Uproar and shouts: "It is not true!") You can shout as much as you want to, but you will not prevent me from telling the truth known to every worker and about which I was just going to talk. When a worker prizes highly his earnings in a bourgeois newspaper, when he says: I wish to retain my high wages because I help the bourgeoisie to sell poison to the masses of the people, I say then that those workers act as if they were bribed by the bourgeoisie. . ."41)

Later on, Lenin began "to safeguard the interests of the working class from the small handful, the small groups and layers of the working class who cling tenaciously to the traditions and ways of capitalism and who regard the Soviet state as they did the employer in the old times. Their attitude is to give him as little and as bad work as possible, to 'squeeze' it for what it may hold. Haven't we got quite a number of such scoundrels among the type-setters of

40) N. Lenin, "The Report of the Council of People's Commissars," p. 377, vol. XV.

41) N. Lenin, "Concluding Statement," p. 353, vol. XV.

the *Soviet Printing Shops,* among the Putilovsky and Sormovsky plants, etc.? . . . The resistance of capitalists and those who cling to their parasitic ways will be broken with an iron hand".42) And since under the then prevailing conditions of frightful want and centralization of food provisioning almost every worker found himself in the position of such "scoundrels" and "idling parasites," the category of enemies and adversaries expanded so as to embrace nearly all workers. It included workers' cooperatives that held on to the idea of independence, and to Lenin "anyone that upholds such a point of view is already an adversary of the Soviet power."43)

**
*

Thus the Marxist centralized state created for the purpose of "violent suppression of its adversaries" resolves the entire population into its adversaries, that is, save an insignificant section of the "proletariat"—its so-called "vanguard". And since "we are the vanguard, we," that is, the Party, "are the Proletariat raised to the ruling power," which enslaves the population for the sake of freeing and enfranchising it, for the sake of creating a "Proletarian Democracy". Yes, it creates a proletarian democracy, for, according to Lenin, "a dictatorship does not necessarily imply the destruction of democracy for the class which exercises this dictatorship over other classes". For instance, "the rebellions of or dissatisfaction among the slaves of antiquity revealed the essence of the State of that Period as the Dictatorship of the Slaveholders. Did this do away with democracy among slaveholders exercised in their own midst? Everyone knows that this was not the case".44) The "Dictatorship of the Proletariat" is thus a slaveholders democracy which, as distinguished from the one of the ancient world, has for its aim freedom, economic equality, freeing the entire population from slavery, and all this is to be realized . . . by enslaving the entire population! Could there be a more absurd theory? Indeed, it is the most absolute nonsense, a theory fit for the madhouse. And it was in the name of this absurdity that the rights of the man and the citizen conquered by the Russian revolution were anathematized, were burned out with a glowing iron and

---

42) N. Lenin, "The Character of Our Newspapers," p. 419, vol. XV.

43) N. Lenin, "On Workers' Cooperation," p. 585, vol. XV.

44) N. Lenin, "The Proletarian Revolution and the Renegade Kautsky," p. 450, vol. XV.

were washed out, reeking with human blood. Since "a free State is pure madness", Lenin, upon reaching power, began to build a Proletarian State in accordance with the recipes given by Marx and Engels. It was "our" State (for "the State it is the workers, it is the vanguard, it is we"), the State of "our Party", of my party, my State, set up for the purpose of "violently suppressing its adversaries", in order to clear the road to freedom, Socialism and Communism. Lenin thus became the opposite of Lenin of 1917, of the Lenin who tried to persuade the masses and to gain their confidence. But now that he began to govern and build a slaveholding democracy, freedom and equality became bourgeois prejudices standing in the way of the new construction and which therefore have to be fought ruthlessly.

"A ruthless exposure of the petty-bourgeois democratic prejudices in regard to freedom and equality".45) "Anyone who speaks of freedom and equality within the framework of a toiler's democracy is thereby a defender of exploiters".46)

Any discussion of and argumentation about freedom began to be branded as "senseless argumentation", "mere prattle and phrase-mongering" about which "one has to rise".47) Freedom of the press and criticism became "meaningless things".48)

Democracy became mere "sentimentality" and "prattle". ". . . All this sentimentality and prattle about democracy has to be cast overboard".49)

"An open proof of one's Menshevism (that is democratic convictions—*M. G.*) should be sufficient ground for our revolutionary courts to confer the highest punishment, that is, shooting."50) In the same manner Lenin made short shrift of the other rights and

---

45) N. Lenin, Sobranie Sochineniy, "Disingenious Speeches on Freedom," (November 11, 1920), p. 379, vol. XVII.

46) Ibid, p. 380.

47) N. Lenin, Sobranie Sochineniy, "A Speech Delivered at the Second All-Russian Convention of Representatives of the Political Sections of the Army" (October, 1921), p. 375, vol. XVIII, part 1.

48) N. Lenin, "The Concluding Speech" (March 9, 1921), pp. 128-129, vol. XVIII.

49) N. Lenin, Sobranie Sochineniy, "A Speech Delivered at the Conference About Work in the Villages" (June 30, 1920), p. 226, vol. XVIII.

50) N. Lenin, Sobranie Sochineniy, "A Report on the Activity of the Central Committee of the Russian Communist Party" (March 27, 1921), pp. 35-37, vol. XVIII, part 2.

liberties of the population which workers and peasants conquered during the revolution. Such became the fate of freedom of press and association, of freedom of conscience, of freedom of parties and nationalities, of freedom of thought and science, of freedom of literary creative work and research, of freedom of agitation and propaganda, of freedom of demonstrations, strikes and independent labor unions, of freedom of teaching and education, of the inviolability of person and domicile, of local autonomy and rights granting a certain measure of independence from the State.

One may ask then whether this does not represent reaction pure and simple, whether this is not in its essence but the reactionary ravings of an obscurantist and despot? For isn't all that a super cynical attempt to replace Socialism with the most primitive gross and barbarous form of despotism? Isn't that the essence of tyranny and absolutism?

Lenin learned this from Marx and Engels and he in turn taught it to his Party. He taught the Party to treat the working masses with a heavy hand, to stifle them. And the Party did stifle the people, placing it in a Procrustean bed, handing on this venerable art —the venerable art of all the reactionaries, to the youth, assuring it that this is the only secure road to freedom, equality, Communism, toward the dying away of the State and the establishment of a free and classless society. . . .

**
*

Is it possible, without using organized violence and terror, to subject the entire population to "the Dictatorship of the Proletariat", that is, to the dictatorship of the Party, that is, of the Party clique, that is, of the leader of the clique and the Party? Is it possible to create a slaveholding democracy without doing away with the freedom and rights of workers and peasants? Of course not! It is impossible because it would be naive to think that workers and peasants, the professionals, could all be taken in by the name "proletarian dictatorship" and that, like St. Augustine, they would come to believe in this absolute absurdity because it is an absurdity. It is improbable that they would believe that freedom can be arrived at via enslavement, equality via inequality, humanity via inhumanity, the abolition of the State via its strengthening and that initiative can be developed by first having it stifled.

Just the opposite is true. Proceeding from the formula of progressive evolution one can and should expect that notwithstanding the artful deceit, this recoiling of progress upon its backward path, its sudden metamorphosis into regress, will meet strong resistance which can be suppressed only by the most frightful terror and arbitrary rule. Lenin knew it, he knew that men are not guinea pigs and that they will not, if they can help it, let themselves be vivisected for the sake of Party experiments. That is why Lenin kept on preparing himself to deal with this certain reaction of the people to his experiments. He studied the revolutions of other countries, and especially the Great French Revolution, he studied terror, for he saw clearly the terroristic nature of the Marx and Engels State. That is why, having in view the seizure of power, he lied when he demanded from the Provisional Government the abolition of the death penalty, he knowingly lied when he promised to restore the liberties trampled down by Kerensky and to abrogate the death penalty. While demanding that, he had something else in view and his indignation was great as testified by L. Trotzky when he learned that Kamenev had published a decree abolishing the death penalty.

Since he was, like Marx and Engels, a Jacobine, he thought in terms and images of the latter. He could not conceive a revolution without terror and he held that the French revolution became great only because of terror, and that the Russian revolution can be great and successful only if it pursues a terrorist policy which being built upon "scientific Socialism", upon "the scientific organization" of Marx and Engels, upon the class struggle, is bound to yield totally different results from the Jacobin terror of 1793.

"The great bourgeois revolutionists of France of 125 years ago made their revolution great by the use of *terror* against all the oppressors, the landlords and capitalists", wrote Lenin in September, 1917, in the pamphlet "The Threatening Catastrophe and How to Overcome It".[51] And on December the first of the same year, he said by way of bringing up his strongest arguments in favor of his latest act outlawing the Cadet Party: "that is the way the French revolutionists acted".[52]

---

51) N. Lenin, Sobranie Sochineniy, p. 207, vol. XIV, part 2.

52) N. Lenin, Sobranie Sochineniy, "The Declaration of the Cadets by Enemies of People," Speech delivered at All-Russian Central Executive Committee (December 1, 1917), p. 47, vol. XV.

Five months after he had arrived at power, Lenin insisted in his pamphlet, "On the 'Left' Infantility and Petty-Bourgeois Manifestations" upon the necessity of applying the most resolute terroristic measures and not to stop short even before their barbarous character.

"While the revolution in Germany still tarries, our task should be to learn from the Germans how to run state capitalism, by all means to copy it from them and not to spare *dictatorial methods* in order to accelerate this process of taking over from the Germans, doing it at an even more rapid pace than the one followed by Peter the First in Westernizing barbarous Russia, without stopping short before the most barbarous means of struggle against barbarity".53) The same demand Lenin reiterated in 1921 in his pamphlet: "On the Grain Tax".54) Those were the guiding ideas of Lenin's policies as well as of those of his faithful disciple Joseph Stalin.

**
*

But a guillotine was not enough for Lenin, he sought out stronger methods of terrorization, methods which combined with the guillotine would transcend anything the world had known until now. Those means he discovered in the "military socialism" of the warring capitalist states—*terror by starvation.*

"The grain monopoly, the rationing card and universal labor service are in the hands of the Proletarian State, in the hands of the Soviets, vested with full powers, the most powerful means of control and accounting. Those means when applied to capitalists, to the *rich* and to the *workers,* will furnish a power unprecedented in the annals of history, which will 'set into motion' the state apparatus, will overcome the resistance of the capitalists and will keep them in subjection to the proletarian state. Those means of control and compulsion to work are stronger than the laws of the Convent and the guillotine. The guillotine only terrorized, it only broke down *active* resistance. *But this is not enough for us.*

"It is not enough to 'cow' the capitalists in the sense that they should feel the might of the proletarian state and should forget about

---

53) N. Lenin, "Left Infantility and Petty-Bourgeois Habit," p. 268, vol. XV.

54) N. Lenin, Sobranie Sochineniy, p. 207, vol. XVIII, part 1.

showing active resistance. We have to break down passive resistance which doubtlessly is the most harmful and dangerous one. And not only do we have to break down any sort of resistance, but we have to *compel* them to work within the organizational framework of the new state. It is not enough to 'chase out' the capitalists (one has to "remove" the unfit, hopeless "resisters") and place the others *in the service of the state*. This refers to the capitalists and the upper layer of the bourgeois intellectuals, high salaried employees, etc".55)

"And—Lenin continues—we have such means in our possession. It is the grain monopoly, the bread card, the labor service conscription. . . . The Soviets will introduce the work book for the *rich* and then gradually for the entire population".56)

When Lenin came to power, he began coolly, warily and cunningly to organize this terror "for the purpose of forcible crushing of its adversaries". And the adversaries, as we have already shown, were all those who were outside the party—and not a few of them were within the party itself. The prevailing spirit of the mass of workers and peasants who became imbued with the agitation against the death penalty carried on by the Bolsheviks in the Kerensky period, was not altogether receptive to an open declaration of terror; nor was it politically expedient to come out openly in favor of a policy which was only recently combatted—this would furnish an additional weapon into the hands of enemies and adversaries. It was necessary to prepare the masses. It was necessary to instill a taste for terror and murder among the members of their own party as well as that of the allied party of the Left Social-Revolutionists. It was necessary to train the working masses to become indifferent toward executions and to regard them as matter-of-fact occurrences. Acting upon Lenin's instructions, the Bolshevik press and agitators raised a furious campaign against the other parties, groups, movements and persons. Slanders, lies, deceit, the most frightful frameups began to rain down from this inspired source, far outstripping the propaganda methods of the pre-October period. At the same time, following the understanding reached between Lenin and the leaders

55) "Peasants and workers."

56) N. Lenin, Sobranie Sochineniy, "Will the Bolsheviks Retain the State Power?" p. 234, vol. XIV, part 2, September, 1917.

of the party, terror in all its forms—that is, persecution and assassination, was gathering momentum.57)

During this period which was "preparatory" to the unloosing of the wave of terror, from October 25 (Nov. 7) to April 29, 1918, Lenin himself was rather reserved in his open encouragement of terror and murder in regard to any one taken in the act of committing a crime. He still remembered the noble act of the Petrograd workers who released general Krasnov upon his promise not to take up arms against the Soviets. And although at that time Lenin grew indignant about this act, branding it as "an intelligentzia-bred prejudice against capital punishment," he nevertheless was restrained by this "prejudice" for five months from coming out openly with the scandalous-in-form and depraved-in-essence bloody propaganda and agitation to which he gave himself up till his very last days.

---

57) As to this understanding, see L. Trotzky's article "Lenin and the Work in the Government," which we cite in full in this work.

CHAPTER III

THE "PREPARATORY" PERIOD OF TERROR

Lenin directed his first blow against the bourgeois papers, which category gradually embraced all newspapers with the exception of the Bolshevik and government publications. "To tolerate those papers," Lenin said at the session of the Vzik (All-Russia Central Executive Committee of the Soviets), November 4, 1917—"is to cease to be a Socialist".[58] Since the Soviets were still in the throes of an armed struggle against Kerensky whose attempts to regain power had not yet been suppressed, Lenin refrained from calling for a terroristic policy: at that time he was demanding not heads, but the suppression of the bourgeois papers.

On November 21, Lenin spoke to the All-Russian Central Executive Committee of the Soviets on the question of recalling and re-electing members of the Constituent Assembly and for the first time following the seizure of power he came out with the idea of organizing violence. "The State—said Lenin—is an institution built up for the sake of exercising violence. Previously this violence was exercised by a handful of money-bags over the entire people; now we want to transform the State into an institution of violence which is to do the will of the people. We want to organize violence in the interests of the people".[59] On the following day Lenin spoke at the All-Russian Convention of Sailors, at which he said: "We are showered with accusations charging us with terror and violence, but we take it calmly. We say: we need a firm government, violence and compulsion, but we shall direct it against a handful of capitalists, against the bourgeois".[60]

On the first of December, 1917, as we already pointed out, Lenin,

---

58) N. Lenin, Sobranie Sochineniy, p. 26, vol. XV.

59) N. Lenin, "On Right to Recall and Re-election of the Members of the Constituent Assembly," speech delivered at All-Russian Central Executive Committee, November 21, 1917, p. 40, vol. XV.

60) N. Lenin, "The Speech Delivered at the Convention of the War Fleet," November 22, 1917, pp. 41-42, vol. XV.

with due references to the French Revolutionists, outlawed the Cadet party; on December 14 he assured the All-Russian Central Executive Committee that "no one, save the Utopian Socialists, ever denied that it would be possible to triumph without meeting resistance, without a Proletarian Dictatorship, without putting an iron hand upon the old world," and that "this iron hand creates while destroying".61)

On January 11, 1918, in his address on the work of the Council of the People's Commissars, delivered before the Third All-Russian Convention of Soviets, Lenin told the delegates that, "the experiences furnished by the civil war shows clearly to the peasants that there is no other road to Socialism save the Dictatorship of the Proletariat and the ruthless suppression of the rule of the exploiters".62) But "we are still far from a real terror, because, for the time being, we are stronger than they are".63)

On the following day, Lenin, in his summary of the previous address, said the following by way of answering the charge made on the floor of combating the Socialists:

"In answer to the charge made here that we are combating 'Socialists' we can only say that in the epoch of parliamentarism the latter have nothing in common with Socialism, that they have rotted away, have become outdated and have finally gone over to the bourgeois. 'Socialists' who, during the war, provoked by imperialist motives of international robbers were shouting about 'defending the fatherland'—are not Socialists, but tuft-hunters and bootlickers of the bourgeoisie".64)

This answer shows clearly that the attempts of the Socialists to enter into coalition with the Bolsheviks were met by Lenin not only with a rebuff, which provoked a crisis in the Central Committee of the Communist Party and in the first Bolshevik government, but also with persecutions. And it stands to reason, for even prior to the seizure of power Lenin wrote in the article "On Compromises": "Our party like any other political party, aims to obtain political power

---

61) N. Lenin, "On the Nationalization of the Banks," a remark made at the All-Russian Central Executive Committee, December 14, 1917, p. 49, vol. XV.

62) N. Lenin, "A Report on the Activity of the Council People's Commissars" (January 14, 1918), p. 76, vol. XV.

63) Ibid, p. 79.

64) N. Lenin, "The Concluding Speech," p. 89, vol. XV.

for itself"[65]) and that "events may place us in power, and we are not going to let that power slip from our hands".[66])

One has to bear in mind that the chief competitors, in the realms of ideology as well as in the struggle for power, were the Socialists and not the bourgeois. Strongest among those competitors was the party of the Social-Revolutionists which, due to its heroic past, became the strongest party after the fall of the monarchy. Already after the October upheaval this party had a predominant majority in the Constituent Assembly and notwithstanding the propagandistic decrees of the Bolshevik government, it still continued to be the party of the majority of the population, having a solid backing in the villages as a result of its pre-revolutionary activity, and its work in promoting peasant co-operatives. It stands to reason that Lenin had to direct his blows against this party and its ally, the Social-Democracy, which had quite an influence among the city workers. Lenin and the Bolshevik party did everything possible to compromise those parties in the eyes of the peasants and workers, to provoke them, to make it appear to the masses of workers and peasants that those parties had placed themselves at the other side of the barricades, that they sided with the landlords and generals. The Bolshevik aim was to annihilate those parties, morally and physically, by making them into a symbol of counter-revolution.

From the first day of the upheaval the legal activity of the parties became the object of persecutions. Their publications were being closed up and at the same time they were being vilified in the most persistant, tenacious, deliberate and systematic manner. They were purposely linked up with counter-revolutionary generals, with counter-revolutionary attempts, they were persistently labeled as counter-revolutionists, agents of the Entente, bootlickers of the bourgeoisie. For instance the Brest-Litovsk peace was resolutely opposed by the Socialist parties, Anarchist groups and even a considerable section of the Bolsheviks headed by Bukharin, Piatakov, Bubnov, Osinsky, etc. who even began to publish their own paper "The Communist" and named themselves "Left Communists." All that, notwithstanding, Lenin on March 7, 1918, at the session of the Fourth extraordinary

---

65) N. Lenin, Sobranie Sochineniy, p. 96, vol. XIV, part 2.

66) N. Lenin, "A Letter to the Party Central Committee," p. 96, vol. XIV, part 2.

All-Russian Convention of the Soviets, in his address on the Brest-Litovsk peace, had the temerity to refer to them in the follwing language.

"The further continuation of the war will lead us to a defeat and a debacle. . ... That is why all the counter-revolutionary advocates of this new carnage, echoed by the Mensheviks, the Chernov, Tzereteli and the "Dielo Naroda" crowd 67) became so vociferous in their demand for war; to them it is a selfish problem, it is demanded from them by their class interests, by considerations of their own personal benefit. That is why they uphold this point of view in their counter-revolutionary writings.

"Outcries: *'Our papers have been closed!'*) Of course, unfortunately not all of them! Soon all of them will be closed. . . . (*stormy applause*) the Dictatorship of the Proletariat will wipe out the shameful purveying of bourgeois opium. (*Stormy applause*).

"We can now very well understand their wailing about the foul peace, the wailing of those who are giving a rapturous reception to the German imperialists, who are now invading the territory of the Revolutionary Republic. They are rooting for war, but what they are really after is to have the Soviet State fall into a trap".68)

At last Lenin succeeded, as a result of this persistent policy, in exasperating the majority of the Social Revolutionists and some groups of the Social-Democratic organization to the extent of provoking them into armed rebellion. In May 1918, that is a half year after the October upheaval, they let themselves become involved in the Czecho-Slovakian adventure. They made common front with the rebels, the front of the Constituent Assembly, the People's Army, and of course they soon were entangled in the snare of Admiral Kolchak. Having ruined forever their standing with the masses, they signed their own death sentence. Lenin got what he wanted.

On April 23, Lenin spoke in the Moscow Soviet. This speech was the prelude to an open turn in Lenin's policies, to the policy of an open struggle against the people with their revolutionary conquests, a struggle waged with the view of building up a "Dic-

---

67) Chernov, leader of the Party of the Social-Revolutionists; Tzereteli, leader of the Russian and Georgian Social-Democratic Parties; "Dielo Naroda" — publication of the Party of Social-Revolutionists.

68) N. Lenin, Sobranie Sochineniy, "Report on the Brest Peace" (March 14, 1918), p. 176, vol. XV.

tatorship of the Proletariat" and carrying out the program laid down by Marx and Engels in the "Communist Manifesto." This was a turn toward an official course of open terror, toward a blind and frenzied advocacy of terror to be directed against each and everyone; in a word, Lenin, following in the footsteps of the French Jacobins launched upon his program of exalting via terror the Russian Revolution into a Great Revolution.

In that speech, Lenin complained that until that time the Soviet Power had been in the nature of "a jellyfish and not that of iron." He held out the threat of ruthless terror not only toward enemies and adverseries, but likewise toward the hesitating members of his own party.

"The Soviet Power," said Lenin by way of writing up his speech, "in many cases did not evince sufficient determination in its struggle against the counter-revolution, thus far proving itself jellyfish and not a thing made of iron, and on this Socialism cannot be built. We have not yet overcome the petty-bourgeois forces." (To the latter category Lenin relegates the entire peasantry, the Anarchists, Social-Revolutionists, Mensheviks, the Left Social-Revolutionists, and all the other non-Bolshevik groupings, workers' unions and cooperatives —G. M.) . . . "We shall be crushed if we do not oppose the threatened collapse, disorganization and mounting despair with an iron dictatorship of class-conscious workers. We shall be ruthless toward our enemies as well as toward all hesitant and noxious elements in our own midst, those that will dare to bring demoralization into our ardous task of building a new life for the toiling people".69)

The impression conveyed by this speech is that the described period from November 7, 1917, to April 29, 1918, was one which did not know of terror, this being the implication of Lenin's complaint that the Soviet power was a "jellyfish." But was the terror necessary in that period? Was the Soviet power in such desperate straits that it had to fall back upon "iron" as the final argument?

According to the reiterated statements made by Lenin at that time there was hardly any civil war. There were only isolated attempts to incite such a war by way of mutinous outbreaks which were rapidly liquidated by the masses themselves.

---

69) N. Lenin, "The Speech Delivered at Moscow Soviet" (April 23, 1918), p. 188, vol. XV.

On March 7, 1918, Lenin addressed the members of the Seventh Convention of the Communist party: "The entire country was swept with a wave of civil war and everywhere we triumphed with great ease because the fruit was over ripe—because the masses have gone through the experience of a compromise policy with the bourgeoisie."70) And further: "We have easily triumphed over Kaledin's troops and have set up a Soviet Republic against a resistance that hardly deserves any attention".71) "Also, that in October, November and December we had a walkover as far as our internal front against the domestic counter-revolution was concerned".72)

At the fourth Extraordinary All-Russian Convention of Soviets (March 14, 1918) Lenin said the following:

"The course of our revolution, from the end of February 1917 to the end of February 1918, is the course of easy and rapid successes".73) "The forces of the people's enemies, as compared to the revolutionary might of the proletariat, proved to be rather insignificant. The Soviet government has triumphed in the Civil War."

"Layer after layer—workers, peasants, soldiers, up to the toiling cossacks, all those forces of the revolution gradually began to split off from the counter-revolutionary bourgeoisie. The Soviet power has definitely established itself in Russia".74)

Two weeks after this speech, on April 23, Lenin addressed the deputies of the Moscow Soviet. In that speech he expressed himself more emphatically on this matter:

"One can say with certainty that the Civil War in its main phases has been brought to an end.

"Of course, there will be skirmishes here and there, shootings will break forth in some cities as a result of the scattered attempts to overthrow the revolutionary power made by the reactionaries, but there is no doubt that at the domestic front the reaction has been stifled by the effort of the people in arms".75)

That is how matters stood as portrayed by Lenin. And in the light of this picture Lenin's complaint about the "jellyfish" character

---

70) Ibid, "Report on Brest Peace" (March 7, 1918), p. 124, vol. XV.
71) Ibid, p. 125.
72) Ibid, p. 128.
73) N. Lenin, "Report on Brest Peace" (March 14, 1918), p. 173.
74) Ibid, p. 174.
75) N. Lenin, "A Speech delivered at Moscow Soviet" (April 23, 1918), p. 186, vol. XV.

of the Soviet Power at that period sound strange and unintelligible. It seems strange to hear him expressing regrets that the Soviet power at that time was too soft, that there was not enough iron in it, that it did not apply terror. For weren't the conditions described by Lenin of the kind which should make possible the free development of the Soviet and Socialist parties, of the Anarchist groups, of the various workers' and peasants' organizations peacefully competing with each other for the possession of power? In other words, according to the earlier statements made by Lenin in his capacity as the head of the state, these were precisely the conditions under which "Socialist Democracy" should have flourished. For this is what Lenin said in his speech on the land question delivered at the Second Convention of the Soviets held on October 26, 1917:

"Being a democratic government, we cannot ignore the decisions of the masses of people, even when they run counter to our own opinions. . . . And even if the peasants follow in the future the party of Social-Revolutionists and give that party a majority in the Constituent Assembly, we shall say:—let it be so".[76] And again speaking in the Central Executive Committee of the All-Russian Soviets, (on November 21, 1917) on the right of recalling and re-electing the members of the Constituent Assembly, Lenin said:

"We have to continue the line of democratization and to make the right of recall essential to the functioning of the Soviets as the most consumate bearers of the idea of state and compulsion. And then the transfer of power from one party to the other will proceed in a peaceful manner, by way of mere elections".[77]

Those statements, however, were a deliberate lie: Lenin said one thing while having in mind something altogether different. His statements were about the same as when he fought against capital punishment, which only two months later he stormily defended on the ground that during the revolution, capital punishment could not be abolished. Nor was the Soviet Power as supine as it was pictured by Lenin. From the very first day of its existence, it was launched upon its infamous terroristic course, and were Lenin's declarations to be taken seriously, he, Trotzky, Stalin and the entire

---

76) N. Lenin, "On the Land Question," p. 20, vol. XV.

77) N. Lenin, "On Right to Recall and Re-elect of the Members of the Constituent Assembly" (November 21, 1917), pp. 40-41, vol. XV.

leadership of the party should have been placed on trial for exceeding power, for murders, and bloody butcheries, which violated the decree abolishing capital punishment.

In spite of this decree, terror by shooting began as soon as Lenin appeared in Smolny. He started off, as related by Trotzky, in the above quoted article, by terrorizing the leaders of the Bolshevik party who published the decree abolishing the death penalty.

The Revolutionary War Committee ("Revcom," for abbreviation), egged on by Lenin, were shooting men at will; it was this practice initiated by them that created the winged phrases: "to dispatch to Dukhonin's staff," that is, to lynch or "to put to the wall"—an expression bequeathed to the newly formed Che-Ka. The idea of the latter was conceived by Lenin,* and acting upon Lenin's idea Dzerzhinsky drew up a plan for the Extraordinary Committee (Che-Ka) which was set up on December 27, 1917 and which started off with shootings, the abolition of the death penalty notwithstanding.

Apart from shootings and murders following the squashing of the attempts to restore the Provisional Government there was the murder, (it took place on January 6) in the prison hospital of Kokoshkin and Shingarev, members of the Central Committee of the Democratic-Constitutional party, (Cadets) the shooting down of the street demonstration in favor of the Constituent Assembly. On January eighth, the Council of People's Commissars issued an order about, "setting up trench-digging battalions made up of men and women of the bourgeois class, with Red-Guard men acting as the 'surveillants.' This order states especially, "Those that resist are to be shot," that is—they are to be killed on the spot. . . . In about a month after this order, the All-Russian Che-Ka declared that "counter-revolutionary agitators" and also "all those trying to escape to the Don region in order to join the counter-revolutionary troops . . . will be shot on the spot by the Che-Ka squads." "Izvestia" (No. 27) contained a declaration to the effect that "Meshechniki", when showing resistance at their arrest, will be shot on the spot. The same threat was held out to those who pass out or paste or stick up anti-government leaflets: "They have to be shot immediately". The air was saturated with such threats, which were more than mere threats: blood was shed and men were assassinated with

* See Lenin's letter in "Pravda," December 27, 1927.

no one fearing to be held responsible for those crimes, because the Central power authorized and invoked those assassinations. It is clear that the further removed from the central seat of power, the more those invocations were conducive toward orgies of brutality. Local authorities felt as conquerors and acted as such. Thus, for instance, in Briansk, drunkenness was threatened with shooting. In Viatka it was "leaving the house after 8 P. M.", that was threatened with shooting. In Rybinsk it was declared that, "shooting without warning" will follow any congregating of people on the streets. In the government of Kaluga all those who failed to pay their levies in time were subject to the supreme penalty of shooting. The same "crime" was threatened in the town of Zmyev with drowning—"with a stone on the neck in the river Dniester."

Krylenko, the Commander-in-Chief, distinguished in the field of Soviet "Justice", (has since been arrested by Stalin, and is himself now threatened with execution), issued on January 22 an order for the government of Mogilev, which runs as follows:

"I herewith empower the peasants of the Mogilev government to take the law in their own hands when dealing with perpetration of violence".

The Commissar of the Northern region of Western Siberia issued an order in which he threatened: "In case the guilty ones are not turned over to the authorities, one person out of ten will be shot, irrespective whether he is guilty or not".

February 23, the German offensive began, and the government declared that "the Socialist Fatherland" is in danger. Upon that occasion a manifesto was issued [78] which stated: "Agents of the enemy, speculators, gangsters, counter-revolutionary agitators, German spies are to be shot on the spot".

Another item of this "manifesto" referred to the organization of the above mentioned battalions for digging trenches, and it stated: "All those battalions are to include all able-bodied members of the bourgeois class—men and women—and are to be placed under the surveillance of the Red-Guard men; *those who resist are to be shot*".[79]

The Ex-Commissar of Justice, I. Z. Steinberg, states in his book that Antonov-Ovseyenko (has since been arrested by Stalin, and is

---

78) See "Znamia Truda," February 23, 1918.

79) The author of this "Manifesto" was L. Trotzky; see his article which was already used.

now waiting for his turn), "motivated by revenge and sheer demagogy, and acting upon his own discretion, dispatched the members of the Council of Metallurgical and Mining Industry of the South, to do forced labor in the mines" and that "Lenin openly approved by telegram this savage act by Antonov."[80] Steinberg also maintained in the same book that "in March 1918, the Executive Committee of the Soviet of Rostov on Don seriously discussed the question of summarily executing all the leaders of the local Mensheviks and right wing Social-Revolutionists; the question was discussed but was not decided upon for the lack of a majority in its favor".[81]

On the night of April 12, an armed force, acting upon government orders, smashed the Anarchist organizations of Moscow. Against those organizations the government forces threw in action not only rifles and machine guns, but also cannons. This "military expedition" resulted, according to M. Y. Latzis,[82] "in 30 casualties—killed and wounded—on our part—12" All that was done under the slogan of fighting "banditry in the Anarchist ranks", but the real cause lies elsewhere. It was laid open by Lenin in his, "A letter to the Comrades" (issued in September, 1917) in which he wrote that: "All agree in characterizing the prevailing mood of the masses of people as one nearing despair and as one giving rise to the generally acknowledged fact of growing Anarchist influence".[83]

In addition to the eighteen killed and wounded Anarchists, it is rather difficult to ascertain the exact number, the Che-Ka killed the arrested Anarchist Khodounov, during an alleged "attempt to escape". From that time on persecutions of Anarchists continued at an ever growing rate and by the use of all kinds of means and methods.

Added to that there were the punitive and requisitioning detachments whose manner of acting in the villages was wild in the extreme. Also there were the "stop-the-way" detachments (military units set up at the time when the grain monopoly was promulgated as the official policy of the Soviet Government). The task of those detachments, mainly operating along the railways, was to prevent

---

80) I. Z. Steinberg, "The Moral Visage of the Revolution," p. 31, Russian edition, Berlin, 1923.

81) Ibid, p. 42.

82) M. Y. Latzis (Soudrabs), "Two Years of the Struggle on the Internal Front," p. 62, Russian edition, Moscow, 1920.

83) N. Lenin, Sobranie Sochineniy, p. 283, vol. XIV, part 2.

the free trade in grain. They operated against the *"Meshechniks."* *
And even that does not give a full picture of the unbridled terror
prevailing at that time, it being difficult to reconstruct the picture of
the terroristic activity of the Military-Revolutionary Committees functioning in 1917 prior to the formation of the All-Russian Che-Ka.

All those terroristic brutalities were committed in spite of the
decree abolishing the death penalty. They were committed without
the approval of the All-Russian Central Executive Committee of the
Soviets, without the sanction of the Convention of the Soviets. Consequently, the Government headed by Lenin and his henchmen are
subject to indictment on the counts of murder and violation of the
rights and liberties of the citizens.

And with all that, Lenin had the temerity to declare that the Soviet
power was "jelly-like and not iron-like," at that period. And well
it might have been "jelly-like," only the jelly was of human blood,
shed by iron. But this was not enough for Lenin: he demanded more
executions and more blood. And so, beginning with April 29, there
was unloosed a mad bacchanalia of terror headed by Lenin himself.

---

* *Meshok* — Sack, bag; the poor people, mostly workers, who against
the State Grain Monopoly were trying to bring from the villages for their
families a bag or two of flour or grain—a bag contains 36-72 English pounds
—were called *meshechniki*, sing. *meshechnik*.

CHAPTER IV

THE BOLSHEVIK COUNTER-REVOLUTION BEGINS
(*Second Period of Terror of* 1918)

The second period of terror lasted until August 31, 1918, that is, until the attempt made upon Lenin's life by the Socialist Dora Kaplan.

At that period Lenin, like a madman, demanded blood, shootings, the "applying of iron", all sorts of terrifying measures to be undertaken against each and everyone. In his "The Tasks of the Soviet Power"—an article and speeches, from which we date the beginning of the Russian counter-revolution—Lenin demanded the strengthening of the dictatorship, the tightening up of the screws, restrictions, repressions and shootings—more and more shootings. From that moment the demand for shootings, the threat of shootings becomes with Lenin an "*idee fixe*" which is emphasized throughout Lenin's writings and speeches beginning with that period and ending with his death.

"The next tasks of the Soviet power" (articles and speeches delivered at the All-Russian Central Executive Committee of the Soviets, April 29, 1918) is a highly significant historic document upon which one should dwell at some length. This document marks a veritable watershed in the development of the Russian revolution, since it was in those articles and speeches that Lenin, for the first time after he arrived at power, presented more or less coherently, although not fully enough, the basic principles of the organization and methods of governing which became the starting points in the basic policy pursued by Lenin and then by his successor—Joseph Stalin.

Already in 1917, prior to the October upheaval, Lenin, alongside his propaganda of the ideas of the Paris Commune, and with the "Communist Manifesto" and the views of Marx and Engels upon centralization and the "workers'" state, as his point of departure, advocated ideas the complex of which became known later under the name of fascism and the totalitarian corporate fascist state built up by Mussolini in Italy. Especially clear were those ideas, namely the ideas of the corporate state, developed by Lenin in his pamphlet "The

Threatening Catastrophe and How to Fight It", written in the middle of September 1917. In that pamphlet, in the chapter called "Compulsory Unification Into Associations", Lenin wrote the following:

"All the manufacturers and industrialists of every branch of industry who employ, let us say, no less than two workers, shall have to be united immediately into county and provincial associations. The responsibility for the steadfast execution of the law is placed in the first place upon manufacturers, directors, management boards, large stock-holders—for they are the real leaders of modern industry, its real bosses. They are to be regarded as such when they shirk their and in carrying out the law, and are to answer with their property in accordance with the principle of mutual responsibility: all for one and one for all. And then responsibility is to be placed upon the white collared employees who shall also have to form ONE union, and upon all the workers with their trade union. The purpose of this unionization is to establish the fullest, most rigorous and most detailed accountancy, and mainly to *unite all operations* in buying raw material, in marketing the products, in *economizing* the national means and efforts. This economy obtained as a result of unifying isolated enterprises into one syndicate may reach gigantic proportions, as it is taught to us by economic science, and as it is shown by the example of all syndicates, cartels and trusts. It is to be repeated again in this connection that this 'syndication' in itself does not change the property relations one iota, does not take away a single cent from a single owner. This has to be stressed over and over again in view of the fact that the bourgeois press keeps on frightening the small and the middle-size owners, by telling them that Socialists in general, and Bolsheviks in particular, want to have them expropriated. It is a deliberately false statement since Socalists, *even in case a thoroughgoing Socialist* upheaval takes place, do not and will not intend to expropriate the small peasant".[84]

Mussolini, as is known, had hardly anything new to add to this program, and Lenin can justly be viewed as the first theoretician of fascism, notwithstanding some very essential points of divergence between modern fascism and Lenin—in the racial, national problem for instance.

The above quoted excerpt embodies the recipe which Lenin pre-

---

84) N. Lenin, pp. 195-196, vol. XIV, part 2.

scribed for Russia. And it was this recipe that Lenin intended to follow when he arrived at power. But something happened which Lenin could not altogether foresee, something which he did not want to happen: while waiting for the tidal wave to subside (and against these elemental forces he was at first quite powerless), he saw that the seizures of enterprises—industrial and commercial—by the workers went too far, having in fact made a clean sweep of the rather feebly rooted Russian capitalists, industrialists and merchants. It had to be changed, and in place of a fascist "socialism" and a corporate state Lenin had to begin building up a "state capitalism", adding on from time to time elements germane to modern fascism. "The Next Tasks of the Soviet Power" was an attempt to trace the basic outlines of this plan of government and social structure.

"The first task of our party"—Lenin wrote—"was to convince the majority of the people that its program and tactics were basically right". This task "was solved in its main aspect." The second task, that of seizing political power and crushing the resistance of the exploiters, "was already solved in the period from October 25, 1917, until (approximately) February 1918." And now we have on the order of the day the next task, giving expression to the unique nature of the present moment, the task of organizing *the administration* of Russia",85) and now this became the *"principal and central task."*

But who was to govern Russia? There were no two ways of answering this question as far as Lenin was concerned.

"We, the Bolshevik party, *convinced* Russia. We *conquered* Russia for the poor and for the toilers, having taken it away from the rich and exploiters. And now we have to govern Russia".86)

This declaration made by Lenin shows how little he took into account the party of the Left Social-Revolutionists which at that time shared power with the Bolsheviks.

What did Lenin suggest as the basic principle of the organization of administration? First of all Lenin insisted that "in the interests of the *further* offensive, it is necessary to halt *right now* the offensive upon capital", that is, to put a halt to the continuing seizures of industrial enterprises by the workers and the organization of workers' management. The offensive had to be halted because "our work

---

85) N. Lenin, Sobranie Sochineniy, "The Next Tasks of the Soviet Power," p. 195, vol. XV.
86) Ibid, p. 196.

(that is the work of the party—G. M.) of organizing a proletarian control and accountancy (by proletarian control Lenin meant state control—G. M.) *lags* behind the spontaneous work of 'expropriating the expropriators'." [87] This meant that the work of the party in regimenting the workers and keeping them under the control of the party met incredible obstacles on the part of the workers who, acting through the medium of the factory committees, were organizing workers' management in the factories and for the first time in the history of the world were introducing industrial democracy in the factories, at the point of production and employment.

This had to be stopped, for it ran counter to the plan of organizing a centralized monopolistic state with the "Dictatorship of the Proletariat" which, according to Engels, was to crush its adversaries.

To stop this offensive and to invite the services of the bourgeois specialists was part of this plan, for "without the guidance of the specialists of various branches of knowledge of technic and accumulated experience, there can be no transition to socialism".[88] To pay those specialists high salaries, although this virtually means a step backwards, and to have them work under the constant supervision of the Che-Kists. And since "the Russian is a poor worker" it is necessary to teach him to work well. To intensify the discipline among workers: to raise the productivity of labor by introducing piece work, "to apply in practice and test out piece work to apply much of what is progressive and scientific in Taylor's system",[89] to introduce elements of emulation into work. A vigorous carrying out of an iron labor discipline with unquestioning obedience to the will of one person. To establish a one-man dictatorship in industry and transport. To introduce labor service *"for the rich,"* "to introduce a labor book and consumption card for every bourgeois, the village bourgeois included".[90] The consolidation of grain monopoly and the maintaining of fixed prices, the intensification of centralization in the work of provisioning the population. It was necessary to introduce state capitalism, for "reality itself tells us that state capitalism would be a step forward," would be "our salvation;" apart from that "state capitalism is a step toward socialism," "from which depends

---

87) Ibid, pp. 198-199.
88) Ibid, p. 200.
89) Ibid, p. 209.
90) Ibid, p. 205.

the success of socialism." Hence Lenin derived the demand "to learn how to realize socialism from the organizers of trusts," "irrespective of their moral qualities": "let him be an arch-knave, but if he organized a trust, if he is a businessman who had something to do with the organization of production and distribution for millions and tens of millions of people, if he is a man with experience in that of work—we must try to learn from him".91)

Such are the basic tenets of Lenin's policies which became fundamental to the further work of the so-called "soviet state." But the workers and the peasants were still imbued with the ideas of the year 1917, and acted accordingly; besides, all those tenets, basic to Lenin's policies, ran counter to the Russian socialist traditions, to the teachings of Russian socialism about the state, individuality and freedom. Lenin realized that there was such a contradiction and that is why he declared all that which militated against his scheme to be nothing but chaos and disorganization, manifestations of petty-bourgeois habits and spirit, manifestations of Anarchist petty-bourgeois elements, petty-bourgeois licentiousness and hooliganism. And those characterizations were meant by Lenin to cover everything and everybody: the Left Communists, Left Social-Revolutionists, Anarchists, Maximalists, Mensheviks, right wing Social-Revolutionists, workers and peasants. And Lenin, on April 29, declared a ruthless war upon all of them, having decided to break down this prevailing spirit of the masses, with the help of terror and physical force.

"In a country of small peasants, which only a year ago threw down the Tzar's regime and which only less than half a year ago freed itself from the Kerensky government, there remained, naturally, quite a great deal of the elemental Anarchism, heightened by the brutalization and wildness which always accompany prolonged and reactionary wars; there is not a little of the mood of exasperation and a feeling of bitter resentment directed at no particular object; if we add to all that the provocative policy of the flunkeys of the bourgeoisie (the Mensheviks, right wing Social-Revolutionists and others) it becomes quite clear that it will require continued and dogged efforts on the part of the best and most class conscious workers and peasants in order to bring about a break in the prevailing spirit of the masses and a turn toward regular, sustained, disciplined

91) Ibid, pp. 236-237.

— 63 —

labor. Only such a turn brought about by the mass of poor people (proletarians and semi-proletarians) will complete the victory over the bourgeois, and especially over the most tenacious and the most numerous peasant bourgeoisie." 92) And further: "the state which for ages was the organ of oppression and spoliation of the masses of people left as a legacy the greatest hatred and distrust on the part of the masses toward everything connected with the state. To overcome it is a very difficult task, which only the Soviet Power can tackle successfully".93)

And since, as Lenin taught his readers and audiences, "the success of socialism is unthinkable without the victory of the proletarian class conscious discipline over the elemental forces of the petty-bourgeois anarchy, this veritable source rendering possible the restoration of the Kerensky and Kornilov regimes," Lenin urged to expose this evil and "to strengthen the Soviet methods of struggle against it",94) that is, the methods of compulsion and shootings which to him became the natural methods of governing.

Lenin ended the article with an appeal "ruthlessly to tighten up on the discipline, to bear down upon any manifestation of laxness." What does this appeal signify? What was the concrete meaning with which it was implemented by Lenin? It meant compulsion and shootings—the Soviet methods of administering and organizing the social, economic and political life of the country.

Thus, for instance, the success in carrying out the nationalization of banks was made contingent, in Lenin's plans, upon the success in catching and shooting grafters and crooks:

"In order to go on with the nationalization of banks and proceed unswervingly toward the transformation of banks into nodal points of social accountancy in a socialist economy, we must prove ourselves successful . . . in catching and shooting grafters and crooks, etc".95)

The success of raising the productivity of labor was again made conditional: first, upon "laying down the basis of a socialist organization of emulation," and, secondly, upon "applying compulsion in such a manner as not to desecrate the slogan of proletarian dictator-

92) Ibid, p. 197.
93) Ibid, p. 205.
94) Ibid, p. 209.
95) Ibid, p. 204.

ship with the practice of a jelly-like proletarian power".96) In other words, he did not stop before shooting those that "violate" the discipline established by the state, substantiating it in another statement to the effect that: "there will not be any famine in Russia, if we take a full census of the grain and other products at our disposal and if we show ourselves ready to mete out the harshest punishment for the violation of the established order".97) And the harshest punishment can be only shooting, which is exactly what Lenin said: "what was expropriated should be counted and not permitted to be squandered away by letting every one grab whatever he can; those that do so, those that violate the discipline, should be shot. . . ".98)

Thieves have to be shot on the spot:

"There was not a single revolution in history when people did not instinctively feel it and did not manifest salutary firmness by shooting thieves on the spot. The trouble with the former revolutions was," regrets Lenin, "that this revolutionary enthusiasm which maintained this state of tension among the masses and which gave them the strength ruthlessly to crush the elements of disintegration, lasted only for a short while".99)

Lenin also demanded that the death penalty be applied to hooligans:

"A dictatorship is an iron power, possessing revolutionary daring and swiftness of action, ruthless in crushing exploiters as well as hooligans. But our power is excessively soft, very often resembling jelly rather than iron".100)

Shooting by way of lynching, however, is to give place, according to Lenin, to legalized shooting via courts in proportion as the organized administration of Russia shapes up:

"In measure that the basic task of the government becomes not military suppression but administration, the typical manifestation of suppression and compulsion will be not shooting on the spot, but trials by courts".101)

---

96) Ibid, p. 210.
97) Ibid, p. 246.
98) Ibid.
99) Ibid, p. 214.
100) Ibid, p. 215.
101) Ibid, pp. 215-216.

But the courts, which, according to Lenin, are to become "the *medium* of training and *discipline*" are not yet sufficiently prepared, they are not sufficiently cruel and ferocious and so Lenin demanded that they begin manifesting those "salutary" qualities:

"Our revolutionary and people's courts," Lenin complains, "are unusually weak. The impression given by the functioning of those courts is that rooted attitude of the people toward them as an alien bureaucratic institution—an attitude born out of the age long yoke of the landlords and the bourgeoisie—has not yet been lived down."[102]

This is what Lenin wrote and spoke on April 29, 1918, to and for the Russian workers and peasants, Russian "citizens," Russian people. And one can see now why this date was chosen by me as one that signifies the beginning of an open Bolshevik reaction and counter-revolution, and why I consider this document as a dividing watershed line in the Russian revolution.

*

I have already pointed out that beginning with April 29, 1918, Lenin became a veritable terror addict—a mental state lasting with him until the end of his days. It is this state that I intend to demonstrate and illustrate with concrete and tested facts. It is a frightfully abominable task to deal with and study: the savage, bloody nightmare and maniacal bestial outcries for blood and more blood coming from the only canonized saint of Soviet Russia, and his fellow champions. But it is a necessary task, for it is necessary that the great masses see, understand and draw the proper conclusions from this ghastly picture of Lenin's terror.

*

One week after the above described Lenin's address on "The Tasks of the Soviet Power," Lenin wrote a polemic article captioned the "Left Infantility of the Petty-Bourgeois Habits," which was printed in "Pravda" issues from May 9 to May 11. In this article which grew into a pamphlet Lenin formulated his attitude to the petty-bourgeoisie (any one who was not a member of the Bolshevik party and who did not obey unquestioningly the dictates of the latter was a petty-bourgeois according to Lenin.—G. M.) and toward state regimentation.

---

102) Ibid, p. 216.

"The petty-bourgeois resists any state intervention, any control and accountancy whether of the nature of state capitalism or that of state socialism. This is an incontrovertible fact of the reality of present day life".103) In accepting this fact Lenin showed that he clearly realized that "the economic basis of speculation is the social layer of petty-owners, very widely diffused in Russia, and the system of private capitalism which has in every petty-bourgeois its agent." 104)

And because Lenin realized the deep social roots of speculation, he at one time resolutely turned down the method of fighting speculations with executions, as it was done by the French Jacobins. Lenin subjected the Left Social-Revolutionists to bitter ridicule and invective for suggesting such methods, but as though forgetting what he had said about them, he demands in the same pamphlet: "our task should be to learn from the Germans how to run state capitalism, by all means to copy it from them and not to spare *dictatorial methods* in order to accelerate this process of taking over from the Germans, doing it at an even more rapid rate than the one followed by Peter the First in Westernizing barbarous Russia, without stopping short before the most barbarous means of struggle against barbarism".105) Further on he demands ruthless measures against speculation and graft, adding rather regretfully that "we still have little of ruthlessness necessary to assure the success of socialism, and there is little of it, not because we lack resolution. We have enough of that, but we don't know how *to catch* sufficiently fast a sufficient number of speculators, marauders and capitalists, that is, our Soviet law breakers. This 'knowledge' is acquired only in the process of organizing control and accountancy. Secondly, our courts lack firmness: instead of shooting grafters they give them half a year in prison. Both shortcomings can be traced to one social root: the petty-bourgeois climate of opinion, the debilitating effect which it produces".106)

On May 22, 1918, Lenin spoke at the convention of the Commissars of Labor where he demanded again and again "the organiza-

---

103) N. Lenin, "Left Infantility and Petty-Bourgeois Habits," p. 264, vol. XV.

104) Ibid, p. 265. All peasants are petty-bourgeois according to the Marxist theory.

105) Ibid, p. 268.

106) Ibid, p. 272.

tion of an iron order," "an iron power," "an iron discipline for workers;" calling for a crusade against the peasantry, "against disorganization and concealing of grain." And in the letter to the workers of Petrograd "On Famine" written on the same day, Lenin, railing at "the contemptible Anarchist windbags," "the weak-willed and shallow people (the Anarchists and Left Social-Revolutionists)," assured the workers that "there will be enough grain for everybody" if the workers establish "an iron order, a ruthless severe power, a genuine dictatorship of the proletariat, which will force the Kulak to knuckle under and will obtain an equitable distribution of grain." In order to obtain that, "the vanguard of the revolution—in Petrograd, as well as throughout the country—has to issue a war-cry, *has to rise en masse,* has to understand that the salvation of the country is in its own hands, that the vanguard has to display a heroism as great as in October 1905, of February and October 1917, that it is necessary to organize a great *crusade* against grain speculators, Kulaks, village usurers, disorganizers, grafters, a great *crusade* against those that violate the strict order established by the state in gathering, transporting and distributing grain for the people".107)

And again. . . . "There should be a crusade of the advanced workers . . . in order to annihilate speculation, grafting, in order to get rid of the slipshod ways of doing things". For that purpose Lenin suggested and demanded that workers single out from their midst armed detachments made of those who "are self-disciplined to such a measure that they will be able to strike off and shoot any one in their own ranks who might be 'seduced' by the profits of speculation".108)

And so workers' detachments went forth into all parts of rural Russia; they went forth and became corrupted; they plundered, killed, executed people and were laying the ground for the famine of 1921. They incited peasants' uprisings which were stifled in blood and were thus preparing the ground for Denikin, for the hecatomb of skulls and utter breakdown of the economic life of the country. But this consideration was of little importance to Lenin: he had to come out

---

107) N. Lenin, "On Famine," pp. 299-300, vol. XV.
108) Ibid.

victorious and remain in power even at the price of the destruction of half of the population. "The worker, by becoming the leader of the poor classes, did not become a saint thereby: he very often became infected with the diseases generated by the petty-bourgeois disorganization".109) It is deplorable but after all it is not so important: the demoralized have to be shot, and in their place there should be ten times as many iron detachments, "there is a necessity of the mass crusade" of the "vanguard workers in all ends of the huge country".110)

And so the war began, blood flowed in torrents: the poor peasants, the middle peasants, and the numerically insignificant Kulaks, the rich peasants, all rose up as one. The country was swept with peasant uprisings—unnecessary, senseless, harmful, destructive uprisings provoked by Lenin's policy toward the peasantry—all of which could have been obviated, since it was possible to find a way toward a peaceful understanding. But Lenin did not want such an understanding, he did not care to find the ground for such an understanding either with the peasants or with the Socialist parties and he did not want to hear of any united fronts with those elements.

Two weeks later, June 4, Lenin spoke at the united session of the All-Russian Central Executive Committee of the Soviets and of the Moscow Soviet held on the question of "The Struggle for Grain". In this speech he made everyone understand that he realized and saw that "hunger and starvation on one hand lead to uprisings and rebellions of people who are wracked with starvation, and on the other hand we see the entire country swept with the fire of counter-revolutionary uprisings that are financed by the English-French imperialists and are being organized by the right wing Social-Revolutionists and Mensheviks. It is when we view this picture as a whole that we say: 'yes, it is pretty clear, let any one who wishes, still daydream about united fronts'." 111)

In his speech made on June 27 at the Fourth Conference of Trade Unions and Factory Committees of Moscow, Lenin admitted that the detachments of class conscious workers which left Moscow and Petrograd for the villages, "very often stray from the right path and de-

109) Ibid, p. 301.
110) Ibid, p. 302.
111) N. Lenin, "The Struggle for Grain," p. 316, vol. XV.

generate into criminals".112) He knew "that it very often came to armed clashes with the peasants" 113) and also that "the detachments which went forth to collect grain turned to drinking, moonshining, banditry . . . we are quite aware of that" 114) "and still, wtih all that notwithstanding, when people tell us about other methods, we tell them what we had already said at the session of the Central Executive Committee of the Soviets when the same question of other methods was brought up: go to *Skoropadsky* (the Hetman of Ukraine placed in power by the German military command—G. M.), go to the bourgeoisie. It is those people that you have to teach your ways and methods of raising grain prices, how to make united fronts with the Kulaks—there you will meet an attentive audience, but we say to the workers: launch a crusade to get bread, a crusade against the speculators, against the Kulaks, a crusade for the purpose of establishing order".115) This crusade was to be launched notwithstanding the fact that "peasants demand an equitable barter, refusing to give up their grain for depreciated paper currency".116) But in order to launch this crusade, it is necessary to possess physical force, "for we are building a dictatorship, we are building an apparatus of violence to suppress the exploiters . . ." "What we need"—Lenin said—"is that the grain collecting detachments go forth into the villages, that our war for food, our war with the Kulaks, our war with confusion and disorder be consecrated and legalized by workers who should use it as a vehicle to carry on Socialist propaganda". 117) Lenin wound up his speech before the members of the All-Russian Executive Committee and the delegates of the Moscow Soviet with the following appeal to workers:

"Join our detachments of fighting agitators, don't be taken aback by the fact that many of those detachments break up and turn to drinking. . . ." 118) Lenin consciously chose the course of bloody struggle, the course of civil war with the peasants in the hope of terrorizing them and subjecting them to a full state regimentation. Lenin

112) N. Lenin, p. 342, vol. XV.
113) Ibid, p. 343.
114) N. Lenin, "The Struggle for Grain," p. 321, vol. XV.
115) Ibid, p. 320.
116) N. Lenin, "On Economic Problems" (December 19, 1918), p. 603, vol. XV.
117) N. Lenin, "The Struggle for Grain," p. 322, vol. XV.
118) Ibid, p. 324.

even glorified it in his polemic with K. Kautsky: "that we brought civil war to the village is something that we hold up as a *merit*".119)

Simultaneously with the organization of a "crusade" against peasants who did not want to give up their grain for "depreciated paper currency", Lenin put forth another demagogic and terroristic slogan which unleashed base passions, "entertained" workers and distracted their attention from the serious food problems and ways of solving it, and that was the searches of the rich and well-to-do undertaken in all the cities. On June 27, in the address on "The Current Events", delivered before the delegates of the Fourth Conference of the Moscow Trade Unions and Factory Committees, Lenin drew a fair and attractive picture of a wholesale search instituted in the houses of the town of Yeletz, urging that the same be done in Moscow.

On the following day, in his concluding remarks, Lenin made an open bid for this method of solving the food problems: "In Moscow there are 8,000 Communists, the trade unions of Moscow will give us 20 to 30 thousand people for whom they can vouch, reliable and steadfast people who will carry through the proletarian policy. Rally those people, create hundreds of thousands of such detachments, start fighting in order to carry out the food policy, to carry out searches among the rich population—and you will have obtained what you need".120)

Simultaneously with the "crusades" against villages and searches of rich houses, that is, simultaneously with the egging on of workers against peasants and other strata of the city population (during the searches there was no distinction between rich or poor; if there were found a few pounds of flour or other food products—it was sufficient), Lenin began to incite one section of the working class against the other in order to discourage them from bringing forth demands about improving their economic lot. All that was done, of course, in the alleged interests of the revolution.

Thus, for instance, Lenin said to the factory committees: "Remember, you will not be able to retain a single revolutionary conquest if you confine yourselves in your committees to problems of a purely technical or finanical nature".121) "Your factory committees have

119) N. Lenin, "The Proletarian Revolution and the Renegade Kautsky," p. 507, vol. XV.
120) N. Lenin, "The Current Events," p. 357, vol. XV.
121) Ibid, p. 346.

to become more than mere factory committees: they have to become the basic state nuclei of a ruling class"; 122) that is, organs of compulsion and suppression in the factories. On the following day he declared in his concluding remarks that "the working class is one thing and certain small layers within it is quite another thing," there are, for instance, those among the printers who are bribed by the bourgeoisie "who strive to retain their high wages".123) A few days later, Lenin placed those workers in the category of "scoundrels" and he demanded that they be hounded and baited.

Thus in the period lasting from April 29 to August 30, the day on which the attempt on Lenin's life (made by Dora Kaplan) took place, Lenin in his speeches and articles called for murders, shootings, in the name of the dictatorship of the proletariat, in the name of Socialism. And he did it while the decree abolishing the death penalty was still in force. Lenin demanded, insisted and spurred on the taming by force of arms "the petty-bourgeois Anarchist elemental forces", that is, the persecution of all Socialist parties and Anarchist groups; he called for the shooting of thieves, crooks, grafters, profiteers, grain speculators caught in the act of crime, "meshechniks" (that is, hungry workers, who were trying to get for their families a pood—40 Russian pounds—of flour without government permission); he called for an armed plunder of peasants; he organized an internecine war within the working class; he demanded iron and blood and called for the highest penalty for those that violate discipline; he demanded that the courts show more and more cruelty and ferocity. How did the country react to those appeals? What was the reaction of Lenin's party and state apparatus to it? What was the reaction of the courts, military-revolutionary committees, countless Che-Ka bodies, the food detachments, the commissars, Soviets, the army and the criminal police?

I shall cite a few facts by way of illustrating the reactions of this period.

*

The above described period was signalized by the legal murder of Captain *Shtchasny*, and the *responsibility for this murder rests in the first place upon the shoulders of L. TROTZKY*. Captain

---

122) Ibid, p. 347.
123) Ibid, p. 353.

Shtchasny saved the Baltic Fleet from being trapped by the German escadrille, having succeeded in bringing it safely to the Kronstadt harbor. *Shtchasny* was charged with treason and put on trial before the Revolutionary Tribunal. The only witness brought forth by the prosecution was *L. Trotzky*. The indictment against *Shtchasny* reads as follows: "*Shtchasny* performed a heroic feat thereby gaining popularity for himself which he intended to use later against the Soviet Power". The Tribunal sentenced Captain *Shtchasny* to die, and on May 22 he was shot for "performing his heroic feat." It is to be pointed out here that the death penalty, abolished by the decree of October 26, 1917, had not yet been officially re-established, and the Tribunal had no right to take orders to that effect from the Council of People's Commissars. Thus, at Lenin's insistence, executions were introduced by courts.

This open and challenging crime perpetrated by the government stirred up general indignation, sweeping even the Communist ranks. Thus, for instance, on July 30, the ex-sailor Dybenko, who was already then one of the top-ranking Communists, came out with the following protest in "Anarchia", daily organ of the Moscow Anarchist Federation:

"Is there not one honest Bolshevik who will publicly voice his protest against the re-introduction of the death penalty? Wretched cowards! They are afraid openly to raise their voice in protest. But if there is a single straightforward Socialist left, he should voice his protest before the world proletariat . . . we are not guilty of this shameful act of re-establishing the death penalty, and by way of showing our protest we are withdrawing from the ranks of the governmental parties. And now that we who fought and are fighting against the death penalty are issuing our protest, let the Communists who are at the helm of the government send us to the scaffold; let them to be our headsmen and executioners."

Later this very Dybenko, under the guidance of Lenin and Trotzky, took an active part in the shooting of the Kronstadt sailors, but he was quite sincere when protesting against the death penalty; the spirit of the ideas of the Paris Commune by which Lenin succeeded in getting hold of the sympathies of the people had not yet been eradicated from men like Dybenko.

In the month of May, in Moscow, the eighth convention of the party of Social-Revolutionists was raided. The net result of this raid was the arrest of ten to fifteen people. On June 14, the Mensheviks and Social-Revolutionists were expelled from the All-Russian Executive Committee of the Soviets, that is, they were virtually outlawed.

On June 7, the Left Social-Revolutionists, aiming to disrupt the Brest-Litovsk peace, assassinated in Moscow the German Ambassador, Count Mirbach, and made an attempt to carry out a revolt of their own. Many leading members of the party of Left Social-Revolutionists were arrested and the party itself was unofficially proscribed. On June 13, a Left Social-Revolutionist by the name of Alexandrovich was shot in Moscow, together with thirteen sailors.

On June 11, B. Savinkov raised a rebellion in Yaroslavl. Following the suppression of that revolt, 428 of those that surrendered were shot.

In August the conference of the Social-Revolutionist organization of the Astrakhan government, numbering fifteen people, was arrested in the city of Astrakhan. All the fifteen were shot.[124] Beginning with the month of June 1918, the arrests of Socialists became a matter of routine procedure with the Bolshevik authorities.

Apart from the murders committed by various foraging and requisitioning expeditions there also took place during that period mass shootings of people who had been implicated in the Tzar's government and administration; and also of criminals. The number of people who were shot on that score will never be fully ascertained.

124) "Che-Ka, the Materials About the Activity of the Extraordinary Committees," p. 248. Published by the Central Bureau of the Party Social-Revolutionists, Berlin, 1922.

CHAPTER V

THE BLOODY ORGY OF THE MASS TERROR

But all that was only in the nature of a prelude to a bloody orgy unprecedented in world history, a prelude to madly-hysterical and sadistic calls for revenge, to individual and mass murders, to bloodshed ever growing in scope, to torture and outrages. This bloody orgy began on the day following the murder of Uritzky and the attempt upon Lenin's life made August 31, 1918.

A week prior to this attempt, one of the eminent figures of the Che-Ka and its litterateurs, Latzis, wrote the following in the "Izvestia" of August 23, in his article "Laws and Norms Do Not Apply in a Civil War". In this article he rejects the "laws" of capitalist war which forbid the shooting of prisoners; instead Latzis demanded that all prisoners be massacred.

". . . One becomes rather ridiculous"—Latzis wrote—"when demanding that we adhere to laws which at one time were held sacred . . . *To slaughter all those who were wounded by taking part in the battles against us—such is the law of civil war.* . . . This law is well heeded by the bourgeoisie, but we hardly take it into account. Therein lies our weakness".

Following the attempt upon Lenin's life, this "law of civil war" laid down by Latzis on the basis of Lenin's homicidal propaganda began to prevail in the war practice: prisoners, that is, unarmed people, were massacred in a body. And in order to carry out such massacres there was no need of any investigation or evidence, nor of definitely framed charges; all that was superfluous. "Don't seek for incriminating evidence as to whether the prisoners took part, by deed or word, in a rebellion against the Soviet government", Latzis wrote in the "Weekly of the Kazan Che-Ka".125) "You have to ask him what class he belongs to, what is his origin, his education and profession. It is those questions that should decide the fate of the defendant—and therein lies the meaning of the red terror".

---

125) No. 1, November, 1918; reprinted by "Pravda" (Moscow) No. 281, December 25, 1918.

The seeds of Lenin's bloody propaganda sprouted, grew ripe and at the time the attempt upon his life took place they began to yield a rich and abundant harvest.

On the day following the murder of Uritzky and the attempt made upon Lenin's life, the "Krasnaya Gazeta" wrote: "For the death of our champion thousands of our enemies will have to pay with their lives. Enough of this sentimentalizing! . . . We shall teach the bourgeoisie a bloody lesson. . . . Death to the bourgeoisie—this should become the slogan of the day".

The same newspaper issued a demand to kill the enemy in hundreds and thousands, so "that they choke themselves with their own blood"; it shouted hysterically for torrents of blood to redeem the blood of Uritzky and Lenin . . . "more and more blood, as much as it is possible to shed now." The "Izvestia," organ of the government, threatened and promised that "the wounding of Lenin will be answered by the proletariat so that the entire bourgeoisie will shudder with fear". Radek in the same "Izvestia" threatened that "for every Soviet active worker, for every leader of the workers' revolution slain by the agents of the counter-revolution, the latter will pay with dozens of heads". On September 2 the All-Russian Central Executive Committee passed a resolution which served thereafter as a standard for further instructions:

"The Central Executive Committee solemnly warns all the flunkeys of the Russian and the Entente bourgeoisie that for every attempt made upon the active people of the Soviet government and the Socialist revolution all the counter-revolutionists and all those who inspire them will be held responsible".[126)]

On September 3, the War Commissar made public in Moscow the following declaration:

"The working class of Soviet Russia arose, threateningly declaring that for every drop of proletarian blood it will shed torrents of blood of those who go against the revolution, against the Soviets and proletarian leaders. For every proletarian life it will seek to destroy the scions of bourgeois families and white guardists. From now on the working class (that is, the Communist Party—G. M.) declares to its enemies that every single act of white terror will be answered with a ruthless, proletarian, mass terror".

126) "Izvestia," No. 189.

On the same day, the People's Commissar of Internal Affairs, Petrovsky (he was later the Chairman of the People's Commissars of Ukraine, then Acting Chairman of the Supreme Council of the U. S. S. R. and now, along with many other eminent Bolsheviks, vanished in the dungeons of Yezhov's Commissariat), sent out by telegraph an order [127] under the following caption: "An Order About Hostages", which reads:

"The murder of Volodarsky, Uritzky, the attempt made upon the life of the Chairman of the Council of People's Commissars, Vladimir Ilyich Lenin, and his wounding, the mass executions—reaching into thousands—of our comrades in Finland, Ukraine, in the Don region, in Czecho-Slovakia, the plot steadily unearthed in the rear of our armies, the admission openly made by the right wing Social-Revolutionists and other counter-revolutionary riff-raff as to their participation in those plots, and at the same time the rather feeble repressions practiced by the Soviets and negligible number of mass executions of white guardists and representatives of the bourgeoisie—all that shows that notwithstanding the constant reiterations about mass terror against the Social-Revolutionists, white guardists and the bourgeoisie, this terror does not yet exist in fact.

"This state of affairs must be ended. Sentimentalizing and laxness must be done away with. All the right wing Social-Revolutionists known to the local Soviet authorities should be placed immediately under arrest. A considerable number of hostages should be taken from bourgeois and officer ranks. The slightest show of resistance or the slightest move made by the white guardist circles should be met unreservedly by mass executions. The Executive Committees of the local Soviets should display special initiative in this direction.

"The administrative sections of the Soviet Executive Committees, acting through the militia and Che-Ka departments, should take all measures toward the ascertaining and arrest of all those who hide under faked names and documents, and toward the unconditional shooting of anyone implicated in the work of the white guardists.

"All these outlined measures should be carried out immediately.

"Any sign of irresolution displayed in the actions of any organs

127) Published in "Izvestia" No. 190 and then in "The Weekly of the Che-Ka" No. 1.

of the local Soviets should be reported by the head of the Soviet Administrative Section to the People's Commissar of Internal Affairs. The rear of our armies should at last be purged from white guard elements and the vile plotters against the government of the working class and the poorest peasantry. Not the slightest wavering or irresolution should be tolerated in applying mass terror.

"Acknowledge the receipt of this telegram and have it transmitted to the county Soviets."

This telegram was accompanied by the following commentaries written by Petrovsky for "The Weekly Che-Ka": 128) "Enough of this long, sterile and vain talk about red terror. . . . It is time, while it is not late yet, to carry out, by deed and not in word, a ruthless and strictly organized mass terror."

On September 6, the Council of People's Commissars issued a decree approving the actions of the Che-Ka and urging to "shoot all those who are involved in any white guardist organizations, plots and rebellions." It is to be noted in this connection that at the time those lines were written, the decree abolishing the death penalty was still legally valid. . . .

These homicidal appeals issued from the center and coming from the most eminent "scientific Socialists" found their echo throughout the country.

The "Rabotche-Krestiansky Listok" of Nizhni-Novgorod wrote: "Every murder of a Communist or attempt at murder will be answered by putting up the hostages of the bourgeoisie before firing squads, for the blood of our murdered and wounded comrades demands vengeance".129) In the city of Vitebsk the demand was put forth to execute a hundred people for the murder of a single person active in Soviet work. The Communist cell of the Che-Ka of the Western region demanded on September 13 that "all the foul murderers be wiped off the face of the earth." The Red Army guards of the Che-Ka of Ostrogozhsk threatened on September 23, "to annihilate hundreds for the life of one Communist, and tens of thousands for attempts made upon the lives of the leaders." One could cite an endless list of such "resolutions," demands, threats, and decisions.

It is clear that the appeals issued from the center did not remain unheeded: rivers of blood were shed in response to those pleas.

---

128) No. 1.
129) "Izvestia" (Moscow), September 3, 1918.

In Nizhni-Novgorod 46 people were shot on September 1. In Moscow, the All-Russian Che-Ka executed at first 15 and then 90 people, among whom were many common criminals; the Petrograd Che-Ka shot 512 hostages. Acording to the figures published by "The Weekly of the Che-Ka",130)—inadequate and minimized figures—9 people were shot in Arkhangelsk, 12 in Kimri, 2 in Vitebsk, 9 in Kursk, 14 in Vologda, 5 in Severo-Dvinsk, 2 in Velizh, 4 in Velsk, 17 in Sebezh. In the town of Poshekhon, entire families were shot by the Che-Ka, altogether 31 people. Eight people were shot in Penza, 3 embezzlers were shot in the town of Chernsk, 8 in Valanov, 8 in Novgorod, and an equal number of people were shot in Mstislav, Riazan, Tambov, Lipetzk. In Smolensk 34 people were shot among them were common criminals, ex-landlords, officers and policemen. In Pavlovo-Posad six "servants of autocracy" were shot, in Pskov —31 people, in Yaroslav—38; among those were quite a few common criminals.

Dora Kaplan, Social-Revolutionist and ex-Anarchist, who served time as a political prisoner under the Tzar's regime, was shot for making an attempt upon Lenin's life. She was executed under circumstances which remained a deep secret to everyone, and that in spite of the universal expectation that Lenin would make the noble gesture of extending her a pardon.

It is difficult to ascertain the exact number of people executed at that period: many official reports of executions were couched in vague terms, as for instance—"a few were shot" (the town of Klin); "many were shot"—Voronezh. The Sestrorietzk authorities report that shootings took place "after a painstaking investigation of every individual case."

This bloody bacchanalia lasted until the end of the year, nor was there a let-up the following year. There was hardly a single town where executions did not take place: shootings were the price of promotions.

According to statistics issued by one of the prominent chekists, Latzis, there were 245 uprisings in 1918. This is much of an understatement on the part of Latzis, but one thing is clear: ninety-nine percent of them were brought forth by the terror of the food requisitioning detachments, by the Soviet food policy and senseless

130) See "The Weekly of the Che-Ka," Nos. 3, 5, 6.

executions. The crushing of those rebellions resulted in the death of 1821 people and 878 Che-Ka soldiers. During the same year, 56 people were shot for espionage, 2431 were implicated in the uprisings, 1637 for taking part in the work of counter-revolutionary organizations, 396 for inciting rebellion, 39 for speculation, 402 for banditry, 39 for army desertion, 57 for criminal breach of trust, 1173 miscellaneous. Total 6,300.

The total of executed and killed—8,121, arrested and imprisoned people (in prisons, concentration camps) and of hostages (3,061?) was given by Latzis at 42,254. This figure at least would have to be trebled in order to bring it nearer to actuality.

**
*

Lenin was not seriously wounded and upon recovery he took the lead in this bloody bacchanalia, having done much to fan the flames of bigotry, inhumanity and licentiousness. Already in his article "On the Character of Our Press," written September 20, he launched his campaign against workers, against entire factories who, according to his words, "clung to the tradition of capitalism," that is, they refused to work while starving, which always irritated and exasperated Lenin.

"The blackboard of backward factories, which following nationalization remained sad examples of deterioration, decay, dilapidation, dirt, hooliganism, loafing—why don't we see it? Where is it? We still have not got it. But we have such factories. We shall fail in our duty if we do not wage a relentless war against those that still 'cling to the traditions of capitalism'. We are not Communists but rag-pickers inasmuch and insofar as we *silently tolerate* such factories. We seem to lack the ability to wage the *class struggle on the pages of our press* just as the bourgeoisie used to do it. Remember the magnificent manner in which it used to hound its class enemies in the press controlled by it! How it used to mock at them, defame them, and finally drive them off the face of the earth. And we? Does not class struggle in the period of transition from capitalism to Socialism consist in safeguarding the interest of the worker from the small handful, from groups and layers within its own ranks who obstinately persist in the traditions and ways of capitalism? They still view the Soviet State as they did the employer of the old times: give 'HIM' as little as possible, as bad work as one can get away with—and 'squeeze' out as much money as possible. Haven't we quite a number of such scoundrels in our own proletarian midst— among the typesetters of the Soviet print shops, among the workers of the Putilovsky and Sormovo plants? How many of them did we nab, expose and pillory?

"The press is silent about it. And if it does write, it deals with it in a *bureaucratic,* jejune manner and not as a revolutionary press, as the organ of the dictatorship of a class which is proving by deeds that the resistance of the capitalists and the loafers who cling to capitalist ways will be broken with an iron hand.

"The same holds true about war. Do we go after cowardly and incompetent commanders? Have we denounced the utterly worthless regiments? Have we 'caught' a sufficient number of those specimens in the army, have we expelled them in order to hold them up before the public eye and thus openly branded every manifestation of truancy, remissness, etc.? We don't wage a business-like, ruthless, truly revolutionary war with the concrete persons who embody this evil. We do not educate sufficiently the masses *upon living concrete examples* taken from various domains of life—and it is exactly this kind of education that constitutes the main task of the press during the transition from capitalism to Communism. We do not pay sufficient attention to the task of giving wide publicity to our acts of censure, to the necessity of *hounding the worthless element,* of calling upon the people to learn from the better element".131)

Thus Lenin introduces into his system of terror a third element: the first was shootings, prison; the second—compulsion by enforced starvation; and the third, which is clearly expressed in the above cited long excerpt, is "the guillotine via public opinion," as Robespierre used to say at one time. This guillotine via public opinion is created by "hounding the worthless," by lying, slandering, by heaping dirt and deliberately false charges against adversaries. Lenin skillfully applied these three basic elements of his terroristic theory, combining them to suit the circumstances. In his pamphlet on "The Proletarian Revolution and the Renegade Kautsky," which Lenin finished by November 10, he falls back upon demagogy by way of answering Kautsky's sharp criticism of terror. Katusky chided the Bol-

---

131) N. Lenin, Sobranie Sochineniy, "On Character of Our Press," p. 419, vol. XV.

shevik government not only with organizing terror against the bourgeoisie, but also against Socialists, workers and peasants. Lenin ignored this reproof, posing before the workers as a true revolutionist and presenting Katusky as the defender of the bourgeoisie. "And if you, exploiters, make any attempt to resist our proletarian revolution, we shall ruthlessly crush you, we shall deprive you of all rights, and more than that: we shall not give you any bread, for in our proletarian republic the exploiters shall be deprived of ordinary rights, of the use of fire and water, for, unlike the Scheidemanns and Kautskys, we take our Socialism seriously. That is the language we, revolutionary Marxists, are going to use, and that is why the oppressed masses will be siding with us."

One cannot deny that Lenin was consistent. His ideas follow directly and logically from Engels' "our state" and Marx's centralization; that is, it is the result of carrying into life the ideas of the "Communist Manifesto" by Marx and Engels.

Following the attempt made upon his life, Lenin took an even firmer course upon a die-hard terroristic policy, and that notwithstanding the seemingly endless peasant rebellions, notwithstanding the frightful destructions wrought by this policy.

In the article "The Valuable Confessions of Pitirim Sorokin," he declares categorically that "it would be absurd and ridiculous to renounce terror and suppression in respect of the landlords and capitalists with their hangers-on who are selling out Russia to the 'allied' imperialists".[132] And since "hangers-on", according to Lenin, embrace all those who show dissent with his policies, this virtually means that terror would be applied against everyone, it means approval of the bloody orgy enacted at that time in the country.

Those "hangers-on" were in the first place: Social-Revolutionists and Social-Democrats. And when Friedrich Adler, who was held in high esteem by Lenin, interceded in behalf of the imprisoned Socialists, Lenin treated this intercession with a mocking reply: "Adler's letter, written toward the end of September and received by us today, contains only one request: 'Will it not be possible to free the imprisoned Mensheviks?' He had nothing else to write about at such

---

132) N. Lenin, p. 564, vol. XV.

a time".133) And that was the end of Adler. He also became a "hanger-on": clubs, streets, military units were no more named after him and his portrait vanished from sight.

In that article Lenin stressed once more that he aimed toward an absolute rule, toward dictatorship of his party which, in turn, was under his absolute rule: "We leave to ourselves the state power, *only to ourselves*".134) Consequently, "it is necessary that everything should be subjected to the Soviet power and all the illusions about some kind of 'independence' on the part of detached layers of population or workers' cooperatives should be lived down as soon as possible"; consequently, "there can be no question of independence on the part of separate groups"; consequently, "there can be no question, now that the world is threatening to strike at the root of capitalism, of independence of individual parties." 135) And again: "we shall fight, just as we have fought until now, all syndicalist, separatist, localist and regionalist attempts which work to the detriment of our cause".136) Those methods (the "Soviet methods": shootings, prison, compulsion—G. M.) are made basic to government and administration, and it is from the point of view of those methods that "collegiate management" (management by boards) was done away with in order to make possible the tracing and the shooting of those who are responsible for red tape: "we should know who is to be held responsible, from the point of view of immediate arrest and martial court, even if he happens to be the representative of the most important union or central administrative board of some important economic trust".137) "Any attempt to substitute deeds by rationalizations, which embody the myopia, the most vulgar stupidity and the conceit of the intellectuals, will be ruthlessly suppressed as demanded by the war situation".138) That meant the shooting of the myopic, stupid and supercilious industrial administrators who were holding their positions with the knowledge and consent of Lenin,

133) N. Lenin, "On the Petty-Bourgeois Parties," a speech delivered at a rally of the active workers of the party, November 27, 1918, p. 569, vol. XV.

134) Ibid, p. 577.

135) N. Lenin, "On Workers' Cooperation," pp. 585-587, vol. XV.

136) N. Lenin, "On Economic Tasks, a speech delivered at the Second All-Russian Convention of the Councils of National Economy," p. 602, vol. XV.

137) Ibid, p. 603.

138) Ibid, p. 604.

the Central Committee or its Politbureau—but why shoot them and not those who appointed and approved them?

Autocratic one-man management and shooting appointed officials became the basic methods of administration.

". . . Definite persons have to be appointed for a definite responsible work, and it is necessary that everyone of those appointees know his job, that he be responsible for it—even to the point of being ready to face the highest penalty: shooting. This is the policy which we are carrying out in the Sovnarkom, in the Council of Defense, and it is to this policy that the entire work of the Councils of National Economy and of the cooperatives has to be subordinated".139)

Thus the year 1918 was replete with the suppression of all liberties and the closing of non-Communist publications; the breaking up of Anarchist organizations and the murder of individual Anarchists; the outlawing of the Social-Revolutionists and Mensheviks, which came as a natural result of their expulsion from the All-Russian Central Committee of the Soviets; the break-up and the shooting of the Left Social-Revolutionists; the shooting of hostages, thieves, grafters, petty speculators, deserters, hooligans, wreckers, delinquent officials, right wing Social-Revolutionists, people arrested by chance and having the misfortune of not belonging to the working class or peasants, saboteurs, strikers, drunks; people who failed to pay the monetary contribution, who were congregating on the streets, who left their house after 8 p.m.; of those who were accused of posting on walls anti-government proclamations, of agitation against the Soviet power or just of performing "heroic deeds" like Captain Shtchasny. The year was replete with executions on account of red tape, administrative myopia and stupidity, intellectual conceit, etc. It was a year taken up with the organization of the "guillotine of public opinion," that is, the "hounding of the unfit" by slander, lies and deliberately false charges, a year crowded with murders, shootings and mass arrests of peasants, ruthless suppressions of peasant rebellions brought about by the pillage and violence of the Committees of Poor Peasants. Oceans of blood, mountains of corpses, tens and hundreds of thousands of people rotting away in the prisons and concentration camps.

War against the peasantry, which the Maxists class with the bourgeoisie, with the petty capitalists, deemed it a densely reactionary

139) Ibid, p. 605.

mass, was declared not only because the peasants did not want to surrender grain for "worthless pieces of paper," but in order to subject the peasantry to regimentation and the control of the party and state, in order to make the revolution "proletarian": "our revolution prior to the organization of Committees of Poor Peasants, that is, until the fall of 1918, was to a considerable extent bourgeois in character".[140] And it was only then "that we saw that the October revolution started in the villages, it was only then that we got to a sound proletarian basis, having imparted to our revolution a genuinely proletarian character, proletarian in fact and not only by its promise".[141] And this was done notwithstanding the fact that "the proletarian layer which actually governed Russia in that year, carrying out all the policies and constituting our power . . . was very thin".[142] Lenin admits that during this "October revolution," because of the inexperience of the Soviet administration, the difficulty of the problem involved, the blows meant for the Kulaks fell upon the middle peasantry.[143]

In Russia it was the poor, small, toiling peasant that prevailed; the Kulaks were but a small minority. Thus the blows directed by Lenin against the Kulaks fell upon the peasantry as a whole: hit out indiscriminately and then we shall find out what's what.

We shall illustrate here the "October revolution in the village" by instances taken from "Izvestia" and "Pravda" which we take from I. Steinberg's book "The Moral Visage of the Revolution".

The "Izvestia" of January 23, 1919, No. 15|567 contains the following item about the Ureni district of the government of Kostroma.

"In the village Ureni, the chairman of the Soviet Executive Committee, Rekhalev and his three assistants, distinguished themselves in quite a peculiar manner. Beating up of petitioners was common practice in the Soviet; the same thing was going on in the other villages; in the village Berezovka, for instance, the peasants were beaten not only with fists, but also with sticks; the beaten up peasants were unshoed and put into snow cellars". "But it was not only Rekhalev and company that distinguished themselves, but likewise members of

---

140) N. Lenin, Sobranie Sochineniy, "The Report of the Central Committee of the Russian Communist Party," Session of March 18, 1918, p. 105, vol. XVI.

141) Ibid, p. 106.

142) Ibid, p. 107.

143) Ibid, pp. 107-108.

the Executive Committee of Varnavino, Galakhov and Makhov, etc. They showed themselves up especially during grain requisitions . . . Upon approaching any village, the Galakhov expedition would start rattling off their machine guns with the aim of frightening the population. The peasants had to put on five and more shirts in order to be able to bear the terrific flogging. But that was of no avail: the lash was made of coiled wire and it often happened that after the flogging the shirt would cut itself into the flesh and dry up so that only warm water could wash it off". "Makhov gave us orders—told a Red army soldier—to give the arrested peasants a good lashing: why drag them along with us, give them a good laying out and let them remember the Soviet power".

"We are being ruined"—is the burden of complaint in the resolutions of one of the village meetings in the government of Kostroma— "our will is being set at naught, and we are being mocked at as if we were dumb cattle".

In the Khvalinsk county of the government of Saratov, tells "Pravda",144)—one of the villages was visited by a Red Army and food requisitioning expedition. "The three commanders of those detachments rallied the peasants at night, told them to heat up the bath house and fetch young girls—'send us the nicest and the youngest girls'. The peasants raised a rumpus about it and soon a general fight broke out. This lasted all night—one of the commanders was killed and the others escaped with their detachments."

In the county of Nicolayevsk, the government of Vologda, "the last supplies and not only surpluses were wrung from the peasants. The village meeting was dispersed by shots. There followed a rebellion not of Kulaks but of poor peasants" . . .

"The Che-Ka locked up the arrested peasants in cold barns, and had them flogged with gun sticks. The instructions from the Center —the local people reported—were that it would be better to overdo than to leave the thing half-done." It was there also that the imprisoned peasants were given a thorough third degree.

"Pravda" in No. 276, 1918, writes: "The common saying in the two counties of the government of Tambov is that if our comrades who obtained soft jobs did not become like the police of old, no untoward developments would take place here." "Pravda" in No.

144) No. 265, 1918.

265, 1918 writes: "The Communists of the Spassk county of the government of Tambov take away everything from the peasants; the slightest objection leads to arrest, beating up and shooting." The name Communist—writes "Pravda," No. 280, 1918—now stands there for "hooliganism, loafing and imposition." "In the county of Belsk, the government of Vitebsk, peasants are being flogged by orders of the Soviet Central Executive Committee".145) In the county of Dukhov, the government of Smolensk, "the Central Executive Committee of Soviets was nothing but a horde of drunkards" who greatly contributed toward the outbreak of a peasant rebellion.146) "Izvestia," No. 7, 1919, reprints the following order issued by a certain Food Commissar to a Committee of Poor Peasants: "You are to announce to the villagers that I am giving them three days to procure and ship out ten thousand poods of grain. Failure to comply with this order will entail on my part wholesale shootings; already some of those scoundrels were shot in the village Varvarinka. My deputies are fully empowered to carry out such shootings, especially in relation to the vile volost." . . . (a small administrative unit—there follows the name of this volost).

One can adduce a great number of such instances during the years of 1918, 1919, 1920, 1921—that is, during the "October revolution in the villages," at the period of requisition by force and the "rasverstka" (assessment in kind—a policy most hated by the peasants), the period of "crusades into the village," but, by way of concluding, I shall confine myself to one instance relating to the year 1920, the period immediately following the Kronstadt rebellion, that is —the eve of the inauguration of the New Economic Policy (NEP) and the restoring of a limited freedom of trade in grain.

While we were kept in the Taganka prison (Moscow), three Left Social-Revolutionists made their escape. Later they were caught and arraigned before the "Revolutionary" Tribunal. One of the defendants, Gan, made the following statement at the court:

"I was arrested not in January 1921, but in September 1920; there was no wide insurrectionary movement in the government of Tambov, although there were detached cases of armed resistance on the part of the peasants to the requisitioning detachments who were

145) "Izvestia" (Moscow), No. 15, 1919.
146) "Pravda," No. 18, 1919.

— 87 —

shamelessly looting the villages. On the day of my arrival in Tambov the Central Executive Committee of Tambov Soviets hung out the following announcement, declaring that 'because of their attempt to disrupt the campaign of grain collecting, the villages Verkhne-Spasskoye (ten thousand population), Koziri (six thousand) and four other villages were burnt, hundreds of peasants were shot, and their property was looted'.[147] During my six months of confinement in the prisons of the Tambov Che-Ka I had a chance to see for myself the nightmarish picture of mass annihilation and ruination of the toiling peasants of the government of Tambov which was carried on by the Communist authorities: hundreds of peasants were shot by the Revolutionary Circuit Courts and the Tambov Che-Ka; thousands of unarmed peasants were mowed down by the machine guns of the students of military schools and Communists, and tens of thousands were exiled to the far away North, while their property was burnt or looted. The same picture, according to the data which the party of Left Social-Revolutionists has at its disposal, can be drawn for a number of other provinces: the governments of Samara, Kazan, Saratov, in Ukraine, Siberia, etc. That was the way the Communist Party carried out its food policy and it is only this party that bears the responsibility for the shedding of the blood of peasants".[148]

We see thus that by his policy of terror, by the destruction of the peasant economy, by exiling thousands of peasants from their native places, by the policy of grain requisitions, etc., Lenin prepared one of the ghastliest famines in the history of Russia, the famine of 1921, which carried away millions of lives and crippled, physically and morally, tens of millions.

And with all that Lenin had the brazenness to declare to an American journalist—July 25, 1919—that "it was only after the exploiters —that is, the capitalists—had begun to resist that we answered by systematically suppressing them, going as far as to inaugurate a policy of terror".[149] Notwithstanding the shedding of torrents of blood and his frenzied urgings for shootings, Lenin had the temerity to

<hr>

147) "Izvestia of the Central Executive Committee of the Tambov Soviet."
148) "The Trial of the Left Social-Revolutionists, June 27-29, 1922." See "The Roads of the Revolution," pp. 295-296, Berlin, 1923. Published by the Left Social-Revolutionists.
149) N. Lenin, Sobranie Sochineniy, "An Answer to a Question by an American Journalist," p. 284, vol. XVI.

declare that Kautsky and "all the heroes of the yellow International" "lie about Soviet Russia on the question of terrorism and democracy".150) Lenin had the temerity and brazenness to state at the Seventh Convention of the Soviets that "terror was imposed upon us," that "people forget that terrorism was brought forth by the invasion of the world power of the Entente".151) Speculating upon a lack of memory on the part of the delegates, or their utter ignorance or fear, Lenin had the temerity to declare that "we have been charged with raising terrorism into a principle; our answer to those charges is: you yourself do not believe that slander".152) We showed that this was no slander at all. But it is remarkable that two months prior to that, September 30, in his polemic against Kautsky, Lenin thundered forth: "It is a lie that the Bolsheviks were opposed to the death penalty during a revolution".153)

150) N. Lenin, "How the Bourgeoisie Makes Use of the Renegades," vol. XVI.

151) N. Lenin, Sobranie Sochineniy, "The Report of the Council of People's Commissars," December 6, 1919, p. 416, vol. XVI.

152) Ibid.

153) N. Lenin, "How the Bourgeoisie Makes Use of the Renegades," p. 320, vol. XVI.

CHAPTER VI

THE FIGHT AGAINST LIBERTY

(*Terror of* 1919)

The succession of peasant rebellions, bringing to an end the year 1918 and inaugurating the year 1919, forced Lenin to put an end to his unrestrained agitation for terror directed against peasants, to his urging for "crusades". He became more cautious but at the same time he did not come out against the terroristic practice and bloody excesses in the villages. He did not renounce but silently carried on the policy of terror in the villages, having changed only the methods of its application. Lenin gave a new formulation to his old terroristic policy in the villages: "The chief lesson to be drawn is that we have to be cautious in our attitude toward the middle peasant and the petty bourgeoisie. This is dictated by the experience of the past. . . . What is demanded on our part is frequent shifts in our line of behavior, which to an outsider may seem strange and unintelligible. Only yesterday you gave promises to the petty bourgeoisie', he will say, 'and today Dzerzhinsky declares that the Left Social-Revolutionists and Mensheviks will be "placed against the wall". What a contradiction.' . . . Yes, it is a contradiction. What else is to be done if the behavior of the petty bourgeois democracy in itself is contradictory. . . . We changed our tactics toward it, and no sooner does it turn half-face toward us than we say: 'Welcome'."[154] And that is why "one has to avoid anything that might spur on abuses in the actual work. Careerists have wormed themselves into our ranks. . . . Those people are only after promotion, and in order to achieve it, they fall back upon methods of compulsion, believing those to be the right methods". (How characteristic this is of Lenin's favorite way of shifting the burden to someone else, to some small fry—G. M.)

---

154) N. Lenin, "The Report of the Central Committee of the Russian Communist Party," March 18, 1919, p. 100, vol. XVI.

But in practice it leads to peasants saying: "Long live the Soviet power, but down with the Communists". The unrestrained orgy of murders and violence which Lenin kept on urging upon the Soviets were "necessary to suppress the bourgeoisie", but to do the same towards the middle peasantry, "is nothing but idiocy, stupidity, ruining our cause to such an extent that only provocateurs can deliberately use such methods".155)

But those "provocateurs" continued their work with the knowledge and blessing of Lenin who was carrying out the "October revolution" in the villages. The peasant rebellions were brought about by the activity of the purveying expeditions and detachments, who were requisitioning cattle, grain and were looting the peasants. Those uprisings were suppressed with great cruelty; this cruelty and brutal senselessness brought on in turn new rebellions.

According to the data supplied by the chekist Latzis, only during seven months of 1919 there were 99 rebellions, most of which were raised by the peasants. But Latzis' "bloody statistics" is rather careless, tending toward understatement in order not to shock even the most unrestrained imagination. The figures cited by Latzis should be increased threefold in order to bring them nearer to actuality. But even 99 rebellions taking place within the domain of the shrunken territory of Soviet Russia of that period—20 governments only— and that with 7 months only—is in itself far from being a small figure.

Instead of facing reality and putting an end to the bloody orgies in the villages and cities, Lenin made use of terror in order to physically exterminate, in accordance with the views of Engels, his political adversaries who seemed to be swept into prominence by the rising wave of popular unrest, and this was to Lenin the worst contingency, threatening the dictatorship of the party which Lenin cherished above everything else. "Yes, the dictatorship of one party! We firmly uphold such a dictatorship and we do not intend to abandon it under any circumstances".156)

Because of this, Lenin began to build up a terrorist sentiment

---

155) N. Lenin, "On the Work in the Villages," pp. 149-150, vol. XVI.

156) N. Lenin, "A Speech Delivered at the All-Russian Convention of Workers in the Field of Education and Socialist Culture," August 1, 1919, p. 296, vol. XVI.

against the Social-Revolutionists and Mensheviks as the inciters of peasant rebellions: "Political sharpers—all kinds of Social-Revolutionists and Mensheviks—egg on the peasants and keep on telling them: 'you are being robbed'." 157)

In order to distract their attention from the real author of their distressful state, Lenin was arousing the hatred and malice of the starving workers, not only against Mensheviks, Social-Revolutionists and Anarchists, but also against the peasants.

"While workers are overstraining themselves in the cities—and nowhere is there so much of agonizing starvation as in the cities of the non-agricultural provinces of Russia—while the peasants, as it is known to everyone of us, having seized the landowners' estates and grain, are working for themselves and the merchants, are now eating better than they ever did before—while the city population of the non-agricultural provinces is wracked with hunger, while the capitalists try to undermine us by an organized famine—at the same time there are people who, decked out in the Menshevik, Social-Revolutionist or some other clownish garb, dare come out with their allegation: 'you are being plundered!' They are capitalist agents and it is as such that they should and will be treated by us".158)

And thus the slogan was given out, the culprits were discovered and all over Russia the Communist papers—there were no others by this time—unloosed a vicious campaign of terror of public opinion. The Soviet political and economic organs began to terrorize the population by using the weapon of hunger, and the various and numerous Che-Kas unloosed a policy of terror along the lines of administrative and physical pressure. Lenin set his terroristic machine into motion, took the rudder into his own hands, accelerating its course and adding more and more fuel as it began its race. The year 1919 was replete with this triune terror. Lenin dedicated to it all his dialectical, sophistic abilities, all his Machiavellian talents, doing everything possible to undermine the workers' illusions about freedom.

"The word 'freedom' is a good word! Freedom at every step: freedom of trade, freedom to sell and to sell oneself, etc. And then there are the Mensheviks and Social-Revolutionary crooks who keep on harping upon this fine word 'freedom', but those people are impostors,

<hr/>

157) N. Lenin, "The Successes and Difficulties of the Soviet Power," March 13, 1919, p. 79, vol. XVI.

158) Ibid, pp. 79-80.

capitalist curs who drag the people back to the old times." 159) "We are not going to let ourselves be deceived by such high-sounding slogans like freedom, equality and the will of the majority, and those who call themselves democrats, the partisans of pure democracy, consistent democracy, directly or indirectly opposing it to the dictatorship of the proletariat—those people we class with Kolchak's accomplices".160) "We declare that we are fighting capitalism as such, the free, republican, democratic capitalism included, and we realize, of course, that in this fight the banner of freedom will be waved defiantly at us. But our answer is . . . 'every freedom is a fraud if it contradicts the interests of the emancipation of labor from the oppression of capital'." 161) The right to clear up those contradictions Lenin reserved only to himself.

Lenin's explanations were that, first, "the French revolution was called the Great Revolution because there was nothing wishy-washy, half-hearted, nothing of the phrases that characterized many of the 1848 revolutions"; secondly, "when only workers remain in the world and people have forgotten that there ever was a society consisting of non-workers—this will take some time yet and its delay is to be laid at the door of the bourgeois gentlemen and bourgeois intellectuals—then we shall be in favor of freedom of assembly for everyone, but now freedom of assembly is freedom of assembly for capitalists, counter-revolutionists. We are fighting them and in the course of this fight we declare that this freedom is abrogated".162) Thirdly, Lenin brought out that "all those who use the terms 'freedom', 'democracy', in order to come out against us, take the side of the propertied classes, deceive the people, for they do not realize that freedom and democracy were until now freedom and democracy for propertied classes and only crumbs for the non-propertied".163) Lenin draws dialectical conclusions to deprive the non-propertied of the crumbs while the propertied elements are being annihilated. Fourthly, Lenin brought out the point that "it is clear that while class differences between the workers and peasants remain, we cannot speak of equality without running the danger of adding grist to the wheels of the bourgeois

159) Ibid, pp. 80-81.
160) N. Lenin, p. 203, vol. XVI.
161) Ibid, p. 204.
162) Ibid, p. 206.
163) Ibid, p. 207.

mill",164) and that is why "we cannot admit the equality of workers and peasants, maintaining that those who uphold the equality are partisans of Kolchak".165) And since Lenin maintained that class differences between workers and peasants would remain during the entire transitional period, "there can be no equality between workers and peasants during the transition from capitalism to Socialism" and consequently, "those who do promise such equality should be considered as abettors of the Kolchak program, even if they are not altogether aware of it".166) It follows hence that "those educated people who do not want to understand this difference will be treated as white guardists, even if they name themselves democrats, Socialist-Internationalists, Kautskys, Chernovs, Martovs." 167) And it also stands to reason that "those who in a country which is engaged in a mortal combat with Kolchak, still continue to struggle for 'the equality of labor democracy', for the freedom of trade in grain— are in fact partisans of Kolchak".168) Incidentally, Lenin did not put himself in one category with the partisans of Kolchak when two years later he legalized free trade in grain . . . but at that moment he held out the threat before the workers: "If we abandon the dictatorship of the proletariat in favor of this freedom and 'equality' demanded by the democrats, Social-Revolutionists, Left Mensheviks and sometimes Anarchists"169) we shall have capitalism, as well as the rule of Kolchak and Denikin, restored in our country. And in order to forestall such a contingency Lenin demanded that a stop be put "to this chatter about 'the democracy of toilers', about 'freedom, equality, fraternity', about 'the rule of the people' and such other matters".170)

The entire Communist press and literature began to work frenziedly upon these retrograde items; the Communist agitators and propagandists carried those ideas to the masses even in a more reactionary form. There began the reactionary training of the Communist rank and file regimented by fear and barrack discipline. The original aim

---

164) Ibid, p. 209.

165) Ibid, p. 210.

166) Ibid, p. 212.

167) N. Lenin, "The Economics and Politics in the Epoch of the Dictatorship of the Proletariat," p. 353, vol. XVI.

168) N. Lenin, p. 211, vol. XVI.

169) Ibid.

170) N. Lenin, p. 255, vol. XVI.

of this "noble work" was to forestall the growing influence of the non-Communist parties and groups, to annihilate them morally and physically so as to prevent them from turning into account Lenin's changed attitude towards the middle peasants. Lenin in his speech of March 23 ("About Work in the Villages") threatened to put an end to his "kindness and patience", if an attempt is going to be made to profit by his retreat and to impress the peasants with the idea that the Communists are flirting with them: "They, the Communists, took stock of your rebellions, and they are already beginning to waver".

"We have shown toward them (that is, toward all non-Communist, Socialist and Anarchist groups and parties—G. M.) much of patience and kindness. We will let them exploit this kindness to a certain limit, but in the near future we shall have to put an end to this patience on our part, and if they do not make their choice we shall have to ask them in all seriousness to depart for the Kolchak territory".[171] This "kindness and patience" was manifested at the time when hundreds of Socialists and Anarchists had already been shot and thousands of others had been incarcerated in prisons and concentration camps. But even this "patience and kindness" lasted with Lenin only until his following speech—that is, for less than two weeks. In that speech, "The External and Internal Situation," delivered on April 4, 1919, before the Moscow Soviet, Lenin admitted that the Socialist press was being persecuted: "Mention should be made of the Social-Revolutionists and Mensheviks. Of late the Soviet power began to close their papers and make arrests among the members of their organizations". It would be nearer to the truth to say that Lenin was finishing off their papers. Lenin fully approved the closing up of the papers, deeming it quite "just", and tried to inculcate the same attitude into the delegates of the convention of "the workers in the field of adult education".

In his speech delivered at that convention, Lenin said that the Social-Revolutionary and the Menshevik papers were closed "quite justly and in the interests of the revolution".[172] At that very convention Lenin threatened to treat Socialists like Kolchak partisans. "Anyone pretending in the name of democrat or Socialist of any shade or variety, who spreads among the people the charges that the

---

171) N. Lenin, p. 42, vol. XVI.
172) N. Lenin, p. 193, vol. XVI.

Bolsheviks are prolonging the civil war, a painful war, while originally promising peace, is a bourgeois defender, and we will answer him just as we answered Kolchak".173) But that was quite true: the Bolsheviks did drag out the civil war, having declared a ruthless war —instead of arriving at an understanding—against the Socialists and Anarchists, and carrying this war into the ranks of workers and peasants, ruthlessly persecuting all those who differed with them in opinion. Moreover, because of their terroristic policy and drive for party autocracy, because of their obstinate refusal to cooperate with Socialists and Anarchists, they bear the responsibility for the civil war which flared out seven months after the Bolsheviks had established their power. Lenin himself said on several occasions that the Czecho-Slovakian rebellion "began over trifles".

And now Lenin discredits by all means the united front with Socialists, designedly heaping all into one lot: Rights, Lefts, the Maximalists, Anarchists, all were indiscriminately heaped together with Kolchak partisans in order to egg on the masses against them— that is, Lenin knowingly drove them under the knife of "the guillotine of public opinion", as well as under the bullets of the chekists. For Lenin knew only too well of the power his lawless gangs in the provinces had—in the party as well as in the various Che-Ka bodies, Tribunals and Executive Committees of the Soviets. "In the provinces," Lenin said by way of trying to whitewash the bloody excesses in the villages, "people who are calling themselves party members are very often adventurers who unscrupulously work violence in the villages . . . they confound the Kulak with the middle peasant".174) Moreover, in his answer to the letter of Professor M. Dukelsky, Lenin wrote: "The author demands that we purge our party and our government institutions from 'unscrupulous fellow travelers, from grafters, adventurers, hangers-on, bandits'. The demand is more than right. We raised it a long time ago and are now carrying it out. 'Newcomers' in our party are not getting much headway. The party convention decided upon a special membership re-registration. Bandits, grafters, adventurers caught by us within the party are being shot and will be shot in the future".175) And it is those

---

173) Ibid, p. 196.
174) N. Lenin, "The External and Internal Situation," p. 176, vol. XVI.
175) Ibid, p. 166.

unexposed bandits and adventurers within the party that Lenin imbues with the idea that Anarchists and Socialists have to be shot, alleging that they are the agents of Kolchak and Denikin.

At the Seventh Convention of the Soviets, Lenin, speaking in reference to the declaration introduced by Martov, stated the following: "When we hear such declarations coming from people allegedly in sympathy with us, we say: yes, terror by the Che-Ka is absolutely necessary".176) "We are told that we represent but a minority within the working class—that is what Wilson, Clemenceau, Lloyd George keep on saying. But when such speeches made by representatives of predatory imperialism are being repeated here by people speaking in the name of the Russian Social-Democratic Party (the Mensheviks), I say to myself: yes, we have to be on guard and bear well in mind that the Che-Ka is necessary!"177)

In his "A Letter to Workers and Peasants in Connection with the Victory Over Kolchak" Lenin impresses upon them that "the Mensheviks and Social-Revolutionists are the accomplices of the white guardists; some of them are such by design and through spite, others because of a lack of understanding and headstrong obstinacy in refusing to acknowledge old mistakes, but all of them are accomplices of the white guardists".178) "The Mensheviks, right and left Social-Revolutionists . . . continue to advocate strikes or the cessation of the civil war. Whatever they do—they tend to aid the white guardists".179) And thus there can be no united front with them: they are to be kept in prisons and not to be allied with; that is why "when a united Socialist front is offered to us, we say: 'this offer is made by the Mensheviks and Social-Revolutionists who were wavering during the revolution, tending toward the bourgeoisie'."180) "The Mensheviks and Social-Revolutionists offer a united front upon condition that we make concessions to the capitalists and their leaders, Kolchak, Denikin, that we, for instance, 'renounce terror'," 181) but

---

176) N. Lenin, Sobranie Sochineniy, p. 424, vol. XVIII.

177) Ibid, p. 428.

178) N. Lenin, Sobranie Sochineniy, p. 306, vol. XVI.

179) N. Lenin, p. 169, vol. XVI.

180) N. Lenin, "A Speech Delivered at the All-Russian Convention of Workers in the Field of Education and Socialist Culture," p. 297, vol. XVI.

181) N. Lenin, "A Letter to Workers and Peasants in Connection with the Victory Over Kolchak," p. 306, vol. XVI.

"we are convinced that those who in Russia advocate the giving up of terror are, wittingly or unwittingly, agents in the hands of those terrorist imperialists who are strangling Russia with their blockades, and the aid extended by them to Kolchak and Denikin".182) "Can it be that with all the experience they had with Kolchak, the peasants, a few isolated individuals excepted, do not yet realize that a united front with Mensheviks and Social-Revolutionists would be a union with Kolchak's aides?" 183) "That is why we say to everyone of them: if you came to help us, you are welcome here, but if you are going to incite and egg on the workers to strike against us, you will be of no help to us, you will have to get out to Georgia, to Kolchak, and if not, you will land in prison. We need state officials from the ranks of the Menshevik Party, since they are not grafters nor ex-members of the Black Hundreds (Black Hundreds—an organization in pre-revolutionary Russia, anticipating by its vile tenets and actions the modern fascists) who try to worm themselves into our ranks and do us damage. If those Mensheviks believe in the Constituent Assembly, we tell them: 'Gentlemen, as far as we are concerned, you may believe not only in the Constituent Assembly but in God Almighty, but stick to your work and keep out of politics'." 184)

Apart from this theoretic campaign intended to arouse the workers and peasants against the non-Communist parties and groups, Lenin handed down the following maxims of good citizenship:

1) "To shun the methods of the disorderly guerrillas, the self-will of individual detachments who refuse to obey the dictates of the central authorities, for all that leads inevitably to ruin. Siberia, Ural and Ukraine have given proof of it".

2) "Those that do not back up the Red Army wholeheartedly and unstintingly, those that do not back up with all their power the forces of order and discipline within the army, are betrayers and traitors, partisans of Kolchak and are to be ruthlessly destroyed".

The destroying was carried out quite in the spirit of this commandment. Lenin himself declared publicly that the discipline of "the Red Army, as a result of many months of propaganda to that ef-

---

182) N. Lenin, "A Speech Made at the All-Russian Convention of Workers and Peasants in the Field of Education and Socialist Culture," p. 298, vol. XVI.

183) N. Lenin, "A Letter to Workers and Peasants in Connection with the Victory Over Kolchak," p. 305, vol. XVI.

184) N. Lenin, "The External and Internal Situation," p. 175, vol. XVI.

fect, was on part with the discipline of the old army. Harsh, rigorous measures, going as far as applying the highest penalty—shooting—were used in the Red Army; even the old government shied from introducing those measures in the army on such an extensive scale. The philistines shout and howl: 'The Bolsheviks have introduced shootings'. Our answer should be: 'Yes, we did! and we did it purposefully'." 185)

3) "Those that do not turn in the grain surpluses to the state are helping Kolchak, are betraying the workers and peasants, are guilty of causing the death and agony of tens of thousands of workers and peasants in the Red Army".186)

4) "Many of the ex-landowners wormed themselves into Soviet agricultural enterprises, the capitalists into various central Trusts . . . they are on the lookout for every mistake made by the Soviet power, for every manifestation of weakness, hoping to be able to subvert the Soviet power to help the Czecho-Slovaks and Denikin. Those bandits have to be tracked down, exposed and ruthlessly punished". bandits have to be tracked down, exposed and ruthlessly punished."187)

Such were the doses of terroristic propaganda which Lenin administered to the country in 1919. Let us see now how and in what forms this terroristic propaganda was carried out in practice.

***
*

The beginning of 1919 was signalized by the strikes in big industrial centers like Petrograd, Tula, Briansk and other cities, having even reached the factories of Moscow. The workers demanded an improvement of the food situation, free trading in grain, the removal of the military cordons stopping the peasants from bringing their products to the cities, and also the reestablishment of civil liberties. This accounts for the character of terroristic propaganda carried on by Lenin during that year and his efforts to discredit political liberties as the stepping stone to the restoration of the rule of Kolchak and Denikin. The striking workers were handled in the most cruel

185) N. Lenin, Sobranie Sochineniy, "A Speech Delivered at the Second All-Russian Convention of the Representatives of Politico-Educational Departments of the Red Army," October 17, 1921, p. 379, vol. XVIII.

186) N. Lenin, Sobranie Sochineniy, "A Letter to Workers and Peasants in Connection with the Victory Over Kolchak," p. 302, vol. XVI.

187) Ibid, p. 304.

and ruthless manner. Here is a description of this treatment given before the Moscow Revolutionary Tribunal by a worker from the "Triangle" factory, a Left Social-Revolutionist by the name of Yeliseyev, who was kept in the same prison with all of us—at first in the prison of the All-Russian Che-Ka, and afterwards in the Taganka prison.

"The plight of the workers in Petrograd was terrible indeed: unemployment was rampant. Most of the mills and factories were not working, and the rest worked only part time; the 'Triangle' factory, for instance, which employed about 17,000 workers during the war, had only 3,000 in 1919; the Putilovsky plant formerly had 35,000, and in 1919, from 8 to 10 thousand. Because of a shortage in currency, workers were not getting paid for six and eight weeks at a stretch; no products were given out save bread, and even that was pared down to one-eighth of a pound per day for every working member of a family. (The rest of the family did not get even that.) The workers sold everything they had in order to hold body and soul together and toward the end were collapsing during their work from sheer starvation. It was this situation that impelled the workers to come out into the streets demanding bread and wages from the Communist government, which styled itself 'a workers' government'. The first one to strike was the Putilovsky plant; following a general meeting the workers came out into the street, where they were met by volleys of rifle shots directed by the chekists. There were many casualties — wounded and killed. The following day a meeting took place in connection with the shooting down of the Putilovsky workers and a delegation was elected to familiarize itself and the workers with what took place: among the elected members of the delegation were two Communists, Strebulayev and Nikiforov, both members of the party since 1905, but who at that time found themselves in disagreement with the tactics of the Russian Communist Party. Having visited the Putilovsky plant, where we found out about the desperate plight of the workers, we called a general meeting of the workers of the 'Triangle' factory at which we made a report of the situation. While I was making this report, a shot rang out, soon it was followed by an indiscriminate shooting. In the ensuing panic a few people were wounded by ricocheting bullets. Among the wounded was Comrade Nikiforov, one of the delegates. Since all the emergency exits were closed beforehand by the

Communists from the factory committee, the panic-stricken workers rushed toward the one exit left open. The stampede resulted in quite a few casualties. As it was found out later, this was the work of the Communist cell. March 16, troops were quartered in the factories —chekists camouflaged as Kronstadt sailors who were to personify the indignation felt by the latter in regard to the Petrograd workers. But the workers soon saw through those sailors, having recognized among them a member of the finks and gendarmes of the Tzar's government. March 17, I was arrested on the factory premises." 188)

The same thing took place in Astrakhan from the 10th to the 16th of March, 1919, under the leadership of K. Mekhonoshin, the member of the All-Russian Central Executive Committee of the Soviets, member of the Military Revolutionary Committee of the Republic and chairman of the Caucasian and Caspian Front, etc.

We are giving here a description of the bloody week in Astrakhan as witnessed by the Social-Revolutionist P. Silin who told about it in his small but ghastly article in the book "The Che-Ka".

Beginning with January 1919, the food situation held out the prospect of vertiable famine for the workers. . . . The workers were called upon to give the utmost in production. . . . Hungry, exhausted, exasperated, having to stand after work in long queues in order to get their ration of one-eighth of a pound of bread, the workers turned those long waits into mass meetings, seeking a way out of the unbearable situation. The authorities sent out special patrols to scatter those extemporized meetings. The most active workers were arrested. . . . Beginning with March 1, work stopped in all factories. Everywhere workers discussed demands to be presented to the government. It was resolved to demand the authorization, for the time being—until the difficulties of the food situation were regulated—of the free purchase of bread and free and unmolested catching of fish. The authorities during all that time were casting about for reliable troops, rallying them around the factories." . . .

The catastrophe broke loose on March 10.

Mekhonoshin relates the following in his official report:

"March 10, 1919, 10 a. m., the workers of the factories 'Vulkan', 'Etna', 'Kavkaz and Merkuriy', following the alarm signal of the fac-

188) "The Roads of the Revolution," see "The Trial of the Left Social-Revolutionists," June 27-29, 1922, pp. 304-305.

tory sirens, stopped work and began holding meetings. The demand of the authorities to disperse was met with refusal. It was then that we fulfilled our revolutionary duty by using arms. . . .

K. Mekhonoshin".

But here is an account of the events themselves given by the same Silin:

"Ten thousand workers peacefully assembled at that gigantic rally were discussing the distressing material situation. Soon the meeting was surrounded by machine gunners, sailors and grenade throwers. The refusal of the workers to disperse was met with a volley of rifle shots. That was followed by the rattling of the machine guns aimed directly at the compact human mass of workers and by the deafening explosions of the hand grenades.

"The mass of workers wavered, shrunk back and fell into an awe-stricken silence. The rattling of the machine gun smothered the groans of the wounded and the agonizing cries of the mortally stricken victims. . . .

"And then this human mass surged forward and with one irresistible sweep broke through the barrier of government troops, running, scattering into every direction, frantically seeking cover from the machine gun bullets. Many of the workers were cornered and shot down on the spot. The site of the recent peaceful meeting was now strewn with corpses. Among the bodies of workers writhing in death agony, could also be seen the bodies of the 'revolutionary subduers' crushed to death by the stampeding crowd.

"People were running in all directions, frenziedly shouting: 'They are shooting, they are shooting!'

"A vast crowd of workers, numbering many thousands, rallied near one of the churches. . . . The rumbling of a distant cannon shot. . . . The church dome crumbled with a crash. . . . Another shell burst somewhere in the neighborhood. That was followed by more and more. The throng was seized with frenzy. It scattered like a panic-stricken pack of animals. The outpost still continued bombarding. The aiming was constantly corrected and the bursting shells took their toll among the scattering crowds.

"The city became depopulated and strangely silent. The people went into hiding; some managed to escape.

"No less than two thousand victims were snatched from the ranks of the workers.

"Thus ended the first part of the Astrakhan tragedy.

"The second part, and the ghastlier, began on March 12. . . . The Chairman of the Revolutionary Military Council, L. Trotzky, was laconic in his cabled answer: 'Give no quarter.' And the fate of the unfortunate prisoners was sealed. The city was swept with a bloody frenzy.

"Shootings were going on in the cellars of the Che-Ka, and in many cases just simply in the back yards of the city's houses. Men were thrown overboard from steamers and barges. Some of those unfortunates were thrown into the river with stones tied on their necks or had their hands and feet tied. . . . In one night 180 people were thrown into the Volga from the steamer 'Gogol.' And in the city itself, in the chambers of the Che-Ka, the number of executed people was so great that the burying facilities utterly broke down. It was hardly possible to bury the corpses; most of them were just piled up in heaps and put down as 'typhus-stricken.'

"The commandant extraordinary, F. Chugunov, issued an order forbidding, under the threat of shooting, to drop off corpses on the way to the cemetery. Almost every morning the people of Astrakhan would find in the streets semi-nude, blood-stained bodies of shot workers. And early at dawn people could be seen wandering among those corpses in search of their dear ones.

"During March 13 and 14 only workers were being executed, but on the following day the authorities 'wised up' to the situation . . . they decided to take any 'bourgeoisie' they could lay their hands on and wreak vengeance on them. The plan followed in this case was rather simple: owners of houses, fisheries, small merchants and industrialists were seized wholesale and shot down indiscriminately.

"Toward March 15 there was hardly a family which was not bereft of a father, brother, husband. . . . The exact number of executed people could be ascertained only by a house to house inquiry. At first the number was set at 2,000, then 3,000. . . . Toward the first days of April people already set this figure at 4,000. And still the repressions did not show any signs of abating.

"On March 16 the entire population was ordered to appear at the burial of the 'revolutionists'. The order ended with the threat: 'Recalcitrants shall be punished with the revolutionary rigor'. The workers refused to come out into the street, whereupon the red cavalry was ordered to drag people out of the houses, from the yards, chase them off the streets and drive them toward the funeral. The brutalized cavalrymen raced all over town in search of recalcitrant workers. Anyone found hiding was given a severe flogging. And thus, after much delay and guarded by lances and whips, did the funeral procession start out toward the city".189)

Silin ends his story with an appeal: "Investigate the Astrakhan tragedy!" It stands to reason, of course, that there was no investigation: it is still left to history. · · ·

That was the treatment meted out to the "scoundrel" workers, as Lenin reviled the workers of the Sormovo and Putilovsky plants.

As to the peasants, the conquerors' policy was still being pursued notwithstanding Lenin's declarations about the need of uniting with the middle peasants. The bloodiest of all was the quelling of peasant rebellions in the Tambov government which took place in the month of November. The harrowing pictures of this quelling are given in "the memorandum" presented to the Council of People's Commissars by the party of Social-Revolutionists.190)

According to that memorandum, the punitive columns operating in the county of Spassk (of the Tambov government) subjected the peasants to floggings and other forms of bodily punishment; in a number of villages they shot many peasants; in the town of Spassk the shootings took place in open view of the townsmen whose presence was made compulsory. Ten peasants and a priest were shot in this manner. In the prison of Spassk 30 people were shot; all of them were forced to dig their own graves. In the county of Kirsanov tortures were practiced; those that were subjected to these gruesome tortures became insane. Even after the punitive column had left the villages, the chairman of one of the Committees fo Poor Peasants, Nashtchokin, kept on shooting down the peasants. In the county of Morshansk the number of executed people reached into hundreds and those that suffered otherwise—into thousands.

Some of the villages were nearly destroyed by artillery. Peasant property was not only looted, but burned down together with the

---

189) "Che-Ka. The Materials About Activity of Extraordinary Committees." Published by Central Committee of the Party of the Social-Revolutionists, Berlin, 1922. Silin's article: "The Astrakhan Shootings," pp. 248-255.

190) Cited by S. P. Melgunov in his book: "The Red Terror," 2nd edition, Berlin, 1924, published by "Vataga," pp. 153-155. Melgunov took it from "Livre Blanc," p. 131.

grain supplies. In the village of Perkino, which did not take part in the rebellion, the entire organization of the Soviet delegates was shot down. There were numerous cases of rape. One woman had all her hair torn out. The peasants brought to Tambov were maimed and crippled. In Morshansk eight wounded peasants were buried alive by Red Army soldiers. In the county of Tambov many villages were destroyed by artillery; the number of peasants shot was great.

Apart from the punitive columns the authorities were also sending out against the rebellious peasants detachments made up of village Communists who took to drinking, pillaging and burning. Throughout the entire government of Tambov were thousands of prisoners, most of whom were afterwards shot.

Something similar, if not even more gruesome, took place in the Turkestan province.

In the city of Saratov, according to S. L. N., the author of the article: "The Work of the Che-Ka of the City of Saratov",[191] 1,500 people were shot in the years 1918-1919. In Kronstadt, according to the official reports, 19 people were shot on charges of being involved in a rebellion; the unofficial reports place that figure as high as one hundred. The Moscow newspapers of September 23 published 66 names of people that were shot in conjunction with the Shtchepkin case. Among those people was the well-known poet Gumiliev. The sculptor S. A. Ukhtomsky was shot because "he was furnishing information to the 'National Center' on the museums and his reports were published in the white guardist press abroad." The number of people shot in conjunction with this case was more than 66. This is confirmed by the pamphlet written by the chekist Latzis who, upon listing eleven names of people that were shot, adds: "Apart from these eleven there were fifty-seven more shot in conjunction with this case." We have thus 68, and not 66.

September 23, some of the "underground" Anarchists and the Left Social-Revolutionists—the "activists"—brought to a high pitch of desperation by the Bolshevik policy of terror, threw a bomb at the Moscow Committee of the Communist Party. In conjunction with this case two men—Kasimir Kovalevich and Sobolev—were killed on the street. Ten others refused to surrender and burned themselves at a country house in the village Kraskovo. Two members of the Cen-

---

191) "Che-Ka," pp. 196-204.

tral Committee of Left Social-Revolutionists, Cherepanov and Tamara, were strangled in prison, and not shot, as was reported. Baranovsky, Grechanikov, Glasgon, Nikolayev, who were arrested in conjunction with this case, were tortured and shot. Notwithstanding the fact that the Anarchists of Moscow and the representatives of the Ukrainian Anarchist Confederation, who, being opposed on tactical grounds to the use of terror against the Bolsheviks, passed at their united meeting a resolution to that effect 192) about a dozen Anarchists were arrested on October 9 and kept as hostages. Among them were the author of these lines, Olga Freydlin, his wife, the brothers Gordin, Roshtchin, Rottenberg, Dukelsky, and a few outsiders who were caught in the ambush and also some Left Social-Revolutionists, whose names now escape my memory. Later on we found out that the Politbureau was seriously discussing the question of whether we should be shot immediately. It was the single vote of Kamenev that helped to defeat this proposal. The arrested Anarchists were released: some were freed immediately—after having been quizzed on this matter; and the others, on the following day.

The corruption brought on by Lenin's terroristic propaganda reached such proportions that the Communists by that time did not set any value upon human life. Thus, for instance, a certain Goldin, who was deputized by Moscow to the Che-Ka of the town of Kungursk, made the following statement, as attested by the Social-Democrat Frumkin: "We do not need any evidence, interrogation or even suspicions in order to shoot anyone. We shoot people when we find it expedient—and that is all".193) Thus the Anarchist hostages were not shot because it was not expedient—and that was the sole reason.

The "red terror" was especially vehement in Ukraine, just freed from the domination of Germans, and of the Hetman government. There full scope was given to experienced chekists, Peters and Latzis, who by their actions laid the ground for the triumphant sweep of Denikin. In the first place, of course, the Communists, following the Great Russian model, organized Committees of Poor Peasants in

---

192) This resolution was published in one of the issues of the "Izvestia"; see the issues of that paper for the end of September or the beginning of October.

193) A declaration made by Mrs. Frumkin at Ural District Committee of the Russian Communist Party. This declaration was published in the Menshevik paper "Always Forward," January 22, 1919.

order to carry out the "October Revolution" in the villages. The work of those committees was similar to that of the same bodies in Great Russia, and they led to the same results: peasant rebellions and their brutal repression accompanied by executions, lootings, outrages and destruction of villages by artillery bombardment.

The work of the Ukrainian Che-Ka assumed such forms that even Moscow was compelled to send a Committee of Inquiry headed by Manuilsky and Felix Kohn. In view of the sweep of the terroristic propaganda such a course on the part of the government was quite to be expected. Thus, for instance, the Revolutionary Tribunal of the city of Kiev called upon the workers, Red Army soldiers and others immediately to denounce ("telegraph or personally report") the enemies of the Soviet power.[194] A few days prior to that (July 19) the Defense Committee issued a blanket permission "to arrest all those who come out against the Soviet power, to take hostages from the wealthy and to shoot them in case of a counter-revolutionary rebellion; to impose a military blockade upon those villages which refuse to turn over their arms; after the arms had been turned over to make wholesale searches and to shoot those that keep their arms, to deport the leaders and instigators of the rebellion, and to confiscate their property in favor of the poor peasants".[195]

Piatakov (recently shot by Stalin) in his capacity of Chairman of the Extraordinary Revolutionary Tribunal of the Donetzky region published an edict, declaring that "any failure to denounce enemies will be regarded as a crime against the revolution and will be punished with all revolutionary rigor".[196] And Latzis himself, Dzerzhinsky's vice-agent in Ukraine, published in "Kievsky Izvestia" (June 15, 1919) "a warning" which reiterated Dzerzhinsky's ordinance of March the first in reference to hostages from the Menshevik and Left Social-Revolutionary camps:

"The All-Ukrainian Che-Ka therewith declares that any attempt made upon the lives of people active in the Soviet will be followed with the shooting of the imprisoned Left Social-Revolutionists (activists) here in Ukraine as well as in Great Russia. The heavy hand of the proletariat will fall upon the white guardists with the

---

194) "Izvestia," July 24, 1919, Kiev.
195) "Nachalo".
196) "Kharkovskaya Zvezda," June 7, 1919, Kharkov.

Denikin mandate as well as upon the 'activist' Left Social-Revolutionists who style themselves internationalists."

Peters, as reported by the "Izvestia" (of the city of Kiev), August 29, declared that food supplies were found yesterday during the search made in the city. "The owners of such stocks who have not complied with the order to declare those supplies with the respective authorities, will be subjected to the highest penalty: shooting." Terror broke loose in Ukraine; the district and county Che-Ka, the Military-Revolutionary Tribunals were shooting people in batches of tens and hundreds; in Kiev, 127 people were shot at once. According to "Izvestia" of August 29, heavy shootings were taking place throughout the country. As a rule, before abandoning any city the Che-Ka would shoot nearly all the political prisoners.

One of those massacres taking place on the eve of abandoning the city of Kharkov was vividly described in the book issued by the Left Social-Revolutionists, "Kremlin Behind the Bars." Two authors writing for this book dealt with this ghastly incident: V. Karelin in his article "Capital Punishment Be Damned!" and Leonid Vershinin in the article "Upon the Cold Hillock." 197)

At the same time the Bolsheviks, only a few days before the city had been surrendered to Denikin, shot the chief of the Staff of the Makhno Army, Ozerov, two members of the staff—Mikhalev-Pavlenkov and Burbiga—and also a few members of the Military-Revolutionary Council of this army; all those people were lured to their death in the most treacherous manner.198) This took place in accordance with the plan worked out by Lenin and Trotzky laying the ground for the annihilation of Makhno's Insurrectionary Army even at the price of losing Ukraine to Denikin. Both envisaged in this plan the rebellion of peasants against Denikin, which to them was just as inevitable as the rebellion of the Siberian peasants against Kolchak, and which would clear the road for the ultimate victory of the Red Army. The Makhno army was holding a front of a hundred miles long, keeping in check the Cossack army of General Shkuro which was pressing upon Ukraine from the Don region. Notwithstanding

197) Also read my own recollections narrated in the article: "One Day in the Che-Ka's Cellar," published in the second part of this book.

198) See in the second part in this book the article: "Revolutionists Have Been Executed in Kharkov."

this strategic position held by the Makhno army the Bolshevik government sabotaged this army in point of supplies just as the Aragon front was sabotaged by the Stalin-controlled Spanish government in the recent Spanish civil war. But when Grigoriev rose in rebellion against the Soviets (on May 10), Kamenev turned to Makhno for assistance; nor was such assistance slow in coming. By May 15 the Grigoriev rebellion was already dead, while Grigoriev himself was later killed by Makhno.

It was after the crushing of the Grigoriev rebellion that Trotzky opened a vicious campaign against Makhno, his army and the Anarchists. When the Executive Committee of the Military-Revolutionary Council of the Makhno army issued a call for a fourth extraordinary convention of delegates of peasants, workers and insurgents, to take place in Guliay-Polie on June 15, 1919, Trotzky issued an order in the name of the Military-Revolutionary Council of the Republic (order No. 1824, dated June 4), forbidding this convention, and making the very participation in it a state crime of the highest order, punishable by death.[199]

Trotzky demanded that the convention delegates be arrested and brought before the Revolutionary Tribunal; that is, he virtually demanded that they should be shot. Makhno, in virtue of this order, was proclaimed a rebel, while all those caught circulating the call issued by Makhno and the Executive Committee of Guliay-Polie were to be placed under arrest. At the same time Trotzky began circularizing malicious lies about Makhno "invariably retreating before the white guardists." Acting upon this order issued by Trotzky, the authorities seized and shot a few peasants: Kostin, Polunin, Dobroliubov, etc.

Following this order, Trotzky began agitating the Red Army against the Makhno army, calling for the latter's annihilation. A few days later the Bolsheviks removed several detachments from the Grishin sector of the war front, thus opening the front and enabling the Denikin troops to outflank the Makhno army. The Cossacks made full use of this opportunity. There followed a general retreat; thus a plausible motive was furnished to place Makhno under charges of

---

199) A similar order was issued by Dybenko, Telegram No. 283, then the commander of an army division operating in that sector. In that order, issued in regard to a Soviet convention of that region held on April 10, Dybenko declared this convention counter-revolutionary, threatening its organizers with shooting.

treason and have him shot. The Bolsheviks did try to carry out this plan, but Makhno slipped out from their trap. However, some of the Army Staff and its Executive Council were seized and, as already pointed out, were shot in Kharkov. Denikin began occupying Ukraine, meeting hardly with any resistance. And it is still very much of a mooted question whether Denikin would have been defeated by the Red Army, had he not been hamstrung by Makhno's army which rapidly organized in the rear of his troops.[200]

We are giving here a cursory view of the lightning-like sweep with which, following the government-induced breakdown of the Makhno-held front, Denikin began moving toward Moscow, clearing Ukraine, Don, and the lower Volga provinces from the Red Army.

On June 21, Denikin occupied Feodosia and Kalach; on the 23rd, Sinelnikavo; on June 30, Yekaterinoslav; on July 29, Kamishin; on July 31, Poltava; on August 18, Nikolayev and Kherson. At the same time Mamontov's cavalry broke through the front held by the Red Army, swooping down upon Tambov, Kozlov and then continuing its operations far into the rear of the Red Army. July 23 Denikin occupied Odessa, on the 31st, Kiev. September 23, the Red Army abandoned Kursk; October 6, Voroniezh; on the 12th, Chernigov; on the 13th, the city of Orel was already in Denikin's hands; on the 17th, Denikin seized Novosil and was closing in upon Tula.

Thus, in less than four months Denikin seized Northern Caucasia, the Don region, Crimea, Novorossia, Ukraine, part of the Volga region, the southern part of Great Russia, and was closing in upon Moscow itself. The Red Army was hardly showing any resistance. Such were the results of the policy of Lenin and Trotzky aimed at the annihilation of an independent insurgent movement.

At the same time, however, Makhno built up in the rear of Denikin's army a strong army of irregulars which at first retreated under pressure of the numerically and technically superior Denikin troops, 600 miles west—up to the city of Uman. Having defeated there (near Peregonovka) the Denikin troops which were encircling it, this army swept back to its original base; moving in four directions, it swept throughout Ukraine, working havoc in the rear of Denikin's

---

200) See P. Arshinov's book: "The History of the Makhno Movement" (1918-1921)); published by the "Group of the Russian Anarchists in Germany," Berlin, 1923. This book was translated into German and French.

army: destroying military supplies and the army's food stocks, blowing up railway bridges, disrupting railway transport, annihilating military units which it met on its way, rousing the population to active rebellion, etc. This was a tremendous, if not the most tremendous factor, in causing the break in favor of the Red Army.

With the regulars in a state of demoralization as a result of the destructive work of Makhno's irregulars, Denikin's army found it hard to resist the counter-drive of the Red Army. A few well-aimed blows—and his army rolled back avalanche-like with the same speed with which it kept on advancing upon Moscow.

**
*

The terror of 1919 had a larger territory for its field of operations and was, therefore, bound to result in a much greater number of victims. The only statistical data at our disposal are the bloody statistics of Latzis given in his pamphlet "Two Years of Struggle at the Domestic Front." Latzis himself qualifies his data with the statement that his figures are far from being adequate since they cover only twenty governments.

Those twenty governments had 99 rebellions during seven months of 1919 which resulted in the death of 1,236 rebels and 272 of the government forces, all of whom were killed in the process of putting down those rebellions. During the seven months were shot 2,089 people. This does not include the 1,206 people shot by the Petrograd Che-Ka; 234, by the Moscow Che-Ka; and 327, by the All-Russian Che-Ka. Nor does it include the number of people shot by the All-Ukrainian Che-Ka together with the Kiev Che-Ka. (In the government of Kiev the All-Ukrainian Che-Ka executed 825 people. Altogether we account for 4,671. And since 20 governments constitute less than half of the territory held at that time by the Soviet power, one could safely increase this official figure two and a half times; in other words, the number of people shot by the Che-Ka must have been no less than 11,677. But even the most conservative estimates show this figure to be far below the actual number killed. The authorities, for rather intelligible reasons, minimized the number of its victims, cutting it at least into half as a rule. So we can safely double the above quoted figure and state in accordance with rather conservative estimates that the Che-Ka organs of Soviet Russia shot no less than 23,000 to 25,000 people.

That was done by the Che-Ka only! And how many people were shot by the Revolutionary Tribunals, Military Revolutionary Tribunals, the Transport Che-Ka, the Punitive columns, etc.! The number of their victims far exceeded those of the All-Russian Che-Ka and their subordinate Che-Ka organs of the government and counties. Rivers of blood and mountains of corpses! And how many lives were ruined! How many were crippled!

During those very seven months 7,305 were sent to concentration camps, 12,346 to prisons, and 10,050 were taken as hostages. Altogether, 44,639 were put under arrest. This figure is in our opinion only one third of the actual number. And this huge prison population was dying from starvation, typhus and many other diseases.

Let us now pass to the year of 1920, the year when the so-called peaceful construction began, the year of the "bloodless" front.

CHAPTER VII

THE "BLOODLESS" FRONT
(1920)

In 1919 Kolchak and Denikin were defeated and the movements headed by them were virtually liquidated. The vast country was being cleared of white guardist bands. The war with Poland was proceeding rather successfully, the Soviet troops having swept up to Warsaw. Right up to August 21, the date when the retreat from Warsaw began, the Soviet skies were serene and bright. It was clear to everyone that the civil war was virtually at an end; the agony outbursts of counter-revolution, like the Wrangel adventure, were not seriously regarded. The persecuted Socialist parties and Anarchist groups, whose members were being arrested and confined to prison "until the civil war ends," were hoping for the chance to resume legal and normal activities. The average man, who was tired of the terroristic policy, looked forward to the approaching period when he could have a calm, safe and dignified life. And, indeed, the Bolsheviks, as if about to meet those expectations, had the Che-Ka take upon itself the initiative of abolishing the death penalty. (The Che-Ka was made instrumental in promoting this measure in order to raise its moral prestige in the eyes of the population and the workers of the world.) January 15, the All-Russian Che-Ka issued an order to all the branches to forego the use of the death penalty; it also appealed to the All-Russian Central Executive Committee of the Soviets to abolish the death penalty altogether throughout the country. This appeal was granted; the Executive Committee of the Soviet having passed such measure in the month of February. But, as we are going to prove, this was nothing but a masquerade, the usual deceit practiced upon a country wracked by hunger and terror.

Nevertheless, there seemed to have come a temporary break in Lenin's bloody, terroristic spell which until that time expressed itself in maniacal, frenzied calls for more and more shootings; there seemed to have come a change in the form of the terroristic madness of this moral monster, this representative of a degenerating gentry.

Lenin proclaimed a new front, a "bloodless" front, a front of toil and labor, having charted out the course of reconstruction, and the method to be followed by the ruined country toward its rehabilitation.

This program could be reduced to the following points: to consolidate the grain monopoly of the State and ruthlessly to combat all the demands of free trade in grain surpluses; to reconstruct the industries and to replace board (collegiate) management by one-man administration; to obliterate the gulf, which he himself had dug, between the city and the villages; to carry out universal labor service and to militarize labor; to organize labor armies and to transform the trade unions and cooperatives into state organs; to carry out the program of workers' control; to raise labor discipline and to root out the lingering influence of other parties in the country; to grant concessions to foreign capital; to consolidate the party rule, the leadership within the party, and to preserve party unity.

The realization of this program was conditioned, in Lenin's outline, upon the existence of an iron dictatorship of the party, which was incompatible with granting of liberties to the population.

"We—Lenin said at the session of the Moscow Soviet of March 8—must wipe off the face of the earth all traces . . . of the policy of the Mensheviks and Social-Revolutionists who speak about individual rights; their policy is dooming us to hunger and starvation." 201)

On March 21, Lenin spoke the following about the change from board-management to one-man management in his report of the Central Committee presented at the party convention:

"The trade unions are going to be faced with gigantic difficulties. It is necessary that they approach this task in the spirit of a struggle against the vestiges of the notorious democratic procedures. All those shoutings about appointees, all this old harmful rubbish asserting itself in various resolutions, in all kinds of talk, should be definitely swept out. Otherwise we shall not be able to obtain a victory. If we have not learned this lesson in two years, we have shown that we are not keeping pace with life and those that lag behind life are always beaten" 202)

201) P. 49, vol. XVII.
202) "The Report of the Central Committee of R. C. P.," p. 76, vol. XVII.

And again:

"We are being helped now by the Mensheviks and Social-Revolutionists who demand that one-man management be replaced with board management. You will have to excuse us, comrades, but this gag will not work with us! It is past history as far as we are concerned."

In the concluding statement, made on March 30, in which he answered the charges presented by the party opposition, Lenin spoke irately: "All your words are nothing but verbalism pure and simple: self-activity, the rule of appointees, etc.! But when does our centralism come in? Could we hold out for two months, let alone for two years, if we did not appoint people? . . . Because you don't like the fact that we recalled Shliapnikov or Yurenev, you bandy about these phrases and throw them to the ignorant masses of people".203)

And Lenin demanded that the party convention grant the Central Committee the right to place its appointees where it deemed necessary, trade unions included. The very idea that he and the Central Committee had no right to appoint people to the trade unions at their own discretion was to him a wild heresy, and he was genuinely indignant over the fact that the trade union circles viewed his appointees to the Central Executive Committee—Radek and Bukharin—as political Commissars, whose appointment undermined the self-activity of the trade unions by fastening upon them the rule of bureaucracy.

"What?—Lenin asked the opposition indignantly—hasn't the Central Committee of the Party the right to add to the trade union leadership people who are theoretically the best prepared to deal with the trade union movement, who are well acquainted with the German experience and are capable of exerting pressure in the way of correcting an erroneous line? A Central Committee that does not fulfill this task is not fit to govern".204)

It stands to reason that in the political field Lenin remained true to himself in every detail. He is against "a democracy of toilers" (the slogan of the Social-Revolutionists) and against freedom and equality within such a democracy because "freedom and equality within the confines of 'a toiler's democracy' is freedom for the small land owner (even if he carries on on the basis of nationalized land) to sell

203) Ibid, p. 83.
204) Ibid, p. 84.

the grain surpluses at speculative prices, that is, to exploit the workers. Anyone who speaks of freedom and equality within the confines of 'a toiler's democracy'—under condition that the capitalists be overthrown but private property and freedom of trade remain—is a defender of exploiters. And in carrying out his dictatorship, the proletariat must mete out the same treatment to those defenders as to exploiters, even though this defender style himself a Social-Democrat, Socialist or one that has come to see the rottenness of the Second International".205)

Thus even conditions of peaceful construction toward which the country was leading in 1920, Lenin's line of action remains unaltered; no one is to have freedom. Consequently, the working out of the plan of peaceful reconstruction and the carrying out of this plan are to be the concern of one party only, the party headed by Lenin. And this in turn implies that "all this sentimentalizing, the chatter about democracy should be cast overboard". This also meant that "we have to maintain a rigorous discipline and to carry out the program mapped out by the vanguard of the proletariat,"206) —that is, by the party. And insofar as resistance might be shown to this program—which is rather natural to expect—one has to be ready for such a contingency and always bear in mind that in order to obtain victory on "the bloodless front" it is necessary to go through, just as is the case in a regular war, a most strenuous battle; that it is necessary to obtain an iron-bound military discipline." 207) "At this front every worker must be a red commander of labor".208) "Immense difficulties are facing us in this work. I know that some will have to work standing in water, with no proper working clothes. But we must remember that at the bloody front our Red Army men are also without boots, that they carry on under conditions of campaign life, working knee-deep in water and mud, as was recently the case at the southern front where our soldiers obtained a series of victories. We should not say at the labor front:

---

205) "Disingenous Talks About Freedom," p. 380, vol. XVII.

206) "A Speech Delivered at the Conference on Work in the Villages," June 13, p. 226, vol. XVII.

207) "A Speech Delivered at the Third All-Russian Convention of Water Transport Workers," March 15, p. 57, vol. XVII.

208) "A Speech Delivered at the All-Russian Convention of Textile Workers," April 18, p. 108, vol. XVII.

'where do we come to it' or 'this is way above our power to do'." 209)

It means that the workers are to place class interests above craft interests. "Those workers who do not want to make such sacrifices are self-seekers who will be cast out of the proletarian family. This is the basic question of labor discipline." . . . 210) It means that we have to work intensively in order "to eradicate the habit of viewing labor in the nature of an obligatory service to be rendered only on the basis of a definite remuneration".211)

And since, according to Lenin, the basic feature of the Russian character is "to leave tasks undone and to relax when not tightened up by outside efforts," it is necessary to combat such a tendency toward laxity "in the most ruthless manner," and to see that at "any cost discipline and submission to orders are carried out with ruthless rigor".212)

Such was Lenin's policy in regard to workers. As to peasants, the old policy remained in force. Lenin carried on as before a persistent struggle against the free sale of grain surpluses, he kept on inciting the workers against the peasants and waging a struggle against the traders in grain with the help of the special railway cordones, prisons and shootings; as before, he was pursuing the policy of extorting grain and other products from the villages with the help of the Che-Ka, Revolutionary Tribunals, prisons, shootings and ruining the plucked and plundered peasants.

"We ought to apply heroic measures and efforts in order to keep the free trading in grain from spreading out. . . . Our attitude toward the possessors of grain surpluses must be definite: this attitude underlies the dictatorship of the working class. . . . We shall combat it with all the ruthlessness at our power." 213)

The methods pursued at the "bloodless front" remained the same:

209) Ibid, p. 109.

210) "A Speech Delivered at the Third Convention of the Trade Unions," April 7, p. 104, vol. XVII.

211) "From the First Subbotnik to an All-Russian Subbotnik," p. 206, vol. XVII.

Subbotnik—a gathering for collective social work on free evenings or days of rest.

212) "A Speech Delivered at the Convention on Work in the Villages," p. 224-225, vol. XVII.

213) "A Speech at the Session of the Moscow Soviet," March 8, p. 48, vol. XVII.

compulsion and terror, that is, blood and iron; an unrestricted one-man dictatorship of persons appointed from above and not responsible before the people; military discipline and obedience, in a word, brute physical force and the threat to apply this force to all and everything, to every domain of life. When, for instance, the question of cooperation comes up, Lenin recommends measures of police action and sleuthing: "We have in the cooperative organs a number of counter-revolutionists. . . . It was justly said here of the Che-Ka: if you cannot, because of your shortsightedness, expose the leaders of cooperations put one Communist in the cooperative organ, and, if he is a good Communist—and a good Communist is at the same time a good chekist, he will nab at least two counter-revolutionists who are working under the guise of cooperative workers. And we have plenty of decrees telling especially that counter-revolutionists are to be forwarded to the Che-Ka, and where there is no Che-Ka —into the Revcom".214)

Again when it comes to the question of rural teachers, Lenin recommends and demands that violence and terror be applied: "Every teacher—Lenin said at the conference on work in the villages—should have pamphlets of an agitational character; not only should he have such but also he should read them to the peasants; if he fails in this duty he should be deprived of his position." It should be demanded that "every teacher pursue his work in the spirit of the Soviet State, that he consider such work his direct duty, that he be made clearly aware that if this is not done by him he cannot retain his position." 215)

That is what Lenin taught in 1920, that was the course which he charted out for the party, for the Communist sympathizers among the workers and the officials of the State apparatus. How were all those rallying slogans carried out in practice?

**
*

We already pointed out that in all Lenin's articles and speeches referring to this year, the word "shooting" so frequently used in the

214) "A Speech on the Question of Cooperation," April 3, p. 94, vol. XVII.
"Revcom"—Military Revolutionary Committee, the highest authority in the region or city.
215) "A Speech Delivered at the Convention on Work in the Villages, p. 228, vol. XVII.

preceding years was nearly always absent. This seems to point to a change in the character of the terroristic policy, to a change from a wet to a dry guillotine. The fact that the All-Russian Che-Ka took the initiative—and that undoubtedly was done at the promptings of Lenin— of abolishing the death penalty, was to convince everyone that a change was really in the air. In reality, however, the year 1920 was the bloodiest one of all the years of his dictatorship. But even the nominal abolition of the death penalty proved to be short lived. The Bolsheviks got used to bloody lynching, and human life lost all value —that is, granted that it even did have such value.

They could not get along without shootings and so on May 24, the death penalty was reestablished by an official decree. In reality, however, the death penalty had been abolished prior to that only on paper. During all the period of its nominal abolition, shooting continued with unabated vigor.

On January 15, 1920, there appeared under the signature of Dzerzhinsky a prolit ordinance of the All-Russian Che-Ka, the concluding part of which stated the following:

"1) To forego, beginning from the date of the issuance of this ordinance, the application of the highest measure of penalty—shooting—by the sentence of the All-Russian Che-Ka and its local affiliations.

"2) To instruct comrade Dzerzhinsky to lay before the Council of People's Commissars and the All-Russian Executive Committee of the Soviets, the proposal of the total abolition of the death penalty not only by the verdict of the Che-Ka organs but also those of the city, county, regional tribunals and also the Supreme Tribunal of the All-Russian Che-Ka.

"The enactment is to be carried out via telegraph instructions." . . .

In February the death penalty was officially abolished, with the exception of at the war front zones where it was left in force, which, of course, as we shall see later, actually reduced to naught the ordinance of the Che-Ka as well as the decree abolishing the death penalty.

While signing with one hand the ordinance about foregoing "the use of the highest measure of penalty," Dzerzhinsky at the same time issued an order to clear the prisons of the Che-Ka of those who were supposed to be sentenced to die; and so the Che-Ka began to hurry, it began its wholesale shootings only a few days prior to the issuance of the ordinance. . . .

A number of Socialists, who had witnessed those scenes of mass shootings, told of this indecent haste. Thus, for instance, the old Social-Revolutionist (of the left wing), the renowned terrorist under the Tzar's regime, A. Izmaylovich, tells in her diary: "Seven Weeks in the All-Russian Che-Ka," about the shooting of a hundred and twenty people. She maintained that just one night before the issuing of the decree the Che-Ka shot 150 people in the city of Moscow. The prisoners sentenced to death—A. A. Izmaylovich tells in that diary —who somehow got wind of the decree, scattered in the prison court, imploring for mercy, referring to the decree. But all those that re- sisted as well as those that resigned themselves to their duty were slaughtered like cattle".216)

Nadezhdin in his article "A Year in the Butirky Prison"217) main- tains that on that very night the Che-Ka shot 160 people and the shoot- ings continued to January 13 and 14. He states that even those were shot down who had been given prison sentences by the Revolutionary Tribunals and who, like Khvalynsky, for instance, had already served half of their term. (Khvalynsky was convicted in connection with the Lockart case.)

"In the morning—Nadezhdin tells in this article—they brought in to the prison hospital a man from the Moscow Che-Ka; his jaw was shot through and his tongue was pierced with a bullet. Somehow, with the help of signs and gestures, he explained that he was among those who were shot down but that the 'job' was left undone in his case. He already considered himself safe since he had not been "finished off" but was brought into the surgical ward of the prison hospital. He was beaming with joy, his eyes were glowing and it was clear that he was overwhelmed with his 'luck': he seemingly could not altogether believe it. It was impossible to establish his iden- tity or the nature of his case. But in the evening he was taken out with his face bandaged and finished off."

Similar bloody purges were taking place in other cities. For inst- ance, S. P. Melgunov, member of the Socialist-Populist party, main- tains in his book "Red Terror in Russia," from which we borrowed some official (Bolshevik) data for our book, that "In Petrograd on the very eve of the abolition of the death penalty and even on the night following it, 400 people were shot; in Saratov, 52; this informa-

---

216) "Kremlin Behind the Bars," note on p. 112; Berlin, 1922.
217) "Che-Ka," p. 147.

tion having been supplied by a private letter".[218] All this is highly plausible, for the abolition of the death penalty was only a comedy and a mockery perpetrated upon the country, enacted only for reasons of political expediency, for reasons of domestic and foreign policies.

Already on February 5, one could read the following communication in the "Izvestia":

"The Che-Ka of the Kiev government received a telegram from the Chairman of the All-Russian Che-Ka exempting the front zone from the application of the decree abolishing the death penalty. The city and the government of Kiev are to be considered a part of this front zone."

The All-Russian Che-Ka made wide use of this circumvention and on April 15 its Special Department (in charge of military cases), acting, of course, with the knowledge of Lenin, Dzerzhinsky, the Central Committee of the Party and the All-Russian Executive Committee, dispatched the following decree—in the form of a circular letter. We quote from Melgunov's book:

"In view of the abolition of the death penalty we suggest that all those who have been given the highest penalty should be dispatched to the war front zone to which place the decree abolishing the death penalty does not extend."

And all that seemingly found the widest practice. I shall bring here the following illustration. Our comrade V. Volin, the ex-editor of the "Golos Trouda" (when it was published in Petrograd) worked in the Educational and Cultural Section of the Insurrectionary army of Nestor Makhno. On January 14, while stricken with typhus, he was arrested in the region of Krivoy Rog and was immediately forwarded to the Bolshevik Army Staff. The danger of being shot was very real in his case. Only our intervention in Moscow—A. Shapiro, Roshtchin, and I visited the Party secretary, Krestynsky, who knew Volin as a fellow student in the university, and demanded that Volin be transferred to Moscow—saved him from being shot, which seemed inescapable in his case.

But dispatching people to the war front zones was done in special cases; in most of the cases the Che-Ka had little cause to fall back upon the subterfuges, since as a rule it paid little heed to the ordinances of its supreme organs or the decrees of the All-Russian Execu-

218) P. 91.

tive Committee: It merrily kept on shooting people in its cellars. This is substantiated by the "Izvestia," which writes (we are quoting from Melgunov's book): ". . . it was somehow reported that beginning with January, and to May, 521 people were shot; the tribunals had to their credit 176 of those executions, and the Moscow Che-Ka —131."

The retreat of the Russian armies at the Polish front resulted in the reestablishing of capital punishment. It was officially restored on May 24 and blood began to flow freely. Of especially fierce character were the shootings at the war front. I myself read an order issued by Piatakov enjoining upon the respective authorities to detain the runaway soldiers and to shoot one out of ten. And on June 16 L. Tortzky issued the following order:

"1) Scoundrels who exhort soldiers to retreat, deserters who do not carry out military orders, will be shot.

"2) Any soldier who unwarrantedly abandons his military post will be shot.

"3) Anyone who throws away his rifle or sells even part of his equipment, will be shot."

And here is another, no less remarkable order: "The address of the All-Russian Extraordinary Committee (Che-Ka)" which was circularized in 1920, in the Chernomorsky government. The document was directed against the "greens," that is, insurgent soldiers and army men who were hiding in the woods, and who sallied forth from there in frequent attacks upon the Bolsheviks of the cities and villages. We are presenting here the document itself:

"We are herewith making it known to the population that resolute measures have already been taken in regard to the white-green movement. And in calling upon the working population of Kuban and Chernomorye to fight against those bandits, I suggest:

"1) To notify the nearest Soviet authorities as to the whereabouts of those white-green bands.

"2) To take a direct part in the struggle against those bands by disarming them, arresting their leaders and instigators.

"3) To inform the authorities of any suspicious character showing up in the peasant, Cossack and mountaineers' villages.

"4) To notify in time of the raids made by those bands and to furnish assistance to the Soviet authorities in liquidating the white-green movement.

"In case this demand is not carried out and assistance is given to the white-green bands, we shall mete out cruel punishment to those who are guilty of such complicity, namely:

"1) The peasant and Cossack villages which shelter the white and green bands will be razed to the ground, *all the grown-ups will be shot*, their entire *property will be confiscated*.

"2) Anyone caught in giving assistance to those bands will be shot immediately.

"3) Most of the 'green' bandits hiding in the mountains have relatives left in the villages. All those relatives have been listed and in case the bands begin to advance, all the *adult relatives* of those who fight against us will be shot, and those of immature age will be deported to Central Russia.

"4) In case of a mass uprising on the part of any town or village we shall be compelled to use *mass terror* in respect to those localities, the life of every Soviet activist will be paid for with the lives of *hundreds* of residents of those towns and villages.

"Our warning is not an empty threat. The Soviet power has sufficient means at its disposal to carry out those threats.

"We warn the population for the last time, and we declare that participants in the 'green' movement who have turned over their leaders to the authorities will be granted full pardon. The failure to comply with this appeal within seven days will result in heavy punishment for the guilty ones as well as for their relatives. The smiting hand of the Soviet power will ruthlessly sweep away its enemies.

"The plenipotentiary of the All-Russian Executive Committee for Northern Caucasia—Lander".219)

On April 28, Lenin made a statement at the convention of glass workers in answer to the suggestion of the British government, to show a humane attitude toward the remnants of the Denikin and Wrangel armies. He said then that "we don't need the blood of those Crimean white-guardists; the feeling of vindictiveness is alien to us". 220) Nevertheless this blood was shed in the most ghastly and vicious manner. The horrors of this blood shedding were given a succinct

---

219) See Voronovich, "The Green Book," a compendium of materials on the history of the peasant movement in the Chernomorsky government, Praga, 1921.

220) "A Fragment from Speech Delivered at the Convention of Glass Workers," April 28, p. 199, vol. XVII.

description in "Sotzialistitchesky Viestnik" of February 16, 1921, No. 2:

"Crimea, December.—Bela Kun in the Role of the Super Executioner

"When Crimea was being occupied the commander of the Southern front, M. Frunze, promised full amnesty to the officers who were surrendering to the Soviet troops. While he remained in Crimea this promise was being kept. But after he had left, the power passed to Bela Kun, a member of the Revolutionary Military Council of the Southern Front and Crimea. In Simferopol and other towns the officers were ordered to appear for registration. They all appeared, and were arrested, many of them were shot afterwards. *This is a well established fact and you can publish it.* Rumors were spread to the effect that thousands of them had been shot; this, perhaps, is an exaggeration. But the number of executed officers runs well into the hundreds. They were shot in 'batches', without the benefit of trial, without any hearings. There were errors. Thus, for instance, Captain Orloff who fought with the irregulars against Wrangel was also shot along wih the rest of the officers."

In the same year the Bolsheviks routed—by deceit and treachery—the insurrectionary army of Makhno, having shot and arrested thereby a great number of its prominent members. This happened in the following fashion. When the war started with Poland and Wrangel began to creep out from his Crimean bottleneck, the Central Soviet authorities instructed its representatives to enter into an agreement with Makhno for the purpose of a joint and coordinated struggle against Wrangel. A military and political pact was signed between the Soviet power and the staff of the Makhno insurrectionary army. We are citing this accord in full, in view of its special interest:

The terms of the preliminary military and political pact between the Soviet government of Ukraine and the Revolutionary Insurrectionary army of Ukraine (the Makhnovites).

SECTION ONE
Political Pact

1) Immediately to free and to stop persecution upon the territory of the Soviet republics all the Anarchists and Makhnovites, with the exception of those who took up arms against the Soviet government.

— 124 —

2) To grant the Anarchists and the Makhnovites the freedom to spread their ideas, through spoken and written propaganda and agitation, under conditions of complying with the military censorships and of refraining from advocating the violent overthrow of the Soviet government. In the matter of publishing their literature the Makhnovites and Anarchists, in their capaciy of revolutionary organizations which are recognized by the Soviet power, are to get the full use of the technical apparatus of the Soviet state, submitting at the same time to the rules of the publishing technic.

3) Free participation in the election of the Soviets, the right of the Makhnovites and Anarchists to join the Soviets and freely to take part in the work of prepairing to convoke the extraordinary fifth All-Ukrainian convention of Soviets, to take place in December, 1920.

For the Soviet government of the U. S. S. S.—*Ya. Yakovlev.*

The delegates of the Soviet and High Command of the Revolutionary Insurrectionary Army of Ukraine (The Makhnovites).

Kurilenko and Popov.

SECTION TWO
Military Pact

The Revolutionary Insurrectionary Army of Ukraine (The Makhnovites) constitute an integral part of the armed forces of the Republic; while submitting, in its capacity of an irregular army, to the High Command of the Red Army as far as strategic operations are concerned, it retains its already established internal regime and is not forced to adopt the organizational principles of the regular forces of the Red Army.

2) The Revolutionary Insurrectionary Army of Ukraine (the Makhnovites), in their march across the Soviet territory and war front zones will not accept into its ranks units of the Red Army and deserters from the latter.

Note.

a) Red Army units and individual Red Army men who had formerly joined the Revolutionary Insurrectionary (the Makhnovites) Army are to be sent back to the Red Army.

b) The Makhnovite insurgents who were left in the rear of the Wrangel forces, or the local population which is entering the ranks of the Makhno army, are to remain with the latter, even though they were formerly mobilized by the Red Army.

3) The Revolutionary Insurrectionary Army (the Makhnovites), in order to facilitate the task of crushing the common enemy—the white guardists—apprises of this accord the masses of people who follow its leadership / by issuing proclamations and broadcasting appeals to the people to cease waging warfare against the Soviet power; likewise the Soviet government obligates itself immediately to make public the contents of this treaty.

4) The families of the Revolutionary Insurrectionary Army (the Makhnovites) who reside upon the territory of the Soviet Republic are to enjoy the same grants and privileges as the families of the Red Army men, for the purposes of which they are to get official papers certifying their rights.

Signed: Commander of the Southern Front: *Frunze*.

Members of the Revolutionary Military Council of the Southern Front: *Bela Kun* and *Gousiev*.

The Deputies of the Council and High Command of the Revolutionary Insurrectionary Army of Ukraine (the Makhnovites): *Kurilenko* and *Popov*.

The fourth provision of this political pact, which the Bolsheviks tried to hamstring by putting off the date of its signing, was given the following formulation:

"Whereas one of the main features of the Makhno movement is the struggle for self-government on the part of the toilers, the Makhnovite Insurrectionary Army stresses the fourth provision of the political accord, namely: in the region where the Makhnovite army operates, the local population of workers and peasants organizes free organs of economic and political self-government whose links with the state organs of the Soviet Republic are to be based upon the principles of autonomy, federalism and free agreement."

The Bolsheviks held back with the publication of this pact. And only when faced with the threat that the Makhno Army would not go into battle unless the accord were signed by the Soviet authorities, did the later publish at first the military accord, and within a week, the political pact.

As to the additional afore-mentioned provision, the Bolsheviks held back with the signing thereof on the ground that its terms had to be first discussed in Moscow.

The Makhno Army started out in the direction of Perekop, moving to attack the Wrangel forces. Three weeks later they were already at the isthmus of Perekop, having started to cross the frozen Sivash Sound under the hurricane fire of the enemy. This heroic task was fully carried out by the Makhno troops: the enemy was put to flight and on November 13 and 14 Simferopol fell into the hands of the Makhno Army which thus found itself in the rear of the White armies who were defending the narrow and well fortified isthmus. The Wrangel troops fearing encirclement, were forced to abandon the isthmus and began their panicky retreat toward the Southern ports.

That was the end of Wrangel. And that gave the Bolsheviks a free hand to deal with Makhno. While the Makhno troops were busy occupying Simferopol driving the remnants of the Wrangel army toward the sea, the Soviet High Command was working out the plan of a simultaneous attack upon every contingent of the Makhno Army. This attack took place on November 26; it was also well-timed with the arrests of Ukrainian Anarchists and delegates to the Anarchist Convention of Kharkov

Later on Lenin, Trotzky and other eminent Bolshevik leaders fabricated the legend of Makhno having been routed because of looting practiced by his troops and because of his refusal to submit to the order of the High Command of the Red Army bidding him to leave for the Polish front. This was given the lie by the following document which was published for the first time in the Kharkov newspaper "Kommunist," dated November 30. In view of the fact that the Makhnovites did not know of this document, one is led to assume that it was made up for the purpose of justifying the action of the Bolsheviks. But not only does it not exonerate them, it denounces and exposes their perfidy, their studied treachery and beastly cruelty. The document reads:

"Order issued to comrade Makhno, Commander of the Insurrectionary Army. Copies sent to the Army Commander of the Southern Front. No. 001419 Field staff, city of Melitopol. Nov. 23, 1920.

"Whereas military operations against Wrangel have been brought to an end, the Revolutionary Military Council of the Southern front deems that the task of the guerilla army has been fully accomplished and it therefore proposes to the Revolutionary Military Council of the Insurrectionary Army to undertake the work of reorganizing its various units fully incorporating them into the Red Army.

"The existence of the Insurrectionary Army with its special

organization is not warranted any more by the military situation. Just the reverse: the further existence alongside of the Red Army of a special organization with specific tasks of its own leads to events that cannot be tolerated any longer. . . . (There follows the enumeration of cases of murder and disarming of Red Army men allegedly done by the Makhno troops). . . . Therefore the Revolutionary Military Council commands the Revolutionary Military Council of the Insurrectionary Army:

1) "To place all the contingents of the erstwhile Insurrectionary Army quartered in Crimea at the disposal of the Revolutionary Military Council of the Fourth Army, which is charged with the task of reorganizing those contingents and merging them with the regular units of its own.

2) "The combatants of the Guliay Polie region are to join the reservists in accordance with the instructions of the Army Commander of those contingents.

3) "The Revolutionary Military Council of the Insurrectionary Army is to take the necessary measures to enlighten the combatants as to the necessity of the measure that is to be carried out.

Signed: Commander of the Southern front—*M. Frunze.*
Member of the Revolutionary Military Council—*Smilga,*
Chief of the Army field staff—*Karatigin.*"

Some of the documents relating to the arrests of the Anarchists are cited in the second part of this book. As to the number of Makhnovites shot during the operation of November 26, no one knows precisely and perhaps, no one will ever know. One thing is known though: their number was great, while some of them, like Popov, were held in prison for more than a year, after which they were shot by the Moscow Che-Ka. Blood was shed galore. Human life became cheap and worthless. The moral corruption bred by those endless murders affected the mentality of the party and worked toward its disintegration. This corruption found its way to the schools. No, it did not just permeate the schools, but it was consciously introduced there in order to deprave the minds of the children. Thus, for instance, in 1920 was published a book containing problems on educational extension work of the libraries made up by Nevsky and Khersonskaya. We find there the following "problem."

"A girl of 12 years old, is afraid of blood; the father is a prominent Menshevik. To make up a list of books, the reading of which would overcome the girls instictive aversion to red terror. . . ."

"That is the limit," the reader will say. But no, this by far was not the worst. Children were taught to squeal upon their parents, to testify against them in court, openly to renounce them. Children were extolled for doing such things and were held up by the Soviet press as heroes to be emulated. . . .

I shall not dwell any longer upon this bloody frenzy of the year of 1920. It is a vast topic and one could cite many ghastly instances from the practice of putting down peasant revolts brought about by the grain policy of the Soviet government. However, we still have three years more of Lenin's bloody rule to review, and I shall pass therefore to sketching in brief the work of the dry guillotine which worked much more intensively than the wet guillotine.

**
*

The task of the dry guillotine remained the same: to disorganize and suppress the work of the political parties and the independent organization of workers and peasants, to obtain the physical annihilation of the members of such organizations by handing out long prison sentences, by exiling them to baneful places, to break their morale by making them into living corpses, dead as far as political activity goes; to crush the slightest manifestation of the activity in any domain of life. Usually the dry guillotine goes hand in hand with the wet guillotine, as the case was during the French Revolution and as is still the case in Russia. But the first years, this guillotine worked chaotically and with no system at all. Beginning with 1920, it began to work in accordance with a carefully conceived plan based upon the experience of the past years. This plan was given its first clear-cut expression in "the very secret" circular letter 221) of the All-Russian Che-Ka, No. 5, of June 1, 1920. The letter was signed:

"For the chairman— *Ksenofontov,*
Chief of the Secret Dept.—*Latzis,*
Secretary of the All-Russian Che-Ka—*Uralov.*"

The letter was in the nature of an instruction sent out to all the Che-Ka organizations, their Special Departments and the Che-Ka

---

212) The letter was published in "Sotzialistichesky Viestnik" ("Socialist Courier"), April 5, 1921, Berlin.

Regional Transport branches in regard to the ways of proceeding with the extirpating of the right-wing Social-Revolutionists, Left Social-Revolutionists, Mensheviks and Zionists.

The letter urges that serious attention be paid to the work of organizing a Intelligence apparatus for espionage and to constantly improve it "by drawing in new informers, for which purpose money should be used unsparingly. A good espionage apparatus, this is our next task.

"Let us strike at the internal front and let us smash to smithereens the counter-revolutionary fortress".

The letter goes into detailed instructions, telling how to "strike out" at the right-wing Social-Revolutionists; it recommends "resolute measures in order to isolate organizationally the top leadership of the Social-Revolutionists" and also "to pay especial attention to people coming from the capital to the provinces or to those sent to the capital from provincial towns; likewise, an eye should be kept upon administrative, economic, and cultural institutions which shelter in their official service members of the Social-Revolutionists".

As to the Left Social-Revolutionists, the authors of this letter recommended that "once for all the Cherepanov gangs, those 'Socialist bandits' be liquidated". It asks to bear in mind the necessity "of dispatching all the arrested Left Social-Revolutionists to Moscow as soon as the preliminary investigations and hearings in their case are brought to conclusion. *In Moscow it will be possible to make the best use of them and as was done already on many occasions we shall be able to recruit from their midst many valuable workers for the Che-Ka.*"

In dealing with the Mensheviks the circular recommends "to inveigle the local Menshevik organizations into having them participate in the coming October festivals and thus to undermine from within their party discipline and organizational unity." The local Secret Departments of the Che-Ka are urged "to draw special attention to the disintegrating work of the Mensheviks who work in the trade unions, in the cooperatives and especially among printers; painstakingly to gather incriminating evidence against them and *to indict them not as Mensheviks but as speculators and strike instigators, etc.*".

*

It is quite appropriate here to remind the reader of the smashing up of Anarchist organizations in Moscow. This was done, as has already been pointed out under the specious slogan of fighting bandits and not Anarchists. This experience of smashing up Anarchist organizations under the banner of an anti-criminal campaign, of purging the Anarchist ranks from criminals, has now been transferred, in a somewhat changed form, to the campaign against other political parties and groups; the authors of this letter recommend that "in regard to the anti-Soviet political parties *one should try to make use of the martial law and that one should try to incriminate them on charges of speculation, counter-revolutionary activity, delinquency in performance of official duties, undermining the rear-guard and the front, and making common cause with the Entente and its agents.*"

The letter then passes to the Zionists, in regard to whom it recommends the follwing methods of struggle:

1) An ideological struggle, which task is to be assigned to the Jewish Communists. . . .

2) The gradual breaking up of this organization which, however, should be effected within the confines and limits of the following procedure:

a) To have all members registered and kept under close surveilance.

b) To prevent any meetings and assemblies (*to turn down the organizations request for premises*); unauthorized rallies should be broken up *under various pretenses*, the participants should be detained for 24 hours. Every case of that kind should be reported immediately by telegraph to Moscow.

c) *To intercept* the Zionist *correspondence* and to retain or to forward to Moscow, those letters which are of some interest.

d) To refuse granting any railway permits to certified Zionist organizations and their affiliations: "Hertzlin," "Cadima," "Maccaby," etc. However, no obstacles should be put in the way of those Zionists who travel with mandates of Soviet institutions.

e) To dislodge them gradually from their premises, *justifying these evictions by the need of the army or Soviet institutions for quarters.*

"On the whole," this circular letter concludes, "this business of routing the Zionist organizations should be carried out in such a discreet fashion as not to give the impression of officially banning them: notwithstanding the lack of this official ban, the organizations should be constantly hampered in a way as to paralyze them completely."

Those methods were first applied to the Anarchist organizations following their crushing, at first in Moscow and then in the provinces. For instance, we were evicted from the house on the Povarskaya street under the pretext that some sort of Soviet institution had been very badly in need of a place. At the same time all sorts of difficulties were placed in the way of our getting another place; likewise, we were frequently raided, subjected to searches and kept under arrest for a day or more. I. for instance, was arrested more than six times during two years, while searches took place nearly once a month. The same methods were applied in regard to other political parties and groups, and not only toward the Zionists. Sometimes later a similar instruction was sent out by the Central Committee of the Communist Party, laying down the policy to be pursued in regard to the Anarchists.222)

It was in the spirit of this very same instruction that beginning with 1919 the Bolsheviks carried out the destruction of the Russian co-operative movement, brought about mainly by the fact that this movement was built up and brought to its high level of development by representatives of Socialist parties, who were now declared counter-revolutionary. By the decree of March 20, 1919, ("On consumers communes") the co-operatives were merged with the Food Commissariat, its cultural and educational work was altogether wiped out, without being replaced by any other similar work; and its industrial enterprises were turned over to the Councils of National Economy.

Prominent workers in the co-operative movement became the objects of a most intensified persecution drive: they were arrested, thrown into prisons, arraigned on trumped up charges such as keeping and spreading monarchist literature. Such charges were brought up in Saratov against the Regional Co-operative Center; the Management of the Central Union of Cooperatives (Tzentrosoyuz) was indicted for economic sabotage, counter-revolution and "sympathyzing with capitalism." All that was done quite in accordance with the Ksenofontov-Latzis instruction.

---

222) See second part of this book.

Toward summer, 1920, the co-operative movement was smashed to pieces, and the Che-Ka, following up Lenin's cue, kept on fishing out the remnants of the prominent workers in the Russian co-operative movement. The co-operatives furnished an abundant and ever renewed supply of inmates for the prisons and concentration camps.

The trade unions shared a similar fate: some unions, like the Union of Chemical Workers, were just broken up by a government fiat, others were merged along the lines of industrial organization, which enabled the authorities to freeze out the opposition elements in the process of such reorganization; another way was to force reelections of officials, while in other unions, lawfully elected executive boards controlled by opposition elements failed to be ratified. The opposition in the unions was dealt with in the same high-handed manner: arrests, prison confinements, concentration camps, with and without the benefit of trial. Notwithstanding their expressly stated opposition to Communists, the workers were forced to demonstrate under the banner of the Communist Party at the reception of "distinguished foreigners." How this compulsion was exerted is illustrated by the following document: [223]

"Urgent

"To all the workers and employees of the Municipal Drainage Works:

"The Committee of Municipal Drainage notifies hereby that tomorrow, Sunday, August 15 of this year, will take place the reception of the international guests, the delegates to the Second Congress of the Third Communist International, for which purpose all are to appear at the Office Management (Pletnevsky st. No. 2) at 11 A. M. From there they are to proceed with banners unfurled toward the Municipal Service House, and from there at 1 P. M. they are to march to the Hippodrome. The Committee warns most categorically that in case the workers and employees do not appear at the designated place, special attention will be paid, in accordance with the decision of the Communist cell, to the matter

---

223) Published in the "Sotzialistichesky Viestnik," No. 1, February 1, 1921. "The Management of Drainage Works."

of supplying this service personnel with products. Workers on duty should remain at their places.

Chairman of local committees, *S. Ovchinnikov.*

"Secretary (Signature not clear)

"Seal".

The editor of "Sotzialistichesky Viestnik" adds the following note to this document: "The original of this document is kept in the editor's office".

There is an abundance of such documents; some of them contain more drastic threats.

Workers were not only compelled to demonstrate and "manifest their enthusiasm" whenever it was necessary for the ruling party and its policies, but they were being rationed out in respect of their spiritual needs, doled out in doses permitted by the authorities. Thus, for instance, in the town of Gomel the State Department of People's Education sent out to all its branches throughout the region (government) the following order:

"R. F. S. S. R.
The Soviet of Workers
and Peasant Deputies;
Department of People's
Education;
Subsection of Politbureau
December 8, 1920

To . . . . Politprosviet. 224)

"On the basis of the instructions as to revising library catalogues and withdrawing unfit literature we urge you to undertake immediately such revision of catalogues in all the libraries within your county.

"a) All agitational books and pamphlets of a non-Communist content: pamphlets on the Constituent Assembly, universal suffrage, democratic republic, etc.

"b) Books of a 'spiritual' content, the lives of saints, miracles, meditations etc.

"*Note*: Religious dogmatic books like the Bible, the Gospel, the Koran, the Talmud are not to be exempted.

---

224) Politprosviet—educational and propagandistic organ. This document was published by "Sotzialistichesky Viestnik," No. 2, February 16, 1921.

"c) Pornographic literature.

"d) Agitational literature on questions which are now being approached by the Soviet power in a manner differing from that of the first period of the revolution.

"Withdrawn books of pernicious content should be forwarded to the regional Politprosviet organization. The work of revising the library catalogues should be brought to an end by January 1. The Chief of the Politprosoviet and the Chief Librarian are to be held responsible for the carrying out of the instructions contained in this letter.

"In case books of a pernicious character are found in the libraries, those responsible having them there will be charged with counter-revolutionary intent and will be arraigned on such charges before the Revolutionary Tribunal.

"Signed:

Chief of Politprosviet—*Nemanov*
Chief of Educational Dept. ⎞
Chief of Library Section ⎬ *Signatures are*
Secretary." ⎠ *illegible*

Acording to the statement made by Lenin in his article "On the Work of the People's Commissariat of Education" 225) there were 33,940 libraries in Central (Soviet) Russia, that is, leaving out Siberia and Northern Caucasia. One can easily imagine the devastation wrought by similar orders relative to withdraw books of a pernicious character. This circular letter was the forerunner of the famous order issued by Krupskaya (Lenin's wife) about exempting books of a non-materialistic nature.

*

We already saw that Lenin threatened to cast out from the ranks of the working class those who did not want to work under starvation conditions and who were reluctant to sacrifice their craft interests for the sake of the interests of the class as a whole. This resulted in a fierce struggle waged by the Communists against strikes. The punishment meted out for strikes was, and still is, of the most cruel kind. Demonstrations of striking workers were shot down, strikers

---

225) "On the Work of the People's Commissariat of Education," p. 77, vol. XVIII, part 1.

were indicted and given the highest measure of punishment—shooting —or were sent to the war fronts. Mass arrests were made by the Che-Ka and great numbers of workers were sent to forced labor in concentration camps. In the provinces ruled by Trotzky, where an intensive militarization of labor was carried out through the medium of the so-called "labor armies," shooting for "violating labor discipline" was frequently used as a measure of discipline. Thus, for instance, perished the Anarchist Gordeyev, a worker of the Izhevsk Arms factory.

There are many gruesome documents in existence showing the ghastly persecutions of workers during that year. I shall cite here one of the numerous verdicts of the Revolutionary Tribunals. This document is characteristic in many respects, and that is why I find it necessary to cite in full, notwithstanding its prolixity:

The Verdict of the Revolutionary Tribunal of the Government of Simbirsk

July 27, 1920, in the name of the Russian Federated Socialist Soviet Republic, the Revolutionary Tribunal of the government of Simbirsk held its session in the City of Simbirsk, with comrade Gelman as Chairman and comrade Demin and Zavorotnov as associate members of Court, with comrades Arsky and Uziukov as state prosecutors, comrades Ivanov, Shulman and Pliushchevsky as defense attorneys and Salogaeva as the first Secretary. The defendants in the case were: Filippov, Nicolay Filippovich, 43 years old; Kuzmin, Alexander Ivanovich, 44 years old; Mikhnenco, Nicolai Seliverstovich, 26 years old; Stepanov, Mikhayil Ivanovich, 32 years old; Fomin, Feodor Prokopievich; Kiselev, Sergey Andreyevich, 23 years old; Yakovleva, Marya Anisimovna, 24 years of age; Kaske, Wilhelm Martinovich, 41 years of age; Kabanov, Piotr Matvejevich, 29 years old; Vitin, Ernst Yanovich, 35 years of age; Lagoda, Nicolai Matvejevich; Zenkovsky, Nicolai Nicolayevich, 37 years.

All the defendants are brought up on the following charges:

While being employed by the Gun Shell factory of Simbirsk, a munition factory situated in a region in which a state of siege was declared, they indulged in open and malicious sabotage taking the form of counter-revolutionary agitation against the Soviet power with the help of which they succeeded in pulling an "Italian" strike; the result of this strike was to upset the regular and tranquil course of work, to cause a drop in the productivity of labor at the factory, to cause harm to the Red Army and in fact to aid, the armies of White Poland. Taking in view all the circumstances of the case brought out at the trial hearings, and guided by the revolutionary conscience and the interests of the Republic, the Revolutionary Tribunal *pronounces* the following sentences:

1) Citizen Filippov, Nicolai Filippovich, is to be declared guilty of malicious and repeated agitation against the Soviet power, which, during and prior to the strike, expressed itself in besmirching the Soviet power and also openly calling upon the workers to disobey the decree of the All-Russian Executive Committee about an All-Russian "subbotnik" on the first of May; likewise the court definitely establishes the fact that Filippov belonged to the right Social-Revolutionists, and it declares him guilty of inciting the masses of workers against the Soviet power, of playing upon the self-seeking instincts of the unenlightened masses, thus abetting the outbreak of the "Italian" strike, undermining labor discipline and causing great harm to the Red Army, the defender of the interests of the class of toilers.

2) Taking into consideration the fact that citizen Filippov acknowledged his guilt and evinced a desire to reform, and also his proletarian origin, the Court sentences citizen Filippov to be shot. The sentence is not to be carried out but to be considered only conditional in his case; instead he is to be sent immediately to work on the railroad in his special line, with the reservation that if during one year he proves himself an honest and devoted worker of the Soviet power which will be attested by official references presented to the Revolutionary Tribunal, the latter will release him from the conditional punishment.

3) To declare citizen Kiselev Sergey, a member of the Social-Democratic Party (Mensheviks) guilty of having taken part in carrying out the "Italian" strike at the factory, and abetting the breakdown of labor discipline among the employees of the factory working for the defense needs of the Red Army.

4) To declare citizen Kiselev guilty of deliberately misinterpreting to the masses the wage policy of the Soviet government, thus misleading the masses of workers.

5) In view of the fact that Kiselev, Sergey, consented to defend the Soviet power with weapons in his hands, expressing the view that it is a proletarian power, and also taking into view his proletarian origin, the Tribunal decides to send Kiselev via the County War Commissariat to the first lines of the Western front; likewise, the sentence of a conditional loss of freedom for ten years is to be imposed upon the defendant, with the reservation that if during one year of civil war he manifests his desire to defend the Soviet government by distinguishing himself in the discharge of military duties, he will be freed from the conditional punishment.

6) To declare citizen Fomin guilty of labor desertion, simulation of illness, of self-seeking and systematic truancy.

7) To declare citizen Zenkovsky guilty of having joined the Russian Communist Party with mercenary motives, the disclosure of which resulted in his expulsion from the Party ranks.

8) To declare as lacking any substantial evidence the charge of citizen Zenkovsky having taken part in the strike and having carried on an agitation against the Soviet power.

9) To declare citizen Mikhnenko guilty in having carried on agitation against the Soviet government, finding expression in slandering the Russian Communist Party and verbal unpremeditated threats directed at the latter.

10) Taking into consideration their proletarian origin and their repentance expressed in their closing statements in the court, the Tribunal, in order to have them redeem their guilt before the working class and the Soviet power, sentences them, to be sent via the County War Commissariat, to the first lines of the near front.

11) To declare citizen Kabanov, ex-Menshevik guilty of systematic loafing, of being a labor deserter, of speculation and profiteering and also of passing contemptuous references to work—which is the foundation of the proletarian state—and also of baiting the Russian Communist Party. In view of all that the Tribunal sentences him, his proletarian origin notwithstanding, to three years of forced labor in concentration camps, to be served fully with no amnesty applying in his case, his crime against labor being especially grievous and not deserving leniency.

12) To declare Stepanov and Lagoda deserters from the Communist Party and guilty of taking an active part in the strike at the factory which they viewed as a method to counteract the wage policy recommended by the central authorities and opposed by the tool making shop; likewise the Tribunal declares them guilty of aiming to disrupt the system of shifts established by the factory management.

13) Taking into consideration their proletarian origin but also the fact that until now they did not show any signs of repentance, the Tribunal sentences every one of them as pernicious deserters, unscrupulous in their methods of fighting the directives of the central authorities with camouflaging self-seeking, hoggish aims and with "idealistic" saintliness, to three years of forced labor in the concentration camp and the forfeiture of the right to appear at the territory of this gun shell factory.

14) To declare the ex-Social-Revolutionist Kuzmin guilty of having admitted to the general meeting of May 30 that he had no right to be there. However, taking into consideration his proletarian origin, and also his avowed repentance, the Tribunal sentences him conditionally to one year of forced labor; the defendant is to be immediately mobilized for work at the railway transport, the court deeming his further presence in munition factories highly undesirable.

15) In view of the sudden illness of the defendant Yakovleva, the Tribunal withholds its pronouncement until she gets the opportunity to make the final statement before the Court on her own behalf.

16) To declare that the charges of citizens Kuske and Vitin having taken part in the strike have not been substantiated.

17) To declare the foreman Kaske guilty of showing an indifferent attitude toward the strike, whereas in his official capacity he should have taken due measures to counteract it; to administer a public reproof to citizen Kaske.

18) To declare citizen Vitin guilty of negligence in performing his official duties, expressing itself in failure to report in time his absence from work; to administer a public rebuke to citizen Vitin.

19) Until the verdict is handed down in its ultimate form—that is, during the next forty-eight hours—the defendants, with the

exception of Kaske, Vitin and Yakovleva, are to be kept under guard.

Signed: Chairman of Revolutionary Tribune, *Gelman*
                     Associate members of the Court: *Demin* and
                     Zavortncv.
                     Secretary (signature)

This document tells a tragic tale of the struggles of the workers in almost every city of Russia, in the year 1920. Happenings of the kind described above took place with especial frequency in the region of the highest militarization of labor, at the Ural provinces, where Trotzky and Piatakov were trying to run things with the aid of *the labor armies.*

The year 1920 was characterized by the rapid growth of opposition to the Bolsheviks among the workers, and keeping step with this growth of opposition, there also grew the repressions and persecutions of workers unloosed by the various state and party organs, mainly the Committees to Fight Labor Deserters, and the Extraordinary Committees (the Che-Ka).

At the conventions of the provincial Soviets this opposition assumed quite impressive proportions, and that was so notwithstanding the ferocious persecutions. At the Moscow convention of the Chairmen and Secretaries of the Executive Committees of the Volostnikh Soviets,226) Sosnovsky was prevented from delivering his talk; he was even chased off the platform (Sosnovsky one of the most prominent Bolshevik leaders; editor of a popular Moscow newspaper published for the villages; later joined the opposition and was among the most consistent and irreconcilable adversaries of Stalin; and was among the first to be shot by Stalin). In Kostroma the opposition headed by the Anarchist Barmash, a graduate of an agricultural college who was fiercely persecuted by the Tzar's government, received 40% of the votes.

In Nizhni-Novgorod the non-partisans leagued with the disgruntled members of the Bolshevik Party constituted a majority at the convention. The same took place in Ukraine at the convention of poor peasants. In Volchansk the opposition obtained a majority, following which the Bolsheviks made the following threat: "everyone is to vote

---

226) Volost—the primary administrative unit of government and district.

and by this voting we shall know, who is for, and who is against the Soviet power".227) The threat had the desired effect and the second voting gave the Bolsheviks a clear majority. In Kiev, along with the Mensheviks, the Anarcho-Syndicalists kept on growing in influence. Their slogan was: "The factories to the workers." As a result of this growing influence the convention of non-partisan workers held in December, at which the Bolsheviks found themselves in a paltry minority, was dissolved. The ostensible reason for this act of dissolution was that the conference "went beyond proper field, concerning itself with problems of general policies."

A few days later mass arrests took place, the scope of which can be gauged by the fact that among the Mensheviks only the number of arrested people reached the figure of 67. Nor did the authorities stop before applying the highest penalty, shootings. Thus in the town of Vinnitza was shot a Social-Democrat, Vladimir Dudich, the ex-Mayor of the town; in Yekaterinoslav were shot the Social-Democrats Nicolai Meleshko and Fiodor Sidenko; in the town of Yalta, in the month of November, was shot an old Social-Democrat, L. P. Liubimov, the ex-secretary of G. V. Plekhanov, who was indicted by the Wrangel government for "sympathizing" with the Bolsheviks. The same was practiced in regard to other parties: right and left Social-Revolutionists, Maximalists and Anarchists. All of them were "fished out" from the trade unions, Soviets, co-operatives, from Departments of People's Education. They were thrown into prison and kept there for months and years, very often without any court hearings, without being presented with any indictment. A mere administrative order was often sufficient to send away those people to forced labor in the numerous concentration camps, where starvation and diseases were rampant, or to the horrible typhus-infected prisons.

To be sentenced to serve time in those prisons was like being sentenced to be shot or to be sent to the front trenches; the prisons were unspeakably filthy and were hardly heated, or sometimes not heated at all, in the winter. The food was way beneath the lowest physiological minimum, and the inmates lived at the expense of the accumulated fats of their own organism or on whatever their friends or relatives could spare from their wretched food rations.

*

227) See "Sotzialistichesky Viestnik," No. 1, Feb. 1, 1921.

What was the bloody balance of the year 1920? Are there any official data as to the number of the terror victims during that year? There is a statistical "Yearbook," second edition, 1918-1920, in which we find that the Revolutionary Tribunals shot 766 people, of which the Moscow Tribunal shot 189 and that of the city of Smolensk, 255, that is, only two Revolutionary Tribunals shot 444, leaving to all the others throughout the country only 322. That in itself raises legitimate doubts as to how far those figures can be accepted. No less doubtful are the data given by the "Yearbook" about the number of people shot by the Revolutionary War Tribunals, which, according to this "Yearbook," was 5,757 in the year 1920. The same data set the number of people shot by the "Railway Tribunals" as low as 349. As to the number of people shot by the Che-Ka, the answer of the "Yearbook" is that "no information has been obtained as to the activity of the Extraordinary Commissions (Che-Ka)." Thus, according to the "Yearbook", during the year of 1920 the number of people shot was 6,872 plus some unknown number. The size of this total will, perhaps, forever remain unknown. The statistics of the "Yearbook" do not inspire confidence since it contains such remarkable figures as the total membership in the trade unions, which the "Yearbook" sets down for the year 1920 as 6,856,940, while setting at the same time for the very same year the total of persons of "non-agricultural occupations" at 6,402,059. In other words, according to this "Yearbook" there were more members in the trade unions than the total number of workers in the country.

The number of people shot by the Revolutionary War Tribunals was much above that given by the "Yearbook". Much nearer to truth are the data collected by Melgunov on the basis of information gathered from Bolshevik papers. We present here some of the figures:

From May 22 to June 22 (1920) there were 600 people shot; from Juny to July, 898; July to August, 1,183; August to September, 1,206; that is, 3,887 during four months, averaging 972 per month. On the basis of such an average one can set the number of people shot by the War Tribunals during 1920 as 11,664. The "Izvestia" of November 12 reports that the "Vokhra" ("the troops of internal defense"), which are at the disposal of the Che-Ka, shot 283 people. The period during which those shootings took place was not given. And so, taking these official, uncorrected figures only, we have 7,155 as the number of people that were shot in 1920. This leaves out the victims of the Che-Ka and the people shot at the suppressions of numerous rebellions. The total for the year 1920 could be safely set down at 30,000. And how many people perished in prisons, concentration camps during that very year?

Let us now pass to the year of 1921, during which, to our opinion, a crushing blow was delivered to the revolution; a blow which, we hold, was the starting point of the rapid development of the counter-revolution in Russia, now climaxed by the Stalin regime.

This year was the beginning of the process of disintegration which set in within the Communist Party. By that time, as a result of the unrestrained and senseless terror carried out in the name of the dictatorship of the Party and of Lenin himself, the Communist Party degenerated to a great extent into a reactionary force and the mainstay of an undisguised absolutism.

What were the slogans launched by Lenin in that year and how were those slogans applied?

CHAPTER VIII

THE SECOND YEAR OF THE "BLOODLESS" FRONT AND "PEACEFUL" RECONSTRUCTION

(1921)

The second year of peaceful construction was on. Military fronts gave place to "bloodless fronts" bringing in their train new problems. Some of those problems already emerged in the year 1920, but it was the year 1921 that was to bring their complete solution. One of those problems was the role of the trade unions in the new situation brought about by the economic and political reconstruction. The discussion on that question unfolded in the preceding year, bringing to the surface the crisis within the party. It still echoed in the party circles, keeping them highly agitated and disturbed. For the question of trade unions was closely and inseparably bound up with the question of organizing and managing production, and with the question of labor discipline, or the labor question in the totality. The last and decisive word, as in all and everything, belonged to Lenin.

Lenin defended the "sound forms of militarization of labor," ("The Party Crisis",[228]) demanding the introduction of "disciplinary courts," characterizing industrial democracy as "trifles." "The industrial role of the unions, 'industrial democracy'—and let comrade Bukharin take no offense at that—those are sheer trifles when not accompanied by disciplinary courts".[229] He defended "the organization of disciplinary armies of labor"[230] which were introduced in the resolution on electrification adopted at the All-Russian Central Executive Committee, February 2-7, 1920, and he also upheld the principles of preferential treatment in remuneration of labor and encouragement of shock workers.

"The principle of shock work," said Lenin, "implies preferential

228) P. 30, vol. XXIII, part one.
229) "On Trade Unions, on Current Issues and the Mistake of Comrade Trotzky," p. 18, vol. XVIII, part one.
230) "On the Single Economic Plan," p. 82, vol. XVIII, part one.

treatment, and preferential treatment without preferences in matters of consumption amounts to nothing. If I am to be preferred by getting only one eight of a pound of rye bread, I shall say: thanks a lot for such a preference. To show preference to shock workers means to prefer them in matters of consumption".231) And further "In order to carry that into life it is necessary to have unity and not disunity in the party and that is why we have to declare war on this disunity, why we have to include the following provision in the party platform:

". . . . . . It is necessary to combat the ideological disunity and the *unhealthy* elements within the opposition who go so far as to give up the idea of a militarized economy, as to renounce not only the methods of appointing people which have been practiced until now but 'the principle of appointment as such,' that is, they renounce the leading *role of the party* in regard to the mass of non-partisan workers. It is necessary to combat the syndicalist deviation which will ruin the party if the latter does not cure itself completely in this regard".232)

The methods pursued in this struggle, he says, should be persuasion and compulsion: "first we have to convince and then use compulsion". It is necessary to condemn as a syndicalist deviation in the most resolute manner the "All-Russian Convention of Producers" of the Platform of the Workers Opposition.

And since there was little time for persuasion, compulsion remains as of old the only method to be pursued in the country and within the party. Compulsion begets irritation and resistance; and resistance begets the necessity of suppression, which in turn calls for shootings and prisons. In a word, terror to Lenin remains as of old the only and all-redeeming means of action.

Lenin in this respect remains true to himself. In 1921 he repeated everything he said and wrote in 1918, in the article "The Tasks of the Soviet Power" on management, on state capitalism, and its implantation in the country, on the methods to be pursued in introducing state capitalism.

"We convinced Russia, we wrested Russia from the exploiters,

231) "On the Trade Unions." . . . p. 16, ibid.
232) "The Party Crisis," p. 37, ibid.

conquering it for the toilers, we suppressed the exploiters, and now we have to learn to govern and administer Russia".233)

In his pamphlet "On the Food Tax", Lenin reiterates his recommendation "to learn about state capitalism from the Germans, to assimilate their methods, not to spare any dictatorial methods in order to accelerate the westernization of barbarious Russia, not to recoil from using barbarous means of struggle against barbarism. If there are still people among Anarchists who are prone to say that it is not fitting for us, revolutionists, to 'learn' from German imperialism, we have to tell them: the revolution would go to pieces— and rightly so— if it took seriously people of your kind."

In his "A Speech Delivered at the Second All-Russian Convention of the Politprosviet Organizations", October 17, 1921, Lenin deciphered, made clear the meaning of the phrases: "not to spare any dictatorial methods" and "not to recoil from the use of barbarous means". He taught the Politprosviet workers: "Keep up your meetings and discussions, but when it comes to governing, don't show any wavering; govern with greater firmness than the capitalists did. Otherwise, you will not win. You must remember: your administration must be more stringent and firm than the old administration."234) And he cited instances from the life of the Red Army to illustrate the need for this firmness and stringency.

"In the Red Army, following the many months when mass meetings reigned supreme, the new discipline which came to prevail did not yield in any respect to the old discipline. This discipline included harsh, stringent measures, gonig as far as shootings, measures which even the old government did not visualize. The philistines kept on writing and shouting: 'there you have it: the Bolsheviks have introduced shootings.' We must say to that: yes, we did, and we did it knowingly".235)

Lenin demanded that the same measures should be carried over to the factories and applied to workers: "The one that goes back on disciplined order, opens wide the gate to the enemies . . . . . you worked for the capitalist, you worked for the exploiter and, it stood to reason, you worked badly, but now you work for yourself, you work for the workers' and peasants' government. . . . And

---

233) "On the Single Plan," p. 88, ibid.
234) P. 379, vol. XVIII, part one.
235) Ibid, p. 379.

we say just as we said in the army: those will perish who want to ruin us—and we shall use the harshest measures of discipline in order to obtain that—we shall save the country and our Republic shall live".236)

We have already seen that in the past Lenin came out with the demand to apply terroristic measures toward workers who demand improvement of their lot, calling them "scoundrels" and "self-seekers," and he said it although he knew only too well the frightful situation in which the workers found themselves at that time. And those terroristic measures in respect to workers were given the widest applications: we proved it with facts and documents. In 1921 this policy was still carried out by Lenin. In his article "On the work of the People's Commissariat of Education" Lenin states that "the workers are starving, they have no clothes, nor shoes,"237) and, nevertheless, when he had already initiated the policy of concessions to the peasants by granting them the right to trade in the agricultural surpluses left after they had paid to the state the tax in kind, Lenin still regarded as a provocation, typical of the Social-Revolutionists, the workers talk about "wanting the same" . . . . . .

"Some workers say: now the peasants are getting certain allowances, but we don't get anything. That kind of talk one hears now and then, although, perhaps, not too often, and one has to say that it is a dangerous kind of talk, because it echoes what the Social Revolutionists say on that question; we have here an overt political provocation and rudiments of craft, trade, and not class preconceptions on the part of the workers which lead them to view themselves as rightful members of the capitalist society, without realizing that this attitude is grounded in capitalist relationships. It is this attitude that underlies the talk that forsooth, the peasant was given allowances, that he was freed from the assessment in kind, and we, workers who ply the machines, we want the same . . . . To 'want the same' is to violate labor discipline, it is 'hoggish self-seeking,' and 'scoundrels' that manifest such desires fall within the category of those toward whom the harshest measures should be applied: from prisons and concentration camps up to the highest measure of punishment—shooting. Class consciousness and devotion to socialism must be so highly devel-

236) Ibid.
237) P. 80, vol. XVIII, part one.

oped as to be willing to die without a protest, without rebelling against the errors and their authors who in the name of 'socialism' doom the workers to a semi-starved existence, to consuming illness bred by undernourishment, and death from starvation.

"The revolutionary and iron discipline", (Lenin loved this word "iron") must be maintained irrespective of the existing conditions. And this discipline was exemplified by a peasant woman of one of the famine-stricken villages about whom the Bolshevik writer Ingulov tells in his article "On the Topics of the Day"[238] that she introduced at the session to the Soviet Executive Committee of the volost as a matter to be discussed on the "business of the day" the question "whether she should be permitted to eat the body of her deceased husband." . .. .

This is what you call "revolutionary discipline!" ironically wrote the "Sotzialistichesky Viestnik" from where we borrow this fact. "Yes, this is indeed, a revolutionary sense of justice! And how can one, indeed, talk of such things as 'rations.' 'wages' or complain that 'one's belly is giving one trouble.' And to think that there are workers who think of those things, and even talk about it in these great days!"[239]

*

The policy of plundering the peasants brought about the ghastly famine of 1921-1922. The centralization of the food provisioning, the grain monopoly, the "zagraditelny" detachments, [240] the struggle against workers carrying their own grain from the villages stifled in the most ruthless manner the spontaneous self-help and self-activity of the population in the matter of supplying itself with food. By putting into effect those measures, the state virtually told the population: leave it to me and I will get everything into shape and will feed everyone. When the specter of famine loomed upon the horizon in a startlingly realistic manner, Lenin did not show any intentions of calling a halt to the policy of curbing the population, he threw into the claws of famine millions of people, declaring with

---

238) "Krasnaya Nov," No. 3, 1922.

239) "Sotzialistichesky Viestnik," No. 16, Aug. 16, 1922, article "A Little Prose," p. 4.

240) Cordons to stop free provisioning in agricultural products.

unsurpassed cynicism and cruelty that "it is necessary that the republic maintain with the grain surpluses collected by it only that which is necessary for production."241) And again: "it is necessary to supply with food out of the state funds only those employees who are actually needed under conditions of maximum productivity of labor, and to distribute the food provisions by making the whole matter an *instrumentality of politics,* used with the view of cutting down on the number of those who are not absolutely necessary and to spur on those who are really needed."242) And thirty millions "of those who were not absolutely necessary" were thrown off the state rolls, were denied the assistance of the state in the matter of food provisions. "If in the year of 1920 we had 38 millions kept up by the state we have by now succeeded in cutting down this figure to 8 millions.".243)

The city population, abandoned to the rage of famine, was in addition threatened with ruthless repressions. Lenin realized that the peasantry brought to the state of unprecedented ruin and famine would not be able to pay the food tax necessary in order to feed the selected eight millions; and still he refused to seek other ways which would obviate the necessity of using violence and terror:

"We know," he said at the Party convention of March 8, 1921, "that without compulsion things will not be done, without compulsion to which the ruined peasantry will react quite strongly".244) "Without an apparatus of compulsion we shall not take what we need. Never! Anyone can see that," said Lenin at the Party conference of May 27, 1921, preparing the Party for a "crusading campaign" against the villages at the time of the greatest famine in Russia.245)

The goal remained the same: to retain power. To retain it at any price; to retain it in spite of the immense number of the craziest and most crying errors admitted by Lenin himself, in spite of the revealed inability to show creative solutions; to retain power in order

---

241) "A Speech Delivered at the All-Russian Food Provisions Conference," June 20, 1921, p. 292, vol. XVIII, part one.

242) Ibid.

243) "A Report at the Ninth All-Russian Convention of Soviets," Dec. 23, 1921, p. 440, vol. XVIII, part one.

244) P. 20, vol. XVIII, part one.

245) P. 273, the same vol.

to learn to govern and build. To learn at some one else's expense, at the expense of workers and peasants, of the entire population of the country. . . . And in order to realize its goal, every means at the disposal of the terroristic police state was made use of: terror against workers who do not want to starve meekly; terror against peasants who refuse to yield their grain for no price at all; dooming thirty millions of the city population to the terrors of famine in order to save "those that are absolutely necessary," the eight millions of select ones; dooming to death from starvation the peasants of the famine-stricken provinces who were kept by the military cordons from entering the other provinces, and thus forcing them to devour each other, to die in frightful agony, with swollen stomachs: more than five million people perished. . . .

Bare violence, suppression, compulsion, terror with shootings — those are the methods of Lenin's system of governing and solving the most intricate and simple problems. Whatever task he took up, or approached, those were invariably the means used to achieve such tasks. Bureaucracy, the natural result of any centralization and dictatorship, is ascribed by Lenin not to the system but to a wicked will; and he had the same explanation for the abuse of power by state officials with their attitude of overweening contempt for the people and their scandalous outrages. Here again he was clamoring for terror as the cure-all: "We need a terroristic purge: trials held on the spot and shooting as an unreserved measure".246)

Lenin's mind, like the mind of any partisan of dictatorship, of any dictatorship, works only along a single track—the police track. Thus, for instance, in declaring war on bureaucratism, he pointed not at the root causes of it—centralization, dictatorship, lack of social self-activity and wide control—but to the consequences, the results of the system; being himself a hundred percent bureaucrat (every partisan of centralization is bound to be one), he demanded the application of bureaucratic police measures and sleuthing with the aid of stool pigeons in order to combat the natural and logical by-products of the Marxist system carried into life in Russia. In his closing statement made in a speech on the food tax (May 27, 1921), Lenin asked the Party conference:

"And did you arraign anyone on account of this red tape? Where

---

246) "On the Food Tax," p. 226, the same vol.

do we have verdicts of People's Courts passed on cases where a worker or peasant, who is compelled to apply to some state institution for the fourth or fifth time is finally disposed of by a formally correct but essentially a mockingly-evasive reply. You are Communists, why don't you organize such traps for the bureaucrats? Why don't you drag them to the People's Court, why don't you put them in prison for red tape? How many people did you put in prison on that account?" 247)

Lenin's utopian faith in the all-powerful effect of terror is on par with the naive faith of a savage; it is both terrible and ridiculous. With the help of terror he hoped to make even capitalists work for the benefit of Communism.

As is known, the year of 1921 was the year of the "NEP"—the year of the "new economic policy". It was then that Lenin made a number of startling discoveries. The first discovery was that "toward the spring of 1921 it became clear that we had suffered a defeat in the attempt to use the method of 'direct assault', that is, in the attempt to use a short-cut in passing to a basically Socialist system of production and distribution. The political situation in the spring of 1921 showed us clearly that in regard to a number of economic problems it is necessary to retreat to the positions of state capitalism, that it is necessary to change from 'storming by assault' to 'long siege' tactics".248)

The second discovery—at first only a near-discovery—was that "our proletariat became declassed", and then followed the discovery itself, amounting to the admission that "altogether we have neither a big industry nor a proletariat. Comrades say, we are the representatives of the Communist Party, of the trade unions, of the proletariat. We beg your pardon on that score. What is a proletariat? It is a class which is occupied in the big industry. But where is this big industry? What sort of a proletariat is it? Where is your big industry?"249)

---

247) Ibid, p. 278.

248) "A Speech Delivered at the Moscow Party Conference," Oct. 20, 1921, pp. 395-396, vol. XVIII, part one.

249) "A Report at the Third All-Russian Convention of Soviets," Dec. 23, 1921, p. 449, vol. XVIII, part one.

"The industrial proletariat . . . has been dislocated, he has ceased to exist as a proletariat . . . the proletariat vanished. He is still formally listed as such, but he has no corresponding economic roots". 250)

This was the greatest discovery, the logical implication of which is that the country had neither industry nor a proletariat. This can be created only with the aid of capitalism, and consequently, it is necessary to retreat back to capitalism, to become apprenticed to it, and at the same time—to retain the power of the proletariat, the dictatorship of the proletariat. . . . With the proletariat being conspicuous by its absence! . . .

Lenin paints an idyllic picture, showing how capitalism under his dictatorship will create an industry and a proletariat:

"The Socialist state gives the capitalist the means of production now constituting its property: factories, raw material, mines; the capitalist works as a contractor, as a lessee, using the Socialist means of production, receiving profits on his capital, giving back to the Socialist state part of the product".251)

"If capitalism wins, the industrial production will keep on growing—and along with it we shall have the growth of the proletariat. . . . If capitalism is restored, that means that the proletariat as a class will also be restored. . . ."252)

Quite simple, indeed! "The capitalists will be growing alongside of you, you will also have alongside of you foreign capitalists, concessionaires, lessees, they will be making profits on you, they will be making big money on you. Let them! But you in the meantime will learn to manage the economy, and only then will you be able to build up a Communist republic." 253)

"This is one task, and the other task consists in affording the peasant the maximum of freedom in disposing his products and also

250) "A Speech at the Second All-Russian Convention of the Politprosviet Organizations," Oct. 17, 1921, p. 375, the same vol.

251) "On the Food Tax," a report delivered at the Rally of Party Secretaries and Responsible Representatives of the Cells of the Russian Communist Party of the City of Moscow," Apr. 9, 1921, p. 198, vol. XVIII, part one.

252) "A Speech at the Second Convention of the Politprosviet Organizations," Oct. 17, 1921, pp. 374-375, vol. XVIII, part one.

253) Ibid, p. 380.

in raising the small industry in order to grant some freedom to capitalism which grows on the basis of small property and petty trade; we don't have to fear this capitalism, it holds no terror for us".254) Likewise, "concessions hold no terrors for us, if we give a few factories to concessionaires, while retaining most of them; there is nothing terrible about that . . . because this capitalism will be under the control, under the surveilance of the state".255)

This is, indeed, a solution that can emanate from the mind of a genius! How can this idyl be made to work in practice? How to make capitalism willing to work in behalf of Communism? Lenin showed how this can be done: give the capitalists the opportunity to make a hundred percent profit. That is, to foreign capitalists only; as to domestic capitalists—terror remains in force. Terror against one group of capitalists, compromise with the other.

"We can and should obtain now a *COMBINATION* of methods of ruthless suppression of uncultured capitalists, who do not want any 'state capitalism', who do not think about meeting it halfway, who keep on thwarting the Soviet measures of speculation, by bribing the poor section of the population, with the methods of *COMPROMISE* or ransom to be used in regard to the cultured capitalists who are willing to accept 'state capitalism'."256)

No guarantees to capitalism, save one: it will be safeguarded from labor strikes, Anarchists, all kinds of Social-Revolutionists and Mensheviks, who will be carefully isolated in prisons; it will be safeguarded from the population which will be deprived of any freedom and civic right, and a policy of muzzling by police measures will be instituted toward those workers and peasants who say: "we have driven out our own bourgeoisie, and now we are to let in foreign capitalists".

"This question must be put in quite a sober fashion. Ideological talk and phrase mongering about political liberties should be dispensed with; all that is just mere chatter and phrase mongering. We should get away from those phrases." (*p. 375, v. XVIII*). In other words, the propaganda to be carried on among workers and peas-

---

254) "A Report on the Food Tax Delivered at the All-Russian Conference of the Russian Communist Party," May 26, 1921, p. 267, vol. XVIII, part one.

255) P. 199, vol. XVIII, part one.

256) "On the Grain Tax, the Significance of the New Policy and its Conditions," p. 210, vol. XVIII, part one.

ants should be only of the following kind: "The 'freer', or more 'democratic', a bourgeois country is, the more fiercely does the capitalist gang rage against workers' revolution; this is exemplified by the democratic republic of the United States of America".257)

**
*

The brutal crushing of Kronstadt in which Lenin enacted the role of Thiers; Trotzky—that of Galiffet, and the Tenth Party Convention —the role of the Versailles Assembly showed to every one that party dictatorship and terror would be carried on as before. Lenin confirmed it by declaring in his pamphlet, published in the month of May:

"The Mensheviks and Social-Revolutionists have now learned to take on the color of 'non-partisans'. This fact has been fully established. And only fools cannot see it, cannot realize that we cannot let ourselves be fooled. Conferences of non-partisans are not a fetish with us. They are valuable if they help us to get near to the mass of people that have not as yet been touched by our propaganda, with the layers of toiling millions who stand outside of politics; but those conferences are harmful if they become a springboard for the Mensheviks and Social-Revolutionists, who have now taken on the color of 'non-partisans'. Such people help to promote rebellions, they aid White Guardists. The place of the Mensheviks and Social-Revolutionists— those that work openly as well as those that are camouflaged as 'non-partisans'—are in the prisons (or in the foreign magazines, alongside the white guardists; we willingly let Martov go abroad), but not at the conference of non-partisans.

"One can and should find other ways of checking on the mood of the masses and also ways of getting near to them. Let all those who are desirous of playing at the game of parliamentarianism, Constituent Assembly, conferences of non-partisans—let all of them go to Martov, they are quite welcome to go! Let them find out for themselves the delights of 'democracy'; let them find out from the Wrangel soldiers about the fascination of democracy. But as for us we have no time for this game of 'opposition', of 'conferences'. We are en-

257) "The International Day of the Woman Worker," March 4, 1921, p. 100, vol. XVIII, part one.

circled by the world bourgeoisie which watches for the slightest moment of wavering on our part in order to restore 'their own people' to power, in order to restore the capitalists and the bourgeoisie. We will keep the Mensheviks and Social-Revolutionists—those that work under their own colors as well as those that work under the color of 'non-partisans'—in prison.

"We will try by all means to make closer ties with the mass of toilers that has not yet been touched by political propaganda and in order to get close to those masses we are not going to use methods that only afford free elbow room for the Mensheviks and Social-Revolutionists and create the ground for waverings which can benefit only the Miliukovs.

". . . And as to political waverings that can benefit only the Miliukovs, we will ruthlessly combat them".258)

Lenin ends his pamphlet by reiterating the aforementioned threats:

"As to the Mensheviks and Social-Revolutionists disguised in the now fashionable Kronstadt attire of 'non-partisanship', we will see to it that they be safely kept in prison or that they be shipped to Martov, in Berlin, so that they can fully enjoy the blessings of democracy and be able to exchange ideas with Chernov, Miliukov, with the Georgian Mensheviks".259)

Of course, with the exception of a small number of Anarchists, Mensheviks and also of nearly 200 prominent intellectuals, no one was sent to Berlin, for it seemed more expedient "to keep one safely in prison" than to dispatch one to Berlin. And so those people are still kept in prison from which only death brings the ultimate deliverance. The aforementioned threats, which at the same time bore the character of peremptory dictates, were meant not only in respect to the Mensheviks and right wing Social-Revolutionists, but likewise in regard to groupings of a Socialist and Anarchist character. The Mensheviks and Social-Revolutionists were picked out as a target for those attacks because Lenin succeeded in blackening their character to a considerable extent, and to undermine their moral authority. Inasmuch as he directed his blows at those parties, by linking them up with Kronstadt, with which, in fact, they had nothing to do—and Lenin knew it—he tried to bring into disrepute the pro-

---

258) Pp. 232-233, vol. XVIII, part one.
259) Ibid, p. 235.

Kronstadt sentiments of the great mass of people who knew little about events in Kronstadt. Lenin worked hard in order to keep the truth about the Kronstadt events from reaching the masses, in order to keep them from learning that what had happened in Kronstadt was not a rebellion nor an uprising but just a peaceful protest and a peaceful petition presented to the government and backed up by the Communists of Kronstadt, Left Social-Revolutionists and Anarchists.

While yielding under the pressure of famine and utter destruction of the rural economy—and it is Lenin that bears the responsibility for both—to the extent of granting the peasants concessions in the economic domain, Lenin at the same time declared that in the political field the peasantry was to choose between the Bolsheviks and repressions, that there was no question of concessions and loosening up in the political fiield.

"We say to the peasants quite openly that they will have to choose: either the Bolshevik government—and we will grant all kinds of concessions, going to the outermost limits compatible with keeping the power in our hands, and then we will lead the peasants toward Socialism—or bouregois power. All the rest is fraud, demagogy of the purest kind. And against the fraud of this pure demagogy we must declare the fiercest struggle".[260] That is, a struggle against everybody and everything which does not accept this alternative: either the Bolsheviks or the bourgeois power. Hence the inference: no trust should be placed in the power of the working class. And Lenin was not slow in making this inference. In his article "New Times, New Errors in a New Guise," written August 20, 1921, Lenin scoffing at the "fetish of philistine democracy, the Constituent Assembly and bourgeois 'liberties' like the freedom of the press for the rich, for instance."[261] declared in his answer to the ex-Communist (German) Levi that here in this point "Levi coincides in his views with those semi-Anarchists and phrase-mongers and to some extent with some of the erstwhile members of the 'workers' opposition', who like to indulge in loud talk about the Bolsheviks having lost 'confidence in the working class'. The Menshevik-minded as well as the Anarchist-minded people raise this notion of 'the ability of the working class'

260) "The Tactics of the Russian Communist Party—A Speech Delivered at the Session of the Comintern, July, 1921," pp. 336-337, same vol.

261) P. 354, same vol.

into a fetish, without being able to think of the actual, concrete content underlying this notion. Instead of studying and analyzing this content they satisfy themselves with declaiming and reciting this phrase." . . . "The actual forces of the working class consist now of the mighty vanguard of this class (the Russian Communist Party) plus the elements that have weakened as a result of the declassing of the proletariat and which have shown themselves susceptible to the influence of the Menshevik and Anarchist vacilating attitudes.

"Under the slogan 'more confidence in the power of the working class' is now carried out a policy leading to the strengthening of Menshevik and Anarchist influences: Kronstadt has proven it quite conclusively in the spring of 1921. Every class conscious worker should expose and chase away those that now keep on shouting about 'our lack of faith in the forces of the working class', for all those shouters are but the accomplices of the bourgeoisie and the landlords who by extending the influence of Mensheviks and Anarchists are instrumental in weakening the proletariat which is of benefit only to landlords and capitalists.

"So 'there is the rub', if we look soberly into the actual content of this notion 'the forces of the working class'."[262]

Lenin, as is to be seen, openly admitted the fact that the Communists had utterly lost their influence upon the Russian working class, declaring that he will hold on to power against the will of this class by the use of terror and compulsion; and he issues his sloganized order:

"Down with the shouters! Down with the accomplices of the white guardists who now repeat the errors of the hapless Kronstadters in the spring of 1921"[263] and . . . long live the All-Russian Che-Ka, for "without this institution the power of toilers cannot exist as long as there are in this world exploiters who have no desire to hand down to the workers and peasants on a silver platter their rights as landlords, their rights as capitalists".[264]

"You know that our only answer could be given in the language of repressions, ruthless, prompt repressions backed up by the sym-

262) Pp. 356—358, same vol.
263) Ibid, p. 358.
264) "A Report Made at the Ninth All-Russian Convention of Soviets, December 23, 1921," p. 451, same vol.

pathies of workers and peasants. And therein lies the merit of our All-Russian Che-Ka. And we will always stress this point whenever we hear the direct or indirect wails, now frequently coming from abroad, of those Russian representatives who know how to use the word Che-Ka in all languages and who hold it up as the exemplification of Russian barbarism".265)

And so the question of freedom in the country is dismissed by Lenin most categorically. And when one of the old Bolsheviks, a worker by the name Miasnikov, appealed to Lenin with a request to grant freedom not to the bourgeoisie but to workers, Lenin, before putting Miasnikov into prison, tried to convince him by arguing that freedom for people like him—that is, for all workers— is detrimental and altogether useless. In "A Letter to Comrade Miasnikov" written in the first days of April 1921 and published in the pamphlet "Discussions Materials," Lenin answered Miasnikov with the following:

"Freedom of press in Soviet Russia which is encircled by bourgeois enemies of the entire world is freedom for the political organization of the bourgeoisie and its most trusted servants—the Mensheviks and Social-Revolutionists. This is an undeniable fact. The world bourgeoisie is so much stronger than we are. To give it such a weapon as freedom of political organizations (freedom of press, for the press is the basic center of political organization) means to make it easier for the enemy, it means to help the class enemy.

"We do not intend to commit suicide and that is why we will not do it.

"We clearly see the fact: Freedom of press means in reality that hundreds and thousands of writers from the ranks of the Mensheviks, Social-Revolutionists and Constitutional Democrats (a liberal bourgeoise party) will be bought off by the international bourgeoisie for the purpose of organizing its propaganda and waging a struggle against us . . .

"Freedom of press will help the world bourgeoisie. . . . That is a fact. And freedom of press will not become instrumental in cleansing the Party from its many weaknesses, errors, troubles, illnesses (and there are heaps of them). It isn't this that the world bourgeoisie

---

265) Ibid, p. 450.

is after. And the world bourgeoisie is, by far, not dead but alive. It stands alongside of us and is constantly on the watch. It has already hired Miliukov, whom Tchernov and Martov (partly because of stupidity, or because of factional spite, but mainly because of the objective logic of their petty-bourgeois democratic position) serve truthfully and loyally. You started out one way, but you ended by heading in an altogether different direction".[266]

Lenin's cheap demagogy did not convince Miasnikov and so the latter landed in prison—the first Communist political prisoner in Russia. But the first step was now taken, the outline course of struggle with the opposition within the party began to take visible shape and the sphere of persecutions expanded in a new direction. And the logic of this step was fully brought out by Stalin in his recent purge climaxed by the shooting of Lenin's lieutenants. Lenin taught this art of struggle in 1921.

**
*

Now let us give a brief description of how Lenin's terroristic slogans and maxims were carried out by the Party and state organs.

The year 1921 is characterized by an open, naked and shamefully exposed campaign against workers, the crushing of the working class with the aid of the police, military, of shootings, exiles and prisons, an unprecedented sweep of persecutions of Socialists, Anarchists and even Communists, and of all those who expected and demanded from the Communists that they live up to their promises of doing away with the regime of suppressions, which they upheld on the alleged grounds of having to wage a civil war, and of setting about to carry into life, under conditions of civil peace, the ideas of the Paris Commune developed by Lenin and the Bolsheviks in 1917 and at the beginning of 1918.

The four most outstanding events of the year 1921 (the workers' strike movement in February, the Kronstadt revolt—or rather Lenin's revolt against the Kronstadt sailors—the seizure of independent Georgia without declaring war upon it—in this respect the Bolsheviks also set an example to the imperialists—and famine) determined the intensity and the character of the Bolshevik terror, giving work to the All-Russian Che-Ka, which was rather apprehensive about

---

266) P. 349, vol. XVIII, part one.

being left in the position of a superfluous institution when "peaceful" conditions will have finally prevailed. But Lenin took good care of the Che-Ka as well as of other institutions of a primitive character....

The so-called Kronstadt rebellion was preceded by the strike movement of the Petrograd workers, which in March spread to Moscow and a few other industrial centers. This movement on the part of workers who in the first place demanded an improvement of their starvation conditions, and then—a change in the general policies of the government, putting a stop to persecutions and terror, the restoration of freedom and free Soviet elections,—this movement was met by Lenin and his government with the arrests of Anarchists and Socialists throughout the country, with lockouts, with martial law in Petrograd, the formation of a Defense Committee, armed suppression of workers and the dispersal of workers' demonstrations in Petrograd. One of the most prominent Petrograd Communists, Lashevich, sharply assailed the workers at the session of the Soviet, February 28, having introduced the proposal to close the Trubochny plant. This proposal received the backing of the chairman of the Soviet, G. Zinoviev and was adopted by the Soviet. The Red Army detachment, untrustworthy from the point of view of the Communists, were disarmed and kept shut in the barracks: the authorities relied only upon the "Kursants"—the red kadets. The Che-Ka was working full speed, and the prisons and the Che-Ka cellars were being rapidly filled up with prisoners. The Petrograd scene strikingly resembled the last week of the Tzar's absolutist regime. And almost simultaneously labor unrest flared up in Moscow. In the Khamovnichesky district of Moscow the workers of the big factories went out on strike. Workers marched from one plant to the other, closing up the factories on their way and drawing in ever greater numbers of people into their ranks. Toward the end of the day a crowd of 1500 workers started out toward the barracks, demanding that they all be admitted to talk to the Red Army men. Of course, they were not admitted; instead, they were fired at and several workers were killed and wounded. The strike movement spread to other factories and districts of Moscow. A meeting of protest against shootings, participated in by 10,000 people, was organized on the premises of the Women's Higher Courses (University). The Che-Ka was working double shift, filling up all the old prisons and the Bolshevik houses of detention.

And while this tragedy was taking place, Lenin found it possible to come out with a speech before the Moscow Soviet on February 27, and have it published in "Pravda" March 1, in which he kept shying away from the topic of Kronstadt, while misrepresenting the situation in Petrograd and Moscow. This is what he said:

"I have here a telegram from Comrade Zinoviev, from Petrograd, saying that in connection with the arrests made there a leaflet was found on one of the arrested which clearly shows that the latter is an agent of the Intelligence Organizations of foreign powers. There was also found a leaflet entitled 'To the Faithful', of a starkly counter-revolutionary content. And then Comrade Zinoviev reports that Menshevik leaflets calling for strikes have been distributed throughout the city (Petrograd). Here in Moscow there are exaggerated rumors of a demonstration. What did happen was that a gun went off in the hands of an agent provocateur, resulting in the death of a Communist. This was the only casualty during these rather unfortunate days".267) This is very characteristic of Lenin's lying, Jesuitic and utterly unscrupulous nature.

"It is noteworthy that at the questioning of the arrested Menshevik the Che-Ka tried to set the workers against party intellectuals and also . . . Russians against Jews".268)

Lenin kept silent about Kronstadt until March 8, until his second speech delivered at the Tenth Party Convention, until the time when the Bolsheviks began to bombard Kronstadt, which took place March 7, 6:45 P. M. There was a reason for Lenin's silence: he was preparing the greatest and bloodiest provocation, he did everything possible to provoke the Kronstadters into armed self-defense which he might declare a rebellion instigated by French capitalists, white guardists and their Generals. In Kronstadt, however, there was neither a rebellion, nor a plot, and no one had in mind preparing anything of that kind. Lenin, for the sake of party interests, for the sake of absolutism of the party and his own person, deliberately provoked the sailors, Red Army men and workers of Kronstadt into taking up arms in their own defense. The Kronstadters demanded, within the framework of the Soviet Constitution, free reelections to the Soviets, restoration of political freedom, the release of political pris-

---

267) P. 98, same vol.
268) "Sotzialistichesky Viestnik," No. 5, April 5, 1921; "Moscow. The Arrests of Mensheviks," p. 15.

— 161 —

oners who were members of Socialist parties, and a few other reforms. Those demands were adopted March 1, at a mass meeting of 15,000 people, at which were present Kalinin, Kusmin—Commissar of the Baltic fleet, and Vasiliev—chairman of the Kronstadt Soviet, who was presiding at the mass meeting. The resolution was carried by an overwhelming majority, against the votes of Kalinin, Kusmin and Vasiliev, that is, was carried by the votes of the members of the Communist Organization of Kronstadt. We are giving here this historic resolution in full:

RESOLUTION OF THE GENERAL MEETING
OF THE CREWS OF THE FIRST AND SECOND SQUADRONS
OF THE BALTIC FLEET
HELD MARCH 1, 1921

"Having heard the Report of the Representatives sent by the General Meeting of Ship Crews to Petrograd to investigate the situation there, Resolved:

"(1) In view of the fact that the present Soviets do not express the will of the workers and peasants, immediately to hold new elections by secret ballot, the pre-election campaign to have full freedom of agitation among the workers and peasants;

"(2) To establish freedom of speech and press for workers and peasants, for Anarchists and left Socialist parties;

"(3) To secure freedom of assembly for labor unions and peasant organizations;

"(4) To call a nonpartisan Conference of the workers, Red Army soldiers and sailors of Petrograd, Kronstadt, and of Petrograd Province, no later than March 10, 1921;

"(5) To liberate all political prisoners of Socialist parties, as well as all workers, peasants, soldiers, and sailors imprisoned in connection with the labor and peasant movements;

"(6) To elect a Commission to review the cases of those held in prisons and concentration camps;

"(7) To abolish all *politotdeli* (political bureaus) because no party should be given special privileges in the propagation of its ideas or receive the financial support of the Government for such purposes. Instead there should be established education and cultural commissions, locally elected and financed by the Government;

"(8) To abolish immediately all *zagraditelniye otryadi;*

"(9) To equalize the rations of all who work, with the exception of those employed in trades detrimental to health;

"(10) To abolish the Communist fighting detachments in all branches of the Army, as well as the Communist guards kept on duty in mills and factories. Should such guards or military detachments be found necessary, they are to be appointed in the Army from the ranks, and in the factories according to the judgment of the workers;

"(11) To give the peasants full freedom of action in regard to their land, and also the right to keep cattle, on condition that the peasants manage with their own means; that is, without employing hired labor;

"(12) To request all branches of the Army, as well as our comrades the military *kursanti,* to concur in our resolutions;

"(13) To demand that the press give the fullest publicity to our resolutions;

"(14) To appoint a Travelling Commission of Control;

"(15) To permit free *kustarnoye* (individual small scale) production by one's own efforts.

"Resolution passed unanimously by Brigade Meeting, two persons refraining from voting

Petrichenko

Chairman of Brigade Meeting

Perepelkin

Secretary

"Resolution passed by an overwhelming majority of the Kronstadt garrison.

Vasiliev

Chairman

"Together with comrade Kalinin, Vassiliev votes against the Resolution".269)

---

269) "Izvestia of the Provisional Revolutionary Committee of Sailors, Soldiers and Workers of the City of Kronstadt"; see compendium to the book *"The Truth About Kronstadt,"* published by newspaper "Volia Rossii," Prague, 1921.

No one, of course, in framing this resolution or voting for it, ever thought that those moderate, altogether constitutional demands which did not violate the basic principles of the Soviet regime would meet the harsh, martinet shout and chekist threat of a Trotzky who issued his famous command: "To shoot them like partridges". None had the slightest inkling that those demands would result in Trotzky issuing the bloodthirsty order to make a clean sweep of Kronstadt, to get even with the relatives of the Kronstadters and with anyone sympathizing with the Kronstadt resolution. They did not take this possibility into consideration because they did not know Lenin, his unsatiable lust for absolute power, for personal dictatorship disguised under the misnomer "Dictatorship of the Proletariat", a proletariat of which, by his own admission, there was hardly anything left by that time. . . .

But Lenin had in mind something else; he intentionally lied about Kronstadt before the delegates of the Tenth Party Convention; he presented the entire affair to the delegates as "a mutiny which rapidly brought to the fore the well known figure—the white guardist General" as a conglomeration "of most diverse elements who are trying to give the impression of being just a little to the right of the Bolsheviks and perhaps even to the left of them". He assured the delegates that "the White Generals played here a big role" and "that this has been proven". The proof of it? "Two weeks prior to the Kronstadt events, the Paris papers already wrote that a rebellion was taking place in Kronstadt." . . . He assured the delegates that "it was the work of the Social-Revolutionists and the white guardists from abroad", and defying the logic of his own words, he kept on stating that it was "a petty-bourgeois counter-revolution, a petty-bourgeois characteristic elemental force in motion" . . . "it is something new . . . it created a movement flaunting the slogans of free trade (which Lenin granted after having crushed the Kronstadt revolt—G.M.) and always directed against the dictatorship of the proletariat". In the closing statement of his speech, Lenin laid bare his hidden thought which give us the cue to Lenin's tactics of provoking Kronstadt into a rebellion and ruthlessly crushing it. Lenin said:

"The petty-bourgeois Anarchistic elemental forces . . . have once more proved to be the most dangerous enemy, an enemy with a potential drawing power and support in the country, with the power to affect a change in the mood of the masses and even to sweep into his sphere of influence certain sections of non-partisan workers".270)

And so "in the historic days of the Tenth Convention of the Russian Communist Party, 320 delegates from all parts of the country, mainly army men, were flung upon Kronstadt to help in the suppression of the rebellion".271)

Now it becomes clear why the Bolsheviks, with Lenin and Trotzky at their head, gave such a reception to the resolution of the Kronstadters, why they forced the Kronstadters into a position where the latter had to take up arms.

Already on March 2, while Vasiliev and Kusmin were still taking part in the deliberations of the Kronstadt Soviet, Lenin and Trotzky openly announced in a special order issued to that effect, about "the rebellion of the ex-General Koslovsky", about "the Social-Revolutionist and Black Hundred resolution adopted on the battleship 'Petropavlovsk'." Lenin and Trotzky declared war upon Kronstadt.

. . . "The meaning of the latest events has been clearly revealed. Behind the back of the Social-Revolutionists was a Tzarist General. In view of that, the Council of Labor and Defense declares: 1) The ex-General Koslovsky and his accomplices are to be outlawed, 2) A state of siege is to be declared in the city of Petrograd and the Petrograd 'gubernia' 272), 3) Supreme authority in the fortified region of Petrograd is to be vested in the Committee for the Defense of Petrograd". This committee in turn issued the following order, whose closing sentence was:

"In case crowds congregate in the streets, the troops are ordered to fire; those that resist are to be shot on the spot".

Following that, the Kronstadt sailors had no other way out but to take up arms in order to triumph or die; in the latter case—to pay dearly for their lives.

"The Kronstadt mutiny" began. . . . The Committee for the Defense of Petrograd began arresting people in great numbers—all relatives of Kronstadters—keeping them as hostages. The Kronstadters, however, arrested only a few commissars, Kuzmin and Vasiliev included, leaving the great mass of Communists free and unmolested.

---

270) P. 123, vol. XVIII, part one.

271) M. Rafayil, "The Kronstadt Rebellion (from the Diary of a Politworker)" p. 4; published by All-Ukrainian State Publishing House, 1921.

272) Province, government.

The Communists in Petrograd were shooting people right and left, but in Kronstadt not a single person was shot.

Having flung all their forces upon Kronstadt, the Bolsheviks, with the aid of the ex-Tzarist Generals, took Kronstadt on March 18. This cost them quite dearly. There was no mercy for the vanquished.

It would be amusing, if it were not so revolting, to listen to the indignation voiced by one of the Kronstadt hangmen "at the most fierce and brutal counter-revolutionists"—the Kronstadters. While the Bolsheviks were arresting thousands of people in Petrograd, and tens of thousands throughout Russia, while Petrograd was declared in a state of siege and shooting was the threatened reprisal for congregating on the street, while relatives of the Kronstadters were being arrested and kept as hostages, while sailors and Red Army men were being rounded up and shot in batches in Oranienbaum, in other towns near Petrograd and in Petrograd itself—while all that was taking place the Kronstadters abolished the death penalty, left the Communists scot free, save 280 of the most dangerous ones who were arrested, but at the same time were treated humanely and given the same food as the rest of the population. And with all that Mr. M. Rafayil, the future "Trotzkyite" was brazen enough to "resent" the "ferocious" and "brutal" Kronstadters.

"Having started with exalted declarations about the bloodless upheaval", M. Rafayil writes, "the Revolutionary Committee during its two weeks of existence succeeded in rounding up a vast number of Communists, and was ready to have all of them shot but was frustrated in its intent by the rapid advance of the Red Army. While loudly proclaiming their protests against the Communist usurpers, against unwarranted arrests, the rebel leaders only a few days later, began issuing orders for summary arrests; the prisoners were stripped of their clothing and the white terror began. Events unfolded with amazing rapidity, exposing the lies, hypocrisy and vileness of those who were directing the rebellion. On the third or fourth day of the mutiny they restored the very same thing against which they allegedly revolted and against which their outcries were the loudest.

"The Soviet power, guided by the Communist Party, deprived the bourgeois and the counter-revolutionists of freedom. The Soviet government used terror in regard to white guardists, it stripped the capitalists of their possessions, but the Kronstadters, in the person of their leaders, deprived freedom to the vanguard fighters—proletarians—Communists, they stripped Communist workers of their clothing, they took away freedom of speech from workers and it was toward the latter that they used terror. To the great joy of the external and internal counter-revolution (and so after all the Kronstadters were no counter-revolutionists—G.M.) the rebels were rushing toward a precipice, turning by virtue of their actions into most savage, ferocious and cruel counter-revolutionists. Having started out with fraud, they ended up with ignominy".273)

Wherein lay this "ferociousness, savagery and brutality"? How did the "white terror of the Kronstadters" manifest itself?

"The leaders of the mutiny", M. Rafayil continues, "granted on the first day of rebellion immunity of person to the Communists, but on March 11, according to the report of 'Izvestia', the arrested Communists were stripped of their clothing. The report reads: 'Whereas the arrested Communists for the time being do not stand in need of their foot-wear, they are to be deprived of such, in the number of 280 pair of boots, all of which is to be turned over to the fighting troops'.

"The rebels were equipping themselves at the expense of the stripped and plundered Communists, to the great joy of the Black Hundreds".274)

How terrible! What a horrible, ferocious, cruel and savage "white terror"! Can that be compared, indeed, with "the red terror" of the Bolsheviks!

**
*

On March 7th, Trotzky radio-telegraphed to Kronstadt an order signed by him in his capacity as Chairman of the Revolutionary Military Council of the Republic, and by the Chief Commander Kamenev: 275)

"The workers' and peasants' government resolved to have Kronstadt and the rebel ships brought back without delay within the fold of the Soviet Republic. I therefore command all those who raised their hands against their Socialist fatherland immediately to put down their arms. The recalcitrants are to be disarmed and turned over to

---

273) M. Rafayil, "The Kronstadt Rebellion," pp. 62-63.
274) Ibid, p. 59.
275) It was not Lev Kamenev, who was shot in 1936 in Moscow.

the Soviet authoriteis. The arrested Commissars and other government representatives are to be set free immediately. Only those who surrender unconditionally can count upon the mercies of the Soviet government. At the same time instructions have been given to smash the rebellions and the rebels with the armed forces at my disposal. The responsibility for the distress afflicting the peaceful population, will rest entirely upon the heads of the white guardist rebels This is the last warning".

Since none "surrendered unconditionally", Trotzky put into effect his threat; it is reported that 18,000 Kronstadters paid with their lives. Following their "victory" the courts began working on the basis of "mass production". Shootings were going on a long time after the "victory". F. Dan (one of the leaders of the Mensheviks) reports on the basis of information supplied by one of the Kronstadters, who had been his prison mate for some time, that two months after the "victory", Perepelkin, a member of the Provisional Revolutionary War Committee, and many other Kronstadters, were shot by the Che-Ka. Those who were not killed off immediately were dispatched to concentration camps, condemned to forced labor under conditions which spelled almost certain death; and, indeed, the great majority of them perished from hunger and various illnesses. Those that escaped abroad were granted an amnesty, many of them returned to Russia, but only a few of them remained at liberty, the great majority of them, as reported by Dan, having been dispatched to various concentration camps.

The deliberate lies and slanders spread about Kronstadt by Lenin and other Bolshevik leaders was afterwards fully exposed by the Communists themselves, thus aggravating their responsibility, or rather placing it squarely upon their shoulders for the mass murders committed in Kronstadt.

Already in December 1921, there appeared an essay "The Rebellion of the Kronstadt Sailors" printed in the magazine "Krasny Arkhiv".276) This magazine was published as a monthly by the Military Scientific Society at the Military Academy and was edited by the Editorial Board of the Supreme Military Council. The magazine was published exclusively for the narrow circle of the top-ranking Communists and caried an inscription: "Not for Publication".

---

276) "The Red Archive," No. 9, December, 1921.

"The Political Department of the Baltic fleet found itself isolated not only from the masses but also from local party workers, having become a bureaucratic organ lacking any prestige and standing." . . . "The Baltic fleet destroyed all local initiative and brought the work down to the level of clerical routine. . . . From July to November, 1920, twenty percent of the members left the Party." . . . "The Chief of the Organization Department of the Baltic fleet pointed out in the middle of February 21 that 'if the work goes on as it has been going on until now, a mutiny is likely to break out two or three months from now.' . . . "The lack of Party work told heavily upon the organization. At a mass meeting, numbering 15 thousand people, which, of course, was also attended by Communists, no one, save comrades Kalinin, Kuzmin and Vasiliev, voted against the resolution. And this also had its effect in the grievous incidents taking place in the Kronstadt organization: the resignation of 381 members who did not grasp the true meaning of the rebellion and its consequences. Nor did the responsible workers heading the work in Kronstadt understand what was going on, and that is why they failed to take the right measures necessary at the very beginning".277)

Lenin knew it; Trotzky knew it; Kalinin and Zinoviev knew it; every one of the rulers of Russian destinies was very well aware of it and still they kept on besmirching Kronstadt; they drowned it in blood, and following that they kept on ferociously annihilating the Kronstadters and any one partaking of their ideas. As in many other instances we have here a clear case of mass murder subject to criminal prosecution.

**
*

Simultaneously with the Kronstadt drama, another drama, no less cruel than the one of Kronstadt, was enacted at the other end of the country. It was the drama of a small nation, the drama of the Georgian State.

The conquest of Georgia was an act of imperialist terror on the part of Lenin. The conquest took place without war having been declared and was conceived and carefully prepared for quite a long time in advance . The course of this conquest was set forth in the Manifesto of the Georgian government entitled "To All Socialist

277) Ibid, p. 44.

Parties and Workers' Organizations" which it released in Constantinople.

"On February 11—says this Manifesto of the Georgian Socialist government—the Russian Bolshevik troops belonging to the 11th army invaded Georgia from the Armenian side.

"Mr. Sheiman, the representative of the Moscow government, declared to us that Russia knows nothing of this invasion allegedly undertaken by the Armenian government. This declaration was made exactly at the moment when the representative of the Armenian government, Mr. Shaverdov, was reassuring us that Armenia was no party to this act of aggression, that she was ready to solve in peaceful manner any question at issue with the state of Georgia. . . .

"February 15, Sheiman received from Baku a coded telegram from the 11th army: 'It was decided to cross the Rubicon. Act in accordance with this decision.' . . . On February 16, the President of the Georgian government made an attempt to speak to Moscow on the direct wire, but Mr. Karakhan, Moscow's Acting Commissar for Foreign Affairs, who at that time was at the Moscow end of the line, refused to negotiate. . . .

"And in the meantime military action was proceeding apace. . . .

"On February 21, the President of the Georgian Republic radioed to Chicherin. Not having received an answer to this telegram, the President of the Georgian Republic appealed to Lenin and Trotzky, asking them to stop the war, which was clearly national in character.

"This telegram shared the fate of others. . . .

"The Angora Government (Turkey) rushed to the aid of the Moscow government. Having entered Batum, the Turks declared on March 16, that the Grand National Assembly of Angora resolved to annex Batum and its province. . . .

"On March 17, the Georgian government decided to put a halt to further fighting on the shores of the river Rion and to dissolve the army. . . .

"This decision left the road to Batum open to the Bolshevik troops. On March 18, the Georgian government abandoned Batum and a few days later the Bolshevik troops entered the city. . . .

"Such was the course of events leading to the destruction of the state created by the workers and peasants of Georgia and the establishment of a military dictatorship and the arbitrary rule of the Moscow bayonets in place of a democratic republic." . . .

Independent Georgia was destroyed: it was necessary to annihilate the elements which created it—the Socialists. And so a campaign of terror was unloosed against Socialists, workers, peasants with the meaningless cruelty characterizing the Bolsheviks.

In a remarkable document, "The Appeal of the Tiflis Workers to All the Workers of Western Europe," signed by 3,449 workers of the city of Tiflis and dated: "Tiflis, August 7, 1921," the situation in conquered Georgia is thus described:

"From the very first days Georgia was conquered, we were placed in the position of and treated as slaves. We were deprived of freedom of speech, of press, assembly and the right of free association. A regime of military labor service has been imposed upon all the workers of Georgia, irrespective of their occupation. Everywhere Extraordinary Committees (Che-Ka) have been set up and summary arrests of workers for most innocuous remarks have been taking place. Advanced workers are being arrested, fired from their jobs, deprived of their civic rights and deported from their native places. All the elected trade union representatives—party people and non-partisans—have been driven out of the unions and replaced by appointees, by people who are altogether alien to us. Anyone making speeches at rallies, anyone acting in the capacity of workers' representative, is subject to incredibly harsh punishments: confinement in dark, damp cellars during many dreary months, without even being given a hearing or arraigned before the court. The Executive Board of Elections in the Union of Trolley Workers (in the month of April) were dissolved, the elected members of the Board were arrested and even those workers were punished who had asked questions at the mass meetings. The same was done in the Union of Railway Workers and all other trade unions of Tiflis. The Executive Board elected at the Convention of teachers of Georgian elementary schools was dispersed and in its place its authorities put a rubber stamp Board consisting of appointed yes-men. . . . Of late, a new method of smashing workers' organizations has been put to use: deporting railway workers from Georgia into other parts of Soviet Russia. Already one party of workers has been exiled from the country; and now another party comprising more than a thousand railway men is about to be dispatched for compulsory labor on railways outside of Georgia. The material situation of the workers is hopeless. The threat of physical deterioration is hanging over our heads. . . . Wages are paid on the same scale as before when general prices were 40 and 50 times lower than they are now, but even this wretched pittance is not paid out for months. To leave for the villages and pick up some work with the peasants is forbidden under *penalty of shooting.* In the workers' quarters reign hunger, all kinds of diseases, cholera. Workers' families are being wiped out. We workers are deprived of the opportunity to speak of our sufferings, for terror now stalks the country. The advanced workers of Georgia, irrespective of their party affiliation, are thrown into prison where they are being decimated by hunger and diseases. Human life has become of no value. Innocent people are shot, even those who never mixed into politics, who never took part in any political struggle. People were shot because they served the democratic government, the state; because in open war they defended their native country from the invasion of foreign troops." Such is the picture as drawn by the workers of Tiflis. . . .

Additional touches are provided by the central committee of the Communist Party of Georgia which published the following ordinance:

"To all Party Organizations of the Communist Party of Georgia

A Circular Letter

"The Central Committee of the Party received a declaration from the Chairman of the Che-Ka to the effect that some of the members of the Communist Party of Georgia are frequently interceding with him about releasing prisoners or mitigating their sentences. Finding such intercessions unworthy of Communists, of the Central Communist Party of Georgia, we direct all Party organizations of Georgia to bring it to the attention of their members that such pleadings in behalf of prisoners will not be permitted and that in the future Party members will be held accountable and even expelled for such solicitations."

Such instructions notwithstanding, Stalin came to Georgia vested with great power, found that the Georgian Communists were not sufficiently firm. He rudely dismissed Makharadze and put in his place Boodou Mdviani; he fired Tziptzade and appointed Atabekov in his place. (The first two were shot by Stalin in 1938). At the workers meeting organized for Stalin, the latter was hooted by the

278) No. 2, December 2, 1921.

audience: he had to witness a grand ovation in honor of the Mensheviks. Four days later all the Mensheviks were arrested in Tiflis.

The "Sotzialistitchesky Viestnik"[278]) published a letter from Georgia describing the death and the funeral of a renowned Georgian Social-Democrat, Parmen Chichinadze. The author of the letter informs: "Like all the Mensheviks, Parmen Chichinadze was kept in Metekh castle where, toward the end of September, he fell ill with meningitis. The Head of the Public Health Department, Kuchenadze, when asked to place the sick man in a hospital, declared that it was a case of simulation on the part of the prisoner. It was after many efforts on the part of many people that the patient was transferred to a hospital where a few days later he died. . . . . ."

The funeral took place October 8. "On the eve of the funeral day the chekists under the threat of heavy penalties forced the burial committee to bury him at the cemetery and to detour the procession to secluded by-streets of the city. . . . " The coffin was followed by a vast throng of 50,000. Everywhere soldiers were placed with machine guns. Even relatives were not permitted to go beyond the fence of the cemetery.

"Two wreaths were placed upon the grave: one was from 'Entire Georgia,' the other from 'comrades in the prison cell.' This wreath and the black flag (the national flag) hung out at the prison, brought forth reprisals: the prisoners were deprived of the privilege to receive their parcels from the outside, thus dooming them to starvation, since the entire prison ration consisted of a half pound of non-edible bread per day."

On October 24, a delegation of 9 people was sent to the Chairman of the Revolutionary Committee in order to transmit to him a declaration signed by 5132 workers. Mdivani had the delegation wait three hours, after the elapse of which it was turned down. Upon leaving, the entire delegation was arrested and thrown into prison, into cellars. This resulted in a great unrest sweeping the city. In order to quieten the workers, Mdivani announced on October 29 that he had not seen the delegation and that he had no part in the latter's arrest. On October 31 it became known that the delegation was kept in the Metekh castle. On November 1, a general strike nearly broke out in the city. Protest meetings and general unrest continued until November 3. And then new summary arrests swept the city. Two thousand people, most of them Socialists, were seized.

The Bolshevik papers threatened with terroristic repressions. The newspaper "Pravda Grouzii" ("The truth of Georgia") demanded that "Menshevism in Georgia should be burned out with hot irons and that Georgian political prisoners be shipped out to Russia[279])."

In December the time was set for elections to the Soviets. According to the report of the Central Committee of the Social-Democratic Party of Georgia[280]), it was declared beforehand that "the elections of non-Bolsheviks will not be confirmed by the Revolutionary War Committee."

". . . The chekists redoubled their energy in preparing the elections. More than 3,000 workers, peasants and intellectuals were arrested; great many workers (including 2,000 railway workers) were removed from Georgia to various parts of Russia; thousands of Georgian employees were discharged."

And thus Georgia was swept into the field of the Bolshevik terror, paying its share in thousands of prisoners, exiled and executed people. As to the exact number of people shot in Georgia, in 1921, we shall never know definitely. One thing is definite, though: Georgia contributed many thousands at the alter of the Moscow Moloch. Kronstadt and Georgia—tens of thousands of murdered and shot people, tens and thousands of prisoners and exiles, that is, doomed to slow starvation and lingering death from consuming illnesses. But this did not halt the flow of the bloody torrent: blood continued to flow all over the country, and prisons were being filled up as before, only more energetically so, with workers, peasants, Socialists and Anarchists. The lack of rooming space in prisons and concentration camps forced the Bolsheviks to revive the old system of exiling politicals, extending the geographical boundaries of the old exile. But of this we shall have to say more in our story of terror.

Simultaneously with the bloody reprisals in Kronstadt and Georgia the Bolsheviks were carrying on their cooly premeditated policy of physical destruction of the popular insurgent movements, those that were hostile to them as well as those that fought together

---

279) Ibid.

280) See "Sotzialistichesky Viestnik," No. 2, January 19, 1922.

with them against Kolchak and Denikin. Special attention was paid to the Makhno movement, as a movement embodying "the petty-bourgeois Anarchist elemental forces" which, according to Lenin, and as we already saw from the Kronstadt example, was "the most dangerous enemy, which might draw many sympathizers and partisans, which might obtain strong backing in the country and change the sentiments of the great masses of people. . . ." We already saw that the Bolsheviks, having drawn up and signed a pact between themselves and the Makhno movement with the object of jointly attacking and annihilating Wrangel forces, treacherously attacked the Makhno insurgent troops, aiming to smash and destroy them. And like in Kronstadt, it was the Bolsheviks who consciously provoked this attack in order to have the excuse for physically destroying the insurgents instead of obtaining a peaceful understanding with them. The Bolsheviks knowingly placed the insurgent troops in a position leaving no way out for them but to turn against the Bolsheviks and fight in defense of their life and freedom. And that is exactly what was done by those insurgent contigents which escaped destruction after the smash up attempted by the Bolshevik authorities: to surrender meant to many sure death by shooting and to all the others—prison and exile. Having found themselves in the position of hounded beasts, the insurgents tried to sell their life dearly, and for this the revenge visited upon them by the authorities was gruesome indeed: their families and relatives were being ruined economically, were being arrested and shot, and terror was visited upon the native villages of the insurgents. This struggle against the insurgents was in fact not a struggle but mass murder pure and simple. The Bolsheviks did not want to admit back to peaceful work anyone who was connected in the slightest with the insurgent Makhno army; they feared that when the survivors among the insurgents returned to their native villages and lived among their own folks enveloped with the halo of heroes, they might become a standing threat to the regime: the possibility would always be there that they would become the focal points of a crystalizing peasant unrest. And so it was decided to annihilate the insurgents physically, cost as it may in terms of human lives and economic wreckage.

How many insurgents were killed and shot, how many of their relatives, peasants suspected of sympathizing with their cause, were shot and thrown into prison, we shall never know. We do know, however, that their number was vast. Some idea of the cruelty, savage vindictiveness, meaningless and unwarranted murders is given by the account of the shooting of Sereda[281] and Bogush,[282] taking place in Kharkov March 14, and of Victor Popov[283] in Moscow and Ribin-Zonov taking place in Kharkov, January 1921.

The struggle against the insurrectionary troops meant virtually the waging of war against the peasants. With the exception of the Makhno movement, a few guerilla detachments in Siberia and irregular contigents linked up with the Pietlura Army—the Tiutiunik, Zeleny and Angel detachments—which rapidly degenerated into ordinary bandits. (All those irregular armies and detachments standing almost poles apart in their aims and methods had this in common that they

281) SEREDA: Anarchist; one of the commanders in the Makhno army; in the Fall of 1920, when the Makhno troops made common cause with the Bolsheviks in their struggle against Wrangel, Sereda who participated in many of the battles, was wounded in the chest. He needed a serious operation and was sent to Kharkov for that purpose. A week after the attack of the Bolsheviks upon the Anarchists, Sereda was transferred from the hospital to the prison and was shot in the month of March.

282) BOGUSH: Anarchist; emigrant from the United States, from where he was deported to Russia together with Emma Goldman and Alexander Berkman. During the period when the accord with the Makhno troops was in force, that is, in November 1921, Bogush went to the district held by the Makhno troops in order to familiarize himself with the situation and conditions prevailing there. After a week's stay in that region he returned to Kharkov where he was arrested and shot on June 2, that is, in less than a year after he had come from America.

283) VICTOR POPOV: ex-member of the left Social-Revolutionists. Signed on behalf of the Makhno army the pact with the Bolsheviks. During the campaign against Wrangel, Popov, in his capacity of an official representative of the insurrection army, stayed in Kharkov where he was arrested, forwarded to Moscow and put into prison (the Butirki prison). No one expected that he would be shot; nevertheless, he was shot by the All-Russian Che-Ka toward the end of 1921.

284) RIBIN—ZONOV, PIOTR: Anarchist; returned in 1917 to Russia from the United States. Worked in the Union of Metal Workers. In 1920 he fought against Denikin at the approaches to the city of Kharkov; was in the regiment made up of responsible workers of the trade union movement. Following Denikin's defeat he joined the Makhno movement and took an active part in effecting the accord between the Bolsheviks and Makhno troops. Was arrested in Kharkov in January, 1921 and shot in the same month.

had some sort of program against the Bolshevik program of organizing the country: the Makhno troops, the Siberian irregulars were
for free Soviets and free Federations; and the Pietlura irregulars were
allegedly for national independence and for a democratic republic.
All the other insurrectionary movements came into existence by way
of resisting, of defending themselves against Lenin's mad "grain
crusades," which were attended by bare violence, by plundering,
and ruining the peasants, by shootings; all of which had been going
on since the first years of the revolution, without showing any
signs of abatement even in 1921, the year of the terrible famine.

The Bolsheviks themselves accounted in a similar manner for
the causes of insurrectionary movements and peasant revolts. Thus,
for instance, the monthly "Krasnaya Armiya" ("Red Army")[285]
published by the Military Scientific Society affiliated with the Military Academy, (the magazine was intended for a narrow circle of
Communist readers and bore an inscription: "not to be republished")
we find in the article: *The general causes of the rise of bandit movements and peasant revolts*" the following admissions:

" . . . . Ineptitude, economic mismanagement, a criminal
attitude toward the commonwealth property on the part of some
economic organs, play quite a prominent role in fostering and
promoting unrest on the part of the masses of people. Thus, for
instance, one can easily see how disastrously the morale of the
peasants is affected when they witness the deterioration of all kinds
of food products and raw materials collected by the various taxing
agencies, when they see with their own eyes how thousands of
pood of grain, meat, eggs putrefy and go to waste, or entire car-
loads of potatoes are permitted to freeze. How often do such
'representatives' of the tax-gathering agencies (of the tax in kind)
in the villages commit acts that are unjust and at times downright
cruel! The irresponsible provocatory acts of such government
representatives frequently beget uprisings of entire villages. In the
Don and Kuban regions a very unique movement sprang up headed
by Maslakov, an ex-Commander of the Red Army, who fought in
the ranks of the latter, with the avowed aims, as formulated by the
movement itself, of declaring war on the saboteurs of the Soviet
power, on the 'commissar-minded' Communists. Those Communists

---

285) No. 9, December, 1921.

who have not shown themselves obnoxious to the local population are not attacked. But workers sent from the center to carry on work in the outlying provinces, who are not acquainted with local customs, ways of life and general conditions, commit as a result of such ignorance a number of unpardonable mistakes, displaying colonizing tendencies, producing among the population widely diffused unrest and even revolts: (in Baskyria, Turkestan, Northern Caucasia." 286)

Here are the reasons adduced by the magazine "Krasnaya Armiya" (the "Red Army") for the rise and spread of the insurrectionary movement upon the territory of the North Caucasian Military District.

"Annulling the currency issued by Denikin without replacing it with Soviet money, promulgating the tax in kind and the resulting repressions, the almost total lack of commodities, the distressful economic crisis producing a state of near-collapse, the shortcomings of the state apparatus and the ineptitude displayed by the local Soviet officials in their approach to the population, all that produced a state unfavorable to the Soviets even among the loyal elements who became disillusioned in their expectations in regard to the Soviet power.

"The imposition of labor and other services, the deliberately criminal work of some of the government representatives—camouflaged agents of anti-Soviet organizations—personal vendettas, all that impelled the most active elements, who were not altogether free from some offenses in the past, to seek refuge in the rebel detachments rather than put their trust in the proclaimed amnesty.

"Sweeping orders for mobilizing the population for the Russian-Polish war, resulted in a great number of deserters who became outlaws. This and a number of other causes gave rise to a new powerful sweep of rebellions287).

"The basis of all insurrectionary movements—the movement for independence on the part of the Cossacks—a movement which does not set itself broader tasks of conquests, but confines itself to the endeavor of redeeming their regions from the Bolshevik yoke and

---

286) Ibid, p. 34. Quoted from "Sotzialistichesky Viestnik," No. 9, May 2, 1922, where long excerpts from this article are cited.

287) Ibid, p. 57, from the same magazine.

to set up autonomous republics upon the principles of bourgeois-democratic self-governments with various fictitious liberties, all of which finds great favor with the Cossack population. . . .

"The 'separatists' disapprove of and fight against White Guardist agitation."288)

The same explanation is given for the rise of the rebel movement in Turkestan—the Basmach movement—as to Siberia, the "Siberian banditism," the "Krasnaya Armiya" has the following to say:

"The carrying out of the policy of grain collections in the spring of 1920 roused the Siberian peasantry into a state of hostility toward the Soviets. The villages were cleaned out of their grain supplies but nothing was given to them in exchange."289) "The movement in the Ishimsk region was proceding under the same slogans which at one time were put forth by the Kronstadt sailors."290)

Such are the causes of the peasant revolts and their explanation as given by the aforementioned source. But what about the facts of suppression of those revolts?

Did the Bolshevik government take any steps toward a peaceful settlement of the emerging conflicts? Never! Just the opposite, it knew only one method, physical annihilation attended by the utmost cruelty, the object of which was to make the Soviet government feared to the extend of discouraging anyone from rebelling, just as his cause might be, against the policy of the Soviet government and its representatives.

I have no reliable information on hand about the Maslakov movement. But apart from that movement in the Kuban region there was another one headed by general Przhevalsky also operating in the same province. We find the following information about this movement in the "Sotzialistitchesky Viestnik."291)

"The policy of violence and oppression soon led to a revolt on the part of the population. Soon there appeared general Przhevalsky with his Cossack detachments (the so-called "green" detachments). This movement was defeated by Budenny, but not without having left in his trail thousands of victims in various towns and Cossack

288) Ibid, p. 60, from the same magazine.
289) Ibid, p. 69, from the same magazine.
290) Ibid, p. 70, from the same magazine.
291) No. 6, March 21, 1922.

villages, not without having taken the customary toll in shootings, arrests and exiling people. (The Cossack village Yelizavetinskaya, of the Yekaterinodar section, was razed to the ground)."

It would not be amiss here to remind of the afore-mentioned command issued by Lander.

"In September"—the correspondent of the "Sotzialistichesky Viestnik" continues—"when the detachments of general Przhevalsky were on the offensive, the Bolshevik authorities arrested and kept as hostages all the ex-Social-Democrats and present members of the Social-Democratic organization (Piotrovskaya, Kheyfetz, Gaaze, Kalita and others) a number of eminent public figures and plain, ordinary citizens—altogether 300 people. Many of them were shot, others deported. The Communists themselves report that Budenny demanded the wholesale shooting of all the arrested people. Social-Democrats included; it was due to the energetic intervention of the Party Committee that the bloodthirsty warrior was curtailed in his terroristic program of executions, which were brought down to 93 people only."

Melgunov in his book "The Red Terror" maintains on the basis of excerpts from the "Izvestia" of the town of Yekaterinodar, that the latter newspaper published a list of 104 executed people. In Rostov on the Don the picture was about the same: "shootings became especially frequent during the last month when the Che-Ka waged an intensive warfare against banditism which assumed great proportions."

In the same issue of the "Sotzialistichesky Viestnik" was published a very important official document—the verdict of the Circuit Session of the People's Court of the Novo-Nikolayevsk "gubernia" (Western Siberia). The peasants did not fulfill the three-week fuel program, because of their failure they were impressed into labor service. A few of the "volosty" (volost, the lowest rural administrative unit) were arraigned before the court, which passed the following verdict, rare even in the annals of Soviet "justice."

"Having listened to the explanations of the volost delegates and the representatives of the Transport Section of the All-Russian Che-Ka and also taking into consideration the fact that said delegates who on November 23 undertook the obligation of delivering within the ten day limit, at the disposal of Comrade Chebulinsky, the Chief of the Lumber Logging Post, fifty percent of the vehicles and horse power, were not able, notwithstanding their zealous efforts to carry out their duty, to do anything in this respect because of a number of circumstances beyond their control, namely the interference of the armed detachments carrying out the program of the food campaign, whose actions expressed themselves: 1) in failing to recognize the necessity to carry out the order No. 19 (on the delivery of timber); 2) in summary arrests among the population and reaching as high as eighty percent of the population; 3) in forbidding the population to leave and enter the villages at will; 4) in making those who were delinquent in paying their taxes sign a paper pledging that they will not leave the village; 5) in seizing all means of transportation; 6) in confiscating horses and other property and removing it to the Moshkovo station; 7) in keeping people under arrest, threatening them with court action, with shooting on the spot, etc. Also, taking into consideration the fact that the delegates themselves express full readiness to apply their energy and make use of their power for the sake of carrying out the three week fuel program, and that the population itself has also expressed its willingness to discharge its duty in lending its labor for the work of logging timber; also, that the tasks of the three week fuel program can be carried out only under conditions permitting quiet unhampered work, ... the Circuit Session places all the present material at the discretion of the regional Timber Committee, and while it refrains from passing any sentences in the case under consideration, the Court joins in the plea of the Chief of the Lumber Logging Works, as well as the delegates of all the volost of the region, about prolonging the three weeks to a new time limit to be set by the Timber Committee of the gubernia."

Here is a splendid illustration to the afore-mentioned quotation from the "Krasnaya Armiya" in respect to the Ishymsk rebellion, a splendid illustration of how "white-guardist," "bandit," "counterrevolutionary" peasant revolts are brought about. This document gives one an adequate idea of how peasants are driven toward resistance, the outbreak of which is then crushed by summary shootings, deportations and annihilation of entire villages. . . . .

By way of adding a few finishing touches to this picture, I shall adduce here one more instance—one of the innumerable instances— showing how Lenin was carrying out the policy of tax collections in 1921. "Here—he said— we shall not be able to get along without an apparatus of violence" . . . How this "apparatus of violence" was functioning in 1921, the year of the terrible famine, is exemplified by the typical instance which I cite presently: the collecting of the tax in one of the "gubernias" situated near Moscow (the Riazan gubernia).

"Our 'gubernia' is now in a very difficult situation in regard to food supplies. The entire grain tax would not suffice to cover the requirements for seeds let alone the feeding of the cities. It was therefore resolved to gratify the demand for seeds only on behalf of the very needy peasants, that is, only 10% of the general demand. All that notwithstanding, an order was received from the center to ship out as an emergency consignment 250 million poods of grain to the Volga region. There was no source which could yield that much grain. The Soviet State farms (the Sovkhoz) had nothing to give, payments on loans for seeds were hardly to be reckoned with as a source of supply. There remained only one source—and that is the grain tax. The commission was carried out. But how? It was worse than collecting the old tax-in-kind. The picture, as given by the data of the central body of the 'gubernia,' is as follows: at the village assemblies the peasants came out with statements to the effect that the tax had proved too burdensome for them. That was sufficient to cause the closing of such assemblies, as it was done in a number of counties; sweeping arrests of peasants especially in the county of Skopin, took place, whole batches of peasants having been dispatched under convoy to the city. Any petition for reduction of the levy, provided by the law, were not even given a hearing for the fear that any exemptions might endanger the program urged by the central authorities. Not only those who were delinquent in paying the levied tax but even those that were not prompt enough in doing it, were made to turn over their grain immediately, right from the barns, irrespective of whether they had enough left for seeds. That took place in several counties. In the aformentioned county —Skopin—as well as in a few others. It came to keeping the peasants, who failed to turn in their deliveries in full, shut up in the villages, barred even from going out to their fields unless they showed tax delivery certificates. In some counties the markets were closed up. It is clear that all those measures could not but aggravate the situation. Vast peasant throngs were besieging the Food Committees, demanding the whittling down of the levy.

In the county of Zaraysk martial law was declared in a number of villages. Special sessions of the Revolutionary Tribunals were held in many of those places. The agents of the grain collecting state organizations were sending out appeals for military detachments. Not only ordinary peasants but even members of the Central Executive Committees of Village Soviets were being rounded up. As a result there were many resignations from the Communist Party. It stands to reason that this campaign was attended by the rounding up of members of other parties, ostensibly for carrying on agitation against the grain tax. Such were the conditions under which the first installment of the grain collection was fulfilled. This was followed by a demand emanating from the center for 100,000 poods more. And now the prospects are that not enough grain will be left to cover elementary needs. Our leading figures have sent an emergency plea to Lenin and Briukhanov (the Soviet Food Commissar) begging them to ease up on the second installment, declining all responsibbility in case this is not done and demanding that armed forces be sent to the province."[292]

One can easily imagine the way the Special Session of the Revolutionary Tribunals dealt with the peasants. . . . . And this happened in the "gubernia" of Riazan only! How much blood was shed through the rest of Russia, how many peasants were killed off! In connection with that it is necessary to bear in mind what we wrote above about peasant revolts in the Tambov "gubernia" (headed by Antonov); of the unspeakable manner in which the authorities crushed those revolts, of the ghastly executions. That rebellion continued into 1921 and was crushed with even greater cruelty and frenzy.

**
*

Simultaneously with the sweep of terror there came upon the country the gruesome famine, which to a great extent was the result of Lenin's savage, terroristic and plundering food policy and not only of a drought and poor harvest, as it was given out by official statements. A ruined peasantry, robbed to its very last, cleaned out of its last supplies, found itself utterly helpless in face of a famine. It had no accumulated stocks to fall back upon, to sustain it during

---

[292] "Sotzial. Viestnik," p. 16, No. 4, February 23, 1922.

that terrible year and somewhat mitigate the consequences of the elemental calamity. But Lenin, as we saw, was not moved by this famine, for even the latter was viewed and approached by him only from the angle of his pivotal aim, which was—to retain power. The All-Russian Committee to Aid the Famine Victims, organized at one time with the aid of some socially-minded bourgeois elements (Socialists were not included in this committee) was soon dissolved, and its members were arrested or deported. Not being able to aid the famine victims with his own forces, Lenin at the same time prevented others from extending aid, fearing that the influence of the Socialist parties would thereby be strengthened. For the sake of such politics he doomed 30 million people of the city population to starvation, expecting to feed on the accumulated supplies, only 8 millions that "were absolutely necessary." But the peasants of the famine stricken provinces ran out of their grain supplies toward the beginning of the spring and were leading a life of frightful starvation, nearing a state where even cannibalism showed itself.

Thus, for instance, the Samara newspaper "Kommuna" ("the Commune") of August 25, 1921, contains a report filed with the Presidium of the All-Russian Central Executive Committee ("The Economic Crisis in the Samara Gubernia") which says:

"The peasants have been feeding on all kinds of substitutes since early in the spring. In the wooded section they lived on acorns and grass. Right now, however, acorns have become a luxury. The price of acorn flour is 120 thousand rubles a pood. (Note: that was before the official devaluations of Soviet money.) The peasants are ruthlessly slaughtering their cattle, using for food even the skin of the animals. All the marmots found on the fields have been eaten up, there are numerous cases of cats and dogs being used for food; young puppies are considered a delicacy. The drought burned the grass in many places. The population is now beginning to use for food roots, special sorts of clay and some sort of stone derived from peat. Here are some of the food substitutes used for food: chaff, horse-sorrel, the pith of sunflowers, birch tree cones and lima tree leaves, roots of forest hemp, clays with an admixture of ferrous acides. The Public Health Department formed a special research institute for the study of substitute foods. The use of those substitutes results in stomach ailments and death from starvation."

That was in August; and then, toward the winter, cases of cannibalism were already reported. . . . The peasants of the famine stricken provinces, in their frantic attempts to escape starvation, rushed into provinces that were not affected by the famine. But on the way they were met by military cordons who barred them from going any further, forcing them to return and thus dooming them to death from starvation.

Notwithstanding those conditions, Lenin dissolved the Committees to Aid the Famine Victims to which the bourgeois elements—but not the Socialist elements—were invited. Instead of calling upon each and everyone to aid in the struggle against the calamity, Lenin issued orders "to keep the Mensheviks in prison," that is, all the Socialists and Anarchists who, as will be seen from further reading, were being tossed about from one prison to the other.

Above all, the party must retain power. And what if half the population died of starvation, the main thing for Lenin was that the Party—that is, he himself—did not let slip its power. What, indeed, is the life of several millions compared to the triumph of Socialism ! . . .

The famine of 1921, according to official data, carried off 5,200,000 people, whose loss should be credited to Lenin's terror.[293]

*

In the cities the terror against workers and their organizations reached unusual scope and intensity, especially against Socialists and Anarchists, against those that were in prison or those that were still left at large. On March 5, disturbances took place in Moscow, at the Bromley Mills, (the fifth during the year) resulting in arrests of workers. On April 16 the authorities dispersed the convention of Metal Workers and Printers of the City of Vitebsk. In May, strikes caused by food shortages broke out in Briansk and other towns. In June, labor disturbances, caused again by the food situation, took place in Yekaterinoslav. In Moscow, the authorities broke up the Union of Chemical Workers; in September, they dissolved the Executive Board of the Union of Soviet Workers in Vologda. In August, the Bolshevik police bore down upon the workers of the Yuriev Plant and the miners of

---

[293] See "Narodnoye y Gosudarstvennoe Khoziaystvo" ("National and State Economy), published by the People's Commissariat of Finances, 1923, p. 5.

the Don Basin; in September, there were labor disturbances in Yaroslavl, accompanied by the arrest of six Anarchist sympathizers among the workers and ten non-partisans; in August, labor disturbances took place in Saratov; in October, in Smolensk and many other industrial centers. Every one of those disturbances and strikes were invariably attended by arrests and deportation of workers.

Characteristic of the Bolshevik policy in 1921 and indicative of its trends was the trial of the Saratov workers taking place on April 10, 1922, in connection with the "disorders" which broke out at the beginning of the year (1921).

On March 3, 1921, the workers of the Saratov railway shops struck in protest against the paring down of their starvation rations. In addition to this protest the workers also put forth demands of a political nature, such as: restoration of liberties, inviolibility of personal freedom, trade union autonomy. On March 4, acting upon the proposal of a Communist by the name of Zhouk, the workers elected a Central Committee for the purpose of checking up on the food storehouses. As supplemented by the proposal of the Saratov Trade Union Council, the original proposal stood for every factory of the city sending its representatives to this committee. Thus there came into existence a body of workers' control comprising 300 delegates, among whom only four were Communists. The Control Committee placed itself from the very beginning in the position of a *supreme* controlling organ, proceeding to inspect not only the food storehouses but government organs as well: the Food Supply Committee of the "gubernia", the Che-Ka, the prisons, etc.

The Communists were nonplussed by this sudden turn of events. The Committee kept on functioning for two weeks. Then came the expected finale: on one of those nights, presumably acting under orders from Moscow, the authorities carried out summary arrests of workers and members of the Committee—totaling several hundred of them. The prison cells became overcrowded; a harsh regime was established in all the prisons. All the members of the Control Committee were kept in prison for about six months, after which the less active ones were released, and the rest, numbering about forty people, were forwarded to Moscow, to the Taganka prison where they were kept under most dismal conditions until arraigned.

The trial was held in Moscow, notwithstanding the fact that their alleged "crime" took place in Saratov. Among the defendants were

representatives of all parties: Social-Democrats, Social-Revolutionists, Anarchist-Communists and ex-members of the Russian Communist
Party; most of the members, however, were non-partisans.

Altogether 31 people were arraigned on charges. The defendants
brought before the court presented a pitiful sight. They were so
weakened physically by the prison regime that the court permitted
them to testify in a seated, and some in a lying position. Witnesses
were not called.

The sentence meted out by the court was, with the exception
of four people, two and four years of forced labor. But this time—
a rather rare case in the annals of Soviet "Justice"—the sentence
was declared conditional; that is, they were all released, their preliminary confinement having been made to count for the entire term
of the sentence.

The workers of Saratov paid dearly for their attempt to apply
the idea of Soviet democracy: four people died in prison, nineteen
became invalids, five were ruined and their families doomed to a
starved existence.[294]

**

Lenin's slogans in 1921 eventuated in a wave of terror directed
against Socialist parties and Anarchist groups attended by unprecedented violence and intensity. It was seemingly resolved once for all
to make a clean sweep of those elements, to put them through the
dry guillotine, and even to shoot a few here and there. . . . .

Even prior to that the arrests of Anarchists and Socialists were
rather a common occurance. But then the arrests had their aim to
effect a general demoralization of those movements, and that is why
the arrested were not kept for a long period in prisons and Che-Ka
detention places: they were released, rearrested several times in
succession. For instance, the author of these lines, was arrested six
times during two years, in the interim between those arrests he was
constantly harassed by searchers on various pretexts.

In 1921 the situation changed: the arrested were not released
any more but were kept in prisons or were sent to concentration

---

294) This incident was described in "Sotzialistichesky Viestnik," No. 11,
June 3, 1922.

camps where they were subjected to dismal moral and physical conditions.

Kronstadt, Ishym, Georgia, famine, labor disturbances, the ever more frequent cases of the Communist failure to get support of the non-partisan conferences promoted by them at that time, signalized a steady and progressive drop in influence of the Communist Party. It was in order to keep this manifest drop in prestige from affecting the party control, in order to safeguard the interests of party absolutism, that the dry guillotine was put in action. And from that time this dry guillotine kept on working with unabated vigor.

In Russia there was not a single town left, a single industrial center, or any big settlement where sweeping arrests were not made of Mensheviks, Social-Revolutionists—right and left—Anarchists or any one implicated in those movements even to the slightest extend.

These arrests started as soon as the Bolsheviks began bombarding Kronstadt. A perusal of the contemporary non-Bolshevik party magazines published abroad that year, will show much correspondence telling of arrests taking place throughout the country. In Ukraine alone about 1400 Mensheviks were arrested at that time. There was no letup on searches which took place everywhere, in every nook and corner of the vast country. Not only people belonging to parties were subjected to arrest but all those who dared to have an opinion of their own. People were arrested for "anti-Soviet propaganda," for "Menshevism," for being "counter-revolutionists." The dossers of the cases of the arrested Socialists and Anarchists were emblazoned with the letters "C. R"— "counter-revolution". . . . . .

In order to ferret out the "culprits," the authorities began to apply on a vast scale the methods of the agent provocateurs; "inside information" that is, the entrance of Communists, as members, into various political organizations.

The Odessa Committee of the Social-Democratic Party printed in its Bulletin (No. 8-9) excerpts from the booklet *The sum total and the practice of the year's work of the Odessa Che-Ka* (published by the Che-Ka, February 1921 which we are using now as they were reprinted by the "Sotzialistichesky Viestnik." The booklet is, to a great extent, in the nature of a treatise on the sleuthing and agent provocateurs technic. Of special interest is the passage treating of the work of the agent provocateur.

"The work of gathering inside information in the Soviet institutions was proceeding in accordance with the plan of covering everyone implicated to any extend in cases involving deliquency in office. In a given case the agent would gradually track down the culprits, one after the other, beginning with the 'aces' and ending with the mere pawns in the crime game, thus reconstructing in detail a full picture of the particular crime under investigation. *Very often the agent would take part in the crime and even hold a position of trust and leadership in the crime conspiracy.* This work would demand close contact with the criminal to the extent of being able to ingratiate oneself into his confidence, and become an accomplice in the crime. Only such an approach enabled the agent to carry out the tasks facing the Head of the Intelligence Department. In the work of this Department in the struggle against espionage use must be made of all kinds of methods which enable one to get on the inside of the spy ring and work there in a position close to the focal point upon which all threads of the conspiracy converge. The practice of working along such lines already yielded noteworthy results. . . . . Agents of the Intelligence Department worked themselves into organizations and *even drew new members into it, those who were genuinely devoted to the cause of the organization.* But at the opportune moment, due to the trust enjoyed by its agents within the organization, the threads of the latter would be in the hands of the Intelligence Department and those who were to be moved from private apartments to prison quarters would be duly disposed of. . . . If in the work of shadowing, the main attention has to be directed upon the study of *make-up* and *costume,* the work of inside information demanded the knack of approaching people, to familiarizing oneself with the tricks of the criminal, the subterfuges of the profiteer, and in worming oneself into political parties one has to equip himself with a thorough knowledge of the *programs* of all parties and of human *psychology.* It is to be pointed out in this connection that on this basis the Department succecded in recruiting quite a number of valuable agents."

Such was the method of work not only of the Odessa Che-Ka, but of every Che-Ka, including the central body—the All-Russian Che-Ka.

It was by working in accordance with this method that, following our hunger strike in the Taganka prison, the All-Russian Che-Ka, aiming to frustrate the preparations for our deportation abroad, organized in Moscow a hold-up and arrested in conjuction with this "affair" a few of its "Anarchist" participants. Immediately our case was turned over from the Foreign Department to the Special Department of the Che-Ka and our wives were told that we would not be released from prison and that the order for our deportation was revoked. This provocation, however fell through. But the other one succeeded. . . . . .

In Moscow, the "Anarchists," that is the Che-Ka stoolpigeons, Steiner and others, obtained a small machine for counterfeiting and placed it in the apartment of Lev Cherny[295] who did not even try to find out what the whole thing was about. Cherny was soon arrested. A few days later were arrested Potiekhin, who was stricken with typhus, and Kashirin who escaped from his place of exile. They were charged with "counterfeiting" and "banditry."

A few days later were arrested in Moscow nine Anarchists who had escaped from the Riazan prison and also Ivan Gavrilov and Fanny Baron; and in the city of Orel was arrested A. Baron's brother, a Communist who was taking food to A. Baron and the other Anarchists that were kept in the Orel prison. All those were charged with "counterfeiting" and "banditry" and were shot without even having been brought up for trial on those charges.

There are solid grounds for the surmise that Cherny was not shot but tortured to death. And, of course, Steiner (Kamenny) and his co-workers were "miraculously" saved from the lot of the others and sent scot free.

On the whole, however, there was no need even for frame ups to carry on the sweeping arrests which frankly pursued the avowed aim of annihilating Anarchists and Socialists, of removing them from the scene of political activity with the aid of the wet or the dry guillotine.

---

295) LEV CHERNY (Turchaninov)—an Anarchist writer; was personally known as such to many prominent Bolsheviks. Kamenev, who knew him well, kept on assuring Cherny's mother and sister that he would be soon freed, that he—Kamenev—was pleading for him with the Che-Ka.

It is really difficult to see why the Bolsheviks needed those lives, especially the life of Cherny, a sick man and feeble in health. Those cases, however, are a good illustration of the way the instructions of the Che-Ka were being applied. It is a typical case of frame-up which was widely used throughout Russia.

Officially the arrests were motivated by the necessity of fighting "the counter-revolution," but there were motivations of a different character. Thus, for instance, in Sevastopol a worker by the name Movchan was arrested for "giving out official but underscored newspapers." The worker Romanov was arrested and sentenced to two years of concentration camps "for reading and commenting upon the very same papers." In the city of Vladimir a woman by the name of Sobolev was arrested and sentenced to two years of imprisonment in the Kostroma House of Correction "for illegally transmitting correspondence to a political prisoner, etc". . . . . In matters of persecution, surveillance and shadowing political suspects, the various Che-Ka bodies were not the only organizations in the field: they were aided by the Bolshevik trade unions, the organs of economic management and the various Commissariats.

Thus, for instance, the Yekaterinoslav Trade Union Council, proceeding from Lenin's maxim that "a good Communist is at the same time a good chekist," adopted a resolution transmitted to the Bureau of the Communist faction of the Southern Bureau of the All-Union Central Council of Trade Unions and to the Bureau of the Printers' Union.

"The Yekaterinoslav Section of the Printers' Unions has been up to now in the hands of the Mensheviks and together with the Poligraj hic Section of the Council of People's Economy, it serves as the organizational center of the Social-Democratic Party (Mensheviks).

'The endeavor of the Bureau of the Communist faction of the Union, and the Bureau of the Communist faction of the Yekaterinsolav Trade Union Council to wrest the control of the Unions from the hands of the Mensheviks proved difficult because of the lack of a sufficient number of active workers in the Communist factions of the Unions.

"The situation is favorable for the dispersal of the old Union Administration and the setting up of a Communist Administration.

"In order to carry out such measures it is necessary to implement the union with active Communist workers.

"We are requesting your aid through the Southern Bureau of the Central Committee of the Union of Printers.

"Secretary of Communist faction".296)

---

296) This document was reprinted in the "Sotzial. Viestnik," No. 4, February 23, 1922.

Another document, published in the same magazine (No. 5) was originally sent out by the Central Agronomic Administration in the form of a secretly coded telegram, "to all Communist factions of the Railwaymen's Unions" and enjoining those factions to work in the direction of inducing the Union of Railway workers to undertake the task of spying upon the active figures in the rural cooperatives:

"Give directives to road sections of the union as to placing a close watch over the work of the instructors of Rural Co-operative Section and secretly transmit information to Central Agronomic Administration."

The Commissar of Foreign Affairs, Chicherin, went even further; in a decree promulgated on May 11, 1921 (No. 4215) he threatened that "unauthorized leaving of Soviet service abroad as well as forfeiting Soviet citizenship in a manner not provided for by the Soviet law will be regarded as a breach of loyalty in respect to the Soviet Republic and will result in reprisals in regard to the families and nearest relatives of such persons who happen to reside in the territory of the U. S. S. R."

The entire country was turned into a prison. Terror dogged the arrested from one prison to the other, taking on a sadist character. The prisons were overcrowded. Hunger, exposure to cold, shocking anti-hygienic and anti-sanitary conditions, rude treatment, carping at the prisoners, introduction of superfluous and irritating "stringencies," the lack of adequate medical aid, interminable confinements with no charges filed and without trials, etc., up to slugging and shooting in the cell. All that became characteristic of Bolshevik prisons. Thus "the regime in the prison of Gomel (reported in "Sotzialistichesky Viestnik") is hideous and ghastly. Close to thirty people are crowded into every cell, the 'parasha' (the wooden excrement bucket) were not carried out from the cell, daily walks were confined to five minutes, and forced labor."

Not much better were conditions prevailing in the prisons of Petrograd, at that time the satrapy of Zinoviev.

"We are squeezed more and more, by continuing repressions; and there is a method to it, as if its aim were to provoke disturbances. Fortunately, up to now we succeeded in restraining the prisoners from letting themselves be provoked. Beginning with June 9, our cells have been tightly shut and no one of us has been allowed even to go out for an airing. At the same time there is an ever mounting tide of petty persecutions."

In Moscow, on April 25, at 4 A:M the Butirsky prison containing 300 politicals—Socialists and Anarchists— was invaded by a detail of armed Chekists who administered a frightful beating to the prisoners. Men and women were slugged; rifle buts, fists were freely used upon defenseless prisoners. Half-naked women were dragged by their hair and thrown down the steps. The Anarchists believing they were being led to be shot, fiercely resisted and as a result were severely beaten up. Semi-naked prisoners were carted into trucks and taken to railway stations to be shipped out into various cities: some to Orel, others to Yaroslavl, Vladimir and other places. The Moscow Soviet and Kamenev approved this action on the part of the chekists on the ground that . . . . "the prisoners were the attackers." (A detailed description of this frightful atrocity the reader will find in the remarkable book "Letters from Russian prisons".297)

The politicals had no other means of self-defense but to fall back upon moral pressure exerted via the time honored methods of self-destruction by starving themselves to death in sign of protest. There followed an epidemic of hunger strikes, dragging out to such long periods as were never witnessed under the Tzar's regime. We, the prisoners, viewing the Bolsheviks, all their misdeeds notwithstanding, as Socialists, erroneously believed that they still possessed some rudimentary sense of moral responsibility.

Under the Tzar there was some sort of public opinion, feared to some extent by the Tzar's government; and it feared even more the public opinion abroad. But the Bolsheviks annihilated the public opinion within the country; and as to the opinion abroad they felt that it could be easily hoodwinked by denying the fact of political persecutions, by representing any reports of such persecutions as lies fabricated by white guardists; they could easily get away with such denials because they were looked up to as the bearers of the revolution, who, it was felt abroad, simply could not act toward workers and Socialists in a manner attributed to them. And so the Bolsheviks completely ignored the hunger strikes.

---

297) "Letters from Russian Prisons,' published by the International Committee to Aid Political Prisoners; Albert and Charles Boni. New York, 1925

— 193 —

for nine days, the Anarchists and left-Revolutionists, thirteen days; the Che-Ka, however, completely ignored it, while Unshlikht declared: "let them die." Indeed, this was the avowed purpose of the dry guillotine. . . .

In the Taganskaya prison the Anarchists kept up their hunger strike eleven days and they won only because of the pressure of a rather unique "public opinion." The foreign delegates at the International Congress of Trade Unions, most of whom were revolutionary syndicalists, were drawn into this affair, having demanded from the Bolshevik government that charges be filed against the hunger strikers or that the latter be released. The government consented to release the Anarchists and have them deported. That was the first case of deportation abroad of Soviet citizens. The deported Anarchists, under the threat of the death penalty, were barred by the expulsion decree from returning to Soviet Russia.

In the city of Vladimir the strike took on a drawn out character . . . In sheer desperation two women, Lydia Surkova and E. Yegelskaya, during the hunger strike in the prison of Orel, made an attempt to set themselves on fire: they put fire to their mattresses and were dragged out from their cells half alive. They were revived with great difficulty. In Petrograd imprisoned workers, members of Anarchist organizations—Vladimir Novozhilov, Vasilyev and Gerasimchuk —kept up their hunger strike for 7-8 days . . . . . .

Following the hunger strike in the prison of Orel a regime of lawlessness came to prevail in the prison. The sentries shot at will into the cell windows, the result of which one of the prisoners— Barkash, a Social-Democrat—was wounded in the hand, the wound having proven sufficiently serious to demand amputation; another Social-Democrat—Shneerson—was wounded by fragments of broken glass. The soldier who wounded those prisoners was rewarded with a watch, as a result of which the rest of the soldiers began to look eagerly for the opportunity to obtain their "watches" in the same manner. The prisoners were literally starving; "the food was putrid, the fish has to be constantly cleaned from crawling worms." . . .

And at the same time shootings were proceeding apace throughout the country. Especially sweeping were those shootings in Crimea, Northern Caucasia and the Don Basin where the "green rebels" and their relatives were being shot in batches. The same was taking place in Ukraine, Turkestan, Siberia, Bashkyria.

On September 28, 63 people were shot in Odessa.[298] In Piatigorsk were shot 50 people;[299] in Kharkov—215 "Ukrainian hostages" also were shot.[300]

The "Izvestia" of the town of Zhitomir reports the shooting of 29 people; the group of Russian Anarchists reports in the pamphlet "The Persecution of Anarchists in Soviet Russia" (page 7) that in the town of Zhmerinka were shot from thirty to forty Anarchists; the group also reports the shooting of Anarchists in Odessa. The same group maintains that up to the end of 1921, 32 adherents of Tolstoy's teachings were shot for refusing to accept military service.

Vishniak (a prominent journalist and active figure in the Social-Revolutionary movement), in the preface to his book "The Black Year," adduces data as to the shootings in the month of June, taking place by way of carrying out the verdict of the Revolutionary Tribunals: in Moscow 748, in Petrograd 216, in Kharkov 418, in Yekaterinodar 315. The Social-Revolutionary paper "Golos Rosiyi" (The Voice of Russia) reports as it alleges, upon the basis of data given out by the Statistical Department of the Commissariat of Roads and Communications that the Railway Tribunals shot in 1921, 1759 passengers and employes. In Petrograd, in connection with the Tagantzev case, there were shot 61 people; among them the poet Gumiliev, also Professor Tikhvinsky who "at one time rendered important services to the Bolsheviks and in 1905 even kept in his place bombs and arms of the Bolshevik militants".[301]

In Yekaterinburg, as reported by "Revoliutzionnaya Rossiya" ("Revolutionary Russia")[302] following the escape of six people the Chief of the Department of Forced Labor, Ouranov, drew up the officers in a line and picked out 25 of them to be shot.

---

298) "Izvestia," No. 217.

299) "Pravda," No. 81.

300) These figures are taken from Melgunov's book which quoted them from "Frankfurter Zeitung," the latter reprinted those items from the Russian papers.

301) F. Dan, "Two Years of Wandering," p. 188.

302) No. 12-13, 1921.

But shootings were only a part of the comprehensive program of terror. Those were only the victims of the wet guillotine, but the dry guillotine worked just as effectively, its "yield" was of sustained character and it is continuing into our own time.

Let us take the city of Petrograd and trace the workings of this guillotine.

"On the night of February 23, 1921, was arrested the first party of workers of 70 people. Toward February 26, the number of arrested people reached 400-460; there were no more than 60 intellectuals in that group. This wave of arrests kept on mounting from day to day. In the House of Detention the number of inmates mounted from 800 in February to 2300 in May.

"The victims of the Che-Ka were mostly workers: from February up till fall this prison housed the Kronstadters, members of non-partisan labor conferences and workers arrested during the Soviet elections (the purpose of those arrests was to intimidate the voters) numbering from 1200 to 1500 people.

"But this does not exhaust the list of the victims of the Zinoviev regime. Following the Kronstadt events, about 2000 sailors and other Kronstadters were sent through the Novo-Cherkask barracks where a certain 'three man committee to liquidate the revolt' was holding court. The judicial procedure of this three-man court reduced itself to filing a printed form with the name of the defendants and the writing out of sentences of from three to five years. The list of those victims comprised many Kronstadt Communists who handed in their resignation from the Party. Many of the Kronstadters were shot, but the bulk of them 1800 people, were exiled to do forced labor in Murmansk and other dismal places.

"About four hundred of them were kept in the second and third concentration camps, where conditions were just frightful. Almost every one of them was sick with scurvy. The hospital admitted only those that were falling off their feet. The writer of these lines witnessed scenes of starved inmates avidly eating accacia pods, boiling the leaves of bird-cherry trees; and the stunted horse-sorrel that was growing within the prison yard was regarded as a delicacy. Women were ready to sell themselves for a bread ration (half a pound of bread), but the supply greatly exceeded the demand.

"This, however, was not all. In June 3000 sailors and Red Army men who escaped to Finland trekked back to Soviet Russia.

They were promised amnesty, and so for several months they lived under prison conditions in the various barracks and prisons of Petrograd. Altogether during that year more than 6,500 politicals went through the prisons of Petrograd. Those that survived were released toward the end of the year, save those who appeared mentally alert and intelligent to the ignorant Che-Ka agents. Of such there were about 200".303)

Here are a few items taken from the pamphlet *"The prison situation in 1921. The report of the Commissariat of Justice to the Ninth All-Russian Convention of Soviets."* 304)

At the disposal of the Central Correction Department of the Commissariat of Justice were 267 Houses of Detention with a capacity for 60,468; actually, however, they housed 73,193 inmates, that is, on the average 107 inmates per 100 available places; but in 36 Houses of Confinement there were 254 persons per 100 available places. "There is quite a number of prison houses where the density coefficient reaches the figure of 300 and more. Out of the total of prison inmates 47% are under investigation, 2.5% are to be re-routed to other prisons, and only 50.1% have been convicted. 61.4% of the prisoners are in the charge of the organs of 'extraordinary justice'—the Che-Ka and the Revolutionary Tribunals.

"The prisons are not being repaired, they are greatly over-crowded in many cases two and three times over their normal capacity; because of fuel shortage the prisons are hardly heated at all; the prison inmates do not get any underwear, linen, clothes, shoes and are hardly fed: in many places the entire ration contains half or a quarter of a pound of bread per day."

What were the results of these officially described conditions?

In the Ufa prison from 7 to 10 people die every day from mere "inanition"; in the prison of the town of Busuluck a state of torpor set in as a result of "inanition," everywhere sickness is on the up-grade and typhus is rampant as a result of starvation. Who knows how many thousands, or rather tens of thousands of lives have been carried away by the dry guillotine, and shall we ever find out? . . . .

---

303) "Sotzialistichesky Vestnik," No. 7, April 3, 1922.
304) Moscow, printing shop of the Taganka prison, 32 pages.

But this does not exhaust the entire prison population of Russia; the aforementioned figures have to be doubled or trebled in order to arrive at the real number of the prison population of that year. We have to add to those totals the number of prisoners kept in cellars, prisons and other places of confinement maintained by the Che-Ka; likewise we are to add those kept in the houses of confinement of the Transport Che-Ka, the militias and improvised "prisons" in the regions of peasant disturbances and revolts—barns, sheds, pits and just any open places enclosed with barbed wire. . . . .

What was the answer of the Bolsheviks to this report? They reestablished the policy of the Tzar's government by way of restoring deportations and exile places, they turned the Solovetzky and Susdal monasteries into prisons, they built up concentration camps in Pertominsk, Kholmogori and other places.

Beginning with 1921 the Tzar's exile was restored and its geographic boundaries greatly expanded. The first victims of this new policy were young Anarchist girls, students of the Moscow University—Isayeva, Ganshina and Sturmer, who were deported to the Arkhangelsky district for one year; it is a long year—for it has not ended yet. Following this first deportation, another group consisting of opposition Communists—followers of the sailor Paniushkov—were exiled to the Vologda region.

To the Socialists and Anarchists this newly introduced political deportation meant a veritable vicious circle, broken only by death. From prison to exile and back, from exile to prison: once caught in this vicious circle, there was no way out but to continue swinging along this ghastly merry-go-round. The vast majority of politicals who were arrested in 1920-1921 still "stay put" within this vicious circle.

Is it possible to obtain even an approximate idea as to the total number of people shot during this terror, that is, apart from those that were killed during the revolts and those that died in the prisons?

The famine and its victims could be laid to the door of the terroristic policy of former years: the official estimate of such victims is 5,200,000. We can only guess as to the number of people that were shot, it being difficult now to unearth official figures pertaining to this bloody statistic.

Taking into consideration the Kronstadt and the Izhma revolts, the conquest of Georgia, the crushing of revolts in Turkestan and Bashkirya, the peasant rebellions brought about by the food policy, and also the violent, beastly struggle against the Ukrainian Insurrectionary troops, and also against the "green rebel troops," we must arrive at the conclusion that the year of 1921 was the bloodiest year. The number of executed people, judged by the most conservative estimates equals from thirty to forty thousand. . . . An equal number, judging from the report of the Commissariat of Justice, perished in prisons, concentration and forced labor camps. We have thus 70 thousand direct victims of the government terror; altogether, Lenin's policy cost the country in the year of 1921 the lives of 5,300,000. . . . A rather gruesome total!

And now we shall pass to the last years of Lenin's life and activity—the years of 1922-1923. We are coupling them together because in 1923 Lenin was already sick and could not devote himself any longer to the "building up of Socialism."

CHAPTER IX

THE TERROR IN THE LAST YEARS OF LENIN'S LIFE
(1922-1923)

In the preceding year, as we already saw, Lenin, Trotzky and the Communist Party drowned Kronstadt in blood, having dubbed it "white-guardist" and "counter-revolutionary," a place "run by White Generals and agents of the Entente." The entire country was drowned in the blood of peasants and rebels. Workers were arrested in thousands, the Bolshevik authorities going as far as shooting many of the arrested workers. Strike movements among workers and peasants unrest were represented as the underhand work of the "counter-revolution, white-guardist forces, Mensheviks and Social-Revolutionists." It was on the ground of such fabrication that the authorities devoted themselves during that year to the ferreting out of socialists and anarchists throughout the country and to the settling of bloody accounts with them.

This "unpleasant situation" having been overcome by way of fiercely crushing the thinking and independent elements of the country, Lenin came to feel himself securely seated in the Kremlin position of power, sufficiently so as to permit himself the luxury of speaking out candidly, or to be more precise, brazenly and shamelessly. Appearing at the fourth congress of the Communist International, November 13, 1922, he said the following, thereby exposing himself and his policy of the preceding year:

". . . . . In the year of 1921, after we had gone through the most important phases of civil war, which ended successfully, we came across a big—I should say, the biggest—internal political crisis of Soviet Russia. This inner crisis brought to the surface the wide dissatisfaction pervading not only among considerable layers of peasants, but also of workers. This was the first (by far not the first—G. M.) and I hope the last time in the history of Soviet Russia when large masses of peasants—not consciously, but rather instinctively—were against us."305)

---

305) N. Lenin, "Sobranie Sochineniy," "Five Years of the Russian Revolution and the Perspectives of a World Revolution," p. 90, vol. XVIII, part 2.

"In the year of 1921 we were doubtlessly confronted with dissatisfaction on the part of an overwhelming section of the peasantry. And then we had the famine".306) "During one year (the year of the new economic policy G.M.) the peasantry not only coped successfully with the famine, but also paid up the food tax to such a large extent that by now we already have millions of poods of grain, all of which has been obtained without the use of compulsion. Peasant revolts, which determined the general picture of Russia prior to 1921, have altogether dissappeared. We can now safely say that the peasantry is content with prevailing conditions".307)

Lenin, in this case, of course, lied in the most shameless manner. The peasants did not cope with the famine: they were just dying off, abandoned to their fate by Lenin and his government. There was nothing in the actual situation to warrant the optimistic statement made by Lenin: during that very same period the A. R. A. (American Relief Administration) was still busily feeding the famine victims.

"The A. R. A. worked in 12 regions embracing 32 'gubernias,' where it fed adults and children in the eating houses opened by it in the famine-stricken regions: in December 1921 it fed 1,029,376 people, in February 1922—1,562,230, in April—5,712,008, in June—8,876,139, in July—10,387,688. Beginning with that time the number fed by the A. R. A. rapidly dropped off (the number fed by the A. R. A. but not the total of starving people.—G.M.) and toward December this number reached the low of 982,920. In 1923 this number rose again, reaching in April the total of 2,629,952".308)

Nothwithstanding the fact that the famine had not yet been lived down, the levying of the food tax was carried out with as much brutality as it was in 1921. Beaten down by famine and cowed by the use of overwhelming military forces, the peasantry lost its capacity to protest; it kept silent and it was this silence that Lenin took for contentment and prosperity: "it is silent because it is prosperous," said Taras Shevchenko (famous Ukrainian poet) about the Tzar's Russia.

306) Ibid, p. 92.
307) Ibid.
308) N. Lenin, "Sobranie Sochineniy," notes p. 225, vol. XVIII, part 2.

Lenin had no scrupples in handing out the same lie about workers to the members of the Fourth Congress of the Comintern: "the light industry is on the upswing and there is an undeniable improvement in the position of the workers of Petrograd and Moscow. In both cities there was unrest among workers in the spring of 1921. Now it is completely gone. We who follow closely the mood of the workers, we cannot err on this question." 309)

There was an element of truth in this statement made by Lenin. Indeed, the mood of the workers was watched very closely, as a result of which, as we already have seen, thousands of workers went to prisons and concentration camps, and terror hung over the rest; under those conditions it was rather difficult to raise the voice of protest and lay one's needs before the government. But in spite of that the workers succeeded in breaking the silence.

Thus in 1922 Lenin himself publicly admitted that in 1921 he had used lies, slander and other criminal means in his campaign against workers and peasants. One would expect that in face of such admissions Lenin would make an attempt to give up the old methods of governing and begin to use cultured and civilized methods instead of terror. Vain hopes! Swayed by dictatorial Marxist ideas, driven along by a consuming passion for power, he could not, even if he wanted, embrace the course of civilization and humanity without renouncing the Marxist doctrine which in practice always becomes a blend between the Tartar knout and the Prussian barrack, that is, compulsion and discipline.

It was just the reverse of what one might have expected. In 1922, Lenin expanded the sphere of application of the knouts, having included into it—following in this case the inexorable logic of his ideas—his own party: the crushing of the Workers' Opposition, the silencing of Miasnikov, the followers of Paniushkov and other malcontents in the party. We remember how Lenin jusified his terroristic policy by arguing that it was forced upon him by the Entente intervention; we tried to show the speciousness of this argument by pointing out the premeditated character of Lenin's terroristic

---

309) N. Lenin, "Five Years of the Russian Revolution and the Perspectives of a World Revolution," p. 94, vol. XVIII, part 2.

policy conceived as an integral part of his program of seizure of and staying in power.

In 1918, when reproached with the use of terror, Lenin's tactic was to deny the latter, but in 1922 he openly admits it, without finding it necessary to fall back upon the much abused Entente argument as a justification for inagurating and maintaining this policy.

"You (Kerensky and his partisans—M. G.) challenged us to a most desperate struggle in October; we answered that challenge with terror, a threefold terror, and if it be necessary, if you force us to it, we will inagurate that policy again".310) And so terror was pushed to the fore time and time again, especially in 1921 when Lenin was making his retreat.

"When an army is forced to make its retreat, machine guns are placed in the rear of the army (the Bolsheviks did so during their retreat from Warsaw—G. M.) and if this regular retreat turns into a stampede, the command issues the order to shoot. And rightly it does so."

And since in 1921 Lenin's retreat turned into a stampede, he gave orders to shoot, not at the retreating Communists but at the Socialists, Anarchists, workers and peasants. And there was no hesitation in carrying out those orders.

"When certain people, who may even be guided by the best possible motives, begin to sow panic just at the time when we are carrying out a retreat beset with vast difficulties, at a time when it is vitally important to retain good order in retreating, it it necessary to punish severely, ruthlessly, the slightest violation of discipline not only in regard to some of our intra-party affairs, but— one has to keep this in view— in regard to the Mensheviks and the gentlemen from the Second and a Half International."311)

Note, not toward the bourgeoisie and the capitalists, but toward Socialists—"yellow" Socialists, it is true—but Socialists and workers nevertheless.

---

310) N. Lenin, "Speech at the Session of the Communist Faction at the All-Russian Convention of Metal Workers," March 6, 1922, p. 12, vol. XVIII, part 2.

311) "A Report on the Work of the Central Committee of the Communist Party made at the XI Party Convention," March 27, 1922; p. 37-38, vol. XVIII, par 2.

" . . . . Otto Bauer, from whom at one time we learned a great deal, after the war became, like Kautsky, a wretched philistine. Now he writes: 'there they are retreating toward capitalism, but we always said—the revolution was only bourgeois in character.'

"And then the Mensheviks and Social-Revolutionists who advocated such views wonder when we tell them that we are going to shoot them for saying such things. They are amazed at it, but the question is clear: when an army is in retreat, it stands in need of discipline a hundred times more severe than when it advances because in the latter case everyone is eager to rush ahead. But if now everyone is just as eager to rush back, the result will be a catastrophe.

"And when a Menshevik says: 'you are now retreating but I was always favoring a retreat, I am in full accord with you, I am one of your people, let us retreat together,' we tell them in reply: an avowal of Menshevik views should be punished by our revolutionary courts with shooting, otherwise the latter are not courts but God knows what.

"Indeed, what Otto Bauer and other leaders of the Second and a Half Internationals, the Mensheviks and Social-Revolutionists now keep on saying, constitutes their veritable nature: 'the revolution went too far; we were always saying what you are now saying; let us now repeat it again.' But our answer is: if you don't refrain from openly enunciating such views, you will be put against the wall, for if you insist upon airing your political views under the present circumstances when we are finding ourselves in an even more difficult situation then at the time of the white-guardist invasion, we shall have to treat you as the worst and most harmful white-guardist elements".312)

This terroristic raving of a madman, the raving of a maniac, was the call to the physical extermination of Socialists and Anarchists; to the extermination not only of rightwing Socialist elements but also Left Socialists. "Mensheviks" and "Social-Revolutionists" were generic terms which Lenin used as synonims for "malcontents." And, soon we shall see the Bolsheviks concoct the famous Moscow case of the Social-Revolutionists, whose blood was demanded by Lenin, Trotzky, Bukharin, Stalin and the entire Communist leadership. By threatening and exerting undue pressure upon

312) Ibid, p. 38.

the workers, the Communists forced the latter to demonstrate and demand the heads of the Social-Revolutionists. . . . On the following day Lenin declared in his closing speech, in which he replied to Shliapnikov, who took Lenin's reference to machine-guns as an implied threat at the opposition group:

"When we speak of machine-guns, we have in mind people who call themselves Mensheviks and Social-Revolutionists and who jump at the conclusion that, forsooth, we speak about retreating to capitalism and they say exactly the same: 'We fully agree with you. . . .'

"We hear it drummed into our ears, and abroad a gigantic agitation is going on to the effect that the Bolsheviks want to keep the Mensheviks and Social-Revolutionists in prison, but at the same time they themselves admit capitalism. Of course, we do admit capitalism but within the confines necessary to the peasants. We have to do it! Without that the peasant cannot get along nor can he carry on his economy. But, we maintain, he can get along very well without the Menshevik and Social-Revolutionary propaganda. And to those that maintain the opposite we say: we will rather perish than yield on this point. And our courts must clearly realize it. While we change from the Che-Ka to political state courts, we must tell at the convention that we don't recognize courts that allegedly stand above classes. We should have now elected proletarian courts and those courts must know firmly what state capitalism is."313)

In a word: the Mensheviks policy should be worked with Bolshevik hands, but Mensheviks should be kept in prison or should be shot. Likewise, those that expose this policy—the Anarchists and Left Social-Revolutionists—should be kept in prison or be shot.

To keep all and everyone in prison when Lenin is on the offensive, and to keep them there when he retreats. . . .

In 1922, the party line was laid down and it was carried over into the year of 1923, by which time Lenin, who was stricken by illness, ceased to take an active part in the work of the state and the party. Bedridden, he had to confine himself to the role of an observer of the workings of the apparatus created by him. During the year of 1923, Lenin made no speeches and only now and then would he write key articles for the "Pravda" setting the main

---

313) p. 61, vol. XVIII, part 2.

lines for the solution of questions under discussion. In the "Pravda" of May 26 was printed his last article "On co-operation" which was in the nature of a testament. Lenin ends it with the following words:

"We are now faced with two principal tasks which sum up our epoch. This is the task of revamping our apparatus, which is absolutely of no use and which we took over from the former epoch".314)

But even on his sickbed, when he was feeling the approach of death, Lenin remained as terroristic and police-minded as before, still continuing to think and seek solutions to pressing problems in terms of compulsion, detection and espionage. Thus, in speaking of the Central Control Committee and preparing its members to struggle against bureaucracy and red-tape, Lenin had nothing but the following:

"The members of the Central Control Committee will have to prepare themselves for the kind of work which I would not hesitate in qualifying as the one of catching people who are not exactly scoundrels but something of that kind, and are devising all kinds of stratagems in order to camouflage their campaign and approaches, etc. In the institutions of Western Europe such proposals would call forth unheard of resentment, it would arouse the feeling of moral indignation, but here, I hope, we have not become that bureaucratic as to react in such a manner".315)

And that sums up the entire Lenin: his moral aspect, his entire philosophy, emanating from a mentality which is much akin to that of a policeman.

**
*

Thus Lenin continued to call for "pogroms" against Anarchists and Socialists, doing it with even greater intensity than in 1921. Now he openly called for executions of Mensheviks and Social-Revolutionists. And a call issued by Lenin meant in practice a command. How did the dry guillotine work during the last two years of Lenin's life? How was Lenin's command carried out in practice? Let us now turn from theory of terror to its description in practice.

The terroristic practice of 1922 did not differ much from that of 1921, and it proceeded along the same route: struggle against

314) P. 145, vol. XVIII, part 2.
315) "Rather Less But Better," March 4, 1923, p. 131, vol. XVIII, part 2.

workers, struggle against peasants for more grain, finishing off the insurrectionary movement and the "green" bands, purging the country from Socialists and Anarchists. This purge, as is known, was initiated in 1921, but in the following year certain changes were introduced which somewhat modified the nature of this struggle. Since it was rather impossible openly to shoot Anarchists and Socialists for the fear of releasing a powerful wave of resentment and mass protests abroad—and the Bolsheviks did not altogether relish such international repercussions—the authorities reverted to the dry guillotine as a way of annihilating their political opponents. They restored political banishment, exiling politicals to most dismal places; the concentration camps were built on sites which, together with the frightful regime, worked powerfully to decimate the inmates through illnesses and unspeakable privations.

In the prisons, conditions were such that hunger strikes as a way of protest were a common occurance. The Bolsheviks deliberately prolonged those hunger strikes which worked havoc with the prisoners health and nervous system. Generally, those hunger strikes finished off the prisoners, after weeks of painful hunger they would be dispatched to all sorts of dismal places or to concentration camps. In a word, the policy toward Socialists and Anarchists was that of physical extermination. But the wet guillotine was working alongside of the dry guillotine. Shootings—with and without trial—were still carried on, although less intensivly than in 1921.

**
*

On February 10, 1922, the All-Russian Che-Ka was abolished, having been supplented by the G. P. U. (The State Political Administration). The aim of this reform was to establish legal procedure instead of arbitrary rule via administrative fiat. But this reform which came in response to the exigencies of foreign policy and partly to the urgent need of domestic appeasement, proved just as much of a fraud and a comedy as the abolition of the death penalty previous to that. Only the initials changed, but the rest remained the same: the G. P. U. continuing the work of the Che-Ka as if nothing had really changed. Shootings without trial were still going on as before and the degree to which they were applied depended only upon the G. P. U. decisions. The difference between the Che-Ka lay only in the greater reserve shown by the G. P. U. publishing the list of its victims. Not that the Che-Ka was given to much publicity but the G. P. U. went much further in this respect than the Che-Ka. It was very seldom that the list of people shot by the G. P. U. were ever published, which means that it is much more difficult to reconstruct the true picture in respect to the shootings practiced by the G. P. U.

In the first place, of course, people were shot for "counter-revolution," for "banditry" and then for graft and embezzlement; the former "whites" were shot for having been in the white-guardist movement; participants of the white-guardist movement and the former insurrectionary troops, lured by promises of amnesty, were shot upon returning from abroad; peasants were shot for voicing their protests at the manner in which taxes were being collected; workers, for taking part in strikes. In addition to all those cases differing not much from the ones of preceding years, there were the cases pertaining to the "counter-revolution of the Church," that is disturbances arising in conjunction with the confiscation of church property. Persons found guilty of taking part in those disturbances were arraigned before the Revolutionary Tribunals which often passed death sentences in those cases; and there were not a few cases of that kind having been settled in the customary way of shooting the defendants without even a court hearing: an administrative order sufficed for that. Thus, for instance, 11 people, with the Metropolitan Veniamin at the head, were sentenced to death in Petrograd, June 5, on charges of carrying on agitation against confiscation of church valuables and property. Altogether, there were 86 people indicted on the same charges. The All-Russian Central Executive Committee confirmed the sentence in the case of the Metropolitan and four other defendants. In the month of May a similar trial was held in Moscow: fifty four people were indicted and twelve of them were sentenced to die; six of those receiving the highest penalty, were shot.

Similar trials were held in many cities of the country, every trial ending with some of the defendants being sentenced to be shot. How many were shot during that year on charges of conducting agitation against confiscation of church property is rather difficult to ascertain. At any rate the number of such victims was not confined to a few hundreds.

Blood was shed unsparingly in criminal cases and even more so in cases involving "counter-revolution" and "banditry" which also included the cases of insurgents and peasant unrest, etc. There were dozens of shootings taking place in conjunction with those cases.

Very characteristic is the case of M. D. Shishkin, a Social Revolutionist.

"The Social-Revolutionist Shishkin who was kept in the Lefortovskaya prison of Moscow, was suddenly conveyed to the Revolutionary Tribunal, without being given a chance to acquaint himself with the indictment, and was sentenced to be shot; the sentence was to be carried out within 24 hours. The convicted man was brought back to prison. The Social-Democrats who were kept in the same prison (B. Vasilyev, Lockerman, Melsitov and Petrenko) found out about this verdict and "kidnapped" the convicted man into their cell. The authorities were thrown into a panic; they fell to threatening and even summoned troops in order to enforce their threats, but for some reasons they refrained from shooting. The relatives of the convicted and his attorneys kept vigilant watch near the prison.

"And thus for a few days the Social-Democratic prisoners kept on defending with their own lives the life of the convicted Social-Revolutionists, while the case was taken up for review by the Presidium of the All-Russian Central Executive Committee. The issue of this appealed case still remains unknown." [316]

Shishkin's crime consisted in keeping printing type and seals in his place; also it was a fact that he had been a member of the Constituent Assembly and a Social-Revolutionist by party affiliations— that constituted his "major guilt" in the eyes of the judges. Shishkin escaped execution: he was exiled to Vologda where he was re-arrested and deported abroad together with the rest of the "seditious intellectuals" numbering 200 people. That was the third and the last —with the exception of the deportation of Trotzky—deportation of politicals abroad.

Lenin as we already saw, boasted before the delegates of the Fourth Comintern Congress that the collecting of the tax-in-kind was proceeding without compulsion and violence and that the peasants were content with their position, that they coped successfully with the famine and that peasant unrest and rebellions had ceased completely. This, of course, was a deliberate lie, and we gave ample

---

316) "Sotzialistichesky Viestnik," No. 120, October 19, 1922.

proof of it in the previous chapter. The tax-in-kind was collected this year in the same way in which the "prodrasverstka"317) was collected in the previous years, resulting in the same kind of peasant unrest, necessitating the use of military force, arrests, shootings, deportations.

In order not to repeat myself I will adduce here an illustration, typical of the year of 1922, of the way in which the agricultural tax was collected in one of the provinces near Moscow: the "gubernia" of Tula.

"Something is going on here which the population has not seen for the last six years of Bolshevik dictatorship. The 'gubernia' is flooded with detachments which ruthlessly exact the agricultural tax. The harvest this year was very poor and the population itself is faced with starvation, but in spite of that the latter is made to part with the very last it has. The slightest resistance, a mere argument or pointing out at some error in calculation of the assessing agencies, is likely to result in immediate arrest. The rural jails are jammed with people.

"The time limit set for the turning in of the tax was of unusually short duration. The peasant had first to mow and thresh the grain to be turned in for the tax and then go back to finish up the harvesting of the rest of the grain. Not to turn in the tax in time resulted in immediate arrest. At the very height of the harvest when literally every hour is of utmost value to the peasants, the latter were made to waste two days in waiting for their turn to pay their tax, in addition to which they were made to participate in demonstrations. The taking in of the grain tax, which is washed with the peasants tears, is turned into a festive occasion: red flags are waving, the portraits of Marx and Lenin are carried around, the orchestra fires away at the 'International' and the speaker announces to the peasants the triumph of world communism. . . .

"The impression created is that some one tries very hard to finish

---

317) The real meaning of "Prodrasverstka" is distribution or division of food. In this particular case it means the distribution or division of the tax. The peasantry was obliged by the Government to deliver for the State a certain quantity of grain and other agricultural products. The Government summarily prescribed to the lowest administrative village unit to deliver for the State, as the tax, for example, 10,000 bushels of grain, this tax the peasants were supposed to divide among themselves according to their only judgment.

off and utterly ruin the peasant economy, styling it at the same time 'establishing a closer bond with the peasants'." [318]

The above account can be extended to cover the entire country, with the exception perhaps, of 32 famine stricken "gubernias," all of which is indeed, a fitting illustration of Lenin's policy of "establishing close bonds with the peasantry." One can easily imagine the extent of arrests made in connection with the levying of the tax: and in many places the scenes ennacted in the Tula province were attended by bloodshed and shootings.

Workers unrest which started prior to the Kronstadt "rebellion" continued straight through the year of 1921; nor did it vanish in 1922.

In 1922 the metal workers of the Southern region came out on strike demanding seven gold roubles a month, instead of the current wage of five rubles. . . . There were also strikes of metal workers in Sormovo, in Briansk (60 thousand of them) protesting wage cuts. There were strikes in various industries of Odessa, of printers in Yekaterinoslav; there were strikes in Kharkov, in Oriekhovo-Zouyevo (12 thousand), in Moscow and a number of other industrial cities. In Kiev, during the retrenchment period, the first to be fired were the elements of political opposition. In Kharkov the Bolsheviks locked out 2500 workers from the railway shops, after which they organized a committee for rehiring workers, consisting of the Superintendent of the Shops, the Commissar and a representative of the G. P. U. It is clear that politically unreliable workers were not taken back to work. In Odessa "the retrenchment" took on a pronounced political character, "active Mensheviks" having been cleaned out during those cuts in personel; in Kharkov the Trade Unions of the Don Basin put in operation several "blacklists." In Moscow, the Union of Trolley men lent its aid in arresting 38 motormen and conductors. In the Troyitzk Munition Factory, situated in one of the Moscow suburbs, the director of this factory, Saltykov, set up a regular prison for the workers who were locked up for the slightest "back talk" and for manifesting a "too free and easy attitude." In Yekaterinodar, at the Chemical Works, the following resolution was passed (Oct. 30, 1922) on the question of celebrating the five year anniversary of the October revolution: . . . . "those who fail

318) "Sotzialistichesky Viestnik," p. 13, No. 20, October 19, 1922.

to show up at the celebration are to be fined with the sum amounting to their wages for three days, which sum is to be donated to schools affiliated with the Union of Chemical Workers. . . . Following the celebration, a dinner is to be arranged, for which purpose the workers are to turn in one day pay."

A Menshevik worker by the name Plaxin refused to comply with this decision. As a result of that:

"The meeting is unanimous in its decision to oust Plaxin from the factory." The Management Board of the Union resolved: "to approve the minutes of the general meeting. Orders were immediately given to that effect. At the meeting of the Commnist faction of the union, it was resolved to expel Plaxin from the union, to publish this decision in the papers and put his name upon the black board."[319]

In Tula "technical causes" . . . . resulted in cuts which mainly affected the "politically unreliable" elements. . . . The unemployed, numbering several thousand people, found themselves in a tragic position. Negotiations were opened with the District Committee of the Communist Party. The joint session of the Communist Party Committee and the unemployed was set for June 21, but on the 17th, immediately after preliminary negotiations, the authorities arrested and imprisoned close to 20 of those unemployed. Several months prior to that, in the month of April, the authorities of the same city arrested about 20 railway workers; the latter were kept in the same prison in which the unemployed workers were confined. When released from prison, the workers of Tula were made by the Che Ka to sign the following "yellow dog" contract:

"Signed pledge by the workers of the Munition Factory. . . . March. . . .

"I herewith sign in pledge of: 1) In entering employment at the Munition Works, I shall discharge my duties at the factory in the most conscientious manner, trying to obtain the best and utmost results in production; 2) I pledge in good faith not to participate in any attempt to begin or to carry on a strike movement or in any attempt to reduce or lower the productivity at the factory; 3) I herewith undertake not to take part in any rally or meeting which

---

319) "Rabochy Khimik" (the "Chemical Worker"), the organ of the Central Committee of the All-Russian Union of Chemical Workers, December 26, 1922.

may lead to a strike or the lowering of productivity at the factory; 4) In case I fail to carry out loyally the aforementioned provisions, I will declare, as prompted by my own sense of justice, that the Soviet government should apply in my case, the case of a rank traitor to the cause of workers and peasants, the harshest measures of repression".320)

There was no need of such terror-extorted pledges to apply repressive measures: they were widely used without such statements. Every disturbance among workers, every strike was invariably attended by sweeping arrests, imprisonments and deportation of workers. In the "Materials of Labor Statistics" we find some information about strikes during that period. It turns out that in Russia proper, that is outside of Ural, Ukraine and the Don Basin, where the strike movement was especially strong, there were 110 strikes with 43,000 workers participating in those strikes (we saw already that in Briansk alone the number of striking workers reached 60,000) that, of course, leaves out of account disturbances which did not eventuate into strikes but which nevertheless were attended by numerous arrests. If we include Ural, Ukraine and the Don Basin, we can safely maintain that the number of strikes was three times bigger than those given in the official "materials." And, again, proceeding from the most conservative estimate which places on the average 15 arrests per strike, we arrive at the conclusion that labor strikes resulted in the arrest of 5000 workers. . . .

As to the persecutions of Anarchists and Socialists one can say that the year of 1922 saw no abatement in the vigor with which they were carried on. If there was any slackening in this respect as compared with the preceding year, that was entirely due to the fact that an ever diminishing number of Anarchists and Socialists could be found at large. Simultaneously with the launching of new arrests, the terror against the Socialists and Anarchists was transferred to the prison itself. or to the exile places and concentration camps.

The most striking attempt to annihilate physically the Socialists was made by launching the famous trial of the Social-Revolutionists. This attempt was unparalled in the past in cynicism and vindictiveness, and it was bound to release a wave of protest all over the civilized world.

---

320) This document was published in "Sotzialistichesky Viestnik," No. 17, Sept. 8, 1922.

Responding to the blood-thirsty calls on the part of Lenin for vigorous action against the Mensheviks and Social-Revolutionists, the Bolshevik government decided to liquidate in a "legal" manner many of the leaders of the Social-Revolutionary Party. That attempt was undertaken five years after the October upheaval, in regard to people who had been kept in Bolshevik prisons for several years. Some of those leading figures, like Gotz and Timofeyev, spent ten and twelve years in the Tzar's "katorga." This blood-thirsty attempt released a veritable storm of protests abroad. This question was raised at the Berlin conference, participated in by representatives of three Internationals and the representatives of the Comintern—Radek, Clara Zetkin and Frossard—pledged, with the consent of Moscow, that no death sentences would be passed at the trial.

"The conference takes due cognizance of the declaration made by the representatives of the Communist International to the affect that . . . . as it was already stated by the Soviet press prior to the conference the passing of death sentences will be entirely precluded at the trial."

Lenin, in his closing speech on the report of the Central Committee of the Communist Party (March 28, 1922) countered the protests of the European socialists against the Bolshevik intent to kill the Social-Revolutionists with the foul slander:

"The international bourgeoisie is sufficiently clever to push Miliukóv to the left and to supply the Social-Revolutionists with enough money to publish any kind of papers, to stir Vandervelde, Otto Bauer into action against us, to raise a campaign in connection with the trial of the Social-Revolutionists and to raise the hue and cry about the 'Bolshevik beast'."[321]

With the date set for the trial drawing near, the Soviet magnate began to speak a different language. Trotzky wrote on June 9 in the "Rote Fanne" that "it would not be altogether true to say that the demand presented to us by the Internationals about refraining from applying the death penalty in the case of the Social-Revolutionists, a demand to which the Soviet government acceded only on conditional terms, was purely juridicial in character." And Radek, speaking in the Moscow Soviet, came out with the demand to "annihilate the murderers of Volodarsky."

[321] P. 68, vol. XVIII, part 2.

When the Defense Committee comprising E. Vandervelde, Lib-knecht and K. Rosenfeld came to Russia, they were met with staged hostile demonstrations attended with the smashing of windows and loudly uttered threats to lynch the delegates, etc. They were barred from associating with the Russian defense attorneys and prevented from familiarizing themselves with the material evidence in that case.

The factory gates were closed after work and the workers kept on the premises, forced to adopt resolutions demanding the death penalty for the Social-Revolutionists on trial. All those resolutions were printed in the Soviet papers as alleged manifestations of popular will. Next came "petitions" demanding that the defendants be shot. Workers were in no position to refuse their signature under such petitions: "so you don't want to sign, and do you want to get the h . . . . out of the factory too?" There were very few that did want to get out under the prevailing conditions of general starvation which the ousted worker would have to face; in addition, there was the certainty of being arrested for such a refusal. And thus petitions were concocted in the name of the workers.

On the day of the opening of the trial the workers of Petrograd and Moscow were forced to come out on the street—their day's pay was vouchsafed to them—in order to demonstrate publicly, before the whole world, in support of "their" demand of the death penalty for the Socialists. Up to that time the world had not yet seen such an exhibition of shame and moral degredation. And that ignominy was organized by Trotzky, Bukharin, Zinoviev and others, while Lenin kept on chuckling: "how cleverly all that was done." "The people's wrath" was staged and enacted so well that it went like a movie scene, especially, the scene of the "people in the Tribunal" demanding through their enraged delegates the heads of the defendants. Of course, no one was deceived by it, and the shame of it will never be erased. At last, "yielding" to the pressure of the "people's wrath," the Tribunal sentenced to death the leaders of the Social-Revolutionists: Gotz, Donskoy, Timofeyev, Morosov, Likhach, Gendel-man and six others.

The All-Russian Executive Committee confirmed the verdict, commuting it to a conditional sentence, the execution of this sentence being made conditional upon the behavior of the Social-Revolutionist Party; in other words, the prisoners were declared hostages who might be shot at any moment if any one of the Social-Revolutionists were to be found engaged in armed struggle and espionage activities against the Soviet government. And ever since, those people have been kept in prison or in exile, still facing the threat of being shot. Seventeen years! . . . .

Something similar, although attended by less publicity and sensation, was done in respect to the Left Social-Revolutionists. Forty-two members of this party who were confined in the Butirky prison declared a hunger strike, demanding that the authorities present explicit reasons for keeping them in confinement for so many years. They were given such reasons, after having been permitted to persist in their hunger strike for nine days. The official explanation was that the prisoners, beginning with the day this declaration was made, were to serve a sentence passed in their case in the Fall of 1918, according to which they were to be deprived of their freedom from one to three years in connection with their struggle against the Brest peace and the murder of Count Mirbach. Until that time the verdict was deemed to have been abrogated by the German Revolution, which annuled the Brest-Litovsk peace treaty, against which the mutiny of the Left Social-Revolutionists was directed. The Bolsheviks dragged out this verdict now that they had signed the Rapallo treaty with Germany. Germany, of course, never demanded the enforcement of this verdict.

People who had already spent two and three years in prison, were told that they were only starting to serve a sentence passed in connection with an alleged offense—the rebellion against the Brest-Litovsk peace—committed four years before. it was the more amazing that the authors of this peace were soon punished by the German proletariat.

In connection with those cases it is of interest to note the following facts: the sentenced Social-Revolutionists were kept in the inner prison of the Che-Ka and for months they were not told of the commutation of their sentence; just the reverse, everything was done to stress the imminence of their execution. Thus, for instance, when Gotz began protesting against being deprived of his marriage ring, he was told by one of the chekists: "you won't need it in the other world!" . . . . The Left Social-Revolutionist, Mayorov, was through serving his sentence imposed upon him by the Revolutionary Tribunal in connection with his alleged part in the Mirbach murder. He was freed by the prison administration. The G. P. U. upon learning of his release immediately re-arrested him, and put him in its inner prison. After a week's confinement Mayorov entered a declaration threatening to commit suicide if he was not freed within 24 hours. There followed prolonged negotiations which finally convinced the authorities that Mayorov was quite serious about the threat; at last he was released from the Che-Ka prison.

Prior to and during the trial of the Social-Revolutionists the members of this party became subject to an intensive man-hunt; everywhere members of that party were rounded up and arrested. The same was done to members of other Socialist parties and Anarchist groups. If on the whole the number of arrested Socialists and Anarchists was somewhat smaller than in the previous year, that was due not to a lessened zeal but to the fact that most of them had already been rounded up. For the lack of Socialists and Anarchists the authorities betook themselves to intellectuals. In Moscow and Petrograd, and to a lesser extend in all the bigger cities, were arrested all the liberal professors, writers and defense attorneys of the Social-Revolutionists: Muraviev, Tager, Zhdanov and Kariakin. A few dozen of the arrested people, together with their families, were deported abroad. This was the third and the last deportation abroad of entire groups.

Notwithstanding the inaguration of "revolutionary legality" forbidding extra-legal repressions (the decree of the All-Russian Executive Committee, Feb.6) the G. P. U. continued the practice of deporting politicals on the strength of mere administrative orders which it issued to that effect. This practice was fully approved by the All-Russian Central Executive Committee. That was, for instance, the manner in which was disposed a group of Social-Revolutionists which spent from nine to fourteen months in prison without having been given a court hearing.

Another method of discrediting the politicals was the so-called "amalgam" method, that is politicals were implicated in criminal cases and were indicted together with common criminals. Or when this "amalgam" was lacking, they were indicted on a framed-up criminal charge of a purely fictitious nature. This is, for instance, what happened to a group of political prisoners in Petrograd. This group, comprising Anarchists and Left Social-Revolutionists, refused to go to court, having instead handed in an interesting document fully revealing the terrors to which defenseless prisoners were subjected:

" . . . . The Russian Communist Party tries to hang upon us criminal charges that were clearly framed up by Che-Ka provocateurs. What are the proofs? Fictitious papers fabricated in the Che-Ka denunciatory reports by undercover agents of the Che-Ka, and common criminals bribed by the Che-Ka into bearing false witness against us by promises of liberty and good jobs as against prison confinement or shooting in case they refuse to bear witness. There is nothing new about that. Those were the methods used by the absolutist regime at the height of reaction. And the Russian Communist Party, the offspring of the autocracy, now copies the foulest and most infamous aspects of the old regime. And out of the numerous abominations witnessed by us we find it our duty to single out the following facts fully exposing the true physiognomy of the Communist Party and its dictatorship:

"1) The official probing into the charges against us—charges of counter-revolution preferred against Left Social-Revolutionists, Socialists of other parties and Anarchists was turned over to an ex-bailiff of the Tzar's court. It was this 'revolutionist' that was permitted to concoct the indictment and frame us up on criminal charges; 2) Imprisoned Socialists are kept in irons: Bogdanov, Stelmakov, etc. 3) One of our comrades, Mikhayil Nikolayev, was put to torture by the Commissar Komovich and his accomplices: they kept on torturing his sexual organs, squeezing his eye balls, striking his hand with the butt of a revolver; after that he was confined in the 'cork cell'; 4) Torture by sending prisoners to the House for the Insane; against the decision of the doctors, the Revolutionary Tribunal ordered the confinement of comrade Litvinov-Grusdev in the hospital for the insane, and notwithstanding the repeated demands of the doctors to take him away from there, it was the opinion of those doctors that continued confinement in this ward for insane was liable to affect the mind of the prisoner, the latter was kept there for a whole month; 5) "Haase hospital" (hospital for contagious diseases bearing the name of doctor Haase—G. M.) for the Socialists on hunger strike, that is, dispatching the hunger strikers to the hospital for contagious diseases where they were stripped naked and kept in that state in cold places and fed artificially" . . . .

Of the Bolshevik prisons and the regime prevailing there one can judge by reading the following description of a Petrograd prison on the Gorokhovaya street. And we must thereby bear in mind that the further the prison was from the large cultural centers, the worse the situation prevailing there.

"A solitary cell in the prison on the Gorokhovaya street: a wooden coffin three yards long and 1.5 yards wide. The furniture: a wooden cot extending the whole length of the cell and a small board attached to the wall which serves as a table. Not a ray of daylight. A dim electric bulb is on all the time. There is no ventilation and the air is thick and heavy. And it cannot be otherwise: out of four solitary cells of the old times, the Bolshevik administration made cells holding 24 people. Prisoners are not taken out for fresh air walks. Reading is forbidden. Even newspapers used for wrapping food parcels are steadily destroyed. Pencils and writing paper are strictly forbidden. One is not permitted to write to relatives or to receive letters from them. . . .

"The usual device is to 'plant' a chekist as a cell-mate in order to extort as much information as he can.

"The prison has a 'cork cell': a narrow, cold cell tightly corked up, with double walls inset with cork. Not a sound is transmitted. Prisoners are put in for five or ten days, but they are frequently kept there a month and longer." . . .

In prison "there are frequent cases of suicides and people going insane. . . . During the month of November two prisoners commited suicide. . . . One prisoner went insane after a hunger strike lasting seven days. . . .

"A common procedure used at the cross-examination is to shout abuse, swear at the prisoner and to threaten him with a revolver. No less accepted is the practice of urging the prisoners to enter the service of the G. P. U. with the promise of immediate release".322)

Is it to be wondered that there were so many hunger strikes on the part of the prisoners who had to fall back upon this means in order to extort the minimum of rights and tolerable conditions? Beginning with 1921 hunger strikes—waged singly and in groups— became a common event in the life of the prison. We already said that the Bolsheviks studiously ignored hunger strikes, letting them

---

322) "Rabochy Listok," the organ of Central Committee of the Russian Social-Democratic Party, No. 1. Was reprinted in the "Sotzialistichesky Viestnik," No. 5, 1923. We are giving a description of this prison by the Left Social-Revolutionist Shabalin.

drag on their utmost. The hunger strikes of 1922 were marked by their prolonged character. We are listing here a few of those strikes.

On January 4, the Mensheviks in the Moscow prison declared a hunger strike, protesting their deportation to some forsaken little towns. On the fourth day they were joined in an act of solidarity strike by the rest of the politicals of the Butirsky prison. And as a result of this hunger strike some of the Mensheviks were deported abroad.

On January 15, in the same prison, the Anarchists declared a hunger strike, acting in solidarity with their comrade Cherniak, who had been on strike for 11 days. That very night the Anarchists were beaten up and carted away to other prisons. (This event is described in Part Two of this book).

In the same prison 42 Left Social-Revolutionists were out on a hunger strike for nine days.

On January 28, in the prison of the Moscow Che-Ka (situated at the Kiselny Lane) the Anarchists declared a hunger strike; on the third day of the strike they were beaten up and taken out to be shipped out to the concentration camp. The Anarchists continued their hunger strike on the way. The strike lasted 16 days. The horors of this case are described in "A letter from Archangelsk".[323]

June 9: a nine day long hunger strike of the Mensheviks in the Butirsky prison.

October 11: a nine day long hunger strike of women Social-Democrats took place in the Novinskaya Women prison in Moscow.

In October a hunger strike took place in Petrograd.

September 23: the political prisoners were beaten up in Yaroslavl.

May 28, Baku, the Social-Revolutionists declared a hunger strike; they were joined by the Mensheviks. Soon after the arrest, which took place on April 8, torture was applied to the prisoners: they were placed in the cellar of the Che-Ka; the cellar was flooded and the prisoners were kept there until many of them began to faint It was only when it went that far that the tortured prisoners with their feet swollen, were carried out of the cellar.

October 2: for the second time the politicals were beaten up in

---

323) See Part Two of this book. The document also was published in "Letters from Russian Prisons," p. 171.

the Yaroslavl prison. The beating administered was extremely severe. Shouting "you damned Jews," the chekist Kisliakov broke into the cell occupied by F. Bukhter, seized her by the hair and reviling her with the choicest abuse.

In order to aggravate the position of the political prisoners, the Bolsheviks liquidated, toward the middle of September, the Political Red Cross and searches were made in the apartments of the ex-prisoners of the Shlisselburg fortress— Novorussky, Dobychin and Gartman.

**
*

Political persecutions during the year 1923 hardly differed from that of 1922, everything went on as before and the well-oiled terroristic machine kept on working without any hitches.

The shootings of Socialists and Anarchists, with and without the benefit of court trial, proceeded along established lines; the practice of administrative deportations, although against the explicit orders to the contrary issued by the All-Russian Executive Committee of February 6, 1922, continued. Ever new ways of tightening up the political control of the country were being devised and carried into practice. And even in the realm of terroristic practice the year of 1923 saw quite a few innovations: formerly revolts were fabricated by the government and people shot for alleged participation in such revolts; in 1923 the place of revolts was taken by "plots." Wide use was also made of the method of bringing about the moral break-down of the Socialists and Anarchists by way of calling with the aid of the G. P. U., conferences of of "penitents" and the extorting of "penitence letters" which were printed in the "Pravda" and "Izvestia." And, finally, there was the brazen terror, new only in the sense that it was more outspoken in 1923, in the cultural field unloosed throughout the country and headed by Madam Krupskaya, Lenin's wife.

Mrs. N. K. Oulianova—Krupskaya sent out a circular letter to all the Politprosviets, Party Committees, Oblit's (Regional Committees in charge of publishing work) and sections of G. P. U. which bore the following caption: "The Instructions about examining the books in the possession of the libraries and the withdrawal of counter-revolutionary and art-destructive literature."

The "instruction" was accompanied by an exemplary list of living and dead authors whose books were condemned to "the highest penalty" via an auto da fe.

According to this instruction, the following books were to be withdrawn. "those that have become obsolete, or are of little value, and to an even greater extent, harmful and counter-revolutionary books."

Those books were divided into two categories: books that are not of a fundamental nature which were to be unconditionally withdrawn, and fundamental books subject to *conditional* withdrawal: for instance, the works of Kant and the Gospel were to remain only in academic libraries, and they could be given out only "under the strictest responsibility of the chief librarians."

Following in the footsteps of her husband, Mrs. Krupskaya let loose against culture the horde of semi-literate chekists. Auto da fe was the sentence passed upon the books of almost all philosophers, including the works of Descartes, Kant, Mach, Plato, Spencer, Schopenhauer; a clean sweep was to be made of theology—only Soviet anti-religious "literature" was permitted; nor did the psychologists fare so well in this instruction, Vvedensky, Hoeffding, James, Taine, etc., having been included in the "Index Librorum Prohibitorum."

Carlyle, Kropotkin, Maeterlinck, Nietsche, Leo Tolstoy (his novels excepted), Bakunin, Vladimir Solovyev, Lossky (renowned Russian philosopher, philosophical protagonist of intuivist school), Grott, Lange ("History of Materialism") were classed in the same category. In fiction—Lieskov, Octave Mirbeau, Victor Margueritte, Nemirovich-Danchenko were placed on the same list.

Likewise, subject to withdrawal was the entire children's literature and all "the agitational pamphlets directed against the Communist movement, Bolsheviks and peace partisans," and also "the agitational literature of 1917 upholding the constitutional-democratic republic, civil liberties, the Constituent Assembly, universal suffrage, etc" . . .

The third paragraph of this instruction specifies: "small libraries ministering to the needs of the mass reader should be purged of obsolete agitational and reference literature of the Soviet organs of 1918, 1919, 1920, on questions which now find a different solution with the Soviet government (the land question, the tax system, the question of free trade, food problem, etc.)."

This "campaign" was to be wound up by January 1, 1924.

And, of course, this "campaign" was carried out brilliantly, and the counter-revolutionary hydra lost its head, it was fully stamped out. A few years later this "crusade" against culture inspired the German Nazi who burned almost the very same books in the streets of the big cities and destroyed libraries. . . .

The filthy police boot invaded even the cultural domain of the hapless Russian citizen. . . .

**
*

In the other fields terror was proceeding along its regular course. In the villages the same old methods were pursued in collecting the agricultural tax; as before, peasants were arrested and driven to exile and forced labor. In the cities and industrial centers workers were starving and striking, as in Sormovo, for instance, (July 16) where the workers went out on strike; the miners of the Alexandrovsk-Grushevsk district were fired at and beaten up with "nagaykas" (Cossack whips); in Kharkov workers demonstrated in the streets asking "bread and work" which was answered with sweeping arrests; in December workers struck in the industrial centers of Ural—in Zlatooust, Bielorechnaya, Asha-Balashovsk, Miass and other places. There were clashes with the administration and the Communist cell, invariably ending with the arrests of workers.

A new feature in the work of exterminating Socialists and Anarchists was the inaguration of the system of summoning "conventions" of ex-Social-Revolutionists, Mensheviks and Anarchists. The first convention—the convention of Social-Revolutionists took place on March 14, the "Menshevik" convention took place sometimes later. Likewise, preparations were made to call an "Anarchist" congress, which, however, came to naught. The aim of those "conventions" was to repudiate publicly their respective party in view of the latter's "counter-revolutionary activity." Simultaneously with those conventions and immediately following them the authorities reverted to the method of extorting "penitent letters to the editor" in which Social-Revolutionists, Mensheviks and Anarchists publicly declared their withdrawal from the ranks of the "counter-revolutionists, humbly repenting their long errors and their work to undermine the 'workers' government,' faithfully swearing to be loyal and devoted to 'the only defender of the working class'—the Communist Party."

However, these stool-pigeon conventions and letters fell short of the desired effect. The penitents broke off with their respective parties without gaining the confidence of the chekists. They were not trusted and a close watch was kept over their movements.

The arrests of Socialists and Anarchists still continued, but since most of the participants were arrested in 1921-22, the authorities began arresting those who never had anything to do with Socialists and Anarchists. In the center of their attention was now the stabilization of the political exile system, the expansion of the net of concentration camps and the establishment of such a regime in the exile and other places of confinement which would inevitably provoke protests on the part of the prisoners and exiles, thus making it possible to liquidate the Socialists and Anarchists by the quiet and noiseless method of the dry guillotine.

In 1923 the policy of the Party toward the Socialists and Anarchists finally took shape. It was a simple policy: the first step was to arrest the "culprit"; the second step to extort "recantation" and release the penitents; the third step was to keep in prison the non-penitents under conditions impelling protests, hunger strikes; the fourth step was to liquidate the hunger strike by imposing the sentence of exile or confinement into concentration camps; the fifth —was to place the inmates of the concentration camps under conditions provoking protests on the part of the prisoners in the form of hunger strikes, and then have them drag out this strike as long as possible, administering beatings from time to time; the sixth— was to refuse work to the exiles; the seventh—to send to exile those who had served their sentence in concentration camps, and those who were in exile—to arrest and dispatch to concentration camps or to re-exile them to worse places. This became a stock procedure with the authorities and with some variations it is still kept up.

The conditions prevailing in places of confinement were frightful. They drove the inmates to insanity and suicide. Thus, for instance, Timofeyev, who was sentenced to death in the trial of the Social-Revolutionists, could not hold out any longer, declaring a hunger strike on January 27. He demanded from the All-Russian Central Executive Committee that either the sentence be carried out in full or that he be freed. Another one of those who were sentenced to death, S. V. Morozov, committed suicide on December 21, in the inner prison of the G. P. U. He cut his veins with a fragment of glass and bled to death.

The cruelty of the Bolsheviks was extraordinary and their vindictiveness was boundless. Here is, for instance, a case well illustrating the quality of their cruelty. The daughter of the Social-Revolutionist, Vedeniapin, was studying in Moscow at the co-operative courses; knowing that she was actually starving, her friends petitioned the Dean of those courses—an ex-Left-Social-Revolutionist, Mrs. Bitzenko—to grant this student a scholarship allowance. The Dean's answer was: "we will not aid the daughter of a counter-revolutionist."

In addition to Morozov's suicide there were many other suicides and attempts at suicide, as well as many cases of insanity, in many prisons and places of exile. We can point out the following:

In Pertominsk the Social-Revolutionist, Kriukov, went insane. In the same Petrominsk, the Anarchists made an attempt to commit suicide by setting themselves on fire: they wrapped themselves up with straw and set fire to it. The fire was extinguished in time to save them. Following that they declared a hunger strike which lasted eleven days. A special committee arrived from Moscow to investigate conditions. As a result some improvement was made in the regime of the concentration camps. In the prisons of the town of Kem, a youth by the name Aronovich, a member of the Social-Democratic Union of Youth, committed suicide by hanging himself. The prisoner was on his way to the dreaded Solovky exile. In the very Solovky, in the Savateyev cloister, another youth, a Social-Revolutionist, by the name of Sandomir, committed suicide by opening his veins. Depressed by this death, a Social-Democrat Yegorov-Lizlov became mentally ill: he sank into a state of deep melancholy, making an attempt to hurl himself from the window of the second floor. He was taken away in a serious condition. After having been kept for some time in the Moscow hospital, Yegorov-Lizlov was shipped back to Kem, and from there—to Solovky. In the same state was Yevgenia Boguslavskaya, a woman worker from a tobacco factory who had been exiled to Perm. Following the notification received of his sentence, which was exile to the Narym region, Professor A. L. Rafalov who was kept in a Petrograd prison, committed suicide by hanging himself. In Veliky-Ustiug three exiled Social-Revolutionists: I. M. Sidorov, Struzhinsky and Dolomashko (from the Far Eastern Republic), after having served their term in exile, were re-committed to prison for another three years. In protest against this high-handed action, the three prisoners poured kerosene over themselves and set fire to it: all of them received serious burns and wounds. (This took place in 1924). E. V. Trutovsky, member of the Central Committee of the Left Social-Revolutionists and ex-member of the Council of People's Commissars, was set free after having served three years in connection with the case of the Mirbach murder.[324] His freedom lasted only a few days after which he was re-arrested and sentenced to be exiled to Kuldzha (Mongolia). In sign of protest, Trutovsky made an attempt to set himself on fire, but he was saved by comrades.

It stands to reason that if conditions prevailing in the prisons and concentration camps were such as to lead to ghastly suicides, the administration of those places of confinement contributed its share toward bringing conditions to such a state. And, indeed, the attitude of the administration toward the prisoners was of a bullying kind, unrestricted by any laws, controls or any sense of responsibility. Its arbitrary regime has ever since prevailed in all places of confinement. And very often the high-handed action of the administration took the form of bloody attacks on defenseless prisoners. That, for instance, is what took place December 19, 1923, at the Solovetzky islands, where five people were killed in cold blood (they were shot in the back) and three wounded: one of the wounded died as a result of the injury received. The details of this massacre, unprecedent in the annals of prison life, can be found in the book "Letters from Russian Prisons." (pp. 215-217). Here we shall confine ourselves to the description of the scene of this massacre as described by the prisoners themselves.

**
*

"We were warned by the administration on December 16 that it contemplated limiting our promenading hours from 9 in the morning to 6 in the evening. The committee of elders declared a decisive protest. In the course of three days afterwards we promenaded as of old and the conversations with the administration on the subject

---

324) Count Mirbach—German ambassador to Soviet Russia in 1918; was assassinated in Moscow, July 7, 1918 by Left Social-Revolutionists Blumkin and Andreyev.

were not renewed. Suddenly, on December 19, after 5 o'clock in the evening, the political prisoners of the Savvatievo cloister were handed a written order: Promenading is permitted in the future from 9 o'clock in the morning until 6 in the evening. The order is to be announced at the roll-call.

"Since the roll-call is usually taken after 8 o'clock in the evening, it was the clear sense of the order that it would take effect the following day, December 20. Nevertheless, at half-past five, the sentinels began to request the comrades who were out in the open to return into the building, and as they continued to promenade the sentinels fired from the watch-towers several shots, apparently into the air. The promenading continued. Then a chain of soldiers and prison officials, numbering about fifty men, spread out along the fence surrounding the prison yard, covering the building from three sides. The commander of the squad turned to the absolutely peaceable promenaders with the request to enter the building, without warning once that in the event of disobedience he would fire. The promenading comrades formed the definite impression that in the worst event it was planned to push them back toward the building, almost nobody conceiving of the possibility of shooting. But after the third request to enter the building the order suddenly rang out: 'Straight at the targets! Fire!' And immediately afterwards followed a volley and deafening continuous shooting from separate sections.

"The promenading comrades failed to comprehend at first what had happened. They were convinced that the shots were made into the air to terrify promenaders. But the first victims, the groans of the wounded, the warning cries from all sides, 'There are wounded' left no doubt as to what had occurred. The murderers heard these cries, they saw how the comrades picked up those who fell and carried them in the direction of the building, but they had not had enough bloodshed yet, and after the first volley came a second and then a third volley. The firing was aimed not only at those who remained in the yard but also at those comrades who were carrying the wounded and at those returning to the building. The unanimous testimony of our comrades bears witness to it, the marks of bullets around the entrance to the building unequivocally point to it, some of these marks being at the level of a man's height, others a little above. After the third volley the yard was emptied and the firing stopped."

* *
*

According to the testimony of medical experts most of the killed and wounded had wounds in their backs, that is, the politicals were shot down when they were getting away from a detachment of soldiers and not when they were approaching it.

How did Moscow react to this bloody massacre?

An answer to this question is to be found in the appeal sent by the prisoners in the month of June, 1924, to the Socialist International.[325])

"About a month passed from the time of the shooting. Telegrams were sent from Solovky to Moscow and from Moscow to Solovky. The first telegram about he occurrence was dispatched from Solovetz on the night of the murder, but days passed and weeks, and the entire higher administration of the northern camps remained undisturbed in its place. The chief of the department, Nogetv, retained his full authority. Moscow kept silent.

"Finally, about the middle of January, we were informed that a commission was formed in Moscow, composed of representatives of the Central Executive Committee of the Soviets, of the Central Committee of the Communist Party, and of the Commissariat of Justice.

"Apparently, the fact of the shooting in Solovky became public and it became impossible to conceal it. That, in all probability, explains the invitation we received to send to Moscow delegates to testify before the commission of investigation. In the circumstances of interrupted navigation, when communication with the continent is maintained by rowboats which accidentally make their way through the ice floes, we considered this invitation a mockery. We considered that the Government had at its disposal all the means, whether airplanes, an ice cutter, or something else, to convey the commission to the place where the crime was committed in order to investigate the unheard-of act. We considered that only here, in the very place where the blood of our comrades was shed, where all the witnesses and all the direct participants of the shooting could be examined, only here the threads are to be found which would lead the investigation to the tracks of the real culprits. And, above all, we did not for a minute believe in the impartiality of a commission composed of

---

325) This appeal signed by 233 Solovetzky prisoners is cited in full in the book: "Letters from Russian Prisoners," pp. 192-200. We are citing the same appeal here after having checked it with the Russian original.

representatives of the Bolshevist Government only, which is fit in this case, according to our profound conviction, to act the role of a defendant rather than that of a judge. And we answered Moscow by demanding the admission into the commission of representatives of the Amsterdam Federation of Trade Unions, of the Socialist Workers' International and of the Red Cross for Political Prisoners, (Madame Peshkova's organization).

"We agreed, under these conditions, to send to Moscow our delegates, even by rowboats, to testify before the investigating commission. Only a commission in which the representatives of the international proletariat participated could provide us with a minimum guarantee that the truth about December 19 would be disclosed.

"Half a year has passed since then. Moscow sent us no answer. It is more than a month now since navigation has opened, more than one steamer has already arrived from the continent, but Moscow still continues to maintain silence, as if the crime of December 19, had never been committed.

"And everything remains as it was in the past on the Solovky Islands. The same rule of criminal elements in the administration, the same servitude for the criminal prisoners, the same eternal, constant menace to the human dignity and life of the politicals.

"However, there is an innovation. A special correction prison has been established on the Sekirn Hill, where criminal prisoners are kept, for small offences, in such inhuman conditions that the men, as a sign of protest, rip open their own abdomens. The regime of penal servitude is winning new victims: hitherto it was applied only to criminals, now it has been extended to a group of Kronstadt sailors sentenced for participation in the Kronstadt revolt of 1921, as well as to students of both sexes who are exiled by the score to Solovky for participation in the students' mass .movement. They are kept like common criminals under the same regime as all the criminal prisoners, they are driven together with the latter to do hard labor, and those who are fined are thrown into the prison on the Sekirn Hill. And at the very moment we are writing these lines the Kronstadt sailors are on a hunger-strike, declared several days ago, trying to win for themselves the regime of the political prisoners.

"Moreover, gradually, an effort is being made to extend the regime of penal servitude to us, Socialists, too. A score of Socialists, bound together by force, were brought from the continent to Solovky and placed on a criminal regime on the pretext that there was no indication in their cases of their belonging to Socialist parties. Only a hunger-strike on their part and the interference of the Socialist communities saved them from penal servitude. But an effort is being made to thrust even upon us, the "recognized" Socialists, who have spent a year here on a Socialist regime, compulsory labor under the guise of innocent 'self-service.' We have been deprived of the heating service, of the bathhouse, of the laundry. We are being placed in a position unknown to the political prisoners in the jails of the czars.

"And to cap all this, we are deprived of the elementary rights possessed by the inmates of any prison, the right of visits from our relatives. In spite of the fact that navigation has again opened, our relatives are persistently refused permission to visit us 'until special orders were issued."

This was Moscow's answer. . . .

In addition to Solovky the Bolsheviks restored another monastery prison in the month of November; the new prison was located in Suzdal which rapidly became a new Golgotha for the Anarchists and Socialists. The Suzdal monastery was at first intended to be a concentration camp, and not a prison, the difference between the two being the greater measure of freedom enjoyed, on paper at least, by the inmates of concentration camps, the latter's function being to isolate and not punish people. But in practice this difference was rapidly obliterated, the concentration camps assuming the character of a regular prison. The Suzdal camp for political isolation immediately became a dilapidated squalid prison, with tyranny rampant on the part of a prison administration freed from any responsibility for the life and health of the prisoners.

The "starostat" institution, that is, representation of prisoners through elected delegates, was not recognized by the administration. Mutual aid among the prisoners was curbed in many ways. The prisoners were permitted to order food products from the market only once a week—at the prisoners expense, of course. Only 45 kopeks a day—a prepostrously inadequate sum in view of the current prices and depreciated money—was allowed for the upkeep of each prisoner. Physical labor was banned. And, as in all the other prisons and concentration camps, there was no check on the arbitrary and tyrannical action of the administration. One could always expect some kind of outbreak on the part of the prison authorities. Thus, for instance, "on the night of July 26, 1924, a painstaking search was made in all cells. During the search sick men were dragged off their cots and flung upon the floor. Danilin, Bikhovsky were nearly choked by the guards when they made an attempt to cry out, Rabinovich and Brook began to bleed profusely at the throats. The guards also broke into the cells of sleeping women. Common criminals suspected of having dealings with politicals were beaten up."[326)]

Here is another colorful instance from the daily life of the prisoners. We have already referred to the protest of the Left Social-Revolutionists and their motivated refusal to appear in court because of the frame-up implicating them in a criminal case. Nevertheless, the Left Social-Revolutionists, together with the Anarchists, were sentenced and sent to Moscow to the prison of Lefortovo where they found a Communist, Yegorov, who three years before had been sentenced to be shot in connection with the case of the Baku Communists. And thus Yegorov had been kept in the state of a man doomed to be shot and waiting for three years for the sentence to be carried out. Incidentally, Yegorov is an old Bolshevik revolutionist who spent seven years of "katorga" (penal servitude) under the Tzar's regime. February 5, 1924, the G. P. U. agents came to take Yegorov out for execution. The prisoners made an attempt at his rescue, repeating in this case the similar attempt described above, to rescue Shishkin. The issue of this attempt, however, was far less successful. The political prisoners declared that they would all commit suicide if Yegorov were taken out. The G. P. U. began negotiating, holding out the pledge that Yegorov would not be shot but merely transferred to the Butirky prison. To make sure that this pledge would be carried out the politicals demanded that one of them should be given the opportunity to accompany Yegorov. The G. P. U. gave in to this demand.

On February 7, Yegorov, accompanied by the right Social-Revolutionist Khokhlov, was sent away to the Butirky prison. Upon arrival at that prison, Khokhlov was seized, bound hand and feet and thrown into a solitary cell. Yegorov was taken away, following which the G. P. U. bore down upon the politicals who protested this outrage. . . . One of the prominent Social-Revolutionists was

---

326) "Sotzialistichesky Viestnik," No. 24, December 20, 1924.

railroaded to Cheliabinsk, and the Anarchists were transferred into the category of common criminals. . . .

Nor was the situation any better as far as the political exiles went. (For that matter it is not any better even now). Who were those political exiles? They are Socialists, Anarchists who were not confined to prison or to the concentration camp, but who—in the Bolshevik scheme—had no place in cultured and populous centers: they were deemed dangerous because of the alleged possibility of their carrying on propaganda and stirring up workers and peasants. In order to prevent such contingency, the G. P. U. laid down peremptory rules for keeping them away from populous centers. Certain towns and regions are designated by the G. P. U. as the only places those exiles could live in. Usually those places were remote out-of-the way little towns, the hamlets and villages of the distant Northern provinces of European Russia, the Northern and North-Eastern regions of Siberia, the provinces of Turkestan, the Kirghiz steppes and even Mongolia.

In those places the exiles were to enjoy "freedom" under the surveillance of the police; theoretically they were to receive from the G. P. U. for their keep the "magnificent" sum of six roubles a month; in most of the cases they were not permitted to work anywhere, and to find suitable employment. This enforced blacklist virtually condemned them to a life of starvation. In addition, the G. P. U. saw to it that they should not stay too long and acclimate themselves to one place. No sooner did the politicals manage to settle somehow in one place, to adapt themselves to the dismal environment than they would be shifted to other and more isolated places. Or they would be tossed about between the Turkestan, with its tropical heat in the Summer, and cold Siberia. The exiles in Turkestan would be suddenly ordered to leave for Siberia, and the Siberian exiles for Turkestan.

Life in exile was hard enough, but still more distressing was the road to exile, which meant transportation via "etape." "Etape" are halting places for convicts transported from one place to the other in large groups; very often the distance from one "etape point" to the other was covered on foot, and that meant a vile, filthy prison— much worse than ordinary jails—as a "resting place" after a day of painful trudging along the road.

In Europe and America deportation by "etape" means very little, if it means anything at all. But in Russia, and especially in Bolshevik Russia, this term is charged with tragic and gruesome meaning. To follow the "etape" is to go through the torment of Dante's Inferno.

"One party of prisoners was deported under especially savage conditions. There were many common criminals in that group, while the convoy was violent and ferocious. The party reached Novo-Nikolayevsk. There the political prisoners declared a hunger strike, demanding that instead of Turukhansk they be exiled to Yeniseysk. The hunger strike lasted 12 days during which time none of the authorities showed up. At last one of them, Krause, made his appearance, declaring that he was giving in to their demands and that he would re-route them to Yeniseysk. The hunger strike came to an end. However, the pledge turned out to be a spurious promise. The prisoners were brazenly deceived, having been sent to Turukhansk instead of the promised Yeniseysk. The convoy behaved in an extremely bullying and cruel manner. They wanted to drop off one of the prisoners, a worker by the name Ivanov, in one of the God forsaken little hamlets. Ivanov refused to remain; despairingly, he seized a knife intending to cut a vein. The guard shouted at him and threatened to shoot. The tension reached the highest point. It was with difficulty that he was quietened down. The party started out again. Now all are in Turukhansk. Conditions are unbearable. But the comrades say that if they were asked to go back to Moscow via "etape," they would refuse to do it, in order not to go through again the same torment which they bore on their way here.

"A woman, Raskin, (from Petrograd) a political prisoner was deported by "etape" to Turukhansk. She was the only political among the convict gang comprising the riff-raff of common criminals and profiteers. She was beaten up twice. Now she is all shaken up as a result of her experience".327)

It was via such "etaps" or, perhaps, under somewhat better conditions in some cases—that the exiles would be conveyed to their destination; to their surprise, they would very often at first meet with a hostile attitude on the part of the native population. The reason thereof was that the Bolsheviks spread rumors to the effect that those people wanted the restoration of the Tzar and that they were quite capable

---

327) "Sotzialistichesky Viestnik," No. 21, November 10, 1924.

of commiting the felony of arson. And, at the outset, before the population had time to acquaint themselves with the newcomers, the exiles had a rather difficult time. In the cold Pechera region or in the torrid Turkestan—everywhere the situation in which the exiles found themselves was frightful to the extreme: lack of clothes, food, aggravated by the difficulty of finding a place to live in. The same unrelieved want prevailed among the political exiles whether in some God-forsaken (not forsaken by the Bolsheviks, though) little village of the far away North or in some less populated centers with some evidence of "cultured life," and where there might be an opportunity to obtain employment. This opportunity, however, remained in most cases a mere possibility since the G. P. U. enjoined the various state organizations from giving employment to the exiles.

This ban was reinforced by the trade unions who in this respect worked hand in hand with the G. P. U. It was impossible to obtain employment without being a member of a trade union, but trade union organizations, acting upon orders from above, closed their doors to political exiles.

Here are two documents: the first, a resolution of the Trade Union Council of the Perm "gubernia" (January 27, 1923).

"While holding that the reply given by the trade union organizations of Ussolsk was formally incorrect, the Presidium of the Trade Union Council, upon due consideration of the appeal of the members of the Social-Democratic Party (Mensheviks) finds on the whole the trade union organization of Ussolsk acted quite right in making their decision in regard to politicals (barring their membership in unions —G. M.). The Presidium is guided by the following considerations. The members of the Russian Social-Democratic Party who are in the ranks of the Second and Second and a half Internationals, wage a struggle against the Red Profintern (International of Red Trade Union Organizations); the same members do not protest against expulsion from the ranks of European trade unions entire organizations and groups affiliated with the Red Trade Union International."

The second document is the resolution of the Presidium of the Trade Union Council of the town and "gubernia" of Tiumen (January 27, 1927).

"Agenda:

"1). About the attitude of the trade unions to the G. P. U. exiles in respect to employment.

"Resolved:

"1). Such persons are unconditionally expelled from membership in unions. They are to be regarded as such in view of the fact that those people do not uphold the line of revolutionary class struggle.

"2). Work can be given to such people only by special dispensation from the Management Board of the Trade Union Council of the 'gubernia,' to be confirmed by the Presidium.

"3). Those people are to be immediately removed from work if they show the slightest tendency to go against the decisions of the trade unions. . . ."

In many cases employment could be obtained only with the consent of the local Communist organizations. But getting a permit was not the only obstacle in the way of getting work. After having gone through all kinds of trials and tribulation in the attempt to get such a permit—and getting one was no easy matter, the cases of turned-down applications for the permits being quite numerous—the exile would find himself at the mercy of the Communist officials who could oust the exiles from their positions and jobs for the most trivial reason. The G. P. U. did not altogether approve the practice of employing exiles, and many a governmental institution did not want to take any chances of incurring the displeasure of the dreaded G. P. U. In addition to that, Socialists and Anarchists were not immune from arrest and constant harrassing on the part of the local authorities and G. P. U. Since the preponderant majority of Socialists and Anarchists had already been ferreted out and sent to various prisons, concentration camps and exile places, the G. P. U. had nothing else to do but frame up new plots by implicating the exiles and re-arresting them, as was done on a large scale with the Mensheviks, in Turkestan, in the month of May, 1923. All those arrests would generally end with shifting the exiles to new places or with prison confinement.

Correspondence with people abroad, or with other exiles of the widely scattered deportation places, was regarded as a crime sufficient to have people arrested, thrown into jail or railroaded to the wildest places of Siberia and other distant parts of the country. The frequent reshifting of the exiles from one place to the other —rather a favorite method with the G. P. U.—was constituted a veritable torture to the exiles. . . . Distressful dramas were frequent in exile. Here is, for instance, the case of the eighteen year old Anarchist girl, Olga Romanova.

. . . "She was sent to the upper regions of the river Kengha, where it was impossible to get work, where for three months she lived only on bread and hot water. . . . That place turned out to be not a free settlement but a concentration camp set up by the local government of Tomsk, although it was not authorized to do so by the Central government. This camp differed from other camps by its starvation regime. The inmates comprised ecclesiastics, a few peasants and Romanova, the young Anarchist girl.

"The peasants and Romanova left the camp, were caught in the first frosts and had frostbitten feet. Romanova was dressed lightly when she came to the camp; all she had when she finally arrived at the village Parabel was a summer dress, and it was in that village that she found shelter with our comrades".328)

**
*

Thus far we haven't made any references to the shootings taking place during that year, and there was much of it going on at that time.

Georgia and the Far East, especially the Maritime province, were the arena of terror against Socialists and Anarchists. In Georgia the Bolsheviks were finishing off the Social-Democrats and the partisans of national independence of the Georgian people; in the Far East the same was done with the Anarchists, Maximalists, Left Social-Revolutionists and the guerilla fighters of the civil war to whom Moscow was indebted for having cleared Siberia from white-guardists, Japs and other interventionists.

In Georgia, in the town of Ozurgety 12 people were shot, in Batum—19, in Tiflis—92. In the publication of the Regional Committee of the Communist Party of Georgia, "Zaria Vostoka," ("The Dawn of the East"), February 18, No. 38, appeared a statement issued by the Georgian Che-Ka announcing the execution of "bandits." However, among those shot "bandits" were people who "had been registered and arraigned several times"—that is, they were hostages. Among the 92 shot in Tiflis are the names of several well-known members of the Georgian Social-Democratic Party while

---

328) A letter from one of the exiles in "Sotzialistichesky Viestnik," No. 9, February 17, 1924.

among those shot in Batum we find the name of a renowned active figure of the Georgian Social-Democratic Party, Alphes Gogouadze. . .

In the Far East where the Moscow emissaries held sway (Vilensky, Nikiforov, Gubelman and others) we had an almost exact copy of the struggle in Ukraine against the Makhno insurgent army, against the Anarchists and Left Socialists. The irregulars were annihilated in every way and with every means at the disposal of the Bolshevik authorities.

Thus, for instance, in Nikolayevsk on the Amur, the Bolsheviks staged an act of popular resentment, and, as M. Volodin relates in his account of this matter, "taking their cue from Vilensky and Co. the Bolsheviks shot the Staff of the Irregular Army, headed by the Maximalist Nina Lebedyeva and the Anarchist Triapitzin; they also shot members of the Soviet, the Communist Sasov and others who deemed the buffer state (The Far Eastern Republic), an artificially created political body brought to life by the Communist Party for purely partisan purposes".329) Those shootings were carried out in order to maintain friendly relations with the Japanese High Command which suffered a humiliating defeat in Nikolayevsk on the Amur at the hands of the irregulars.

"From February 26 to April 12 summary arrests of Anarchists and Left Populists (Maximalists and Social-Revolutionists) took place in the cities of the Far East; the arrests were attended by the wrecking of those organizations throughout the province".330) Worst of all fared the organizations in Vladivostok, where on February 26 were arrested all the prominent workers of the underground movement during the period of Kolchak, General Ditrichs and Merkulov, such as: people who took an active part in the underground trade union movement, in the contingents of the irregulars, members of underground Revolutionary Committees—Provincial and Regional Committees. On February 26 alone there were 12 of those people arrested in Vladivostok: eight Maximalists and four Anarchists, the latter group comprising the editors of the paper "The Black Flag" and members of an irregular unit—Khanyenko and Ustimenko. Thirty eight of such active fighters against the whites—all Maximalists,

329) "On the Trial of the 'Whiteguardists' in the City of Chita," "Golos Truzhenika," No. 220, September 8, 1923, Chicago.
330) "A Letter from Russia," "Golos Truzenika," No. 220, September 8, 1923, Chicago.

Anarchists and Left Social-Revolutionists—were arrested in the town of Blagoviestchensk on April 10."

The arrested were all brought to the city of Chita. The authorities released a statement to the effect "a white-guardist plot was unearthed;" the name of those "plotters" were published but no mention was made of the fact that those "white-guardists" were Anarchists, Maximalists, Left Social-Revolutionists and non-partisan fighters of the irregular detachments who took an active part in the struggle against the white army. The official release stated that those people were organizing guerilla detachments, were arming them, etc. but it did not say against whom and in the name of what that was done. . . .331) The actual cause of the arrest and the framing of a "white guardist plot" is pointed out by the author of *"A Letter from Russia"* which, according to him, was that "backed up by the Left Social-Revolutionists and Anarchists, the workers and peasants put up during the elections to the Soviet their own independent revolutionary but non-partisan ticket and refused to vote for the Communists".332)

The director of the G. P. U., Bielsky, declared quite openly:

"You had to be arrested in the Amur province under the guise of white-guardists: this was tactical camouflage used by us with an eye to the local situation. We won't harm you except that we are going to send you out into the central provinces of Russia and Siberia, and keep you at some distance from the Far East. Amur—and this is due to the influence of the Maximalists, Left Social-Revolutionists and Anarchists—is a seething volcano and we don't know where white guardists begin, where they shade off into Shliapnikovites (the workers opposition) and where they finally merge with Maximalists and Anarchists".333)

During the cross examination the prisoners were offered freedom upon giving a written promise to forego political activity and advocating their ideas. Such an offer, for instance, was made to E. Kokhanovich. Upon the latter's categorical refusal, the investigator declared:

"In that case we shall have to put you through a long course of treatments".334)

The trial began in Chita, on July 9, and ended on the 19th.

---

331) Ibid.
332) Ibid.
333) Ibid.
334) Ibid.

Eight men (Baturin, Tkachenko, Bernis, Beziazikov, Petkevich, Tzigankov, Zabielin and Frolov) were sentenced to be shot, and ten other people—to long prison terms. Only forty-eight hours were granted to appeal the case. A telegram was sent to the All-Russian Executive Committee and to Kuybishev, the Commissar of the Workers and Peasants Inspection, who personally knew Baturin. Kuybishev's answer was: "I can't do anything." All the sentenced people were shot.335)

The terroristic activity of the Bolsheviks at that time was not exhausted by the above cited facts from their terroristic practice in Georgia and the far East.

In the rest of Russia shooting were still widely practiced; true, they slowed down somewhat as compared with 1921 but they still constituted an important item in the work of the G. P. U. and other organs. The Special Investigating Committee of the All-Russian Executive Committee noted 826 cases of extra-legal shootings of the "lynching" kind carried out by the G. P. U. *Five hundred and nineteen of those victims were politicals.*336)

People were shot for all sorts of reasons. The prelate Butkevich was shot, the protests abroad notwithstanding, on charges growing out of the cases of church counter-revolution. People were shot for printing illegal, agitational literature, for bribe-taking and bribe-giving, for embezzlement, theft; people were shot on charges of being "nepmen" profiteers, currency speculators from the "black course"; they were shot on account of their past—like some of those, for instance, who returned to Russia on the strength of an officially proclaimed amnesty; they were shot for taking part in the insurrectionary movement or in their capacity of hostages; on charges of being bandits—and many Socialists, Anarchists, and active workers were being framed and shot on charges of "banditry;" They were shot for counterfeiting railway tickets or banknotes. A new term appeared in the usual indictments and verdicts, the phrase: "shot for economic counter-revolution," foreshadowing the trials of the later period—the so-called "trials of wreckers"—so widely used after Lenin's death and still being used in our own time. This term

---

335) Ibid.
336) S. P. Melgunov, "The Red Terror in Russia," p. 131.

covered charges of mismanagement, and sabotage which generally drew death sentences.

There were murders in prisons and concentration camps, as in Solovky, for instance; suicides and the dying out of prisoners in exile places; murders committed by punitive detachments in their struggle with the remnants of the guerilla movements and with the peasantry in the struggle for grain.

Lists of executed people were published at rare intervals, nor were they ever adequate. The bloody statistics which at first had been made public, although in a highly falsified form, had now virtually discontinued; the same might be said about the strike statistics now banned by the unions themselves. Under such conditions it was virtually impossible to ascertain not only the exact number of the terror victims, but even a rough approximation thereof. There remains the bare facts of terror, of shootings having taken place; and one can get some idea of the degree of terror only by modifying the qualifying adjective: "feeble terror," "intense terror," "very intense terror," "frightful terror."

Toward the end of 1921 the number of terror victims began to drop off, although at times this decline was arrested, and even reversed, by fitful coleric outbreaks of the same terroristic delirium. But even up to now the number of such victims has been rather high, the yearly minimum average being expressed in no less than five ciphers.

The approximate total of shootings during the period of Lenin's terror, lasting from November 7, 1917, up to January 24, 1924—the day of Lenin's death—equals, even according to most conservative estimates, no less than 200,000. Some place it as the much higher figure of 1,500,000—and that for the shorter period of 1917-1923. For our total we shall take the "modest" minimum figure of 200,000. To those we must add other victims: those that died in prisons, concentration camps, in exile; those that died throughout the country from inanition and epidemics; those that were killed at the suppression of revolts and guerilla movements; victims of civil war and finally victims of the famine which, according to official data, carried away 5,200,000 lives. The total, according to the most conservative estimate, would be from eight to ten million people. But this really does not sum up the total: this latter should also include the victims of white terror and the casualties on the part of the Whites during the civil war—and that means millions of more victims. Thus Lenin's Marxist experiment cost Russia, the general havoc and destruction excepted, from ten to twelve million lives. That does not include the victims of the famine of 1924, which came as a logical sequel of Lenin's policy and whose devastating power, as admitted by Rykov, was one fifth as great as that of 1921, that is—it resulted in 1,040,000 victims.

CHAPTER X

THE TORTURES

I completed the study of Lenin's role in the terror during the revolution. The study begins from the day of the seizure of power and it was brought up to the day of Lenin's death. I feel, however, that not everything has been said. I have not touched yet upon another feature of the terror, no less ghastly—perhaps even more gruesome—than the shootings. I have in mind tortures. . . . Yes, tortures. . . . The reader, perhaps, has already noted quite a few of the above cited facts which could nicely fit into the category of *"Torture."* . . .

I have no doubt that the reader, upon acqainting himself with such facts, will ask himself the question: were these casual incidents, casual acts committed by people who happened to drift into the Bolshevik movement—raw, ignorant and cruel people with a sadistic complex, mentally unbalanced or morally degraded people for whom Lenin, Trotzky, Dzerzhinsky and their party cannot bear any reponsibility? Or were all those incidents a part of a system cooly designed in the inner recesses of the Che-Ka—G. P. U. and approved by Lenin and the Central Committee of the Party, the Council of People's Commissars and the All-Russian Central Executive Committee?

Of course we shall not find any explicit decrees authorizing the use of torture. This mildly speaking, would be too shameful for the "builders" of Communism and the social engineers of the Marxist school. But we have something virtually amounting to a decree. The All-Russian Che-Ka began to publish in 1918 its oragn "The Weekly of the Extraordinary Commission" (Che-Ka). And it is in this "Communistic organ," No. 3, October 6, 1918, that the reader will find a document, immortal by its own right. The document is a "Letter to the Editor" sent by the Bolsheviks of Nolinsk (city of the "gubernia" of Viatka), signed by the chairman of the Che-Ka of the Nolinsk county and other Communists; the letter was entitled: "Why do you sentimentalize?"

In this letter the Communists of the city of Nolinsk grow indignant over the fact that the British consul, Lockart, who had been implicated in a plot, was freed and not shot; the authors of this letter express their indignation over the fact that Lockart was not tortured and they insist that the later be used in the future:

"Tell us why did you not subject this very Lockart to the *most refined* torture in order to extort from him information and addresses which that goose certainly had in his possession? Tell us, how is it that instead of putting him to tortures, the very description of which would strike terror into the heart of every counter-revolutionist, you permitted him to leave the Che-Ka greatly embarrassed? Let every British worker know that the official representative of his country is engaged in such dealings that he has to be put to torture on account of them." . . .

The letter ends with an appeal: "Enough of sentimentalizing! . . . A dangerous scoundrel was caught. What should have been done was to extort all possible information from him and dispatch him to the other world." . . .

Why did "The Weekly" print this letter? Was it to administer an open rebuff to the savage, beastly demand—to warn other Che-Ka organizations against such a misdirected "enthusiasm" and to steer them along the channels of the plain, everyday humanism of the average man, that is, if Socialist humanism was too exalted a guide for the daily practice of the Che-Ka? What were the comments on this letter on the part of the editors of the Communist "Weekly of the Extraordinary Commission" (Che-Ka) whose aim was to guide the provincial Che-Ka, to steer them along the lines laid down by the All-Russian Che-Ka and have them carry out the "ideas and methods" of the latter?

The editorial point of view upon questions raised by this letter was expressed in the following laconic formula held out before the provincial Extraordinary Committees (Che-Ka):

". . . . The All-Russian Che-Ka does not object in principle. . . ."

It was a virtual order to use torture! . . .

And did Dzerzhinsky, the Chief of the All-Russian Che-Ka, a member of the Central Committee of the party, a member of the All-powerful Politbureau and all the highest organs of the Soviet power —did he come out flatly against it? No, he did not commit himself upon this question even with a single phrase. And Lenin? And the others—Trotzky and Co.? Did they open a campaign against this manifested tendency? Did they launch an educational campaign in the spirit of Socialism in order to bar such outbreaks of bestiality? Did they struggle against introducing the mores of medieval torture chambers and inquisition? Not one of them saw fit to say a single word about this affair. But sometimes prior to publication of this letter, Latzis (one of the most prominent figures in the All-Russian Che-Ka) was already philosiphizing on this subject, arriving at the conclusion that "there are no written laws for a civil war. . . ."

The same Latzis, together with Ksenofontov, the Chairman of the All-Russian Che-Ka, issued orders to the provincial Che-Ka bodies bidding them to forward all the Left Social-Revolutionists to Moscow. The order was accompanied with a significant hint of the following nature.

"Here we shall be able to make the utmost use of them, and, as the past practice has already shown us, we shall be able to recruit from their midst valuable collaborators for the Che-Ka. . . . "

The use of torture, as already made known, was officially introduced by a secret circular sent out by the All-Russian Che-Ka at the beginning of 1921: "If neither cross-examination nor confrontation with eye witnesses, nor usual threats are of any avail, one should be guided by the old, tested means."

That there was such a secret instruction in existence was revealed by the investigating committee of the Revolutionary Tribunal of the Stavropol "gubernia," whose aim was to probe into charges of tortures allegedly practiced in the Criminal Investigation Department. Similar information of this case is to be found in "Sotzialistichesky Viestnik" and also in the large book of collected articles issued by the Left Social-Revolutionists under the title "The Roads of The Revolution".337)

"The committee established," writes the correspondent of the "Sotzialistichesky Viestnik," "that apart from the usual beatings, suspending prisoners, and other forms of torture, the Criminal Investigation Department of Stavropol uses the following means in order to extort evidence:

---

337) "Sotzialistichesky Viestnik," No. 18, September 21, 1922, the article: "Legislation of Torture," p. 7; "Puti Revolutzii" ("The Road of Revolution"); the article: "The Torture-Chamber of Stavropol," p. 336, Berlin, 1923.

"1) *A hot cellar* consisting of a blind, windowless cell in the basement—three feet long and 1.5 feet wide. The floor consists of three small steps. Into this cell, by way of torture, 18 people are crowded, so that not all of them have enough standing room on the floor, some of the prisoners being kept in a suspended position by hanging on to the shoulders of others who were lucky enough to plant their feet upon the floor. The air in this cell is so thick that a lighted lamp goes out immediately, and matches cannot be lighted. People are kept in this cell for two and three days; not only are they deprived of food during that time but also of water, and in addition, they are not let out of this cell even for a minute, not even to relieve the wants of nature. It was ascertained that women were put into this cell together with men (in particular, a woman, by the name of Weitzman).

"2) *A cold cellar.* This is part of what was formerly a refrigerator; the arrested is stripped naked and then let down along a movable ladder. The ladder is then taken away and water is poured upon the naked prisoner. This is done in the winter, on cold frosty days. Cases have been registered when 8 pails of water were splashed upon every prisoner in the pit (among other prisoners Gursky and Weiner were put through this torture).

"3) *Measuring the skull.* The head of the cross-examined prisoner is tightly bound with cord into which a small stick, a nail or a pencil is inserted; by rotating this inserted stick the cord wound around the skull tightens to such an extend that finally the skull is scalped, the skin with the hair of the head coming clean off the skull.

"Along with these tortures used in order to obtain 'confessions' on the part of the prisoners, there were cases, officially established by the Investigating Committee, of assassination of prisoners at alleged attempts to escape. (Thus in April, 1922, was killed a prisoner by the name Mastriukov).

"All these facts were established on the basis of the testimony furnished by the victims and witnesses of torture scenes, of the data of the medical experts, of the evidence obtained as a result of autopsy, of the confessions made by the agents who were administering those tortures and who testified that they had acted on orders from the Chief of the Criminal Investigation Department (the latter was a member of the Executive Committee of the Stavropol Soviet, a member of the Communist Party Committee of Stavropol and Acting Chief of the Stavropol G. P. U.), his assistant Povetzky and Topyshev, the legal adviser of the Department. The third degree methods were applied under their personal direction and with their personal participation.

"The Tribunal resolved to indict those guilty of such methods and issued orders for their arrest. No one, however, was arrested, the Chief of the G.P.U.—Chernobroviy—having tucked the indictment away on the premises of the communal quarters of the G. P. U., and also having produced a secret circular of the All-Russian Che-Ka authorizing, as we already pointed out, the 'use of the old, tested means.'

"The origin of this document," the correspondent continues, "is such. Toward the middle of 1921 a complaint was made about Voul, the well-known investigator of the Moscow Che-Ka, to the effect that he was using third degree methods at his hearings. Voul wanted to resign and to forego all responsibility in respect to the development of banditry in Moscow. In view of this threat Menzhinsky—the Chief of the G. P. U.—allegedly permitted the continuation of the former methods; following that, a circular was sent out authorizing the use of 'the old tested means.' The finale of this story is rather common. None of the authors of the third degree methods were arrested. But instead persecutions were showered upon those who showed excessive zeal and ardor in aiding to unearth the mysteries of the Criminal Investigation Department."

This letter published in "The Roads of the Revolution" (Putyi Revoliutzii) dealing with the aforementioned tortures makes reference to . . . ."the use of branding irons" . . . .

There exists a quantity of vast material bearing upon tortures in use during those years; it especially abounds in the reminescences of the active figures of the white-guardist movement and the non-socialist anti-Bolshevik elements. Many of these narrated facts show remarkable coincidence in the various versions presented by the authors of those reminiscences. Even if one hundredth of those narratives are true, we have an amazing picture replete with hair-raising horrors. But, in view of the legitimate distrust shown toward those sources, I shall refrain from using them until an opportunity arises to check up on these sources. Throughout this study we confined ourselves to Socialist and Bolshevik official sources, and in this case we are going to the very same source. Let us at first turn to the Bolshevik papers.

If we unfold the Moscow "Izvestia" of January 26, 1919, No. 18, we shall find there a letter from a Communist—a casual victim of this system. In this letter entitled "Is it a medieval torture-chamber?" he complains and gives vent to his indignation:

"I was arrested by accident, right on the premises where, as it turned out, counterfeiting was being done. I was kept ten days in confinement before being taken out for cross examination, and during that time I went through an experience which sounds almost unbeliev-able." (The author of the letter refers to the Investigation Committee of the Sustchevo-Mariyinsky district in Moscow) . . . "Men were beaten to pulp, beaten till they fell into a swoon, in which state they were carried into the cellar or refrigerator where the beating was resumed, this keeping up for 18 hours a day. This scene affected me so much that I nearly went mad as a result of it."

The "Pravda" of February 22, of the same year, released the information that the Che-Ka of the town of Vladimir had a special "corner" where "the heels of the prisoners are pricked with needles."

R. Reisner (a Communist; daughter of a renowned professor of Political Science, also a Communist, who played an important part in framing the first Soviet Constitution) wrote about the Petrograd Che-Ka in December 1918: "Your torture-chambers make me blush." And in February 1919, the Petrograd "Pravda" descanted on the usefulness of make-believe shootings.

"In one of the villages a Kulak was assessed twenty poods of grain. He did not pay. He was arrested—and still he was adamant. He was put up against the wall—the Kulak did not budge. A bullet whizzed by near his ear—and, oh, miracles! He gave in!" [338]

The same kind of make-believe shootings "for the sake of a practical joke" are described by F. Dan in his book "Two Years of Wanderings." (P. 40). F. Dan recounts instances of such "practical jokes" as told to him by one of the organizers of such "shootings." In one case this "make-believe shooting" resulted in the death of the victim from a heart attack.

Third degree methods were widely used and, as the Moscow

---

[338] This fact and the excerpts from the papers are cited by S. P. Melgunov in his book "The Red Terror in Russia," p. 205.

trials and confessions have shown us, they are still used not only in respect to common criminals but also political prisoners and exiles.

We have already cited a number of cases illustrating the use of such third degree methods; the description of the concentration camp of Solovky, the declaration of the Left Social-Revolutionists; the case of Olga Romanova, the eighteen year old Anarchist girl; cases of prisoners setting themselves on fire; hunger strikes; the case of the Social-Revolutionists that were sentenced to death, and many other similar cases. We shall therefore confine ourselves to a few additional illustrations.

I was told by the brothers Tiamin (the brothers Tiamin were implicated in the case growing out of the explosions at the Leontievsky Alley; both bought their life and freedom by turning state evidence) that the prisoners, especially Baranovsky, were kept in the cell in a standing position, and that everyone of them was guarded by a Che-Ka agent who kept on preventing the prisoner from falling asleep. Baranovsky and others were tortured at the cross-examination: they were dealt a number of stabs in the back with a dagger. At the same time there were persistent rumors in Moscow to the effect that Tamara and Cherepanov, Left Social-Revolutionists of the activist orientation, were put to torture and that in the end they were strangled and not shot, as it was given out officially. There is ground to believe that the well-known Anarchist theoretician, Lev Cherny, died under torture, since only a few days prior to his alleged shooting he was transferred to the hospital of the Butirki prison where only one day prior to this shooting he accepted a parcel sent to him from the outside and even signed for it. In addition, only on the eve of this date of his shooting assurances were received from Leo Kamenev to the effect that Cherny would soon be freed; on the day following those assurances, Cherny's name was put on the list of people that had been shot. Those, however, were mere rumors, but here are genuine facts.

In the month of March, Tikhon Kashirin, Anarchist, and Yeliseyev, Left Social-Revolutionist, who were kept in the Inner prison of the All-Russian Che-Ka, were beaten up and thrown into the prison cellar. The solitary cell where I was kept was located in the same corridor where comrades Kashirin, Yeliseyev, Feldman and Surkova were confined. Upon hearing the cries of the beaten up comrades, the vile abuse on the part of the chekists, the crash of the broken window panes, I began to knock frenziedly at the door, trying to draw the attention upon myself and halt the slugging to some extent, but no attention was paid to my "obstruction," that is, not until the recalcitrants were fully subdued. Two months later I met those two comrades in the Taganka prison, and they told me the full story of the beating and the third degree given to them. This story was told in full by Yeliseyev in the court. Here is how it happened:

"I was kept in cell No. 19 together with Dr. Dubrovin from the Union of Russian People,[339]) a stool pigeon and a profiteer. On March 11, I entered a declaration wtih the Presidium of the All-Russian Che-Ka demanding that I be transferred to Butirsky prison and also registering a protest against conditions under which I was kept in the prison of the All-Russian Che-Ka. On March 14 I entered a similar declaration, pointing out that I was reserving freedom of action in case this declaration remains unanswered. Not having received any reply by March 15, I began carrying out my plan at 4 P. M. on the very same date, having broken the window pane in sign of protest; an hour later the Warden, accompanied by a few guards, came to my cell and led me away to the cellar; the door of one of those dungeons was opened. I was kicked in there with a blow in the back. There I found the Anarchist Tikhon Kashirin, with only one shirt on his body; he was also thrown into the cellar for making an 'obstruction' . . . Two hours later the prison warden Dukis, accompanied by other chekists, came down to the cellar and heaping the choicest abuse upon Kashirin, they pounced on him dragging him away, showering intermittent blows in the meantime. Then Dukis turned around and threatening me with his fist, he said: 'as for you, I'll get even with you yet'. Indeed, an hour later Dukis came together with his assistant and both, swearing and shouting, pounced on me—one from the right and the other from the left—and began hitting me on the head. I don't remember the rest: my ears began to ring and sparks flew from my eyes. When I woke up I heard someone groaning, and it was only sometimes later that I realized that there was no one in the cellar but myself and that it was myself that was emitting those groans. The ice around me melted; I found myself lying in water, with chills going through my body, and at

---

339) "Union of Russian People"—an extreme reactionary and anti-Semitic organization of the pre-revolutionary period.

the same time I had no strength to get up. My sides and chest ached so that I could not even touch them. At last I managed with great difficulty to get up. Then I began to feel thirsty. I somehow sidled over to the door and asked the sentry to get me a drink. The latter summoned the guard in charge of the detail, who came over and told me: 'one is not allowed to fetch water to those who are kept in the cellar, but, if you want I'll bring an icicle from the drainage pipe.' I agreed. He fetched the icicle and I avidly ate it, after which I began to feel somewhat better. It was a terrible night on the whole. At 10 A. M., the door opened and both Dukis and Adamson entered. The second one unloosened a torrent of scurrilous abuse, demanding that I get up and show them my hands. I showed them my hands but I refused to get up. They seized me by the collar of my overcoat, lifted me from the floor and began beating me up again; after a while they dragged me upstairs and flung me into an empty cell with a broken window pane. Dukis said: 'There is your place, you cur.' And he left. . . . I was kept there for two days, March 16 and 17. I felt worse and worse. . . . The cell was devoid of everything: there was no cot to sleep on, nor was there even a table or chair to sit on. March 17 I was taken out for cross examination. I refused to go saying that I could not walk. In a little while two guards came in and led me away to the investigator.

"I told the latter that I had been on a hunger strike for seven days and that I did not feel well. The investigator replied that he knew nothing of the hunger strike, 'but I am giving you the word of a Communist that tomorrow you will be remanded to the Butirky if you agree to testify.' I did testify, but in the state that I was then in I could not even be aware of what I was saying. Following that I was transferred to another cell —No. 16—and again I had that miscreant—Dr. Dubrovin from the Union of Russian People—as a cell mate. On the following day I accepted bread.. . . . It was not until April 1 that I was called by the investigator Kozlovsky who asked me about the beating. I testified in full in respect to the latter and demanded that I be transferred to the Butirky prison. He grinned, saying: 'You have not recovered yet;' he did, however, promise that I would be transferred on the following day. The promise was not kept and I was left in the same cell until April 17; on that day I entered again a declaration

— 250 —

demanding a hearing. I was brought to Piukenen to whom I declared: 'If you don't transfer me today, I'll break every window in your cabinet and will refuse to budge from here.' In the evening of the same day I was transferred to the Taganka prison".340)

The well-known member of the Left Social-Revolutionists, I. A. Shabalin, was kept in the Inner prison of the G. P. U. known as the Gorokhovaya House of Preliminary Detention (in Petrograd). Ignoring completely the possible consequences resulting from having his letter published abroad, he signed it with his full name.

"Do not forget that I am writing this from a torture-chamber, in comparison with which the Russian Bastile fortresses—Shlusselburg and Petropavlovsk—the casements where I languished in the old days as 'state criminal,' pale in their regime and in their special measures.

"The conditions prevailing in the present prison make for continuous torture."

Shabalin thus describes the regime of solitary confinement.

"A room 15 yards by 14 wide was subdivided into 29 cells, every one of which is 2.5 yards by 1.5 wide. More than half of the cell is occupied by a little table and a bench. This is all the furniture, except a dim electric bulb, of about five candle-power, right under the ceiling. Nothing else. No windows. No mattresses, no quilts, no pillows, the prisoners sleep on bare bunks in those old cells. The doors of the cells are locked day and night. Here everything is forbidden: open-air exercises, conversations, reading of books. One is allowed only to breathe the poisonous air, to eat during the day two little bowls of soup, prepared from dried fish or herring, and a pound of bread, to drink three cups of hot water with a teaspoonful of granulated sugar. And that is all."

Such were conditions prevailing in the first building of the prison. In the latter part of the letter Shabalin describes two kinds of torture cells: the "cooler" and the "cork cell," both of which are located in the second building.

"The first kind (the 'cooler') is rather simple in construction. There are windows in them without glass. The 'coolers' where people spend weeks in terrible sufferings, partly due to undernourishment, are provided in order to 'freeze out' the prisoners' 'heresy'.

---

340) "The Roads of Revolution": "The Trial of the Left Social-Revolutionists, June 27-29, 1922," pp. 307-308.

"The 'cork cells' are the acme of prison craft. The walls, ceiling, and door are inlaid with cork. There are no windows, no bed. The 'furniture' is like that of the first building. There are only 2 'cork cells.' (I was confined in one of them).

"The 'cork cells' are considered as the most 'terrible' and isolated of all. I am convinced that it is enough to spend three or four months in such a 'cork cell' to have one's health completely shattered. The absence of natural light (in the mines even horses go blind), of fresh air walks, of beds and bedding, the meagre nourishment, the absence of a change of underwear, the cold and the dampness! One must add the ban on books, the wealth of huge spiders, wood-lice, mice, rats and other 'creatures.' It taxes anyone's power of endurance to spend even a short time in such a cell."341)

"E. Litvinova, a member of the Left Social-Revolutionist Party, was put into 'cooler' No. 10, to 'freeze out' her party loyalty and convictions. This was in the month of March, when the frost in Petrograd reached 10 degrees (Reomur). All she had was a light Fall overcoat. She was doubled up in convulsions from cold. . . . She was kept a whole week in this 'cooler'. . . .

. . . "In the 'cork-cellar' No. 1 was kept a young man, a worker of the Putilov Plant, by the name of Misha. He related that he was cross-examined by the investigator with the aid. . . . of a block of wood."

An insane prisoner, a common criminal, on February 28, 1922, was subjected to "cauterization" by way of testing whether his insanity was genuine or whether it was a case of simulation.

A Kronstadt sailor Yakovenko, the Associate Chairman of the Kronstadt Revolutionary Committee, was arrested upon his return from Finland. Shabalin tells that he was cross-examined 15 hours a day, the aim of this third degree method of examination being to extort a "confession" from Yakovenko and also a letter calling upon the escaped Kronstadters to return to Soviet Russia. . . .

"When Yakovenko categorically refused to send such a 'message,' the 'experts' of the Gorokhovaya advanced a more convincing argument. Behind a curtain was mobilized 'the public opinion' of Kronstadt. Several women (rather the wives of Communists) began to 'persuade' Yakovenko that before and after the revolt they were

---

341) "The Roads of Revolution": "A Letter From the Prison on Goro-khovaya," p. 329-331.

satisfied with existing conditions, and they demanded of him, as the leader, that he return their 'sons' to them. Yakovenko would not budge; then the women began to spit in the face of the imprisoned revolutionist. . . . Yakovenko was hand-cuffed upon his arrest." 342)

Of himself Shabalin relates the following episode taking place upon his arrest.

". . . The automobile started. Then they started to give me 'the works.' With one blow the cap was knocked off my head. I was beaten with the butt of a revolver over the hands and feet (my fingers still hurt me, and in the first days it was difficult to hold a spoon). But that was not enough for the sadists. I was put to real torture. . . . It is distressing to recall. . . . They tortured my eyes. . . and sexual organs. . . . I lost consciousness. . . . When I felt the first blow, I firmly resolved not to emit a single sound, a single groan. And biting my lips hard, I kept silent. My grave-like silence was taken as a sign of 'weak pressure.' They began 'stepping on it.' Again I lost consciousness. When I came to myself, blood was streaming from my nose and left cheek. . . ."343)

A. A. Izmaylovich, a renowned Left Social-Revolutionist who had served time in Tzarist penal servitude, tells in her "Seven Weeks in the All-Russian Che-Ka"344) that in the case of Lydia Surkova, a member of the Left Social-Revolutionists there was "a rehearsal of shootings."

The examinations carried on at night under conditions of ceaseless shootings are in themselves a dreadful torture. This is how Izmailovitch describes her experiences in this respect:

"In the evening people are taken out for cross-examination. Sometimes one is taken out from eleven to one o'clock at night. When that takes place I and Sakharov lie in our bunks all tense with expectation: *Will he or will he not come back.* Sometimes we have to wait quite a long time: two or three hours. If the party comes back we breathe more easily and begin dozing off".345)

The same Izmaylovitch tells of a cell-mate who was charged with having taken part in the explosion at the Leontievsky Alley and in

342) Ibid, p. 332.
343) Ibid, p. 334.
344) "Kremlin Behind the Bars," p. 113.
345) Ibid, p. 110.

the hold-up of the People's Bank. This man had proofs that when those events charged to him took place he was staying in a small county town in the "gubernia of Smolensk." "Latzis told him on December 2 that by December 15 he would be either shot or released".346) One can easily imagine the torture which this man went through those two weeks, harrowed by the incessant thought: will he or will he not be shot? . . . .

If such sadistic "performances" were going on in the metropolitan cities, in the most cultured centers of the countries, one can easily imagine what was going on and is still going on in the provinces—far away from those "cultured centers! . . ."

Here is an illustration. In 1920, on April 12, six Left Social-Revolutionists and one Anarchist escaped from the prison of the Cheliabinsk Che-Ka. When the escape became known, everyone of the remaining politicals was grilled about this event.

"The Chief of the Secret-Operative Department, Kosopoliansky, (he was shot afterwards as a white guardist), who was in charge of the exiled comrades, suggested that all prepare to die as soon as 'the other skunks (the remaining comrades) are examined.' Meanwhile, all of them were taken to the 'cooler.' Comrade Osipova who gave sharp answers at the cross-examination, was kept for an hour and a half in a rat infested pit. . . . Karbikov was taken to a barn, placed before a firing squad; orders were already given to shoot, but the firing was halted in the last minute; after that fire was brought in to torture him by burning, etc".347)

One could tell at much greater length of the use of torture in regard to political prisoners, but I believe that the facts already cited will suffice to give one an idea of the brutalization and moral degradation overtaking any person who is vested with unlimited and uncontrolled power over defenseless people. Lenin's appeals for shootings which he tirelessly flung forth from rostrum and the press were translated into departmental orders of the All-Russian Che-Ka —G. P. U. And in order to carry out those appeals there came into existence, with Lenin's consent and approval, an "oprichina"348) which began to disintegrate in the moral sense, losing its human

346) Ibid, p. 125.
347) "Kremlin Behind the Bars": "The Escape from Cheliabinsk," pp. 195-196.
348) The Life-Guards of the Tzar John IV.

aspect, infecting the entire party and stirring fierce hatred among the people.

Lenin is not only responsible for the shootings, for the terror; to an equal measure he is responsible for the brutalities manifested during the terror, for the sadism, for all the torture-chambers. Even if he did not write the instructions as to "the use of the old tested means," he surely was aware of it. He surely was not ignorant of the letter of the Bolsheviks from Nolinsk and of the fact that this letter was approved by the "Weekly of the Che-Ka," that is, by Dzerzhinsky. Even granted his ignorance of both—the letter and the instructions about the use of torture, (this is an absolutely unlikely assumption), he still bears the responsibility for it in his capacity as the Chairman of People's Commissars to whom the Che-Ka—G. P. U. was subordinated. History cannot and will not free him from this responsibility.

Lenin, as the high-priest of a sect, bears the responsibility for the degradation and cheapening of human personality which is un-precedented in the history of mankind; for the absolute lack of regard for human life, for the moral disintegration of the horde of his followers and the corrosion of the basic moral principles without which men sink to a state below that of a brute. He set up medieval torture-chambers, an outwardly "modernized" inquisition in Russia which is still flourishing. . . . Lenin's works were deter-mined by a determined philosophy—the philosophy of Marxism or as it is wrongly styled, the "scientific" Socialism; and it follows that it is this essentially absolutist, barbarous, reactionary and anti-scientific philosophy that bears the entire responsibility for the mountains of corpses in Russia, for the racking and tortures, for economic ruin and famine, for brutality and slavery, for the Asiatic absolutism, for the German barrack system—and for Lenin as its end-product.

CHAPTER XI

LENIN'S TERROR WITHIN THE PARTY

Taking as point of departure the Marxian theory of centralization, of the "dictatorship of the proletariat," of the state and its role in the period of transition from Capitalism to Communism, during which the state is supposed to be not a free institution but the organ of repression and annihilation of the enemies and adversaries of the Proletariat, Lenin inescapably and logically arrived at the conclusion that the "dictatorship of the proletariat" in reality is something like the "slaveholding democracy" of ancient Greece. This was, as we have already showed, the argument he used against K. Kautsky.

But he overlooked the very elementary fact that (as every high school boy knows) the slaveholding democracy of ancient Greece was torn by internecine struggle within the slaveholding class itself— a struggle for power and privileges, for the right to rule over the demos. As a result of this bitter conflict democracies often degenerated into oligarchies and tyranies.

The state, Lenin said, is the proletariat; it is the vanguard of the proletariat; it is we, that is the Communist Party. Consequently, under the "dictatorship of the proletariat" "*our*" party must be the slaveholding class; it must, therefore, inevitably repeat to some extent, the history of the slaveholding class of democratic Greece and undergo the same internecine strife as that between the partisans of the slave-holding democracy and oligarchy.

In 1920 the Communist Party entered into this degenerative phase of development. Lenin was a demagogue: having brought "his class," his party, to power under the banner of democracy, he immediately established an oligarchy, and his own preeminence as the first among the oligarchs has never been challenged. As long as common danger existed, the party "demos" suffered this tyranny; but no sooner was the danger alleviated, no sooner did the civil war come to an end, then the lower strata broke into rebellion against the oligarchy; this opposition was met with ostracism, which resulted only in intensifying the struggle.

We saw that, according to Lenin, the Marxian "dictatorship of the proletariat" connotes the dictatorship of the vanguard of the working class, and since such a vanguard can be only the party, the "dictatorship of the proletariat" is in the last analysis, the dictatorship of the party, and by the same logic, the adversaries and enemies of this dictatorship inevitably are, as we have shown, all those who do not belong to this ruling party. And since the state of the transitional period is also the party, and since this state must ruthlessly suppress its adversaries, it follows logically that terror has to be applied against all, save a very small handful of the "vanguard of the proletariat" organized into a party.

The party is organized upon the principles of centralization and subordination to the leaders. In order to maintain their own positions, the leaders organize around themselves a clique with whose aid they get control of the party apparatus, manning it entirely with their own people. Hence we have the dictatorship of the leaders within the party, and the "dictatorship of the proletariat" becomes the dicatorship of the leaders. The state becomes first the state of the leaders, and then the state of one single leader. Such was the role of Lenin, and, in our own time, Stalin. When Lenin said: the state it is we, by "we" he meant himself; hence to oppose Lenin was to oppose the state, the dictatorship of the proletariat, which necessarily had become the state of one leader.

Having become the state, Lenin proceeded ruthlessly to suppress his adversaries. But just as the dictatorship of the party inevitably brings forth resistance within the country, (a resistance ruthlessly suppressed by terror), so does intra-party dictatorship inevitably beget among certain of its members discontent, then protest, and finally overt rebellion. These discontented and rebellious members of the party, according to the essence of the "workers' state," are the objects of the suppression and terror. So intra-party terror, just as terror within the country, has the same source: centralization, dictatorship and the state.

The revolt within the party began when Lenin was still alive; he kept on suppressing it through terror, ever tightening the inner regime to prevent open rebellion or to quell it in its incipient phases. The dictatorship of Lenin and his clique early accumulated much discontent but the members themselves restrained their differences during the years of civil war.

But a conflict was developing in the party along two lines: the ideological issue and the actual struggle for power within the party and the country. Despite Lenin's efforts, the rank and file had not lived down the ideals of 1917, the ideals of the Paris Commune. Whereas they put up with the dictatorship both in the Party and the country during the civil war, upon its termination they demanded that the oligarchy give place to a genuine workers' democracy. Opposed to the rank and file was the Party bureaucracy which defended its own position of power. To disagree with the bureaucracy was to place oneself outside of the "vanguard of the working class," to deviate in the direction of "petty-bourgeois Anarchism, which threatens the unity of the Party and the maintenance of the dictatorship of the proletariat. . . ."

The *Workers' Opposition*, which emerged during the 1920 discussion concerning trade unions, could not subscribe to this interpretation. Thus, there arose along with the trade union question, a complex of other problems, such as: bureaucracy and democracy in the party as well as the state, freedom, the role of the party, syndicalism, labor discipline, etc. There were many other issues and many sides to each issue, but notwithstanding all their differences, the representatives of these several platforms were unanimous in their condemnation of the *Workers' Opposition* headed by Shliapnikov, Medvediev, Kolontay and others.

*

Following Lenin's historic analogy, we may say that intra-party strife immediately assumed the character of a struggle between the Communist patricians and the Communist plebeians, with the difference, however, that the Communist Grachii perished without having obtained any improvements for the plebeians of the party.

Lenin, as head of the Communist patricians, and experienced in matters of party strife, immediately realized the seriousness of these discussions. "The bitter truth should be faced courageously," he wrote in the article "The Party Crisis".[349] "The party is shaken with fever. The question becomes: is the malady limited to the upper layers and exclusively those of the Moscow party or has the entire organism been stricken? If the latter be true, can this organism be

---

349) P. 29, vol. XVIII, part 1.

fully cured within a few weeks (prior to and following the party convention)? Can it be immunized against recurrence of the malady, or will its illness assume a long drawn-out and dangerous character?"

The malady, as we know now, proved a chronic affair. The party organism was stricken with a cancer which demanded surgical treatment. Since that time, it has undergone constant painful and serious operations which made it unrecognisible; but the cancer has not yet been cut out and a dreadful death is imminent in the near future.

*

Lenin addressed himself to this problem. "What is to be done," he asked, "for the quickest and surest solution?" And he answered, "We need a close examination of all participants, an examination guided by a certain partiality".350) And he evolved those methods of maintaining obedience which he applied outside of the party, in the country as a whole: threats, intimidation, in a word—terror.

"The Party Crisis" was intended as a warning to the participants in the party discussion who were getting out of control, and especially to the Workers' Opposition and kindred groupings who were demanding freedom and democracy.

"We must combat ideological disharmony and those unhealthy elements of the opposition who renounce any 'militarization of economy;' thus rejecting not only the 'methods of appointment' which have been in practise until now, but any possible 'system of appointments' (rather than elections); in the last analysis this means the denial of the leading role of the Party in regard to the mass of non-party people. We must fight against this syndicalist deviation, which will ruin the party, if adopted".351)

To Lenin, the "unhealthy elements of the opposition" were the party plebs who demanded the abolition of the oligarchic party regime and of the dictatorship of the patricians. Having reviled them as "loud mouths," having stygmatized their demands as "the worst forms of Menshevism," he frightened all other dissenters into submission by declaring that "the capitalists of the Entente will undoubtedly take advantage of our party's weakness by invading

350) Ibid.
351) Ibid, p. 37.

— 259 —

us again, and the Social Revolutionists will organize plots and rebellions".352)

These warnings and threats were made in the midst of the discussion on the role of the trade unions, in January, 1921, but since the tenth convention of the party was scheduled for March, actual repressions were postponed. Lenin was confident that since the party apparatus was in his hands, all his recommendations would be adopted and terroristic measures against any and all opposition groups would be legalized.

**
*

The tenth party convention began on March 8 and ended on March 16, 1921. In his "Inaugural Speech," Lenin of course, did not fail, to cut short the discussion by impressing the delegates with the danger inherent in party wrangling and disagreements; and naturally he called for unity, which meant for him the stabilization of the party status quo.

"You, Comrades, must know," he declared, "that all our enemies —and their name is legion—in innumerable foreign publications repeat and amplify the countless rumors which our bourgeois and petty-bourgeois enemies circulate here within the soviet republic, namely: if there is discussion, that means there are wranglings; if wranglings, there must be dissensions; and dissensions mean that the Communists have weakened and the time has come to take advantage of their weakness. This has become the slogan of a world which is hostile to us. We dare not forget it for a single moment. We must show that, whatever luxury of discussion we permitted ourselves, rightly or wrongly, in the past, we now recognize the need for greater harmony and unity than ever before. We must tell ourselves, after having duly considered the profusion of platforms, shadings, delicate gradations of opinion at our Party convention, that much as we may disagree and wrangle here, we have so many enemies, and the task facing the dictatorship of the proletariat in a peasant country is so great, that formal solidarity is not enough. Henceforth, we cannot afford the slightest trace of factionalism, regardless where and how it might have occured in the past".353)

---

352) Ibid.

353) P. 104-105, vol. XVIII, part 1.

On that very same day Lenin, in his "Report on the Political Activity of the Central Committee of the Communist Party," regretted that he had allowed so much discussion in the party, "On my own account I must add that this luxury should not have been permitted, and that in allowing it we were no doubt in error".354)

Lenin complained that when he pointed out to the comrades the difficult situation of the country—poor crops, army demobilization, economic crisis and ruin—saying that under these conditions it was necessary to maintain the closest unity and that "the atmosphere of controversy is becoming highly dangerous, some comrades, to whom I happened to talk a few months ago, and to say, 'Beware, here is a definite threat to the rule of the working class and its dictatorship' replied, 'this is a method of intimidation, you terrorize.' I had to listen several times to this libeling of my remarks but I always answered that it would be ludicrous for me to terrorize the old revolutionists who had undergone all kinds of trials in their lives".355)

The speakers of the Workers' Opposition and similar groups who took the floor on Lenin's report, charged him and the Central Committee with administrative wilfulness and with gagging opinion; they demanded freedom of criticism and broad discussion. Osinsky accused Lenin and the Central Committee of having ousted Sapronov from the Presidium of the convention; while all the left groupings complained of lack of democracy in the Party, exposing all Lenin's talk of unity as insincere since neither he nor the Central Committee had any confidence in the working class.

Lenin's answers were demagogic and rude: Do you want to carry on discussion? You can do it in the pages of "Pravda," they are open to you. Sapronov was ousted? But that is a trivial matter which should be ignored. Lack of confidence in the working class? "This is wholly untrue. We are looking for and are ready to take from the ranks of workers any one with the least administrative ability. We examine him".356)

Lenin assailed chiefly the Workers' Opposition. His target was a clause in Kolontay's pamphlet, which stated that "organizing the management of the national economy belongs to the All-Russian

354) P. 111, vol. XVIII, part 1.
355) Ibid, p. 113.
356) Ibid, p. 132.

Convention of Producers, united into trade and industrial unions, which is to elect a central organ administering the national economy."

Lenin's refutation was: "After two years of Soviet power we openly declared at the Communist International to the entire world that the dictatorship of the proletariat is possible only through the Communist Party. . . . Despite all this, there are people 'class conscious' people, who tell us that 'organizing management of national economy belongs to the All-Russian Convention of Producers.' An All-Russian Convention of Producers—what would that be? Should we waste our time on such oppositions within the party? It seems to me that we have had enough of this. All this talk of freedom of speech and freedom of criticism constitutes nine tenths of the meaning of the speeches of the 'Workers Opposition,' which in reality have no meaning at all".357)

And further: "The All-Russian Convention of Producers should manage production? I am really at loss when I try to characterize this jumble of words. But I am comforted by the thought that we have here party and soviet workers who have been engaging in revolutionary activities for the last one, two or three years, and it would be a mere waste of time to criticize such phrases before these comrades, for they themselves close discussion when they hear such speeches; these are boring and it shows a lack of seriousness when people talk about an All-Russian Convention of Producers which is to manage the national economy".358)

"Way back last summer at the second congress of the Communist International I referred to the resolution on the role of the Communist party. This resolution unites the Communist workers in the Communist parties of the whole world. And this resolution explains everything".359)

Lenin's patrician sentiment was outraged by the Workers' Opposition. He refused to even consider the idea that a convention of producers and not the party—that is, he himself—should administer production. And at the same time he ridiculed personally the representatives of the Workers' Opposition: "Thus, Comrade Kolontay and Shliapnikov, and the 'class-conscious' people who follow them, want to subject to their guidance the Councils of National

357) Ibid, p. 128.
358) Ibid, p. 130.
359) Ibid, p. 127.

Economy, the central organs and principal committees as well as the Rykovs, Nogins and other 'nonentities' and to lay down theoretical tasks for them. Can we be expected, comrades, to take all this seriously?"360)

One of the planks of the platform of the Workers' Opposition reads "it is the decision of the Workers' Opposition to remain in the party when defeated at the convention and to uphold firmly the point of view of the opposition, saving the party and rectifying its line."

Lenin comments ironically: " 'Even when defeated at the convention'! what foresight, indeed. But begging your pardon, I, for one, can confidently declare that the party convention shall not permit this".361) Hence, before the convention had passed its decision, Lenin had already resolutely proclaimed, "The Opposition is finished. The lid has been clamped down on its activities. And now, enough of the Opposition for us".362)

What measures did Lenin suggest in the fight against the Workers' Opposition?

"We will sift the healthy from the unhealthy in the Workers' Opposition. . . . We will take those whom we want, and not those whom they want. . . . We shall win over to our side, the side of the Party, whatever is healthy and proletarian in the Workers' Opposition, leaving behind the 'class-conscious' authors of syndicalist speeches." 363) Sifting meant on the one hand disciplinary penalties and expulsions from the party, and on the other, outright bribing: "to draw the desirable elements nearer to the work and to promote them to higher positions".364)

Lenin suggested, and the convention adopted, a long resolution censuring the Workers' Opposition for its syndicalist and Anarchist deviation; it also declared that the propaganda of those ideas was incompatible with membership in the Communist Party. Moreover, he found the view of this group and of all similar groups and persons "politically incorrect and a direct danger to the maintenance

360) Ibid, p. 131.
361) Ibid, p. 129.
362) Ibid.
363) Ibid, p. 130.
364) "A Speech on Trade Unions," p. 135, vol. XVIII, part 1.

of power by the proletariat".365) In a word, the Workers' Opposition and similar groups were declared counter-revolutionary, and the apparatus, that is Lenin, was granted the right to react accordingly. This was precisely what Lenin sought and, as we shall see, did not fail to avail himself of this right.

*

The discussion on trade unions marks the beginning of the disintegration of the Communist Party, the beginning of the struggle for power, which, with Kirov's assassination assumed a highly dramatic and gruesome character. But at the time of the tenth party convention it was difficult to foresee that the discussion on trade unions would take such a turn.

This convention prohibited all factional groupings within the party. The several groups which had emerged from this discussion— Trotzky's group, Bukharin's group, Ignatov's group, Sapronov's group of "democratic centralism," the Workers' Opposition—all fell in line with the decision although the adherents of the Workers' Opposition did not cease to propagate their ideas in the party. Thus Lenin's group or "the group of ten": Lenin, Zinoviev, Stalin, Kamenev, Tomsky, Lozovsky, Rudzutank, Kalinin, Petrovsky and Sergeyev (Artem), scored a full victory. It was an easy victory for the apparatus. The bureaucrats, seeing themselves threatened by the rank and file who were demanding the realization of the ideals of 1917, hastened to close their ranks and to build a united front against workers' oppositions.

Apart from the official Workers' Opposition, there emerged another workers' opposition group, "The Workers' and Peasants' Socialist Party"; the latter was not represented at the convention. It was headed by the sailor, Paniushkin, and was joined by those elements of the Workers' Opposition who remained dissatisfied with the submission of their leaders (Kolontay, Shliapnikov, Medvedev, Kutuzov) to the party bureaucracy.

The new "party" declared that it "stood on guard of the October conquests"; it put forth the demand, "all power to the soviets and not to the party"; it sharply assailed the party intellectuals, and it demanded the abolition of privileges and a more just distribution

---

365) Resolution, p. 163, vol. XVIII, part 1.

of rations. It branded the leaders of the "Workers' Opposition" as renegades who fell for soft jobs and comfortable positions in the party and state.

The newspaper "Pravda" hastened to label Paniushkin as a "self-seeker" and "Jew-baiter" (his anti-Semitism is doubtful and has yet to be verified), accusing him of raising "the inglorious Kronstadt banner". Then Paniushkin and a few other workers were expelled from the party.

On the other hand, however, this new opposition for a while was not only to be unmolested but even assisted in sundry ways: it was given quarters for a club; it was permitted to issue its publication ("Nabat"). Yet simultaneously, efforts were made to seduce the leaders with offers of position and power and to liquidate the membership in a painless manner. The active partisans were secretly put on the official list for surveillance. The attempt to disintegrate this movement from within the opposition itself proved futile. The opposition enjoyed great popularity among the workers: its meetings were crowded, its speakers were greeted with stormy applause, while the official Communists were met with catcalls. But on the night of June 7th, thirty-three prominent figures of this opposition were arrested, their publication was closed, and their program was confiscated in the printing shop. The prisoners were put in the Butirky jail, and some were afterwards sent to exile, notwithstanding the fact that many of them were old party members, dating their revolutionary activity back to 1903-1905.

Thus, under the blows of intra-party terror, fell this workers' opposition group.

The repressions against dissidents did not bring, however, all the desired results: the discontent of the party rank and file was not only unchecked but actually augmented. The workers' opposition remaining in the Party continued to rebel against the bureaucracy, its privileges and luxuries. It was for the purpose of curbing the growth of the opposition that Lenin introduced party purges. At the party conference held in May, purges were accepted under the guise of a concession to the oppositionists who did not suspect that along with the "self-seekers", "hangers-on" and other harmful elements they themselves would also be victimized. While the first purge was directed against the bourgeoisefied upper strata of the party and little affected the opposition, subsequent purges became a powerful weapon of terror in the hands of the apparatus against all the discontented elements of the party.

**

In line with this oppression was Lenin's persecution of Miasnikov and the party organization of Motovilikha (of the government of Perm) which he headed. The Miasnikov episode is of much interest and we shall therefore dwell upon it at some length.

A worker and one of the oldest members of the party, G. Miasnikov was the leader of the party organization of Motovilikha in the period of the trade union discussions. Capable, thoughtful, extremely devoted to the cause of proletarian emancipation, Miasnikov could not be reconciled to the abandonment of the party principles of 1917, the growing power of the oligarchy, the terror of the Central Committee and the bourgeois transformation of the upper layers of the party. He undertook to expose these developments toward the end of 1920 in Motovilikha. "It was because of this," Miasnikov writes, "as I found out later, that I was exiled . . . to Petrograd, to mend my ways."

There he had an opportunity of witnessing the drunken debaucheries of Zinoviev and the complete divorce of the party from the workers; the result of his observations was a memorandum sent by him to the Central Committee. Lenin replied in a letter with which Miasnikov in turn answered and disagreed. Lenin did not deem it necessary to continue this correspondence. His attempt at "persuasion" having failed, he, as we shall see, was soon to resort to "force".

Meanwhile, failing to hear from Lenin, Miasnikov published in pamphlet form his memorandum, his statement of principle together wih Lenin's letter. Let us examine the content of this pamphlet.

Miasnikov wrote to the Central Committee of the alienation of the working class and their enmity toward the party: "When I came to Petrograd, the city was in a festive mood; all the papers rejoiced that 'the sleeper was awakening,' that Petrograd industry was beginning to breathe freely, etc. But this was only Potemkin villages. Upon closer examination I began to see that, to my great amazement, all was not well in Petrograd. Mills and factories were frequently on strike, the Communist influence was lacking and the workers had no sense of participation in the government. It seemed

— 266 —

far away and not their own. In order to get something from it, they had to exert pressure: without pressure, nothing could be gotten. . . . The government threw the blame for the frequent strikes—the Italian strikes—upon the Mensheviks and the Social-Revolutionists, those pernicious agitators who were being arrested in order to save us from their seditious propaganda. But despite repressions, strikes did not stop".366)

Miasnikov explains later: "In Moscow, Petrograd, in the Ural region, in all factories, the workers now show keen distrust of the Communists. Non-partisan workers gather in groups, with the Mensheviks and Social-Revolutionists leading the discussions; but no sooner does a Communist approach than the groups scatter or change the topic. What does this mean? In the Izhorsky plant the workers expelled all the Communists from their meeting, including those actually working in the plant. On the very eve of what was virtually a general strike in Petrograd (prior to the Kronstadt revolt), we did not even know that this strike was about to come off although we had Communists in every department. We only knew it was being prepared and led. What does this mean? It means that the working class has fenced itself off from the Communists by an impenetrable wall and the party is no more aware of this than were the sleuths of the Tzar's time. The workers dubbed the "comcell" (Communist cell) "comsleuth". Why did they do so? Will you tell me that they penalize the Communist Party for no reason at all? That freedom of the press was granted and is still granted to the working class? My answer must be in the negative. The working class penalizes the party because the methods which the party worked out in 1918-1920 to deal with the bourgeoisie are now (in 1921) being practised upon the working class. This cannot go on".367)

Miasnikov continued: "We have freedom of speech in the markets, at the railway stations, in the trains, at the docks, but not in the factories and the villages. There the Che-Ka vigilantly watches over the good behavior of workers and peasants".368)

He exposed the intra-party dictatorship and the servility and wor-

366) *The Material of Discussion* (The statements of Com. Miasnikov, the letter of Com. Lenin, the answer to him, decision of the Organization Bureau of the Central Committee and the Resolution by Party members of Motovilikha). Only for Party members. November, 1921. Printed 500 copies." see p. 4.
367) Ibid, p. 24.
368) Ibid, p. 25.

ship of rank which was developing: "Freedom of opinion in the party is being suppressed by the foulest means".369)

"If one of the party rank and filers dares to have an opinion of his own, he is looked upon as a heretic and people scoff at him saying, 'Wouldn't Ilyitch (Lenin) have come to this idea if it were timely now? So you are the only clever man around, eh, you want to be wiser than all? Ha, ha, ha! You want to be cleverer than Ilyitch!' This is the typical 'argumentation' of the honorable Communist fraternity.370)

"Comrade Zinoviev told me in the presence of many comrades at the party conference of three districts: 'You'd better stop talking or we shall have to expel you from the party. You are either a Social-Revolutionist or just a sick man.' . . . Any one who ventures a critical opinion of his own will be labeled a Menshevik or Social-Revolutionist, with all the consequences that entails. This is the background of the disintegration and drunkenness in the upper strata of the party, under the motto of 'one hand washes the other'; in the soviet institutions one has to announce his presence before being able to see any official, and everything is complicated by red tape. Political 'pull' is the essential factor in attaining public office. Astoria, guarded by machine guns, is the talk of the town: it is a resort for drunks".371)

Miasnikov describes the situation in greater detail: "People keep quiet here. The silence spreads and they remain quiet until suddenly they understand each other and realize that there is nothing to talk about. Then, directly, they begin to fight violently among themselves. If one dares to express an opinion of his own, he is a self-seeker or worse—he is a counter-revolutionist, a Menshevik or a Social-Revolutionist. Such was the case with Kronstadt, too. Everything was nice and quiet there. And suddenly, without a word, the wallops started.. You ask, 'What is Kronstadt? A few hundred Communists fight against us. What does that mean?' But whose fault is it that the higher-ups in the party have no common language with either the non-partisan mass of people or with the rank and file Communists; that the misunderstanding is so great that it leads to

369) Ibid, p. 14.
370) Ibid, p. 20.
371) Ibid, p. 5.

violence? What is the significance of all this? This is the absolute limit. . . . ."372)

Miasnikov points out the emergence from this situation of a new type, the Communist sycophant: "A special type of Communist is evolving. He is forward, sensible, and, what counts most, he knows how to please his superiors, which the latter like only too much. Whether this Communist has influence among workers is of slight concern to him. All that counts is that his superiors be pleased".373)

He describes the lack of confidence in the working class and the peasantry, and counters with his demand for workers' democracy: "The party rank and file are permitted to speak of the peccadillos, the very little sins; but one must keep silent about the larger ones. Responsibility before the Central Committee? But there is Comrade Zinoviev, one of the 'boys'." 374)

"It stands to reason," Miasnikov continues, "that workers' democracy presupposes not only the right to vote but also freedom of speceh and press. If workers who govern the country, manage factories, do not have freedom of speech, we get a highly abnormal state". Consequently Miasnikov demands the abolition of the death penalty and "for all—from Monarchist to Anarchist—a freedom of speech and press such as the world has never seen before".375)

"We must base ourselves upon first, the working class and, second, the peasantry," Miasnikov counsels Lenin. "To believe that without active cooperation of both it is possible to restore the productive forces of the country and to create even a minimum of material welfare, is to try to realize the essential ideas of the Social-Revolutionists; it is to put our faith in bureaucrats, Communist heroes in this case, who will have everyone and everything from all ills and misfortunes.

"People argue in this fashion: you workers and peasants must not stir, nor strike, nor rebel; and don't get too subtle, for we have nice fellow-workers and peasants like you, whom we put into power; and those people will manipulate this power so that, unawares, you will find yourself in the Communist paradise".376)

"Another contention of the bureaucracy is: If we grant freedom

372) Ibid, p. 5-6.
373) Ibid, p. 14.
374) Ibid, p. 5.
375) Ibid, p. 14.
376) Ibid, p. 23.

of speech to all, everything that has hitherto been hidden from the non-partisan masses of people and the enemies of the soviet power (such as strikes, rebellions, hunger, etc.), will become known.

"But we reply: it is not true that the masses are unaware of these disorders, but they learn of them not from our paper but from living people. Moreover, they know more than those in the leading circles of the provinces. The provincial Che-Ka continues to arrest people for spreading false rumors, but those people know more than the Che-Ka. The result of this 'secret' is that people do not believe our papers at all.

"Those who fear to let the working class and peasantry speak out, always fear counter-revolution and see it everywhere".377)

Lenin recognized the pertinence of the foregoing sentence; so he replied: "Freedom of press in the R.S.F.S.R. surrounded by bourgeois enemies everywhere means freedom for the bourgeoisie,"378) "we do not want to commit suicide and that is why we will never do this" (i.e., what Miasnikov asks).379)

"I hope," Lenin concludes, "that after sober reconsideration, you will not insist, because of false pride, upon a flagrant political error (freedom of press) but that having quieted your nerves and having overcome the panicky feeling, you will set yourself to work: to help maintain connections with the non-party people, to check up the work of the party people with the aid of the non-partisan names.

"In this field there is no end of work. And it is thus the malady can and should be treated, and slowly cured; but this cannot be done by befogging your brain with 'freedom of press'—a lustrous will-o'-the-wisp".380)

Lenin's ineffectual letter, calculated to impress naive and ignorant people, reiterating the same idea over and over again, could not, of course, convince Miasnikov and in his reply to Lenin he wrote: "Words, words, as Hamlet said. You yourself realize that all that is not serious. It is strongly worded, but far from convincing".381)

"You say that I want freedom of press for the bourgeoisie; on

---

377) Ibid, p. 25.
378) N. Lenin, Sobranie Sochineniy, "A Letter to Comrade Miasnikov," p. 339, vol. XVIII, part 1.
379) Ibid, p. 340.
380) Ibid, p. 342.
381) "The Material of Discussion," p. 31.

the contrary, I want freedom of press for myself, a proletarian, who never had anything, a proletarian who has been in the party for fifteen years, who has been a party member in Russia and not abroad (Miasnikov hints broadly at Lenin, Trotzky, Zinoviev and other leaders in the party . . .) I spent seven and a half of the eleven years of my party membership before 1917 in prisons and at hard labor, with a total of seventy-five days in hunger strikes. I was mercilessly beaten and subjected to other tortures. I had to 'hobo' my way back and I escaped not abroad, but for party work here in Russia. To me one can grant at least a little freedom of press, at least within the party. Or is it that I must leave or be expelled from the party as soon as I disagree with you in the evaluation of social forces? Such simplified treatment evades but does not tackle our problems." 382)

Then Miasnikov vigorously attacks Lenin thus: "To break the jaws of international bourgeoisie, is all very well, but the trouble is that you lift your hand against the bourgeoisie and you strike at the worker. Which class now supplies the greatest number of people arrested on charges of counter-revolution? Peasants and workers, to be sure. There is no Communist working class. There is just a working class pure and simple".383)

"Don't you know that thousands of proletarians are kept in prison because they talked the way I am talking now, and that bourgeois people are not arrested on this score for the simple reason that they are never concerned with these questions? If I am still at large, that is so because of my standing as a Communist. I suffered for my Communist views; moreover, I am known by the workers; were it not for these facts, were I just an ordinary Communist mechanic from the same factory, where would I be now? In the Che-Ka, or more than this, I would be made to 'escape', just as I made Mikhayil Romanov (Tzar's brother) 'escape', as Luxmeburg and Liebknecht were made to 'escape'. Once more I say: you raise your hand against the bourgeoisie, but it is I who am spitting blood, and it is we, the workers, whose jaws are being cracked." 384)

This reply sealed the fate of Miasnikov. Lenin was not the type

382) Ibid, p. 29-30.
383) Ibid, p. 32.
384) Ibid, 34.

to allow back-talk from people whom he regarded his inferiors; his overbearing character would not brook reprimand or interference. So there began for Miasnikov a period of trials and tribulations. He became the object of ceaseless terror. On August 23, the Central Committee of the Communist Party resolved "to recognize the thesis of Comrade Miasnikov as incompatible with party interests; to impose upon him the obligation to refrain from proclaiming these viewpoints at official rallies of the party." He was recalled from Motovilikha and placed at the disposal of the Central Committee, that is, he was actually put under their surveillance. The party organization of Motovilikha and the "Workers' Opposition" attempted to intercede on his behalf, but that only worsened matters; charges of infraction of party discipline were proffered against all his supporters. And six months later he was officially expelled from the party: "For anti-party activity and infractions of party discipline, G. Miasnikov is expelled from the party by the decision of the Central Committee of February 22, 1922".[385]

No one intervened on behalf of the expelled Miasnikov at the eleventh convention of the party. Lenin spoke only a few words on the matter, assailing the Workers' Opposition for its appeal to the Comintern: "One must tell those who are using their legitimate right to appeal to the Comintern that in the Miasnikov case it was not altogether lawful for them to intercede. The Miasnikov incident took place in the summer of last year. I was not present in Moscow then and I wrote him a long letter, which he put into his pamphlet. I saw that the man had some abilities, that it was worthwhile to talk matters over with him, but that we had to tell him that any open criticisms on his part would be regarded as incompatible with party discipline. He, however, wrote a letter advising us to rally in every district all the discontented elements. Yes, of course, to get such people together in every district is not at all difficult".[386]

Miasnikov was soon sent to prison, and thence into exile. In his letter to the Industrial Workers of the World (I.WW.) (unpublished) of November 27, 1927, from Constantinople, he wrote: "From 1922 up to the present time I have never been free from kind

---

385) 'Pravda," March 3, 1922.
386) N. Lenin, Sobranie Sochineniy, "The Closing Remarks on the Report of the Central Committee of the Communist Party," p. 69, vol. XVIII, part 2.

attentions, sometimes of the G. P. U., at other times of the Intelligence Departments of various foreign govrenments." Lenin began settling accounts with Miasnikov and Stalin finished the job.

*

In the same period, between the tenth and eleventh party conventions, the Central Committee of the party, headed by Lenin, waged a vigorous campaign of terrorization against the Communist fraction of the trade unions. In this regard "The Report of the Central Committee of the Communist Party, from May 1 to June 1, 1921"[387] furnishes quite interesting reading. We find here a description of the struggle of the Central Committee of the Party with the refractory Communist fraction of the All-Russian Trade Union Convention. The issue was the "independence" of trade unions from the party. Riazanov always pleaded for trade union independence along the German pattern. The Communist fraction of the trade union convention adopted Riazanov's resolution. Tomsky, who was instructed by the Central Committee of the party to see to it that its own resolution was carried out, failed to do so. Hence the Central Committee of the party rejected Riazanov's resolution and instructed Lenin, Bukharin and Stalin to deliver talks before the fraction "explaining why the resolutions adopted were unacceptable." It further resolved to remove Tomsky from the group of five appointed to guide the convention of the trade unions, and to put Bukharin in his place. The reorganized group of five was instructed to call a meeting of the Communist fraction of the convention for reconsideration of Riazanov's resolution.

The Central Committee of the party confirmed the presidium of the All-Russian Trade Union Convention, having removed Tomsky and Riazanov therefrom, and the latter two soon felt the heavy hand of Lenin's Central Committee. "The Report" is here quoted in part:

"Whereas the resolution made by Comrade Riazanov, especially his speech at the meeting of the fraction, showed the utter disagreement of Riazanov's views with those of the party upon the so-called 'independence of the trade unions', and whereas Comrade Riazanov violated for a second time the party discipline and the resolutions

---

387) "Izvestia of the Central Committee of the Communist Party," No. 32, August 6, 1921.

of the tenth convention, the Central Committee resolved to remove Comrade Riazanov from participation in the trade union movement. The organization which elected Comrade Riazanov as delegate was instructed to replace him by another delegate.

"The Central Committee voted to administer an official rebuke to the Comrades Artem, Shliapnikov and Kutuzov who permitted an anti-party resolution to be carried at the party fraction of the convention without fighting for the party resolution;

"To release Comrade Tomsky from duties in the All-Russian Central Trade Union Council and in keynoting the convention, his place to be taken by Comrades Tziperovich and Lozovsky; to grant Comrade Tomsky's request for permission to absent himself from today's session of the Communist fraction as well as from all other sessions of the trade union convention; to instruct Comrade Tomsky to transfer his obligations in the International Council of Trade Unions to Comrades Lozovsky and Tziperovich; to appoint a committee consisting of Comrades Stalin, Frunze, Kiselev, Dzerzhinsky to review the facts in this case and to determine whether in view of Comrade Tomsky's infraction of party discipline, it is within the jurisdictional power of the Central Committee to penalize him or whether a party conference with powers exceeding those of the Central Committee need be called for that purpose; to hold the decision of the Committee as final if passed unanimously."

And in this fashion Lenin's Central Committee dealt with the most eminent party workers and members of the Central Committee like Tomsky. The Communist fraction of the convention, terrorized by the Central Committee, and subjected to the report of Lenin, Bukharin and Stalin, rejected by an overwhelming majority Riazanov's resolution which only the previous day it had adopted by the same overwhelming majority.

The investigation committee passed its decision on May 19, declaring Tomsky guilty "of a gross violation of party discipline and a criminally frivolous attitude toward the interests of the party, demanding moreover, the sternest party punishment." But taking into consideration "the existence of opposition sentiments among a considerable section of the trade union fraction," the investigation committee, having confirmed the decision of the Central Committee, found it necessary to add its decision "to administer a stern rebuke to Comrade Tomsky." Riazanov, deprived of his rank and insignia, was dispatched abroad "to get an airing," while Tomsky was sent to Turkestan for meditation.

*

Having made a clean sweep of the Communist trade union fraction which seemed infected with the spirit of the Workers' Opposition, the Central Committee betook itself to the union of metal workers. Here it clashed with the Workers' Opposition on the question of the composition of the All-Russian Central Committee of the Metal Workers Unions. The Workers' Opposition, which was strong in this union, wanted to carry its own slate of candidates, but the Central Committee of the Communist Party approved instead the slate of the Petrograd organization, which was loyal to it, and in which the Opposition was given only a very small representation. Shliapnikov protested, declaring that he would resign from the committee appointed by the Central Committee to run the metal workers convention and demanded that his name be struck off the slate. But he was not permitted to do as he wished. The Communist fraction of the convention of metal workers rejected the slate approved by the Central Committee of the Communist Party "by a majority vote of 120 to 40." Thereupon Lenin's Central Committee simply issued an order to have the slate of the new Metal Workers Central Committee approved. The representatives of the Workers' Opposition began boycotting the newly appointed body, absenting themselves from its sessions, as a result of which its Presidium came to include only one member of the old Central Committee of the union. Then the Central Committee of the party took charge of the whole affair appointing at will the entire Presidium of the Central Committee of the Metal Workers Union.

The Communist fraction of the convention, roused to indignation by the violence of the Party's Central Committee, adopted the following resolution: "The Communist fraction of the convention of metal workers, while submitting to the decision of the Central Committee, resolved to protest against it at the next convention of the party." They decided to complain to Pilate about Pontius!

From Lenin's terroristic regime in the party, there emerged an illegal intra-party literature and groups who carried to the rank and file the struggle against the dictatorship of the Central Committee, against the party oligarchy and patricians. Thus "The Bulletin of

the City District Committee of the Communist Party of Moscow"[388])
reports that during the soviet election the leaflets of "The Group of
Revolutionary Left Communists" were spread among the workers.
One of those illegal leaflets contained the following: "All leaders
betray and become turn-coats, even the leaders of the Workers' Opposition, who, perhaps, do it unconsciously, but they do betray the
interests of the poor. . . . Let us spur on the timidly silent oppositionists—the Kolontays, the Shliapnikovs, the Perepechkos, the Igna-
tievs—in the name of revolutionary principles, for workers' opposition, for its organization!" Further, "The Bulletin" reports another
leaflet as saying: "One elects the bureaucrats Lenin and Trotzky in
Soviets twenty times and over, despite that they are absolutely worthless for the Soviets." . . . "Organize, agitate and fight for Communists from the rank and file, the trade unions, the workers' opposition, for Left Communists." This agitation seems to have met with
some success for after the elections (according to the "Bulletin") more
than 200 deputies, expelled members of the Communist Party, were
elected but nevertheless were deprived of their seats in the Moscow
Soviet.

At the same time the Workers' Opposition took its case to the
Communist International. The latter, wholly depending upon Lenin's
Central Committee, decided, of course, in favor of Lenin and Trotzky
and against the Workers' Opposition. The declaration presented to
the Communist International is known as "the declaration of 22",
but actually it contains more than 400 signatures, chiefly those of
metal workers. Dissatisfied with the decision of the Communist International, the Workers' Opposition took this question to the rank
and file, demanding that the Comintern reconsider its solution. In
some places its resolutions were carried, as was the case, for instance,
at the district conference of the metal workers union of Zamoskvo-
riechie.

This activity of the Workers' Opposition vexed and frightened
the party leaders who, therefore, extended their drive, though they
still were shieing away from too drastic measures. All those who
signed the declaration presented to the Comintern were dispatched
under various pretexts to localities which were undisputedly loyal to
the Central Committee. Shliapnikov, who had previously been sent

---

388) No. 1, February 20, 1922.

as an honorable exile to Astrakhan, was now ordered to take a trip to Northern Caucasia.

But the struggle of the higher-ups with the genuine proletarians of the party became every day more intense: replacements, removals, exiles, expulsions and arrests became more frequent; but still no bloodshed.

*
* *

Communist blood was shed for the first time on February 16, 1922, only a month before the eleventh convention of the party; in the struggle against the Workers' Opposition, the blood of a Finnish Communist emigrant, Voita Eloranta, was spilled.

There exists a legend to the effect that Lenin tried very hard to eliminate capital punishment as a way of solving party disagreements. While this may be so with regard to outstanding party leaders (though we doubt it very much), it certainly was not true with regard to rank and file party members. It is only necessary to point to the executions of the Kronstadt Communists, the Communists of Baku (*e.g.*, the old Communist Yegorov) and Trotzky's terroristic activity on the fronts of Civil War, in order to refute this legend; the shooting of Eloranta tells us that Lenin would not stop even at the shooting of party leaders when he believed the situation warranted it.

The legal murder of Eloranta is characteristic of Lenin and worthy of note. Here is how it happened. On August 31, 1920, a group of young Finnish Communist immigrants, who had found refuge in Petrograd following the destruction of the revolutionary movement in Finland, attacked the Central Committee of the Finnish Party and killed nearly all its members. The toll was eight dead and eleven injured. The cloud of mystery over the case has never been completely cleared away, although the investigation dragged on for quite a long time. It was only on February 12, 1922, that the case came up before the Supreme Revolutionary Tribunal. The perpetrators of the murders were sentenced to five years of prison, but Eloranta, who did not take a direct part, was sentenced to die.

Who was this Eloranta and what role did he play in the mass murder? What were the motives back of it and why was he singled out for extraordinary penalty?

The verdict of the Supreme Tribunal, published in the "Izvestia" of February 17, 1922, states that Eloranta was a journalist, an old member of the Finnish Social Democratic Party. Following the split of this party he became "an influential member of the Finnish Communist Party," heading "the growing Communist Opposition." Because of that he was considered morally responsible for the murder and its ideological instigator, on which grounds he was sentenced to be shot.

We can well see now that Stalin was not breaking new ground when he shot Kamenev and Zinoviev as "morally responsible" for Kirov's murder: here, too, Lenin left beautiful examples to be copied by his successor.

The charges against Eloranta were formulated thus: "He carried on a demagogic agitation against the Central Committee of the Finnish Communist Party"; then: "taking advantage of the distressed condition of the Finnish workers after the defeat of the Communist revolution in Finland, he gathered around him a group from the growing workers' opposition, involving it in squabbles with the Central Committee of the Finnish Party"; "he used his experience as an old member of the Finnish Social-Democratic Party to instigate the younger and politically inexperienced comrades, pushing them toward a bloody reckoning with the Finnish Central Committee, while himself playing the hypocrite and hiding behind the backs of the comrades from the workers' opposition." Further: "He induced members of his group to adopt a collective decision to commit a terroristic act." The slightest analysis of these charges will indicate insufficient ground for a sentence of capital punishment. The court could not even accuse Eloranta of direct incitation to murder. The verdict shows clearly how political accounts with the opposition were settled; moreover, the Presidium of the All-Russian Central Committee of the Soviets resolved, contrary to the decision of the Supreme Revolutionary Tribunal: "To countermand in this particular case the amnesty of the third and fourth anniversaries of the October Revolution, and to execute the sentence as originally passed by the Supreme Tribunal." And on that very night "the sentence in respect to the citizen Voito Eloranta was carried out." Thus a preconceived political murder, the assassination of an eminent ideologist of the Finnish workers' opposition, was committed, with the aim of intimidating the workers' opposition within the Communist Party, which, despite the decision of the tenth party convention refused to cease its propaganda. The charges against Eloranta were formulated in such a way as to announce to leaders of the workers' opposition that they could likewise be applied against them, too. This murder could not have been carried out without the intervention of the Central Committee, or rather its Politbureau; that is, the intervention of Lenin, for the Presidium of the All-Russian Central Executive Committee of the Soviets could not make independent decision, especially in political cases of such a nature. Once more the oppositionists were reminded that in the struggle for power in the party and in the country, Lenin would not stop even at shootings.

**
*

In fact, at the eleventh party convention Lenin made a statement to the effect, threatening Shliapnikov, the opposition and all violators of party discipline with machine guns.

"To retreat after a victorious offensive is very difficult; but in this case we have a different setup. In an offensive—even without discipline—everyone rushes forward eagerly; in a retreat, the discipline must be more conscious and is a hundred times more necessary; for when the entire army is in retreat, it does not see clearly where to stop; under these circumstances a few panicky voices can cause a general stampede; here is a paramount danger. When a real army has to retreat, machine guns are placed in the rear, and whenever a regular retreat turns into a disorderly stampede, orders are issued: 'shoot!' And that is quite justified.

"If certain people, even though they are guided by the best intentions, cause a panic at the moment when we are engineering an unusually difficult retreat, and when the main task is to preserve order, it is then necessary to punish severely, brutally, ruthlessly the slightest violation of discipline. *This holds true not only in regard to some of our intra-party affairs,* but—and one should particularly bear this in mind—also in regard to such gentlemen as Mensheviks and those of the Second-and-a-half International".[389]

Lenin, however, was a bit frightened by his own threats and so in his closing speech he tried to tone them down somewhat: "Poor Shliapnikov! Lenin was going to set up machine guns against him!

---

389) N. Lenin, Sobranie Sochineniy, "A Report on the Work of the Central Committee of the Russian Communist Party," p. 37-38, vol. XVIII, part 1.

"We speak, of course, about ways and means of exercising party pressure and not about machine guns. We are in earnest about machine guns only in regard to people whom we now know as Mensheviks and Social-Revolutionists. . . ." 390)

However, the fate of Eloranta was staring everyone in the face, and Lenin's mention of machine guns remained in everyone's consciousness as a threat and a warning. Who knows: had Lenin's work not been interrupted by illness and eventually death, machine guns might have rattled much sooner and with greater force than under Stalin, who in the field of terror only slavishly emulates his teacher.

The eleventh party convention was the last at which Lenin was present. There all oppositions had vanished except for the Workers' Opposition, which had been quite active in the interim between the two conventions. Its rebellion against Lenin's "New Economic Policy" had, as we have already seen, provoked a threat of machine guns. The Workers' Opposition presented a protest to the Communist International, wherefore the Central Committee headed by Lenin bore down vehemently upon it at the eleventh convention. What exasperated Lenin and the higher party bureaucracy most was the demand to limit the autocratic rights of the Central Committee, especially its control of allocating party members.

"If the Central Committee," Lenin said, "is to be deprived of the right of placing party members, it will not be able to direct and shape party policies. Though we do commit errors here and there in relocating people, I still take it upon myself to say that the Politbureau of the Central Committee made only the minimum of mistakes. This is not mere bluster on our part".391)

The Workers' Opposition insisted that this right be circumscribed in view of the fact that the Central Committee misused its prerogative in the struggle against all those who took issue with it. Lenin confesses that even "long before" the Appeal of the 22, an attempt was made to get rid of Shliapnikov: "A big majority in the Central Committee was in favor of having him expelled: but the vote for expulsion fell short of the two-thirds majority required by statute".392)

The eleventh party convention, on the basis of the data furnished by the investigation committee recognized that "the continued activ-

390) "The Closing Speech," p. 60-61, vol. XVIII, part 1.
391) Ibid, p. 63.
392) Ibid, p. 68.

ity on the part of the Workers' Opposition during the past year, contrary to the unconditional decision of the tenth convention against factional groupings, conferences, and struggle, injures the party." The convention resolved "to subscribe to the decision of the Executive Committee of the International in regard to comrades Shliapnikov, Medvediev and Kolontay, and to instruct the Central Committee to expel those comrades from the party if in the future they manifest a similar anti-party attitude".393) The convention resolved to expel Mitin as "a malicious disorganizer," and Kuznetzoff "as alien to the proletariat."

**
*

Following the expulsion from the party and the arrest of the members of the Paniushkov's "Workers and Peasants Socialist Party," there followed, as we have already seen, the expulsion and the arrest of G. Miasnikov, and the shooting of Eloranta. Now came the turn of the Workers' Opposition. But neither did the intra-party terror nor that in the country brought the desired appeasement. On the contrary, the discontented elements, mainly workers, were driven to organize illegal factions and wage an underground strike against Lenin and the Central Committee; soon underground Communist literature made its appearance.

Apart from the above referred to "Revolutionary Communists" of the fall of 1921, there emerged the group, "Rabochaya Pravda" which published an underground magazine of the same name. Its position was outlined in its illegal "Appeal to the Revolutionary Proletariat and All Revolutionary Elements Who Remain Faithful to the Struggling Working Class".394)

This group was begotten by the NEP (New Economic Policy) or as "The Appeal" has it, by "the restoration of normal capitalist relationships." It maintained that in the present situation Russia should be transformed into a country of advanced capitalism from which a new working class and new working class party would arise. Said they: "Following a successful revolution and a civil war, wide perspectives have opened up before Russia. In the rapid transformation

---

393) Note 207, on p. 231-232, vol. XVIII, part 2.

394) This "Appeal" was reprinted by the "Sotzialistichesky Viestnik," No. 3, January 31, 1923, p. 12-13, from which we quote.

into a country of advanced capitalism, lie vast potentialities for the October revolution."

In analyzing the actual Russian situation, the group asks, "In what way did the position of the working class change?" And it answers, "The working class of Russia are disorganized and confused. Are they in the country of the 'dictatorship of the proletariat'—as the Communist Party carelessly repeats in press and propaganda—or in the country of arbitrary rule and exploitation, of which life convinces us daily? The working class drag out miserable existences whereas the new bourgeoisie (that is, the people holding responsible positions, the factory directors, directors of trusts, soviet chairmen, etc.) and the 'Nepmen' live on the fat of the land—reminiscent of the bourgeoisie of other days . . ."

And again: "An intelligentzia composed of technicians and organizers who direct and conduct the entire organization of production is coming increasingly to the fore.

"In its ideology and methods of work it is thoroughly bourgeois and all it can build is a capitalist economy. A new bourgeoisie is now being created by the merging of the business elements of the old bourgeoisie and the rising class of intellectuals—the organizers of social life.

"The soviet, trade union and party bureaucracy and the organizers of state capitalism are placed in material conditions differing markedly from that of the workers. Their security and material prosperity depend upon the extent of exploitation and subjection of the toiling masses. There rises inevitably a contradiction between the interests of the workers and those of this ruling group—a divorce between the Communist Party and the working class.

"The social existence of the party leaders necessarily determines their social consciousness, and the interests and ideals which run counter to those of the struggling proletariat.

"The Russian Communist Party became the party of the intelligentzia who are the organizers of every branch of our existence. The gulf separating the party and the working class is becoming deeper, and this fact cannot be glossed over by any resolutions and decisions of Communist conventions, conferences, etc. . . ."

The group held that in the near future the dominant role in Russia would belong to commercial capital, along with which there would also grow the influence of the State "as the representative of the national interests of capital" and that the proletariat, because of its constant subjection as well as the lack of its own party, would not be able to play a dominant role. Hence "Rabotchaya Pravda" demanded the organization of a party of the Russian proletariat. The tasks of that party were to include the struggle against the exploitation of the proletariat and for democracy as opposed to the arbitrary rule of the administration.

"Rabotchaya Pravda" was against the Workers' Opposition on the ground that "the Workers' Opposition was valuable to the extent that it contained revolutionary elements, but objectively it is reactionary, aiming to revive the slogans and methods of military Communism which by now have been antedated."

The group claimed further. "that the Russian working class—once the vanguard of the international proletariat—had now retrogressed to its position of several decades past." Consequently, the organization of a new party would be a long and difficult job. It would proceed by way of illegal groups within the Communist Party; the members of these groups were to be carefully selected and to operate in strictest secrecy.

Before it was finally suppressed, "Rabotchaya Pravda" managed to issue another document, entitled "An Appeal to the Twelfth Convention of the Russian Communist Party." Here it demanded improvement in the conditions of the working class and cessation of their exploitation, rationalization of production, restoration of militant trade unions, granting the workers the elementary rights of class struggle and self-organization.

In the same period between the eleventh and twelfth conventions, there appeared within the Russian Communist Party a new illegal group which sharply criticized the party's reign of terror, the growing inequality of income, favoritism and bureaucracy. This group sought the salvation of the revolution in the establishment of intra-party democracy, but it went no further in its demands. It urged that Zinoviev, Kamenev and Stalin be removed from the Central Committee as the persons most bureaucratized and most instrumental in suppressing freedom within the party. This group, we see, was the precursor of the "Trotzkyite" opposition.

**
*

The first party convention to be held without Lenin—the twelfth —was conducted under the direction of the all-powerful triumvirate: Zinoviev, Kamenev and Stalin. There was no articulate opposition at this convention. On the surface, everything seemed quiet, although underneath, discontent was simmering. New factions were being formed constantly. The Central Committee was expanded and renewed, but none was admitted who showed any oppositionist leanings: all those suspected of "Trotzkyism", all those eliminated from the Central Committee after the trade union discussion, were excluded. Some, like Ossinsky and Rakovsky, were dispatched abroad, as ambassadors to a sort of honorable exiles. While the triumvirate deprived him of power, Trotzky was forced to play the role of the most loyal interpreter of the party line. I. N. Smirnov, the ex-ruler of Siberia, was not re-elected to the Central Committee.

In only one respect was the unity genuine, for unanimity existed in the struggle against the proliferous rank and file oppositions. And the new Central Committee took drastic steps to suppress the opposition within the party. At the September plenum a decision had been passed to arrest members of the opposition; in the latter part of September arrests of the members of "Rabochaya Pravda" occurred all over the country. About 400 were taken, among them the old Marxist philospoher and economist A. A. Bogdanov (Malinovsky) who was suspected of being the ideological leader of "Rabochaya Pravda".

In order to bring the group into disrepute, the official party press hinted about its alleged connection with the Entente Intelligence Department. (This method, as we already know, was widely applied by Stalin against the executed Kamenev, Zinoviev, Preobrazhensky, Piatakov, Bukharin, Rikov, and against the exiled Trotzky). In answer to these vile insinuations "Rabochaya Pravda" issued an appeal to the workers of the Western countries. Mass arrests succeeded finally in smashing this group. Two months later the illegal printing shop of the Workers' Opposition was uncovered in Moscow.

*

Lenin's terror against the discontented members of the party drove them to underground work within the party. This greatly exasperated the ruling strata and terroristic methods were intensified. Expulsions and arrests occurred more and more often. Toward November, 1922 there were so many expelled Communists that a special police surveillance became necessary, as is attested by "The Secret Circular Letter of the G. P. U., November, 1922."[395]) We quote from this remarkable document:

"Of late it has become quite common for people who were expelled from the party during the purge to assert themselves as anti-Soviet in their attitude; to openly criticize the Soviet power, the Communist Party and its eminent leaders; to set themselves up as 'true Communists' in contra-distinction from the mere 'holders of party membership cards'. Their attacks always revolve around the role of the trade unions in production and they are distinctly counter-revolutionary.

"It is to be noticed that the expelled members of the party who formerly belonged to other parties, revert to their original platforms, act upon the instructions of those parties and put forth such slogans as 'freedom of speech and assembly', 'free soviets', 'full political rights and liberty'—of which all anti-Soviet parties, Monarchists included, take full advantage.

"These expelled party members represent quite a force in their capacity as agitators and organizers, and very often they not only sow seeds of discontent among the young members of the party but also mislead those in responsible positions, especially in peasant localities. Organized into anti-Soviet parties (Mensheviks, Social-Revolutionists, etc.) they carry on their work of demoralizing the young Communists.

"There are cases where ex-members of the Communist Party establish connections with bandits in their area, extending all kinds of aid to them. Since this involves them in some of the most pernicious anti-Soviet activity, every method of repression may justifiably be applied against them. Therefore, it becomes necessary: 1) to register all ex-members of the Communist Party who have come out at rallies, meetings, conventions, conferences with anti-Soviet agitation and false rumors; local registration should be coordinated with that of the district and county party committees; 2) to investigate those who are most active in this subversive agitation and to place them

---

395) This "Secret Circular," reprinted in Berlin by "Sotzialistichesky Viestnik," No. 8-9, April 24, 1923.

— 285 —

under secret surveillance to determine their connections with other groups and parties; 3) to find out who of the expelled members of the party are still holding responsible positions (especially in the village soviets, the sections of the county party committee, at the mills and factories), to observe their behavior, and in case of any anti-Soviet action, to request their removal; 4) to accomplish this work in strict secrecy, in view of the fact that many of those expelled from the party formerly held responsible positions, such as chairmanship of the executive committee of the provincial soviets, and they have not yet lost their connections."

Incidentally, the only ones whom the "Circular" did not recommend to be placed under surveillance were those who had been expelled for self-seeking and criminal activity.

One more group—the so-called "Workers' Group"—was suppressed while Lenin was still alive. Relevant information is available in V. Sorin's pamphlet: "The Workers' Group" published by the Moscow Committee of the Russian Communist Party and written on the basis of the data of the G. P. U., materials taken away from the arrested and their depositions.

According to Sorin's pamphlet, "The Workers' Group" grew up in the spring of 1923. Its platform was based upon the brochure by G. Miasnikov, "Disquieting Problems" which, with a few editorial changes and corrections (by Miasnikov, Kuznetzoff and Moyseyev) was issued as "The Manifesto of the Workers' Group of the Russian Communist Party." In April, Miasnikov was arrested and the group disrupted, but soon it recovered, and on June the fifth it already had an illegal conference in Moscow. It carried on negotiations with the leaders of the former Workers' Opposition—Kolontay, Shliapnikov, Medvedev, Ignatov and Lutovinov[396])—who differed with the manifesto only on problems of tactics since they insisted that propaganda should be carried on among party members only. Negotiations were carried on with Riazanov, Nevsky and Kuznetzoff who declined to ally with the faction, although (to the surprise of the Workers' Group) they did not advise the Party Central Committee of its existence. The membership of this group is difficult to ascer-

---

396) U. X. Lutovinov, the member of the Presidium of Russian Central Executive Committee of Soviets and Trade Unions, committed suicide in 1924. He was disappointed in the revolution and the party. He was close to the Workers' Opposition.

tain. V. Sorin believes that there were never over 200 members in Moscow. In the summer the Moscow organization of the Communist Party conducted a purge, having first expelled the partisans of the Workers' Group. In August, the latter intended to organize a general political strike, but the G. P. U. getting wind of the matter, succeeded in liquidating it by September.

This was, as we have said, the last intra-party opposition to be liquidated by police and party terror while Lenin was yet alive. And this, perhaps, was the last workers' opposition within the party to be crushed by the united efforts of the party's upper crust, which itself soon began to disintegrate.

**
*

The struggle for power, the dividing of the inheritance, took on the character of a personal strife among the Bolshevik magnates; they resorted to every means evolved by Lenin: the seizure of the party apparatus, removals and replacements, honorable exile, the threat to expel and actual expulsions, arrests, deportations by administrative decree, prisons and finally, mass shootings.

The eleventh convention of the party was held without Lenin who could not attend on account of illness; there was no hope for his recovery and before the twelfth convention a new discussion commenced, the real issue of which was the competition for power between the triumvirate—Zinoviev, Kamenev and Stalin on the one hand —and Trotzky and other party leaders on the other. The party rank and file were nonplussed, unable to understand what the struggle was all about. On December 11, 1923, at the meeting held by one of the Communist cells of Moscow, the worker Gourov declared: "The workers will ask me what are the basic disagreements. To say quite truthfully, I do not know what to tell them."

Gourov's reaction was typical. And we shall understand it better when we familiarize ourselves with the character of this discussion, as shown at least by the excerpts from "Pravda" and "Izvestia". We may use in this connection the splendid summary entitled "At the High Court: What the Great Men Think of Each Other" which appeared in "Znamia Borby",[397) the publication of the Left Social-Revolutionists:

---

397) No. 2, May, 1924. Berlin.

Sapronov: "Now we hear everyone harping, as Comrade Kamenev does, upon the name of Lenin. . . . To keep on referring to the fact that one has been Lenin's friend and to imply that one will remain a Leninist all his life is demagogy pure and simple. Those people merely seek their salvation by hiding behind Lenin's back." ("Pravda," No. 284).

Stalin: "The Opposition has made a habit of extolling Lenin as the greatest of all geniuses. I am afraid that this praise is not altogether sincere. They want, by raising the ballyhoo about Lenin's genius, to camouflage their own abandonment of him and to stress at the same time the weakness of his disciples. . . . But permit us to ask you, Comrade Preobrazhensky, how is it that you found yourself in profound disagreement with this great genius on the question of the Brest-Litovsk peace? And Comrade Sapronov, who now falsely and pharisaically showers praises upon Lenin, is the very same Sapronov who at one time dared to label him an 'ignoramus' and 'oligarch'." ("Izvestia," No. 18).

Preobrazhensky: "Comrade Kamenev said here that this bait'ng of one section of the Party by the other is intolerable. But did he not indulge in baiting himself when he stated here that they are people who are burrowing underneath the rock of the Party structure. But who does this undermining? We must state concretely—who and when. . . . Some comardes in the Central Committee arrogate themselves the monopoly of defending Bolshevism. Other comrades are also old Bolsheviks and have been in the Party for no less a period than Comrade Kamenev. Why does he, then, seek to be exclusive in the defense of Bolshevism?" ("Pravda," No. 286).

Bukharin: "After October our party experienced three crises: the crisis of the Brest-Litovsk peace, the trade union crisis and the present one. In all those stages of party development, Comrade Trotzky was in the wrong." ("Pravda," No. 294).

Preobrazhensky: "The policy which is now being carried out is not class policy within our party, but a policy of petty squabbles and splits. When we spoke of Lenin's role in the party we had in view a program that was benefiting the working class as a whole. But you cannot completely replace Lenin: you have so much less talent but so much more presumption." ("Pravda," No. 12).

Stalin: "Comrade Trotzky identifies himself with the Bolshevik

Old Guard, thus opening himself to whatever criticism may fall upon the heads of an Old Guard if they take the road leading to degeneration. This readiness for self-sacrifice no doubt bespeaks a noble character. But I must defend Comrade Trotzky from Comrade Trotzky, since he, for obvious reasons, cannot and should not bear responsibility for the possible change for the worse of the basic cadres of the Old Bolshevik Guard. Do the Old Bolsheviks stand in need of this sacrifice? I do not believe so. . . . But on the other hand, the party does contain certain elements which lead toward degeneration: I am thinking of those ex-Mensheviks who willy-nilly joined our party and who have not lived down old opportunist habits," ("Pravda," No. 285).

Kamenev: "We know that our state apparatus is utterly worthless. And when the same is implied of our party apparatus as in the speeches of the oppositionists, we ask them: 'What is it that you want us to do?' The state organization is utterly worthless and now you (Preobrazhensky, Sapronov, Drobnis) try hard to make the party appear in the same light. You said in your resolutions that the Central Committee, impelled by fractional aims only, by its urge to retain power, turned this apparatus into a seat for cowards, sycophants, careerists. . . . But what instruments are we to use for governing the country if, as you say, our state machinery has to be destroyed while the party apparatus, you maintain, is manned by sycophants?"

Ossinsky: "Kamenev made reference to Comrade Lenin. But Comrade Kamenev, Lenin was one thing, and you—all three of you and your backers—are quite another thing. You, dear comrades, need the same kind of a majority and the same kind of prestige and moral standing which Lenin had. . . . What do you intend to do now? To say on the one hand: 'Let us embrace each other and make peace', and on the other hand: 'I'll wallop you so that you won't have time to think?' And do you believe it possible to pacify thus the minds of the people, or to develop intra-party democracy under such conditions?" ("Pravda," No. 11).

Kamenev: "Some oppositionists say: you did write a good resolution, but you acted like Tzar Nicholas II did with the manifesto of October 17. Well, overlooking the comparison of the Central Committee with this personage (a comparison which reveals much concerning those who advanced it), what is its political meaning when decoded? It means: Under pressure you wrote a good resolution, but you will deceive the party . . ." ("Pravda," No. 10).

Preobrazhensky: "You have shown here in regard to Comrade Trotzky a monstrous lack of consideration. First, we of the opposition headed by Comrade Trotzky, are alleged to be political bankrupts. But then we are told that Trotzky is indispensable. This is ambiguous. If the charges preferred against him are true, he should be eliminated not only from the Politbureau but from the party as well; but if your charges are false, then you are attempting to deceive the party." ("Pravda," No. 11).

Sapronov: "The victory which Comrade Kamenev and others have just celebrated is such that, if repeated, would leave Comrade Kamenev and others, despite all their victories, without an army." ("Pravda," No. 12).

Stalin: "There can be no double standards as far as discipline goes: one for workers and another for magnates. Comrade Trotzky's error was that he set himself apart from others, believing himself to be a superman standing above the Central Committee and its laws." ("Parvda," No. 17).

Preobrazhensky: "I believe the basic error admitted by the politbureau in regard to Comrade Trotzky was that of treating him as an alien in our midst. With such an attitude, no joint work is possible. This should be clearly understood." ("Pravda," No. 17).

Zinoviev: "Comrade Radek did everythink possible as well as impossible to prevent the Comintern from carrying out its decision. He utterly refused to submit to the decision of the Central Committee of our party. We asked him: will you carry it out? He said: no, for I was elected by an International Congress, and not by you. . . . Comrades Trotzky, Radek and Piatakov wrote counter-theses appealing to the German workers over the heads of our Central Committe." ("Pravda," No. 20).

Preobrazhensky: "Comrade Bielenky talks always about 'genuine factory workers', but at the same time you overlook what has actually been going on among these workers. As a result, bigotry developed —'genuine factory workers' you say—and at the same time we ignore what is going on among workers and thereby we bring the party on the brink of a great disaster." ("Pravda," No. 12).

Stalin: "There are people who are the masters of their tongue; they are average folk. There are others, however, who are swayed by their tongue, who are governed by it; they are more extraordinary. Comrade Radek belongs to the latter category. Such a man can never tell beforehand what his tongue is liable to blurt out . . . Can we, then, rely upon such a comrade as Radek?" ("Izvestia," No. 18).

**
*

. . . Such is the character of the "discussion" which the leaders of Lenin's "slaveholding democracy" were carrying on. The plebian elements of the party were crushed by the joint efforts of the ruling strata, but no sooner was the danger from that direction obviated than the Communist patricians began their internecine strife—a naked, shameless struggle for power in the party and in the country. The party was torn by this conflict of groups and cliques who, failing, however, to unite in their oppsoition to the Central Committee, suffered one defeat after an other.

CHAPTER XII

STALIN'S TERROR WITHIN THE COUNTRY

(1924-1939)

Lenin's death did not lead to any material change in the policy of violence. To this day the terroristic machine continues ceaselessly, unhesitatingly. Its mechanism has improved with the years. But the line of terroristic activity marked out by Lenin was strictly adhered to by his heirs: by the first triumvirate—Kamenev, Zinoviev and Stalin; by the second triumvirate—Stalin, Rykov and Bukharin; and finally by the uncrowned emperor—Joseph Stalin—Dzhugashvili.

Socialists and Anarchists have been the principal victims of the Bolshevik guillotine from the time of Lenin. Howver, a novel feature in the post-Leninist period was the staging of "the wreckers" trials (the possibilities of which had occurred to Lenin but which he himself never carried out). The object of the trials was to vindicate the bureaucracy in the eyes of the masses and to shift the responsibility for the breakdown of the national economy. The prevailing disorder was blamed upon the technicians and specialists whose only guilt lay in slavishly carrying out the mandates of the central authorities, though these were often dictated by political, non-economic considerations.

The old system of political exile restored by Lenin was supplemented by the so-called "minus" system—that is, forbidding those who had served their term of exile to reside in the capitals, the industrial cities or politically unstable areas. Socialists and Anarchists were doomed forever to prison and exile, with "minuses" as brief respites between times.

Practically speaking, all political groups and parties had been smashed and their membership dispersed and imprisoned even before Lenin's death. Ex-members of Socialist or Anarchist organizations (however long the time since they severed these connections) met the same fate. Even relatives, friends and acquaintances of suspects were arrested, imprisoned or exiled. The country was purged (much more carefully than under the Tzars) of Socialists and Anarchists who, in accordance with Lenin's instructions, "were to be kept carefully in prison". Despite all this, the main blows of the G. P. U. in the post-Leninist period were still directed against Socialists and Anarchists. Terrorism and torture were systematically inflicted within the prisons and exiles. Prisoners were provoked into long drawn out hunger strikes, were shifted from one prison to another, from one concentration camp to another, were frequently beaten and driven to suicide. Those sentenced to exile were arrested and incarcerated upon their settlement at the place of exile, or banished to more remote areas of unbearably rigorous climate. These practices continue to this very day.

We do not wish here to describe the horrors of the Bolshevik prisons and places of exile after Lenin. In Part II of this book, data and documents combine to give a fuller picture of the terrors of the dry guillotine and the hopeless situation of the political prisoners.

There is an acute need for a complete and accurate account of terror in the Russian revolution. It is only on the basis of a truthful history that a movement can be founded which will seek to restore the value of the individual, of his sovereign rights, that will agitate against not only the terror itself and its agents but also against their ideologic sources—centralization, dictatorship and state. But although the terror has lasted in Russia for more than twenty years, a complete story cannot yet be written, for most of the historic documents are inaccessible. For this reason and many others, our aim is not to tell the full history of terror in the Russian revolution, but merely to expose its sources and nature. For that purpose we chose the Leninist period, during which the theory of terror was established and its practice institutionalized. We cherish the hope that our aim has been accomplished in the present work, and that we have enabled the reader to realize that terror in the Russian revolution was not the result of the wicked will or personal cruelty of Lenin, Trotzky, Stalin, or those whom Stalin executed; nor was it the result of the Asiatic character of Russian life, its coarseness and lack of culture. It was, rather, the logical outcome of the European social philosophy followed by Lenin and by the Bolshevik leaders executed by Stalin. It is the same philosophy now professed by Trotzky and Stalin alike; it is the soc.al philosophy of consistent political Marxism whose practice necessarily results in terror and absolutism. It is precisely because of this that Stalin continues to act as Lenin had acted, and in Stalin's place

Trotzky, Kamenev, Zinoviev and Bukharin would have done likewise.

Wherever this social philosophy is put into practice, whatever the personnel, it must necessarily create an absolutist regime and yield the same results.

***

Inasmuch as we are not writing the history of terror in the Russian revolution, but are only laying bare its sources, we need concern our- selves now with only the most striking manifestations of the post-Lenin- ist period.

First let us record the bloody orgy in Georgia. In addition to the usual causes motivating terror, there was in this case the stimulus of Bolshevik imperialism (which is blossoming so wonderfully today in its union with Hitlerism).

Georgia had fallen victim to Lenin's imperialist policy in 1921. When foreign oppression and Bolshevik arbitrary rule became intoler- able, she rebeled on August 28, 1924. Stalin and Ordzhonikidze, two Great-Russian Georgians, flooded their native land with the blood of Socialists, workers and peasants. Thousands were shot—including not only active participants in the rebellion, but even those Socialists who had been incarcerated since long before the rebellion. Thus, for instance, Iracly Tzereteli, the leader of Georgian Social-Democracy, pointed out that in the first group of 24 executed Socialists were a number who had been in prison at the time of the rebellion: Noah Khomeriky, who had been imprisoned since October, 1923, George Salukvadze, since 1922, Gogit Pagava, since January, 1924, Valiko Dzhugeli, since August 6, 1924, Benia Chikvishvili, since June, 1924, Assatiani, since 1923. Other eminent Georgian Socialists also executed were Mikha Sabashvili, Rafayil Tchkheidze, Victor Tzentradze.

The crushing of the rebellion was directed by a Georgian, Sergo Ordzhonikidze, head of the Revolutionary Military Council of the Sep- arate Caucasian Army. Like Stalin, he was avenging himself upon his ex-comrades who had expelled him and "Koba" Stalin from the party in 1908 for "the Erivan hold-up". Ordzhonikidze was moved also by a resentment of more recent origin: in 1919 when he had in- flamed the national hatred of Osetin against Georgians and had at- tempted to overthrow the Georgian government with the aid of the Ose- tins, he had been defeated by the detachment of Valiko Dzhugeli. Prison sentences and mass executions of Socialists were his revenge. Thousands of Georgian workers and peasants were deported to Russia, mainly to the northern regions where they succumbed to diseases aggravated by he harsh weather conditions. The Bolsheviks swept through Georgia with fire and sword, and left silence in their wake. . . According to official soviet data more than 4,000 people were shot in the crushing of this rebellion.

**
*

In Russia itself, the cruelty assumed such forms as to arouse indignation abroad. A group of eminent Socialists and world notables called upon the democracies of Western Europe to protest against Bolshevik terror and to aid its victims. This appeal was signed by E. Bernstein, G. Garlakh, P. Peretz, K. Kautsky, R. Hilferding, P. Loebe, G. Strebel, Sheinakh, G. Kessler and others. Simultaneously there appeared— a sign of the times—a protest of *"The International Group of Communists"*, addressed *"to the international Communist and sympathizing proletariat"*. The proletariat of the world was asked to come to the defense of the "Workers' Group of the Russian Communist Party" whose members were recently arrested in Russia. Interestingly enough these opposition Communists of the International Group did not see the necessity of protesting against all terror; they complained just as Trotzky does now only about terror directed against their own partisans.

**
*

Revenge began to figure more and more in the motivation of terror. The Bolsheviks were avenging themselves against their ideological adversaries whom they "kept carefully in prison", trying to break them not only physically but also morally. They began to persecute the nearest relatives of the prisoners. Thus, in the case of the Social-Revolutionists sentenced at the Moscow trial of 1922, the wives of Gernstein, Lvov and Liberov were arrested and exiled with no definite charges against them. The same fate befell Liberov's sisters and Arseniev's wife; the sister of the Social-Revolutionist Shestakov was arrested and exiled following the visit she paid him in the Solovetzky islands; the son of the prisoner Hendelman was arrested immediately after an operation and sent to exile while his wounds were still open; Outgoff's wife, a physician by profession, who supported an old mother and three young children, was discharged from work, as was the wife of Ivanoff, who supported her husband's mother, sister and brother; Hendelman's and Helfgott's wives could not obtain work. And these are only a few examples. . . .

**
*

The degree of moral degeneration, cynicism and brutality to which international Communism under the influence of Russian terror had sunk by this time is strikingly illustrated by the action of the *International Society to Aid Revolutionists* (MOPR). It had been organized to aid the imprisoned Communists of Europe and America and it appealed through the press to the Socialist International *"to organize an exchange of Communists arrested in Europe for Socialists and Anarchists kept in the Russian prisons"!*

The foreign delegations of the Russian Social-Democratic Workers' Party, of the Party of Social-Revolutionists, of the Party of Left Social-Revolutionists, the Union of Maximalists, the Moscow Society to Defend Arrested Russian Anarchists, and the United Committee for the Defense of the Confined Russian Revolutionists answered the MOPR by a collective appeal: "To the Workers of the World":

"No one can suspect us of being indifferent to the infinite sufferings of our comrades in the inner prisons of the Che-Ka, in the cork cells of Leningrad, in hard-labor prisons retained from the time of the Tzar and in the new concentration camps. More than anyone else do we know the tragic conditions of the prisoners of Solovky, Suzdal, or the Siberian exiles near the Arctic Circle and among the hot sands of Central Asia. And though we know all this, we Russian Socialists and Anarchists *categorically reject the exchange suggested by the MOPR.*

"We reject it as morally inadmissible to trade in human heads and to sanction a system of hostageship which is the worst form of military barbarism. We reject it also because it involves the deportation of the comrades and their denaturalization. Our aim is to achieve in Russia itself the freedom of political and economic struggle.

"Moreover, this exchange is not practicable. Even if it were acceptable in principle to the Socialist parties of Europe, the governing classes would never agree to accept the Socialists and Anarchists of Russia, who are even more odious to them than the persons they would be exchanging.

"Still more, this exchange would lead only to the intensification of terror within Russia, furnishing the Bolsheviks with an added incentive for arresting hundreds of new victims in order to extort new 'exchanges'.

"There is only one way to aid victims of terror: it is to fight for an amnesty, for the release of prisoners, for political freedom." 398)

**
*

According to the estimates made by the "Svobodnaya Rossiya" (No. 8) on the basis of data of the soviet press, 1,804 persons were shot in 1924 (not including the 4,000 that were shot during the crushing of the rebellion in Georgia). This estimate is far too conservative but we have no other figures at our command. The number imprisoned and exiled, as was cited at the tribune of some European parliaments, reached 90,000. We should add to these the 1,040,-000 victims of the famine who died from starvation. Like the famine of 1921-22, the one of 1924 was the result not only of natural forces but—to a very great extent—of the terrorizing and plundering grain policy of the government.

**
*

The year 1924 ended with a fourteen-day mass hunger strike of the Anarchists and Social-Revolutionists who were confined at the Solovetzky islands. The year 1925 opened with a nine-day hunger strike of the Social-Revolutionists of Butirky prison in Moscow, who had been sentenced to death. Such hunger strikes—the prisoners' only method of protest and defence against the arbitrary actions of the prison administration—became a common occurrence under the Bolshevik regime; and in contrast with those of the Tzar's times, when public opinion at home and abroad had to be considered, these were characterized by unusual endurance. For instance, the hunger strike carried out by the Social-Democrat A. F. Deviatkin lasted, with an intermission of three days, twenty-four days.

In the three years of its existence as a political place of exile, the Solovetzky islands gained greater notoriety than the French Devil's island. The shooting of Russian politicals at Solovetzky released a storm of indignation in Western Europe. Yielding to this, the Bolsheviks were compelled to liquidate Solovetzky camp. But having done so

---

398) Bulletin of the Joint Committee for the Defense of Revolutionists Imprisoned in Russia, No. 10, January, 1925, Berlin. Reprinted in "Golos Truzhenika," monthly magazine of the Russian Branch of the I. W. W., pp. 28-30, No. 4, February, 1925. Chicago.

they built concentration camps in Kem, where the regime was rigorous and inhumane. The politicals of the Solovetzky islands were distributed to the prisons of Suzdal, Cheliabinsk, Tobolsk, Vierkhnieouralsk, etc.

We present here, instead of our own description of the cruelties and chekist arbitrariness of those prisons and concentration camps, an excerpt from a letter written by the prisoners of the hard-labor prison of Tobolsk. (This letter has been published, at one time or another, in almost every Socialist newspaper in Europe.)

"All those transferred from the Solovetzky islands were sentenced to concentration camps and not prisons. Despite the terrible conditions at the Solovetzky islands, we had enjoyed there a certain measure of freedom within the wire-fenced area allotted to us. There had been no surveillance within the camp, our cells were open and we could freely commune with one another and walk around in the yard from one roll-call to the other. But in Tobolsk we found ourselves in a regular prison, with tightly shut cells, with the well-known air-poisoning prison 'parasha',[399] with a staff of turnkeys specially transferred from Moscow's Inner Prison of the G. P. U. who proceeded to lay down their own rules and regulations. New and more drastic penalties were meted out to us although none of us committed new 'crimes' and our sentences were not subject to revision. People who had lived many years in the Tzarist and Bolshevik prisons were put into common cells containing from fourteen to seventeen persons which, of course, renders impossible any serious study. Our food rations, compared with those of Solovetzky, were greatly reduced and the prisoners had no control of the distribution of products. The starostat (board of delegates elected by the prisoners) is not recognized by the authorities. Hospitals and medical aid are virtually non-existent, for we can hardly dignify with the name of hospital a tiny little surgery accommodating only three or four persons, lacking the most elementary medical equipment. And our sick, among whom are those suffering with nervous illnesses and tuberculosis in advanced stages, are compelled to live in common cells, under the general prison regime, deprived of special diets and

---

399) *Parasha*—the wooden or metallic bucket or tube placed in cells of Russian prisons, used instead of a toilet. Due to this *parasha* the cells always have ammoniacal atmosphere.

almost any medical care. The prison is a two-storied building; the cells of the lower floor are damp and dark. It is in those cells that sick comrades have to live; even healthy ones who are kept there are under the constant threat of illness.

"Abandoned in this forsaken place, 3,000 miles from the capital, almost 300 miles from a railroad line, we are completely torn away from our dear ones; only very few of us can anticipate ever receiving a casual visit. At the same time we are curbed in our *correspondence*, in the choice of people to whom we can write (we can communicate only with our nearest relatives) and in the number of letters to be written and received. Even the Tzar's prison administrators did not introduce such restrictions as have been invented by the G. P. U. And to round out the picture, there are the specially selected administration and surveillance staff and Red Army men, who are imbued with a great hatred toward us, a hatred which is frequently expressed in savage attacks. Although we were theoretically permitted to look out the window, we were threatened with gunfire whenever we came close to the window. Thus, during our short stay there we were actually shot at twice. Fortunately there were no casualties. But casualties are possible; the repetition of the Solovetzky shootings of December 19 is almost inevitable under the present Tobolsk conditions. This is clearly indicated by the incident of August 7: following just such shooting at prisoners near the window we tried to summon the authorities by loud knocking; in answer to our efforts, rifles were aimed at the windows and revolvers were shoved through the peep-holes of the tightly shut doors. There were shouts like 'Menshevik scum', 'don't spare any cartridges' and 'Judases', from the drunken jailers who were wildly dashing around in the corridors threatening to shoot the inmates kept in the locked cells. All that shows clearly into whose hands the G. P. U. delivered us in the Tobolsk prison.

"Bolshevik brutality was also suffered by a group of Anarchists (including a pregnant woman) transferred from the Yaroslav prison and placed in the Tobolsk prison under a regime established only for common criminals. It was only after a prolonged hunger strike that the Anarchists succeeded in being transferred to the political prison. But the same struggle is still facing dozens of Socialists and Anarchists to whom the G. P. U., using various pretexts, refuses to grant the status of politicals. . . .

"These 'counter-revolutionists' are in the majority of cases old party workers who had joined the labor and Socialist movement long before 1917. .... And now, exhausted by many years of Tzarist repression, they must struggle desperately in the Bolshevik prisons for their most elementary human rights, their *human dignity* and their *very lives*. The story of this struggle includes the beatings administered to the 300 Socialists and Anarchists in the Butirky prison in 1921, the brutal thrashings in the Yaroslavl prison toward the end of 1922, and the Solovetzky shootings on December 19, 1923.

"*Hunger strikes* in Bolshevik prisons have become common occurrences. Only in this way can the prisoners get transfers to the political prisons, protest against crowded cells or relieve the intolerably harsh conditions of confinement. Even under the Tzar's regime the hunger strikes were not so widespread and intense as now. The prisoners strike individually and collectively. In the fall of 1924 in Solovetzky, a hunger strike was carried on for 15 days by 150 people.

"As time passes, the record of hunger strikes under the regime of the Bolshevik jailers reaches new heights. The last ones, in Cheliabinsk and Suzdal, established a record of 24 *days*. There are comrades among us who have undergone two hunger strikes: one lasting 17 and the other 24 days. One woman, a Social-Revolutionist, was *beaten up* by the agents of the G. P. U. on the fourth day of her strike until she completely collapsed. Is there any wonder that the prisoners ceased to believe in the efficacy of hunger strikes and reverted to *suicide* as a means of protest? *Once in the clutches of the G. P. U.*, a Russian Socialist cannot hope to free himself unless he is ready to publicly recant in the Bolshevik press. Only at that shameful price can he buy freedom for himself and a piece of bread for his starving family. Otherwise there lies before him only the endless road: from concentration camp to prison, from prison to exile and from exile back into prison. This is not a consequence of new offenses against the government, but merely of faithfulness to one's original convictions. We are sentenced to three, five, ten years of concentration camp or prison, but what meaning can these sentences have when upon their completion we are not freed but exiled to the Siberian tundras, to Turkhansk, Obdorsk, Mezen, Pechera, near the Arctic Circle? And this is no exaggeration. *Out of the hundreds of thousands who came to the prisons from the concentration camps, only a handful have ever been freed.*[400] The others are in distant exiles—mothers with their babies, invalids, old men with long years of imprisonment at hard labor, young men who had only recently joined the labor movement. Torn away from relatives and friends, lacking all means of support, deprived by the G. P. U. of the opportunity, and sometimes the right, to earn a living, constantly kept on the move, banished to ever more remote and less habitable corners of the country—such is the lot of our comrades. They serve their terms and are again exiled; very often they land in prison for some unknown crime allegedly committed in those desolate wildernesses—and again suffer years of confinement. . . . Only three or four years ago people were banished to Turkestan, Ural, Viatka and other points of European Russia; then Narym became the favorite place of exile, then the Pechera swamps; now there is talk of the nomad's tents of northernmost Obdorsk. Even the Tzar's government did not resort to those wildernesses.

"In this respect, neither the vilest courts of the Tzar's regime nor the bourgeois courts of Europe and America, which cruelly persecute the revolutionists, ever went as far as the G. P. U. This is the horror of the Bolshevik regime which should be exposed to the Socialists and to the workers of the world. In the 'free' Bolshevist Russia, which long ago emerged from civil war, which boasts of the strength of its government—in this country the *Socialists find themselves outlawed! There is not a single Socialist or Anarchist* known to the government and within the reach of the G. P. U. who is not languishing in some concentration camp, prison or in exile! And as long as this regime exists, none of its prisoners will see the day of liberation!"

There is little that we can add to this stirring document. We can only say that the conditions it describes have remained the same to this very day.

And only a short while after this letter had appeared in the press,

---

400) The authors of this letter add the following by way of a footnote: "Here are the data concerning the Solovetzky camp: of the 47 people who had served their terms in the Solovetzky islands in the years of 1924-25, 29 were sent to exile; 9 are under the surveillance of the G. P. U. and their choice of residence is limited (that is, residence in the large centers is forbidden them); 3 were placed under the surveillance of the G. P. U., permitted to choose their own residence; 6 were sent to their native districts under the surveillance of the G. P. U."

another tragedy occurred in the Tobolsk prison. The following telegram received by the Foreign Delegation of the Russian Social-
Democratic Party (dated April 24, 1926) reveals: "Sometime ago
the 130 Socialists confined in the hard-labor prison of Tobolsk declared a hunger strike. One prisoner has already died; another one
is about to die. Many of those on strike had participated in the 17
day hunger strike in Solovky."

More shootings occurred in 1925. According to the estimates of
'Svobodnaya Rossiya" (No. 8), made on the basis of data of the soviet
press to which we already referred, 275 people were shot by order
of the courts in the first three months of 1925. How many were
executed in the other nine months of that year, we do not know and
cannot even guess. But apart from these cases there were many
extra-legal shootings. Thus, for instance, about 200 "licey'ists"
(*i. e.*, aristocrats who at one time graduated from the Imperial Lyceum
or the Page Corps) were arrested in Leningrad. The G. P. U. tried
to fabricate a plot but failing in this, they simply selected 30 people from the group and shot them.

**
*

Apart from the mass hunger strike in the Tobolsk prison in
1926, there were the beatings of politicals in Izhma, the details of
which the reader will find in the second part of this book. Large
scale shootings took place in Georgia, where, as stated by the Foreign
Bureau of the Central Committee of the Social-Democrats of Georgia,
"in the years of 1925-1926, more than five hundred people fell as
victims of the chekist executioners. Most of the executed people are
peasants and workers, among them there were a great number of
Socialists."

In 1927 the authorities again began (this time on the quiet) to
exile political prisoners to Solovky. First they exiled the Georgian
Social-Democrats and the Armenian Social-Revolutionists (the
Dashnaktzutiun Party) and then the Russian Anarchists, Socialists,
workers and peasants. "All those prisoners are not recognized by
the administration as politicals and they live in nightmarish conditions."401)

---

401) "Sotzialistichesky Viestnik," No. 4, 1927.

Hunger strikes continued to be the order of the day. Before granting the most modest demands of the hunger strikers, the administration would drag out the negotiations so as to prolong the hunger strikes to the limit. Thus, for instance, it required long drawn-out hunger strikes to establish the right of a wife to stay in the same politisolator as her husband. Ladzovsky, Social-Revolutionist, and Fedorov, Social-Democrat, obtained that right after a hunger strike casting 17 days; the Anarchist Pokrovsky and his wife Federmeyer obtained this right after a hunger strike lasting 22 days with the former and 17 days with the latter.

Under those conditions it was to be expected that the number of suicides should increase. The prisoners of the Tobolsk prison in the above cited letter wrote that this was the case. This was true in the other prisons as well. In the Yaroslavl solitary confinement cell Grigoriev, a peasant Anarchist, attempted to commit suicide by setting himself on fire. In the Tashkent prison in the first days of December, 1928, A. I. Logachev, Left Social-Revolutionist, poured kerosene over his body and burned himself to death.

**
*

In 1928, in order to distract the attention of the people from those responsible for the continuing collapse of the national economy, there was fabricated in Donbass the famous Shakhta trial of Russian and German engineers who worked at the rehabilitation of the mines and factories; they were accused of "disrupting Socialist construction" and all except the stool-pigeons of the government were shot.

Two years later came other sensational trials. There was the trial of "The Sabotage Council" headed by the best Russian expert on railroads, the engineer Palchinsky, an ex-minister in Kerensky's cabinet; all the defendants were shot. This was followed by the even more sensational trial of "the Industrial Party," which ended with the shooting of forty people from at least four different political groups, but all of whom were united by the legerdemain of the G. P. U. into one "Central Bureau of Counter-Revolutionists." A new case was fabricated—that of the "Menshevik Bureau," involving Groman, Kondratiev, Bazarov, Sukhanov, etc.; these last escaped shooting and were exiled to the Solovetzky concentration camp.

During the cross examination certain methods were applied which later were used extensively at the famous Moscow trials of the Bolshevik leaders. In order to extort "confessions" the G. P. U. applied "third degree" methods. The arrested were quizzed for 48 hours without pause by a series of inquisitors. The prisoners were shuttled back and forth from overheated rooms into very cold rooms. By such methods they were reduced to a state where they were ready to sign everything demanded by the G. P. U.

In August of the same year (1930) a number of bacteriologists were arrested. An epidemic had resulted in the death of a great many horses, and since vaccinations did not help, suspicion was turned upon the bacteriologists. They were arrested upon charges of *wrecking*.

*

In 1928 came the well-known adoption of Stalin's "general line." In the field of agriculture this general line meant dekulakization (getting rid of "kulaks") and carrying out a program of collectivization. Both of these policies immediately unleashed a gruesome and unprecedented terror. The years of 1929-1933 were the most terrible. During those years millions of peasants were utterly ruined, exiled or subjected to forced labor—cutting trees in the northern forests, digging canals (the Bielomorsky and Volga canals)—building roads and railways. The conditions prevailing in those forced labor camps were utterly brutal, and thousands of the peasants died from exhaustion, exposure and disease. Deportations of peasants resisting collectivization were most sweeping in scope, embracing entire villages and even larger units, as was the case in Northern Caucasia. The first result of this mass terror was the appearance, as was in 1921-22, of millions of homeless children who became diseased, semi-savage, brutalized. Inevitably, they died by the thousands. Famine swept over Northern Caucasia, Ukraine, part of the Volga region and White Russia.

The collectivization of agriculture was carried out at a rapid tempo, crude force being the means of effecting this transformation. In 1928, according to Stalin,[402] there were only 45,000 house-

---

402) J. Stalin, "A Report at XVIIth Convention of the Party on the Work of Central Committee of All-Union Communist Party (Bolsheviks)", p. 26; Russian edition; Partisdat (the party publishing house), Moscow, 1934.

holds in the collectives, in 1929 there already were a million of them, in 1930—6,000,000, in 1931—13,000,000, in 1932—14,900,000, in 1933—15,200,000. That the concomitant process of degradation of agricultural economy proceeded at the same tempo, can be seen from the following figures showing the dwindling numbers of the peasant livestock. The figures were cited by Stalin at the seventeenth convention of the Communist party.[403] (The figures are given in millions.)

	1916	1929	1930	1931	1932	1933
Horses	35.1	34.0	30.2	26.2	19.6	16.6
Cattle	58.9	68.1	52.5	47.9	40.7	38.6
Sheep and Goats	115.2	147.2	108.8	77.7	52.1	50.6
Pigs	20.3	20.9	13.6	14.4	11.6	12.2

This table eloquently bespeaks the peasant resistance to collectivization. The growth of agricultural collectives was paralleled by the destruction of the peasant livestock and households in general, and the result was famine. And so the years 1929-1933 were the most terrible years. And though the famine in 1921-22 was partly due to the drought, the famine in 1931-1933 must be laid entirely at the door of Stalin's policy. This famine was not produced by unfavorable climatic conditions, but was man-made, the result of a definite government policy, of frenzied terror against that section of the population which had not yielded to the State's control. The famine gave the State this subjection and control.

The collectives became State grain factories, and the peasants became hired laborers at those factories. With the establishment of the collectives, Lenin's aim of building an absolute totalitarian State was accomplished, but at the cost of millions of peasant lives.

The Bolsheviks, of course, tried to hide not only the extent but the very existence of the famine. Only at the fourth session of the All-Union Central Executive Committee of the Soviets held on December 28, 1933, was there any admission of the famine, and even then there were only hinted intimations of its scope. Taking the floor on Molotov's report, the representatives of Ukraine made references to the "break" in the agricultural economy of Ukraine, that is, to the famine.

At that meeting Kossior spoke as follows: "Throughout the two-year period, much as we tried to revive the agricultural economy, we

---

403) Ibid, p. 25.

failed to do it. You, comrades, all know that considerable aid in the form of food and seeds was given, not only to Ukraine but to other districts and regions of the Soviet Union. This must be credited to the exceptional persistence on the part of Comrade Stalin, who succeeded in accumulating, even under such circumstances, certain reserves which were afterwards used to aid a number of provinces. These reserves helped considerably to plug the gaps which were a result of our errors in many localities.

"The cause of this 'break' (that is, the famine—G. M.) lay not in objective conditions, but mainly in the low quality of our local work, the calibre of our local leadership." 404)

Another representative of Ukraine, Zatonsky, no less influential a Bolshevik than Kossior, uncovered a little bit more, giving data enabling us to form some idea of the scope of the famine. Zatonsky said: "For two years in succession Ukraine did not get over the break in agricultural production. . . . A colossal loan was necessary, amounting *to almost 35 million tons of seeds, in order to carry the collectives through the break and enable thousands of them to continue the sowing.*" 405)

The fields sown in localities stricken with famine were guarded by armed forces and the so-called "light cavalry," that is, specially organized children's detachments consisting of "Pioneers." The fields were guarded against "shavers" and "barbers," that is, against starving peasants, who were secretly cutting down the green stalks and using them for food in order to hold out till the next harvest. The property of the collectives first of all is State property and the violators of that property—*"thieves"*—were ruthlessly persecuted and even shot.

Is it possible to establish the number of victims of famine and terror during those years? Not the exact number, of course, but an approximation? The Russian press gives figures varying from 3,000,000 to 9,400,000. The fiirst figure is given by the Russian Social-Democrats in their publication "Sotzialistitchesky Viestnik."406) The

---

404) "Izvestia" and "Pravda," December 29, 1933.

405) Ibid.

406) A. Yugov, "Prosperity and Increase of Population," Nos. 7-8 (435-436), April 28, 1939, Paris.

second is given by Populist-Socialist S. N. Prokopovich, a prominent Russian economist, a publisher of "The Economic Bulletin."[407]

The Social-Democrat, A. Yugov, questions the figures of the famine victims given by S. N. Prokopovich:

"With all due respect to the scientific standing of S. N. Prokopovich, we deem the figures given by him to be highly improbable. The figures exceed the number of people killed on both sides, during the great World War, by heavy artillery, machine guns, bombs and gases. To accept them means not only to lose all sense of objectivity but the very sense of figures. The erroneousness of the statistical method applied by Prokopovich is indicated by the fact that the same method is used by the *Bulletin* to calculate the actual population in 1938 which they set down as 154,686,000 while the second census gaves the figure of 170,100,000. A critical attitude toward soviet statistics does not free one from the necessity of observing a certain objectivity and scientific detachment'."

A. Yugov's objections are based in the first place upon a "sense of objectivity" which cannot admit such a hecatomb of human corpses, and secondly upon inaccuracies in the method employed by Prokopovich. A "sense of objectivity" that consists solely of an unwillingness to conceive such great numbers offers no proof of error in the figures, and need not be considered here. As to the inaccuracies of the method of calculation used by Prokopovich, it must be admitted that he did err, but his error was one of *understatement*. His general population figures were about 10 percent less than those of the soviet census. If the same error prevailed in the estimate of famine deaths, then of course his figure there is not too high but rather too low. But let us even assume that in calculating the number of famine victims Prokopovich committed a great error in the opposite direction—on the side of overstatement. Then, making allowances for such a mistake, we get the figure of 8,460,000 as the probable number of victims. Like A. Yugov, our senses revolt at the idea of so great a human sacrifice. . . . And yet, when we include in this number not only the direct victims of famine, but also those who were shot in the process of liquidating the "kulaks" during the collectivization, as well as those that died in prisons, exile, during the normality among the homeless children, the figures given by Proko-

---

407) "Economichesky Bulletin," No. 139, 1938, Paris.

povich, with the necessary allowances made for the errors in method, will probably be nearer to reality. One has to bear in mind that the sweep of the terror was so great that the peasants came to estimate the number of people who were deported to do forced labor at 7,000,000! [408)

The mortality from famine was very high. Entire families and at times villages were wiped out. Even toward the end of 1933, as a peasant from the Kiev province writes, whole families were dying off. In a letter of May 9, 1933, a peasant by the name of Affanasy wrote to his sister in the United States that "a great many people dies from starvation, and in every village they are buried this way: they are piled into carts like so much manure and are taken away to a common pit where they are heaped up, covered with earth and that is all" (that is, without any church ritual). "All this I am writing you is true." Affanasy continues: "Abraham, my uncle's son, and Pavel Mikhaylovich died from starvation. Gavrilo Kalenikov is all swollen up. He looks as if he will surely die, for he has nothing to eat. He grieves very much over the fact that he came to Russia and he keeps saying: 'I would rather do the heaviest kind of work in America and exist on scraps from the garbage cans than to live here, in Russia'." In the next letter, dated September 3, 1933, Affanasy informs his sister that "Gavrilo Kalenikov and his family died of hunger." [409)

**
*

Beginning with 1934, the terror policy underwent a sharp change: the guillotine began its terrible work within the Party, without ceasing, of course, to snatch victims from the midst of workers and peasants. Before describing briefly the work of the guillotine within the Party in the period following Lenin's death, let us summarize its work within the country at large.

During the six years and three months of Lenin's regime, as we have already established, Russia experienced the dire famine of 1921-22 which cost 5,200,000 lives. On the basis of the most conservative estimate, no less than 200,000 people were shot by the different Che-Ka and the Tribunals; from three to five million people

---

408) "A Letter from a Peasant in White Russia," *Dielo Trouda,* No. 75, March-April, 1933, Chicago.

409) "Dielo Trouda," No. 78, January-February, 1934.

at least perished in prisons, exile, in the civil war, in suppressing peasant rebellions and from epidemics; that is, *Lenin's regime cost Russia from eight to ten million lives.* We should add to these figures the losses of the Whites and the victims of the White Terror, which amount probably to two million lives. Thus six years of revolution and civil war destroyed from ten to twelve million lives. In the first ten years of Stalin's regime, with the civil war already a thing of the past, Russia lost several millions more (exclusive of the victims of the intra-Party terror). By very conservative estimate there were about two thousand people shot every year, which gives a total of 20,000 in ten years. The famine of 1924 killed 1,040,000; the famine, collectivization, the struggle against the kulaks with their sequels took 8,460,000 lives. *In general, Stalin's regime until* 1934 *meant to Russia the loss of* 9,520,000 *people.* Hence in the entire period of 1917-1934 Russia lost from 20 to 22 millions! Twenty millions! And this huge figure does not include the White emigres —perhaps two millions of them—or even the greater number imprisoned or exiled. . . . And then there is the material havoc and moral disintegration. . . .

The figures numb one's brain—the statistical statement of the deaths deadens one's comprehension of the ghastly truth. Paint the hideous picture in numbers—let the heads, the bodies, the persons, become digits to be totaled—and it is possible for us to argue over whether the correct figure is 22 millions or only 20 millions! Let us assume that our calculations really are very much exaggerated. Does it change the ghastly actuality and character of the epoch described by us? No amount of quibbling can do so.

CHAPTER XIII

STALIN'S INTRA-PARTY TERROR

1. *The Leaders Unmasked*

Lenin's death deprived the factional disputes of their pretensions of being a struggle for principles.

Although it had been expected for some time, Lenin's death greatly shocked the Party and the struggle temporarily slackened. The triumvirate availed itself of this calm in order to prepare the coming XIIIth Party convention. In this connection terror was widely used. For refusing to submit to the Party leadership, that is, the leadership of the triumvirate, some were arrested, others exiled, removed from their positions or shifted to other regions. Refractory students were deprived of their scholarships or even expelled from colleges and universities. The Party purge, directed by Soltz and Yaroslavsky, led to the expulsion of 40,000 members. Under the guise of fighting Menshevism the Party was being purged of all opposition groupings. Including the opposition headed by Trotzky, they were ruthlessly and cruelly crushed. The vanquished could do nothing but submit. The Party was kept in a state of siege.

The triumvirate, of course, was fully victorious at the XIIIth Party convention held in 1924, the first convention after the death of Lenin. Trotzky stressed his loyalty, coming out against factions in the Party.

The opposition having been crushed, a struggle broke out within the triumvirate. Zinoviev's decline had begun. A Party purge was instituted in Leningrad, Zinoviev's patrimony, and all his important partisans were removed from their Party and State positions and replaced by persons completely loyal to the Politbureau. At the XIVth convention, the old Bolshevik cadres split asunder, and feeling ran high among warring factions. Dzerzhinsky, at the plenum of the Central Committee of the Party, held on July 20, 1926, threatened to use armed force against the defiant opposition, while Molotov in the "Pravda" of August 20 of the same year, threatened to abandon "mild measures" and employ "the most extreme measures of violence."

The July plenum of the Central Committee of the Party was marked by the break up of the triumvirate. Kamenev and Zinoviev joined Trotzky in a bloc opposing Stalin, who had become more and more powerful. Dzerzhinsky died during this plenum, allegedly of a sudden heart attack. His death followed the activity by his G. P. U. sleuths in unearthing a vast, secret organization of the Party opposition, spreading throughout the country with Zinoviev as its head.

An excerpt from the unpublished in plenum reports of Dzerzhinsky's speech shows clearly not only his state of mind, but the atmosphere of mutual rancors and hatreds prevailing among the leaders of world Communism.

We are citing here a small excerpt from that speech: 410)

Dzerzhinsky: Comrade Piatakov has already revealed his ignorance and now he can indulge in shouting."

Trotzky (from his seat): "And you, Comrade Dzerzhinsky, were you always silent?"

Dzerzhinsky: "You have been witnessing for several days how the minority tries the patience of the majority. As for myself, I shall not pay attention to these outbreaks, lest we give the opposition opportunity to disorganize our regular business."

Kamenev: "It is necessary that Dzerzhinsky be kept from wasting 45 millions of rubles."

Dzerzhinsky: "Yes, yes . . ."

Kamenev: "You have held your position of People's Commissar for four years, while I have been at it only a few months."

Dzerzhinsky: "And you will be at it 44 years and you will still fail at it (laughter), because you are busy playing politics and not doing work. . . . I don't believe you attend the sessions too often."

Voroshilov: "He is busy with his literary work."

Dzerzhinsky: "I told Rykov a number of times: either you accept my resignation or have me take over the Commissariat of Commerce (Kamenev's Commissariat) . . . You, Comrade Piatakov, are the greatest disorganizer of industry. . . ."

Dzerzhinsky died during that plenum. And no sooner was he buried than Zinoviev was expelled from the Politbureau, his partisans were scattered, Kamenev was deprived of his Commissariat, Lashevich was dismissed, in a word, the opposition was routed and chastised.

---

410) "The End of Zinoviev," "Znamia Borbi," Nos. 18-19, September, 1926, Berlin.

Our task here is not to write a history of the struggle within the Communist Party; we are concerned only with showing that the intra-Party terror was begun by Lenin and that it springs from the same source as the general political terror in the country, that is, from the principles of centralization and dictatorship, which are the very cornerstones of political Marxism. So we do not find it necessary to give a detailed description of Stalin's terror in the Party which led to the physical destruction of all the Bolshevik leaders and almost all the old Bolsheviks.

We dwelt upon the July plenum of 1926 because it enables us to anticipate the forms of the struggle that was to follow, and of the causes underlying the shootings—with and without "trial"—of our own period.

But we can concentrate only upon those moments of intra-Party struggle which, in our opinion, are most essential to an understanding of the logical development of terror within the Party and its intrinsic nature.

After the July, 1926, plenum of the Central Committee of the Party, the most important development in the struggle was the plenum of the Central Committee of the Party, held in August and in September, 1927.

At the July plenum of 1926, Kamenev and Zinoviev, having formed a bloc with Trotzky, joined the opposition against Stalin. The majority consisted of the Stalin bloc, the Bukharin-Rykov-Tomsky group, the so-called "right" opposition, and the adherents of Dzerzhinsky, mainly notables of the Che-Ka or G. P. U.

The minority bloc, or "Trotzkyites," or as they called themselves, "Communist-Leninists," opened a vigorous campaign against the majority. Their chief demand was democracy within the Party, although they themselves had fought against this when they were at the helm of the Party and State.

During the Jubilee festival of the paper "Pravda," Zinoviev sharply criticized the members of its editorial staff. Martinoff, an ex-Menshevik, and Sliepkov, an ex-member of the Kadet (Constitutional-Democratic) Party, had by that time become the ideologists of the Communist Party. Afterwards, when Smilga, an eminent Bolshevik, was banished (the exile camouflaged in his case by a transfer to another official position), the opposition organized an impressive demonstration in Moscow near the Yaroslavl railway station, with Trotzky and Zinoviev as the main speakers. On this account, both were placed on trial before the Central Committee of the Party. At the same time there appeared the platform of Sapronov and V. M. Smirnov, signed by 15 people and called the platform of "democratic centralism." Simultaneously there developed a "buffer group" headed by eminent but non-influential members of the Party, including Ovsianikov, Schklovsky and Kasparova. It was in this atmosphere of exacerbated factional struggle and personal rancor that the August plenum of 1927 of the Central Committee of the Party carried on its deliberations lasting 12 days.

This historic plenum was described in the September issue of the "Bulletin Communiste" published by Boris Souvarine, a French Communist of Russian descent, who was expelled from the Comintern:

"Polemics reached the highest point of embitterment. Stalin's faction was openly holding separate sessions. It was somewhat nonplussed by the violent onslaughts by Trotzky and it had to resort to maneuvering. When the debate reached the point of arguing about who was the hero of the October Revolution, Zinoviev made public Stalin's letter written before the October revolution, in which he expressed the opinion that it would be sheer madness to seize power and that some kind of an understanding should be reached with the Mensheviks and Social-Revolutionists. . . . One can easily imagine the sensational effect produced by this letter. Enraged, Stalin took the floor in his own defense. It is well known, however, that at the famous April conference of 1917, at which Lenin brought forward his theses, Stalin declared openly that 'Ilyich (Lenin) is out of his mind' and suggested a bloc with Tzereteli.

"Another storm broke out on a different occasion: Trotzky's opponents accused him of shooting Communists at the front during the civil war. Trotzky then stunned everyone by presenting a letter written to him by Lenin in which the latter gave full approval to his actions and especially to shootings, granting Trotzky full freedom of action in the future. To everyone's astonishment, Trotzky produced blank sheets of paper *signed by Lenin* and granting Trotzky the right to take any decisions he deemed fit. Lenin's most intimate friends could not boast of that degree of confidence. After that Stalin forced upon the plenum the decision to expel Trotzky and Zinoviev from the Central Committee. But this took place against the will of the chairman of the Control Committee, Ordzhonikidze, who was at that time confined to his bed, due to nervousness about the entire affair. When he was able to attend the following morning, he moved that a reconciliation be effected with the oppositionists on the condition that the latter declare their willingness to defend the Soviet Union in case of war, etc. Trotzky and Zinoviev were invited to appear before the Central Committee and then came a long period of dickering as to the text of their conciliatory declarations. The result was their declaration of August 8, which no one took seriously. It is to be pointed out in this connection that Stalin hurled his defiance at the opposition: 'We will not let you get into power without a civil war!' 411)

Following this plenum, the opposition renewed with greater vigor its struggle against the majority of the Party. It began organizing underground printing shops where illegal literature was issued. The discovery of one of those printing shops resulted in the expulsion from the Party of 13 people with Mrachkovsky as leader. Preobrazhensky, Serebriakov and Sharov took the responsibility upon themselves, whereupon the Central Control Committee was forced to expel these three from the Party, notwithstanding the fact that the first two—Preobrazhensky and Serebriakov—had once held the position of Secretary of the Central Committee of the Party.

Trotzky presented in the Comintern (on September 27) a defense of the expelled leaders and assailed the high officials in control of the Party, whereupon the Comintern expelled Trotzky from its ranks. The Central Committee of the Party waged an energetic campaign throughout the country against all oppositionists. These latter began appealing to the trade union rallies and the non-Party workers. The "Trotzkyites" printed at the government printing shop 1,200 copies of their platform; this was discovered and all those involved were expelled from the Party and arrested. Expulsions took place in Baku (Sarkiz—a prominent oppositionist), in Kiev—about thirty people, in Khabarovsk and a number of other cities. The struggle for power assumed a most violent character. And it was

411) Not having this Bulletin at hand we are citing excerpts from the Russian translation of this description given in the magazine "Znamia Borbi," the organ of the Party of Left Social-Revolutionists and Maximalists, edited by I. Z. Steinberg, ex-Commissar of Justice in the coalition government of Bolsheviks and Left Social-Revolutionists. See Nos. 22-23, November-December, 1927.

in this atmosphere of seething enmity that the October plenum was scheduled.

We find a description of this plenum in the above mentioned issue of the magazine "Znamia Borbi." The description corresponds almost exactly with the picture given by Boris Souvarine in his book "Stalin." 412)

Menzhinsky, the Chief of the Che-Ka, presented an official report stating that the organizers of the printing shop had entered into an agreement with non-Party intellectuals—Schtcherbakov, Tversky, etc.—who in turn had established contact with a Wrangel army officer planning a military coup. Trotzky and Zinoviev furiously attacked this report. Zinoviev said: 'I saw several official records of the searches carried out by the G. P. U. in the apartments of Communists. Among the evidence taken away by the G. P. U. agents one invariably sees Lenin's testament. Lenin did not hide Bukharin's opposition platform, although in 1918 Bukharin formed a bloc with the Left Social-Revolutionists directed against the Central Committee of our Party. . . . Here in Russia the workers have been voting during the revolution in a rather *unique manner*. In the demonstration taking place on October 17, 1927, the Leningrad workers also voted in their own way. The opposition already had become a mass movement within the Party and the working class. You shall have to allow us to address the Party or arrest all of us. There is no other choice.'

"Trotzky's speech was delivered in an atmosphere of outspoken hostility, and was punctuated by vile and violent abuse from his opponents. He said: 'Why did the leading faction find it necessary to dupe the Party by trying to press a G. P. U. agent for a Wrangel army officer? Stalin's organizational victory at the present is only a forerunner of his imminent political downfall. The *latter is inevitable*, and, as is fitting to the essential character of Stalin's regime, *it will come suddenly*. . . . The Stalin-Bukharin faction imprisons such Party leaders as Nechayev, Shtikgold, Vasilyev, Schmidt, Fishelev and many others. It is a thoroughly opportunistic faction, trailed during the last year by the Chiang-Kai-sheks, the Purcels, the Hyxes, the Ben Tilletts, the Kuusennens, the Schmerals, the Peppers, the Raf-

---

412) Boris Souvarine, "Stalin, Apercu Historique du Bolshevisme," pp. 422-23, Paris, Libraire Plon, 1935. The book recently appeared in English.

feses, the Martynovs, the Kondratievs and the Ustrialovs. The basic feature of the prevailing Party course is the faith in the omnipotence of violence—even in regard to its own Party. . . . Lenin had his misgivings about Stalin, in the latter's capacity of General Secretary, from the very beginning. "This cook will prepare only spiced dishes" —Lenin said of Stalin.

"Trotzky ended his speech to the accompaniment of hooting and shouting: 'The grave-digger of the Revolution!', 'Down with the snake!', 'Down with the renegade!'

"The expulsion of Trotzky and Zinoviev from the Central Committee came as a matter of course. But the struggle went on. The Stalinists published in "Pravda" Lenin's two sharply worded letters written against Kamenev and Zinoviev on the eve of the October upheaval. In those letters Lenin demanded their expulsion. Molotov delivered a speech in which he declared: 'The opposition is training elements which show their readiness to adopt any methods of struggle against the Party. Therefore stress laid now on baiting individuals (especially Comrade Stalin) may eventually be instrumental in stirring up criminal *terroristic* sentiments against the Party leaders.' Nor did Demyan Biedny, the court zany, lag behind in this task of baiting the oppositionists. In speaking of Trotzky, he said: 'One is offended when one hears people compare Trotzky with Lenin. We have one measure for grain and quite another for chaff. . . . Kamenev now for the first time became a complete Trotzkyite. We have in this man, Kamenev, a peculiar combination of Byzantine features with fatal stolidity. He is a Bolshevik inside out, but he is a parliamentary Bolshevik. . . . '

"Reporting Zinoviev as recently declaring that 'strange as it may sound, there is more freedom in Hindenburg's Germany than here; there one can write and speak as he pleases,' Bukharin answered significantly that 'he who likes Hindenburg's bourgeois republic more than the Soviet Republic is free to go there; we will not stop him.'

"On November 7, the pompous anniversary festival of the Bolshevik dictatorship, the oppositionists took one step further in their struggle; they came out on the street to protest before the masses against Stalin. A group of them, including Chinese students from the University of the Orient, carried their own flags and portraits of the 'leaders'. They made an attempt to speak in various sections of the city. On that very day (November 7) Zinoviev, Radek, Lashevich, Zalutzky, Yevdokimov and others made public appearances at the square in Leningrad. They did not mount the official rostrum but took their stand alongside of it. According to the 'Pravda' report, those participating in the official government demonstration broke through the cordon, trying to rush the opposition group. Fighting began during which the oppositionists shouted at the workers attacking them: 'fascists!' Had it not been for the timely intervention of mounted militiamen, Zinoviev and his followers might have been beaten up by the enraged workers.

"In Kharkov, Rakovsky attempted a sort of *protest strike*. Having been prevented from speaking at a meeting where foreign delegates were present, he turned to the foreign workers with the words: 'You see, then, what kind of democracy we have here!'

"At the same time the Moscow Control Committee made public a report about underground meetings in Moscow, about the seizure of the auditorium of the Moscow Politechnical College, during which the representatives of the Party line were beaten and an armed guard of the opposition placed outside. Following that, *the Central Committee expelled Trotzky and Zinoviev from the Party,* and Kamenev, Smilga, Yevdokimov, Rakovsky, Avdeyev, Muralov, Bakayev, Schklovsky, Peterson, Soloviev and Lizdinia from the Central Committee and from the Central Control Committee.

"At the same time all branches of the Communist Party were instructed to expel all oppositionists taking a leading part in the illegal rallies, and to disperse such rallies by *force*. More than 600 men were expelled. What the opposition can expect in the future can be seen from Tomsky's declaration of November 15: 'If you attempt to carry your fight to the mills and factories, we shall have to ask you: sit down, please, for under a dictatorship there can be two, three and four parties, but only under one condition: one party will be in power, *and the others in prison.* We saw many Left Social-Revolutionists and we went through many situations when we had to break off with former allies'."

The XVth Party convention in December was composed of partisans of the Party apparatus headed by Stalin and the leaders of the right bloc: Bukharin, Rykov, Tomsky, Kalinin, Voroshilov. At the convention the oppositionists were expelled from the Party. They were soon driven into exile, following the road already trod by the

Anarchists and Socialists who had been banished by order of those very oppositionists when the latter were in power. The opposition was smashed and henceforth at the disposal of the G. P. U. rather than the Party. Thirty of its most eminent leaders were banished: among them Trotzky, Radek, Yevdokimov, Rakovsky, Serebriakov, Smilga, Sosnovsky, Bieloboradov and also Kamenev and Zinoviev who recanted and betrayed their own comrades. The places of exile ranged from the north of Russian and Siberia to Central Asia, Mongolia and other remote corners of the immense country.

**
*

In 1928 the Party was thoroughly purged of opposition: the victims were expelled, arrested, exiled or made to publicly renounce their errors. Early in 1929 Trotzky was driven from Russia; that is, Stalin applied toward him the same measure which the latter applied when he was in power, toward Anarchists, Mensheviks and intellectuals. According to B. Souvarine, about 300 Party members were expelled on suspicion of membership in the "illegal Trotzkyite organization," or of "anti-soviet activity." From 2,000 to 3,000 were thrown into prison, including several of Stalin's old comrades in Party work in Caucasia: Mdivani, Kavtaradze, Okoudzhava, Kote Tzintzadze.

In October 1928, Gregory Butov, one of Trotzky's secretaries, died in prison while on a hunger strike. Bliumkin, a prominent agent of the G. P. U., was shot in November 1929 for having visited Trotzky in Constantinople and for accepting a letter from him for his fellow oppositionists. V. Smirnov, the leader of the group of "The Democratic Centralism," perished in Siberia.

Having already made a clean sweep of the "left" opposition with the aid of the "right" groups, Stalin turned his attentions to the latter in 1929. This was a comparatively easy job and did not require any noisy discussions. In July, Bukharin was expelled from the Bureau of the Comintern; in August he was removed from the editorship of "Pravda," in November he was expelled from the Politbureau. Tomsky and Rykov got off with a mere censure, and Ouglanov and three others recanted. Ouglanov begged "to be corrected but not crippled." Some time later the frightened Bukharin, Rykov and Tomsky made public acknowledgment of their "error" and openly recanted. At the same time the exiled "lefts" began breaking off with

"Trotzkyism" and with Trotzky, repenting and capitulating to Stalin. Radek, Preobrazhensky, Smilga Serebriakov and Drobniss recanted in July and a few weeks later I. Smirnov, Bieloborodov and hundreds of others followed suit. The last to go to Canossa were Rakovsky, Sosnovsky, Muralov, V. Kossior and their friends.

The Party as a body was vanquished, Stalin was recognised as its supreme leader; the heads of the opposition preferred to recognize "the great genius" of Stalin and to be in places of power rather than to rot away in exile. "Peace" came to reign in the Party; struggle gave place to gossip and behind-the-scenes intrigues which later proved fatal, as we know, to many ex-oppositionists. That continued up till Decmeber 1, 1934—until the murder of Kirov, after which there broke loose in the Party a bloody hurricane of death, the most terrible in the annals of world history.

2. *The Bloody Hurricane of Death.*

The murder of Kirov by Nikolayev, occurring at a time when the country was deeply perturbed by a widespread unrest among the embittered peasants, was seized upon by Stalin as an indication that the opposition had renewed its struggle for power. And he hastened to put into effect his threat not to yield power without a civil war. He launched this civil war with Hitlerian promptness and resoluteness. He went to Leningrad where he personally cross-examined Nikolayev. His role in that case was analogous to the role of Tzar Nicholas the First in the case of the defeated Decembrists.

In connection with Kirov's murder, 49 men were shot by secret tribunals, while 150 were shot without any trial. Thousands were arrested and banished.

The terror of 1934-1938 was the means whereby a new class consolidated its newly won positions, and succeeded in removing the latent opposition of the old members of the Party—its founders and builders. These (whether becausce they had not been changing rapidly enough to suit the needs of the emerging class or because of other reasons, we cannot say) became the natural core of the forces militating against the final completion of the Russian Thermidor which began in 1918. Everywhere in every corner and crevice of the dictatorship various sorts of oppositions had sprung up. Hence the unprecedented sweep of the terror which began after Kirov's murder and which ended with the triumph of Stalin—a Russian Napoleon in civilian disguise. A triumph representing the climax of the Russian Thermidor.

The entire country was combed carefully—from the Council of People's Commissars of the U. S. S. R. and its component republics to the managements of factories and peasant collectives. The Communist Party was not merely beheaded; its corpse was trampled in mud. One after another fell the founders of the Party, its builders, organizers, theoreticians and practical workers.

Trotzky is in exile. Kamenev, Zinoviev, Mrachkovsky, Smirnov, Yevdokimov, Tervaganiatz, Pikkel, Goltzman, Bakayev and seven others were shot in August, 1936. Piatakov, Serebriakov, Muralov, Boguslavsky and other Communists were shot in January, 1937. In May, 1937, the Red Army leader Marshal Tukhachevsky, Yakir, Ouborevich, Kork, Feldman, Eideman, Putna and Primakov were killed. In July, 1937, came the destruction of the oldest and best known leaders of Georgian Bolshevism: Mdivani, Okoudzhava, Toroshelidze, Kurulov, Chikhladze, Eliava and Karpivadze. In December, 1937, Karakhan, Sheboldayev, Enukidze, one of the old Bolsheviks, and a number of prominent diplomats. In March, 1938, Bukharin, Rykov, Krestynsky, Yagoda, Rosenholtz, Grinko, Chernov, Ivanov, Ikramov, Khodzhayev and eight others. Then Tomsky, Marshal Gamarnik, Cherviakov and Luibchenko committed suicide, and Ordzhonikidze "died suddenly," his death being announced not by radio but through the press on the morning of February 19, while he died on the 18th at 5:30 P. M. Radek, Sokolnikov, Rakovsky were sentenced to long prison terms. Krylenko, the marshals Yegorov and Blukher, Bubnov, Antonov-Ovseyenko, Morris Rosenberg, Osinsky, Yakovleva, Mezhlauk, Petrovsky, Chubar, Kossior, Rukhimovich, Rudzutack, and the oldest chekists of Lenin's school: Unshlikht, Ksenofontov, Peters, Latzis and Mantzev, have been arrested and, if they are not already dead, are being held for "trial". And we have mentioned only the killings of the leaders. At the same time thousands of second and third rank Bolsheviks and tens of thousands of rank and file active Party members were shot with or without trial or were exiled or are still languishing in prisons.

Arrests, removals, open and secret shootings of people suspected of "Trotzkyism" and "Bukharinism" swept the entire country. Communist blood flowed freely.

All of this could take place only after a violent overthrow of the

Party's rule. And precisely such an overthrow had really occurred. Stalin carried out a coup d'etat—in the state as well as in the Party. This Russian Napoleon followed abroad of his own, a road which has no parallel in world history. Consequently many who follow historic analogies too closely have found themselves unable to comprehend the nature of the changes effected by Stalin.

The destruction of the Party was a complete physical and ideological annihilation. It was a genuine break with Bolshevism, with the revolution and with their tasks and goals: a stateless, classless society based upon economic equality, organized upon an international scale. It was because of the international aspects of the change that foreign Communists who found refuge in Russia were exterminated: Polish, German, Hungarian, Finnish, Bulgarian, Macedonian, Yugoslavian, and other Communists suffered this fate. Russia entered a new phase of historic development, the phase of socialistic Caesarism based upon the bureaucracy—the new class which sprang from the Marxist State.

The authors of this upheaval used shootings to create a favorable popular sentiment toward the new exploiting class. Charging old Bolsheviks with espionage, they aroused the crudest sort of patriotism and xenophobia, in an effort to justify their militarism. Charging sabotage, deliberate poisoning of water and spreading of disease, they tried to gain the people's sympathies and to shift responsibility for economic failures. All the charges were intended to stupefy the people and produce a state of mind that is far from the revolution but near to the spirit of the Stalin upheaval.

And who has been lauding this White Terror? Not the people! There is no doubt in this case *that while the people have little sympathy for the victims, they nevertheless hate the executioners intensely also.*

Who, then, offered praise? The same types of people who long ago applauded when Robespierre was carted away to the guillotine: *Sovbours* (the soviet bourgeoisie), *Savburs* (the soviet bureaucracy) and *Comkulaks* (the Communist kulaks), in one word—*Nazcoms* (national Communists or fascist bureaucracy).

With Bolshevism and its Party completely annihilated, the new class needed a new Party; one has been created which, having substituted imperialism for socialism, now fraternized with Hitler.

The first step in this direction was the artificial creation of a "public opinion" which is climaxed in the deification of Stalin, the leader. The second step was the abolition of the soviet system and its replacement by a Hitlerian sort of parliamentarism. The third step was the destruction of the old Bolshevik Guard and those elements of the Party which emerged in the heroic epoch of the revolution and civil war, and which have not become so reactionary as to be entirely immune to a revival of the spirit and ideas of that epoch. The final step is the imperialistic state capitalism which is so beautifully expressed in the alliance with Hitler. Exhausted by the terrible poverty, exploitation and dictatorship, the masses are silent; they take no part in this greatest Russian drama. They despise equally the executed and the executioners. The coup d'etat in Russia is an accomplished fact; the Socialist Empire, the first of its kind, has come into existence, erected over the dead bodies of old Bolsheviks and cemented by their blood.

This new Empire is based upon a new class which for the first time in the history of mankind has come into power and this new class is *bureaucracy*.

3. *The Final Phase of the Terroristic Cycle.*

Bolshevism is reactionary in its essential nature. Having been reared upon the idea of centralization and the absolute power of the state over society, of the Party over the state, of the leader over the Party, it develops logically along the line of socialistic absolutism. Believing fanatically in the correctness of its methods, it does not tolerate any difference of opinion, any opposition. Terror exclusively it its weapon of persuasion. Not to agree with the leader's line of reasoning is to doom oneself to destruction.

As we have seen, Lenin, the father of this socialistic Mohammedanism, constantly demanded blood. Revolution without terror was to him not revolution at all, and the All-Russian Che-Ka he founded carried out his terroristic designs on a scale unprecedented in history. He demanded more and more death sentences from the courts; he demanded that every Party member act without scruple as a Che-Ka agent, an informer, a spy, a stool-pigeon.

This machine continued its ceaseless drive, breaking the heads of rights and lefts alike, of enemies and refractory friends. It demanded more and more food, became more and more voracious; and when actual plots gave out, new ones were fabricated. The bloody wheel began spinning at a mad tempo which has not yet been slowed down. "Plots are being fabricated," said the late Martov, "in order to terrorize by executions. And executions are carried out in order to provoke plots, so that there is no end to the orgies of frenzied terror." And there can be no end, we add, until the last and the most just act of terror against this terroristic machine is accomplished, until it itself is shattered by the revolutionary upsurge of the laboring masses.

The whole history of Bolshevik domination is one of bloodshed. The epoch of the civil war is crowded with ceaseless executions of "Whites," of "meshechniks," with routing of Anarchists and Left Social-Revolutionists, the methodical extermination of Mensheviks, Right Social-Revolutionists, Tolstoyans, religious people, with armed crushing of workers' strikes, peasant rebellions and revolutionary insurgents. All were painted the colors of the Denikin-Kolchak-Wrangel, indiscriminately classed as counter-revolutionists, agents of the Entente, and were shot as such or were left to rot away in prisons. This epoch ended in 1921 with the smashing of the Kronstadt rebellion which Lenin represented as an Entente plot; with the beating up of Anarchists and Socialists imprisoned in the Butirky, with the shooting of the group of 61, including the poet Gumilev, on charges growing out of the fabricated Tagantzev case.

In 1922, the Bolshevik authorities concocted, with the aid of all sorts of stool-pigeons, a frame-up trial of the members of the Central Committee of the Party of Social-Revolutionists, aimed at their legal annihilation. In 1923 there occurred the slaughter of political prisoners at the Solovetzky islands. In 1924, Georgian Social-Democrats were shot down. In the same year also the authorities provoked a hunger strike of political prisoners at the Solovky, following which a regime of dry guillotine for Anarchists and Socialists, for all politicals, was established that continues to this day. It is a regime marked also by the fabrication of "show trials," trials of "wreckers."

The red-hot iron with which Kerensky threatened at one time became a terrible weapon in the hands of the Bolsheviks. With this red-hot iron they burned out their political adversaries, reducing the country to utter silence, to the uncontrolled domination of the Bolshevik Party, and elimination of all criticism and responsibility.

There was no trace of democracy (which had been anathematized by Lenin). The triumvirate—Zinoviev, Stalin and Kamenev—heirs to

Lenin's empire, followed the precepts of their teacher, uprooting every democratic vestige in the Party.

There appeared a new enemy, a "pretender" to Lenin's throne: Trotzky. A struggle ensued in the course of which Trotzky was driven to exile and then deported abroad (which Stalin now regrets exceedingly). There followed a conflict within the triumvirate, in which Zinoviev and Kamenev lost and were driven out of the Party and into exile. Stalin alone remains, inspiring fear rather than respect.

Then came the epoch of annihilation of old Bolsheviks by means of the dry and wet guillotine. The victims of Stalin's intra-Party guillotine recanted, crawled on their bellies, kissed the slipper of the dictator and assumed full guilt for every frame-up crime imputed to them. In accordance with the demands of the dictator they heaped false accusations on one another. They publicly indulged in moral self-flagellation, glorifying the wisdom and the great genius of their hangman.

This behavior of the Bolshevik leaders during the three Moscow trials astonished the world. In an effort to explain it, "the Russian soul" theory has been introduced, the assumption being that the Russian soul is made of material different from that of American, English or French souls; or explanation is sought in parallels with Dostoievsky's sick heroes, who are as much Russian as they are American, English or French. Attempts to account for the "confessions" envelop the whole affair in a fog of mysticism so dense that nothing can be seen through it. In reality, however, the matter is quite simple indeed: if Europeans of the middle ages who fell into the hands of the Holy Inquisition could confess dealings with the devil, if Galileo recanted his view to the effect that the earth revolves around the sun, why are we so shocked that Stalin's victims do the same? The second, and more important, consideration is that the defendants were not revolutionists who fought for the overthrow of the existing regime, but Communist satraps, potentaes and bureaucratic dignitaries who built that regime and had been in power for a long time. Through many years of undisputed rule they had lost all their revolutionary qualities. They came to that trial, not as revolutionists, not as dauntless fighters against an intolerable system, as such, but as magnates intriguing and scheming against the head of the regime. The regime itself remained as sacred to them as the monarchy was to the high officials of the Tzar's regime, guilty of some minor opposition.

They went through a moral compromise (for which they had been promised, no doubt, that their lives would be spared) quite easily, for they were men who had been corrupted long ago by power, by the struggle and intrigue for power. During this time they had suffered defeats and had been made to recant by both Lenin and Stalin; now they felt their current sins were no greater than those earlier ones. Moreover, when they themselves had been in power they had made people of other parties undergo the same humiliating procedure; hence they were psychologically prepared for such behavior. Finally, their own personal interests, the interests of their families and the Party must be taken into consideration. In short, revolutionary consistency and steadfastness could not even be expected from those high-ranking Bolsheviks (who had already been subjected to moral execution a number of times), when they were arraigned by their own Party: to think otherwise, would be to show the profoundest incomprehension of the last twenty-year period of Russian history.

One must also remember that by this time a moral cesspool has been formed that poisons everything with its stench. Byzantine and Tartar morals and vices have come to prevail in the Party and at the court of the Most August Ruler of All Russia—*Joseph the First.*

With the execution of Zinoviev, Kamenev, Bukharin, Rykov and others, the terror reaches its logical end—the head of the Most August Ruler; when this head falls, the terroristic cycle will have been completed in classical French style.

4. *Formation of the New Classes and Stalin's Most Recent Intra-Party Terror.*

Dictatorship, like other forms of absolutism, is the highest expression of political centralization. But socialist dictatorship, "the dictatorship of the proletariat," is absolute centralization; it denotes a totalitarian state which is not confined to the realm of the political but centralizes all industries, all human activity. Every sphere of life is subject to its control and regulation. The state becomes not only the sole capitalist, the sole monarch, but likewise the sole teacher, landowner, policeman, philosopher, priest; in a word, it becomes God, omnipresent and ubiquitous. It dominates man completely from the cradle to the grave; death alone frees him from its power. It is this kind of a state that the Marxists have built in Russia.

In order to execute its infinite authority, such a state requires a great number of officials. And so, a bureaucracy has stepped forth into the arena of world history which is utterly free from political and economic dependence upon capitalism, a bureaucracy which constitutes a new class.

If capitalism is based upon the right of private ownership of the tools and means of production, state capitalism is based upon the private ownership of knowledge; that is why the dominant class under state capitalism (the bureaucracy), as distinguished from the capitalist class (the bourgeoisie), does not need the right of ownership of the tools and means of production. It strives rather for a monopoly of legality, of government, of industrial management, for the monopolist right to organize the political and economic life of the country and to distribute all the products in accordance with its own appraisal of personal merits, and contributions to the state, that is; to itself. These rights give it unlimited power over the entire population. The army, fleet, police, courts and a monopoly of legal murders, being at its disposal, are powerful weapons for the consolidation and perpetuation of its domination and privileges. Through the schools and universities its ranks are replaced by way of an artificial and hereditary selection.

Stalin's "general line" gave the strongest impetus to the process of the consolidation of the bureaucratic class. With this process completed, a new class has become stabilized, and now it occupies itself with the finishing touches a la Europe: in the political realm it imitates Hitlerism, as the new constitution shows, and in the realm of every day life—the bourgeoisie.

It stands to reason that the new class tries not only to secure for itself the "legal" possession of its class privileges and licenses but also to live in accordance with its status; it wants to enjoy the fruit of its victory. Hence its tendency to keep aloof from the rabble—from the workers and peasants—to exploit the national economy for the satisfaction of its own needs and pleasures: extravagant furniture; country villas; expensive automobiles; servants; all kinds of bread and pastries while the masses are starved. Class distinction in transportation; fashionable stores of women's clothes (charging for a single dress prices many times greater than the average monthly wage of workers); beauty salons; stores of cosmetics and perfume; expensive restaurants and cabarets with excellent cuisines, with the choicest wines, with the ultra-modern music and dances; high-priced food stores with innumerable native and imported delicacies; fashionable hotels favorably comparing in their luxury with those of Europe and America. In short, the new class wants to live like the old rich classes: in luxury and joy.

The slogan of Abbe Sieges *"enrich yourselves,"* reiterated by Bukharin in the *NEP* period, has now been replaced by the slogan, "enjoy yourselves."

The words "Communism," "Socialism," "Economic Equality," "Freedom" have lost their original meaning and have become indispensable abracadabra—mumbo-jumbo of the new sorcerers.

The ideology of Bolshevism has now as its basic principle: to each according to the services he renders to the state, that is, the bureaucratic class. The fighting slogan of this ideology at home is "struggle against leveling" and abroad, "aggrandizement of the Fatherland." Economic inequality is consolidated and justified by Socialism. Conditions have been created which are similar to those of the capitalist states: *everyone has equal rights, but not everyone has the equal opportunity to make use of these rights.*

A new ruling class took definite shape, expanded numerically, and henceforth there is no more and cannot be any more of that wide access to its ranks which took place in the initial period of its formation.

Access to the new ruling class has already become very limited. A sharp line of demarcation has been drawn between it and the mass of workers and peasants. But the ruling class must have some sort of backing in the lower classes. In capitalist states the bourgeoisie depend for support upon the well-to-do farmers and, in the cities, upon the small property owners and the highly skilled, well paid workers. Those categories were hostile to Bolshevism and it destroyed them. Instead, it built up its own petty, well-to-do bureaucracy, its own Communist kulaks in the villages, and its own categories of well paid workers in the cities.

It is these elements that the soviet bourgeoisie leans upon, and glorifies. They are being imbued with an anti-social, anti-socialistic, petty-bourgeois psychology. They are fully aware that they owe their prosperity to the existing regime and they are devoted to it body and soul. Those classes want not revolutionary progress but the preservation of the status quo, the enjoyment of the fruits of the revolution and some easy military victory for glory's sake. Stalin gives them these opportunities and that is why they overwhelm the Great Leader with hosannas and manifestations of loyalty. They accord him almost divine honors. Stalin is the Hitler of the new class in Russia and the fact that the new constitution replaced sovietism with Hitlerian parliamentarism is hardly surprising. In Russia there is a unique sort of fascism: social-fascism, com-fascism.

It is quite natural that in the process of this transformation of Bolshevism, oppositions should arise. It does not follow, however, that had the power been in the hands of the oppositionists the development would have taken a different course. Its intrinsic nature destines Bolshevism to develop along fascist lines, irrespective of personnel.

Had Trotzky been in power, Kamenev, Zinoviev, Stalin and others would have become the victims of terror; had Zinoviev and Kamenev been in power, Trotzky and Stalin would have shared the fate now meted out to the former. Whatever the distribution of roles among the acting characters of the Russian drama, the essential characters of the parts would remain: there would be the executioner and the victim.

Whatever it is, the new class cements with the blood of the old Bolsheviks its class solidarity in the struggle for existence and for its privileges. The first and most decisive step, the most difficult step has been taken: *October Bolshevism has been shot down.* The next steps proved to be much easier.

The leaders of various oppositions were shot several times: they were shot morally and politically. That was followed by their physical execution, preceded by a campaign of vilification and character accusation which was based upon absurd and fantastic charges and extorted confessions of complicity in crimes that were never committed.

The oppositionists were killed by the new ruling class in order to destroy the banner under which the inchoate unrest within the

Party and among the people began to crystallize. Their murder was meant to intimidate the discontented and to reassure the international bourgeoisie of the regime's stability and its rapprochment policy.

These murders characterized the nature of the new ruling class which emerged from the state capitalism ultra-centralism and dictatorship, and which began its existence in Russia. These murders mark also the full triumph of counter-revolution in Russia, the completion of the fascist transformation of Bolshevism, just lately crowned by the Stalin-Hitler pact.

Such are the sources and causes of Stalin's most recent intra-Party terror.

CHAPTER XIV

WHITHER RUSSIA?

As we have said, the reaction begun by Lenin in 1918 was brought to a victorious completion by his worthy successor and disciple whose aim is to outdo his master in everything. The length and painfulness of the Russian reaction is to be accounted for by the tremendous sweep of the revolution and its great depth; these factors had delayed the counter-revolutionary transformation of the Party into national Communism and the consolidation of a new class.

Thus, beginning with 1918, Lenin and Trotzky charted their course toward the dictatorship of the proletariat, meaning by it the dictatorship of the vanguard of the proletariat, the dictatorship of the Party, the dictatorship of the few, "the democracy of slaveholders." They succeeded as fast as they went but they did not complete the process. Stalin did it for them and it is he that is resolutely leading the country toward political and economic slavery.

Economics and politics are two sides of the same medal; if economic life is built upon state slavery and exploitation, politics must necessarily rest upon lawlessness, arbitrariness and terror. If the economic set-up leads to physical and cultural degeneration, the political process must follow the same incline, down the road of civil degeneration, of the transformation of man and citizen into a slave.

What, then, can be expected in the field of morality?

It does not take much of an effort to picture the state of mind of the Russian "citizens": for under conditions of terror, of absolute material dependence upon the state (that is, the bureaucracy), man's behavior can be actuated only by fear. Yes, in Russia fear is the foundation of morality. It fully determines the behavior of the citizen in his relation to the state, to the powers that be—whether low or high. It determines his daily behavior toward his fellow men. It determines the attitude of the worker, peasant, doctor, engineer, writer, artist toward their work and their fellow workers.

Fear reigns everywhere and always. It pervades the entire life of the Russian citizen. The relatives of one that has escaped abroad tremble with fear for their lives. If a soviet employee abroad refuses to come back to Russia, his relatives live in constant fear. Relatives of a deserter are in perpetual fear, for they are threatened with shooting, economic ruin, prison or exile. Parents fear for the life of their twelve year old son who has encroached upon state property, for in Russia twelve year old boys are subject to execution. . . . 413) The family of an executed oppositionist, and all those holding positions or accepted into the Party by his recommendation, exist in constant fear for their fate, for the fate of their near ones. Every Party man is in fear of being suspected of oppositionist leanings. Every citizen trembles lest an incidental phrase of his expressing criticism or dissatisfaction become known. . . . Fear, fear and fear!

This historic factor of enslavement operates in Russia with the power of a primitive force.

And doesn't this horrible anxiety affect the historically established character and morality of the people? No doubt it does.

To retain one's position, to get an extra piece of bread, an apartment, a pair of pants or some kind of promotion, one has to cringe before one's superiors or inform upon one's neighbors. And in order to prevent any one from undermining one's position, to hold out in the struggle for self-preservation, one has to dissemble, to prevaricate, to praise things one hates, to act affectionately toward those one is ready to betray. All that leads inevitably to the loss of elementary moral sense, of the ideas of good and bad crystallized by the

---

413) The decree of April 7, 1935, "On Methods of Fighting Against Criminality of Nonadults," declares: "The nonadults, from 12 years old, who are convicted on charges of larceny, violence, bodily injury, mutilation, killing or attempts to kill, are *to be called before the criminal court and exempted from none of the measures of criminal punishment.*" One of these is the "highest measure of the social defense," that is, a capital punishment.

In connection with this decree, Article 8 of "The Fundamental Principles of the Criminal Legislation of the U. S. S. R. and Allied Republics," was abolished because this article, according to the General Prosecutor of U. S. S. R. Vishinsky, "had permitted only so-called medico-juridical measures; even in dealing with nonadults from 16 to 18 years old the application of the juridico-correctional measures (that is, the measures of criminal punishment) was conditional." ("Izvestia," April 10, 1935).

Pre-Bolshevik Russia in general did not know capital punishment for capital crime. After 17 years of their rule the Bolsheviks introduced capital punishment even for 12 year old children!

thousand year old moral experience of the people, that is, it leads to the replacement of human morality by animal instincts, it leads from humanization to brutalization.

A grasping individualism takes the place of moral responsibility, and a responsible attitude toward labor, property and collective opinion, toward man as such, his sense of dignity and the value of life. Pride and human dignity are becoming rare qualities. Contempt for the life of others undermines the last vestiges of respect for it. Friendship is stained with blood and betrayal; it is an object of fear and suspicion.

Fear cultivates slavish loyalty to the superiors, heaping of flattery and unrestrained praise upon the Leader, the God-Man, Joseph the First. Moral corruption reaches its climax in the loud, hypocritical public manifestations of approval of the crimes and murders of the Leader. To promote this corruption has become the duty of every Russian citizen, irrespective of age, sex, and status. One can easily see the blighting effect of all that upon the people, to what extent it cripples its entire character. Its morality, stable as it may be on the whole, must necessarily change under the powerful impact of the pervading fear; and thus, instead of free, proud, independent, enterprising and daring men, the people have become a multitude of slaves, of moral and mental eunuchs.

Russian literature, the bold, rebellious, enlightening Russian literature, which never bowed its head to any despot, a literature representing the highest pinnacle of morality, has now become fear-ridden, an instrument for turning the people into slaves and eunuchs. It has become a prostitute, forced to cohabit with every high-ranking scoundrel. It is corrupted and polluted and is infecting the people with its moral syphilis. It writes on assignment, it praises and reviles by order from above, defaming to-day what it praised only yesterday, and it extolls the very same thing which only recently it trampled under foot.

Art and music have the status of literature and have to submit to every high-ranking idiot. There is the case of Shestakovich who fell into disgrace only because one of the asses in high position found it difficult to whistle his music. Even science has bowed its head to Marxist metaphysics and is compelled to use dialectical methods by which nobody ever discovered anything anywhere. And this state of things prevails all along the line.

Can socialism exist in such a country? Can it breathe its air and not become contaminated? In this connection we have an anecdote:

Stalin summoned a sage, asking him: "Is socialism possible in one country?" The sage's reply came after long reflection: "Socialism in one country is, of course, possible, but to live in that country is utterly impossible."

Can any honest person defend or assist such a regime? It is a sign of the times that this question is worrying liberals and some Socialists. It is the beginning of awakening of social consciousness, of humanism, of the growth of the demand for freedom. It is the growth of feeling and state of mind which approach more and more closely to the immortal, eternally young and new Michael Bakunin's thought: "Without freedom there is no equality, without equality there can be no morality" and that "freedom without equality is slavery and equality without freedom is brutishness."

Against this brutishness and slavery in Russia, which has been so vigorously defended by international liberals, radicals, Socialists and even some Anarchists, a rebellion is brewing: reason and honor are entering the battle, the victorious outcome of which has been secured by the immutable nature of historic progress, which proceeds, fascism and Bolshevism notwithstanding, from animality towards humanity, from lesser to greater freedom, from poverty to prosperity, from inequality to equality, from darkness to light, from God to man.

People are beginning to understand that there can be no two criteria of one and the same phenomenon; they are beginning to understand, and act accordingly, that evil remains evil irrespective of who and in the name of what it was done.

Liberals and Socialists, who a long time had been more than partial toward Communists, following the consecutive Moscow trials and especially after the concluded alliance with Hitler, have begun to drift away from them. They are now faced with a problem as to whether progress is possible under a "dictatorship of the proletariat" and ultra-centralism. But they still seek the cause of Russian horrors in persons rather than in the Marxist theory itself. We rae firmly convinced that under centralization and dictatorship no progress is possible.

Dictatorship leads to regression, to physical, social and moral decadence, toward slavery, toward complete, integral slavery, toward a sea of blood and an ocean of tears. It is natural, for dictatorship bases itself upon terror, upon the death penalty. But the death penalty, whoever uses it and wherever it is applied—on a large or small scale—results in moral corruption, brutalization, loss of human values, stultification of individuality, lack of respect for the rights of others and consequently lack of respect for civic liberties, which in turn sooner or later leads, with the inevitability of a natural law, to the complete loss of all rights and liberties, to slavery, to a latent or expressly manifested dictatorship of a power-greedy and egoistic minority.

Let Russia serve as a lesson to all other nations, let the mountains of corpses and the oceans of blood shed by its people be a redeeming sacrifice for all nations, for the toilers of all countries.

**

The people of Russia have been brought very closely to the verge of degeneration, to the fatal boundary line. And, seemingly, there are no signs intimating that even this line will not be passed. Hopelessness, seemingly, is the dominating state of mind. There are no bright vistas as far as the future is concerned. The future appears to be worse than the present. And, as an anecdote relates, when a soviet citizen is asked: "How are you?" he answers with a cheerless: "Better than tomorrow." Hopelessness is a clear indication of disintegration and death of the individual and the nation.

Were this the all-prevailing mood of the country, one might as well give up hopes for it and say: This is a country of dead people, and its people are fertilizing manure for other nations. But this is not so. If we take into consideration the objective conditions within and outside of Russia, we must arrive at the conclusion that the Russian people and all other peoples living alongside of it under the same slavery, threatened by the same integral decay and degeneration, will be compelled by the course of history to raise again the banner of freedom and social justice, the banner of the struggle to free itself from fascist club-law and the Marxist State metaphysics which crucifies the individual in the name of the latter's emancipation.

The present state of things in Russia is gloomy and forbidding. Many, very many indeed, have cast overboard or given up under duress the centuries-old values accumulated by the historic experience of their own people and by the peoples of other countries.

Russia abounds in living corpses—and which country does not have its share of them?—but notwithstanding the horrors of Russian actuality, notwithstanding the boundless fear prevailing in the country for the last twenty years—Russia is far from hopeless.

The gruesomeness of the terror, its unprecedented sweep in the last years—doesn't all that tell that the terror is directed not upon living corpses, not upon submissive slaves, upon men with broken wills and hollowed souls? Only those who have no fear are the objects of intimidation. Only those that do not bend of their own will are made to bend by force, and only those are persecuted who do not submit and who keep on rebelling. And if in all those years of unrestrained terror, the Bolsheviks did not succeed in terrifying the people, if they did not stifle within them the urge to rebel, to protest, that means that the people are still alive, that their will is strong and the drive for freedom and justice is irrepressible. Such a people have a great future and unlimited opportunities. It means that this people cannot be dragged down to degeneration.

For twenty two years Russia has been dragged to slavery and degeneration, while it has resisted, seeking to drag in turn its executionists to the scaffold, in which it will no doubt succeed, much sooner than the general belief warranted by the apparent state of things is prone to admit.

A bloody and ruthless elemental popular revolution is brewing in Russia. A Jacquerie on a vast scale is bound to break out. A war will probably disrupt the iron discipline of the terrorists and unleash popular passions.

The new ruling class of Russia cannot and should not live forever. With all its force and persistence it cannot glorify for history a "fatherland" of bureaucracy and wealth. It will be succeeded henceforth, by libertarian Socialism: not the bookish, dogmatic libertarian Socialism but the people's Socialism—elemental, not clearly outlined, crude, with numerous survivals of state, church and Marxism. But gradually this Socialism will be purged of these survivals by the practical common sense of the people developed in their daily labors. Objective conditions are forcing this evolution.

Is it conceivable that after this rebellion the workers would want the capitalists back in the factories? Never! For it is precisely against exploitation by the state and its officials that they are now rebelling; they wish to replace these with factory committees of their own workers, to unite these committees into an All-Russian Federation. They seek a free factory regime, and equitable distribution of the products of their labor. This is their only way out.

And the peasants—will they want to bring back the landlords? Never! Millions of lives were lost when they were driven into collectives. But the object of their dissatisfaction is not the collectives themselves but the regime of serfdom that has come to prevail therein: state slavery, forced labor, embezzling and exploiting officials. They wish to institute their own regime within the collectives, to make free use of products of their labor and establish an equitable exchange with mills and factories. The situation is such that even die-hard peasant individualists and property owners have come to realize that there can be no reversion to individual economy; and should such attempts occur the peasants will soon be convinced of the impossibility of individual peasant economy. The only solution is collective labor on the collective farms and cooperation of the collectives throughout the country with the factory committees and other workers' organizations. This is libertarian Socialism, free people's Socialism—the only basis of true Socialism, an edifice of freedom, equality and brotherhood.

**
*

Twenty-two years ago the resplendent rays of freedom brightened the vast expanses of Russia. Despotism, centuries old, vanished overnight. And the common people swept over the land like spring floods and washed away the debris of the old regime. Cleansed by a bloodless revolution Russia appeared before the astonished world in all the splendor of a bold, young and vigorous country.

For the first time she ceased to be a stepmother to her many nationalities. Never before had such horizons of brotherhood, equality and freedom been revealed. And the people who experienced those thrilling moments of history will never be wiped off the face of the earth; they can never make a perpetual peace with slavery, even with the slavery of the state cattle troughs in which food may be abundant.

The Russian people have chosen their own road: the expansion of the program of the October Revolution under the political freedom of the February Revolution. And far as they may be shunted off this road by deceit or brute force, they will go back to it again and again.

Scourge and scorpion will be of no avail: nor will the torture racks, the crucifix and the cellar of the Che-Ka. They may slow down this process of rediscovery, they may cause unnecessary suffering, but they cannot succeed in thwarting the historic evolution of the social organism which must proceed toward individual freedom, general prosperity and justice.

**
*

All Russia is dark in the long arctic night. But the morning is inevitable.

And Russia's dawn will be a dawn of the toiling people of the whole world.

We joyously greet its approach.